Woven Shades of Green

Woven Shades of Green

An Anthology of Irish Nature Literature

EDITED BY TIM WENZELL

Bucknell UNIVERSITY PRESS

UNIVERSITY | PRESS

LEWISBURG, PENNSYLVANIA

Library of Congress Cataloging-in-Publication Data
Names: Wenzell, Tim, editor.
Title: Woven shades of green : an anthology of Irish nature literature /
edited by Tim Wenzell.
Description: Lewisburg, PA : Bucknell University Press, 2019. | Includes
bibliographical references and index.
Identifiers: LCCN 2018057382 | ISBN 9781684481378 (pbk. : alk. paper) |
ISBN 9781684481385 (cloth : alk. paper)
Subjects: LCSH: English literature—Irish authors—History and criticism. |
Nature in literature. | Ireland—In literature. | Natural history—Ireland.
Classification: LCC PR8722.N3 W68 2019 | DDC 820.8/03609415—dc23
LC record available at https://lccn.loc.gov/2018057382

A British Cataloging-in-Publication record for this book is available from the
British Library.

∞ The paper used in this publication meets the requirements of the American
National Standard for Information Sciences—Permanence of Paper for
Printed Library Materials, ANSI Z39.48-1992.

www.bucknell.edu/UniversityPress

Distributed worldwide by Rutgers University Press

Manufactured in the United States of America

For my father,
who showed me the balance
between hard work and humility

Contents

Part III: Nature and the Irish Literary Revival

Part IV: Modern Irish Nature Poetry

Part V: The Literature of Irish Naturalists

Foreword

Woven Shades of Green should be welcomed as generously as the anthology itself welcomes Irish nature writing, offering it to the reader in ample servings. This is because Irish literature has been, as Professor Wenzell points out, selected and read chiefly through the lenses of cultural politics, thus putting nature writing at a severe disadvantage. The century-old neglect of Irish nature writing (broadly defined) is in contrast to its abundance and variety, though until now mostly reposing undisturbed on library shelves. It must also be said that some of that literature of the past century, which celebrated nature on its own terms, was written in tacit or explicit defiance of the narratives and value systems prevailing in much of the island, which required nature to play an auxiliary role and to be a means to political and cultural ends beyond itself.

Of course, nature as a vehicle or vestment could still be served literary justice, particularly when it is the intimate particularities of creatures and vegetation that are the means to an end. The beautiful and often wistful medieval poems of the hermits celebrate nature as divine allegory and the occasion for pious worship. The editor quotes George Moore as writing (with possibly some patriotic hyperbole), "Ancient Ireland, perhaps, more than any other country, understood the supremacy of spirit over matter." Even if true, there is some resemblance between the verbal litany of animals and plants that recurs in the poetry and the species checklists of modern naturalists and a closeness of observation that makes the anchorite's shieling resemble at times the ornithologist's blind or his hermitage an observatory.

The end in sight is very different for the British colonialists, who surveyed and inventoried Irish nature (especially its forests and streams) for the purposes of commodification and plantation. (The woods provided valuable timber for shipbuilding and were hewn on an industrial scale.) But as in the New World at the same time—the seventeenth and eighteenth centuries—these early inventories, however utilitarian, could result in valuable, pioneering nature surveys and writings. We have here Thomas Gainsford, but there are others to be read and learned from.

During forest clearing and agriculture, by the Anglo-Irish in the south and the Scots-Irish in the north, nature was something to be confronted, bested, and made productive, and description and celebration played minor roles. Exploration and survey were succeeded by adventurous travel, which came of age in the eighteenth century and produced quantities of place writing. The fashion for the picturesque later that century (exploited by the tradition of "loco-descriptive" poetry) meant that startling and remote, as well as beautiful, topographies were sought out by painters, engravers, and poets, with ruins and mounds bonuses to cliffs, crags, and painterly lakes. Literature of the picturesque, gothic, and sublime, which emphasized a prescribed set of generic experiences, became, in its toned-down popular form, travel writing, which is still practiced today in the commercial literature of Irish tourism. Nature as a resort once primarily involved field sports, including game and coarse fishing and hunting, and the writing these inspired over a couple of hundred years has been considerable and occasionally literary in the very best sense.

Romanticism at its outer edges internalized the transports and terrors of the wild landscape and its creatures, and it outlived Shelley in its mythopoetic drive. One has only to compare Padraic Colum's poems "Humming-Bird" and "Snake" with D. H. Lawrence's poems of identical titles to see late Romanticism in action in both poets. At a lower voltage, the dialogue between nature and the poet's mood and thoughts ("we receive but what we give," wrote Coleridge of our traffic with nature) also helped generate mainstream Romanticism. That movement gained permanent purchase in English-language literature even after the deaths of Wordsworth and Keats; when William Allingham in the mid-nineteenth century sets the songs of woodland birds to words, and knowledgeably, in "The Lover and Birds," he is engaging in the dialogue between self and nature. Seamus Heaney's imagined living relations between language and landscape or Michael Longley's footprints in the sand beside those of the sanderlings prove them late Romantic poets, though Longley goes farther than most poets since John Clare in honoring what he observes for its own sake and bringing it intrinsically alive with his metaphors.

But if the remote and outlying were the data of the picturesque, the sublime, and the romantic, they were also the data of potential social improvement. The traveling surveys of concerned Victorians, who wanted their own eyewitness accounts of life in the deprived or obscure Irish countryside, gave readers and policy makers along the way a good deal of place writing as well as social anthropology. Professor Wenzell gives us Thackeray, but there were also, for example, Henry Inglis, Thomas Carlyle, and J. A. Froude.

The geologists, too, were early abroad, and an inspired amateur such as William Henry Drummond exploited the capaciousness of the topographical epic tradition to recount the importance of the Giant's Causeway, County Antrim, as a case study in geological explanations while versifying that natural phenomenon's alarming majesty. John Tyndall was a trained surveyor, professional physicist, prominent field-worker, and experimental scientist but wrote with a pen impressively eloquent enough to qualify him as a major nature writer. His study of nature confirmed for him the truth of Darwinism, and his brilliant career as a science popularizer and polemicist reminds us that the Irish understanding of nature was constrained and directed for its faithful by the Roman Catholic Church. Biology, practiced mostly by Protestants, was seen as a threat, yet it was Scots-Irish Protestant ministers who were also keen and expert amateur field naturalists who protested eloquently against Tyndall's notorious and magniloquent "Belfast Address" (1874), which threw down the gauntlet to Christianity. Their protest resulted in a neglected library of anti-Darwinian literature to supplement their library of fieldwork, their local nature studies, and surveys. (The influential Belfast Naturalists' Field Club, which ironically was begun by those who were deeply involved in the industrialism of the Lagan Valley, started in 1863 and is still in active operation.)

In a parallel constraint, the celebration of Irish nature that was not harnessed to the cause of nationalism from the mid-nineteenth century, and was demonstrably "literary," was seen as somehow frivolous or at least too "aesthetic" and so marginalized in a national canon that could be conveniently politicized. (The natural history of the Great Famine and the social history of the subsequent land disturbances played large roles in such a politicization.) And even if nature writing were scientifically sound in a conscious way, as in the hands-on naturalizing of Robert Lloyd Praeger, it could be thought to be insufficiently Irish: and so Heaney thought Praeger's relationship to Irish nature lacked a necessary native dimension. But the Irish canon will have to accommodate Praeger rather than the other way round.

Nature was to play a signal role in the cultural nationalism of the Irish Literary Revival of the early twentieth century, spearheaded by Yeats, but the spectrum of its representation encompassed the entrancing lyricism and beauty of Yeats's early poetry, the mystical outdoor visions of George Russell (Æ), and the ear-to-the-ground observations of John Millington Synge in his prose and plays set in the rugged west of the island, where nature was elemental and powerful. True, Yeats later developed a philosophical vision that led him to exalt that which was out of nature, escaped from life and death, an artifice of eternity; in one poem, he extolls "Great works constructed . . . in nature's spite." Yet despite his symbolism and archetypes, he is remembered by Glencar waterfall and Ben Bulben headland, indisputably there, while Yeats Country in County Sligo is part of the well-worn map of tourist Ireland.

Ecocriticism has recently helped clear nature literature from any lingering charges of being marginal or being mere belle lettres and at the same time substitutes the needs of the local and the global for the needs of the nation. Certainly it retains the Romantic notion of the intimate interaction between humanity and nature; it retains a sound scientific basis that Tyndall, Praeger, Viney, and other field-workers and theorists would approve of (the concept of ecology); and it retains just sufficient of the nationalistic (the desirability of conserving a country's natural heritage) to gain the approval of the people. But it has inspired at once the study of nature, the re-creation of nature in literature, and the vigilant activism that conservation and sustainability require. Ecological concern has been Professor Wenzell's timely motivation behind *Woven Shades of Green*, giving "green" a less political and divisive, more salutary meaning than has been usual.

John Wilson Foster
Senior editor, *Nature in Ireland:*
A Scientific and Cultural History (1997)
Portaferry 2018

Preface

Much pride has been taken in Ireland's rise from one of the poorest countries in Europe to one of its richest. Ireland's history of brutal conquests, from the Danish plundering of villages to Cromwell's atrocities on the Irish people to the long history of British imperialism, have been well documented as both artifact and analysis. This dark period of Ireland's history, at the dawn of the twenty-first century, appears to be over. However, a new menace—the underbelly of this Celtic tiger—has moved from the threat of British imperialism to the threat of world capitalism and globalization and is now rising across the Irish landscape in the form of urban sprawl. This new topography of pavement is threatening to undermine the rich natural history of Ireland and the rich legacy of nature literature from the beginning of Irish civilization. As Mark Lynas states in "The Concrete Isle," an article that appeared in the *Guardian* (London) at the end of 2004, "This land has been mauled by the Celtic Tiger, chewed up by double-digit economic growth—and what's left is barely recognizable."[1]

Statistically, Ireland has been ranked near the bottom of countries in Europe on the environment, and urban sprawl is growing faster in Ireland than anywhere else in continental Europe. This is mainly because people can no longer afford to live in the cities of Dublin or Cork, which has led to a huge increase in long-distance commuting and a more congested network of roads, and with this the amount of urbanized land is expected to double in twenty years. As a result, Ireland has been transformed into one of the most car-dependent countries in the world. Irish drivers average twenty-four thousand kilometers per year, far above Great Britain's sixteen thousand kilometers per year and even surpassing the United States at nineteen thousand kilometers per year, already reaching levels that the Irish government had predicted for 2010. Tony Lowes, a cofounder of Friends of the Irish Environment, is spearheading a plan to tighten planning laws as a means of slowing down urban sprawl and whose aim, he declares, is "to save Ireland from the Irish." Further, he states, "We've turned our back on everything. The environment, the past. . . . There are no victories. Everything is being demolished around us."[2] Or as Frank McDonald, the *Irish Times* environmental editor, puts it, "What is going on across the board in this country is immensely destructive. The level of house-building spells catastrophe for scenic landscapes and the countryside in general if it continues. . . . It's quite clear to me that by 2020 this country will be completely destroyed."[3]

What is clear is that the advent of progress has manifested itself in a landscape that is quickly diminishing Ireland's natural world. This is implicit in places such as the famously scenic road between Galway and Connemara, where the natural world is being wiped out through villages merging together like strip malls; the building boom in Killarney has impacted the once picturesque view there, and as Lynas points out, "Where once only the cathedral spire stood above the famous lakes, Killarney's skyline is now dominated by cranes."[4]

These cranes symbolize the progress that a surging economy and onrushing globalization have brought to Ireland, replete with possibilities of future financial success for both businesses and Irish citizens; but these cranes also symbolize the ugliness that is replacing the lush natural beauty of this land. Sadly, these changes are meeting with little or no resistance.

So this anthology is a response to these changes, as it emphasizes the importance of understanding the significant importance of the natural world of Ireland as it collapses under the weight of human progress. Thus, it is vital to examine the breadth of writing that has embraced Ireland's natural world since the first written poems, as a way of understanding the human relationship to nature over the course of time and the wealth of writing devoted to observations of nature over that time. I have subtitled this collection *An Anthology of Nature Literature*, instead of "Nature Writing," because this volume covers, more accurately, the contents of the collection of all writing about nature: a blend of nonfiction with the genres of poetry, fiction, and drama, all of which approach the subject matter from very different perspectives yet which, as a whole, offer a more complete observation of the significance of Ireland's natural world—not only to naturalists but also to poets and fiction writers. Though some critics might cite scientific inaccuracies in the observations of more poetic and creative reflections on Irish nature, these responses from various authors indeed offer a more imaginative, emotional response, which is just as important, and arguably more important, than rational, scientific observations. So this anthology, as a result of this two-pronged approach to nature writing, comprises a balance of perspective—a collection of these emotional, imaginative approaches to nature crafted into poetry, fiction, and drama, paired with close observations of nature informed by science, biology, and geography. However, even here, in nonfictional observations of Ireland's nature, there is a literary component that is subjective and imaginative, where personal observations of the writer are layered beneath texts informed by a scientific understanding of the natural world, including, most importantly, what is most valuable: the great spiritual connection between the Irish and their landscape. W. B. Yeats, in the last stanza of "The Lake Isle of Innisfree," writes,

> I will arise and go now, for always night and day
> I hear lake water lapping with low sounds by the shore;
> While I stand on the roadway, or on the pavements grey,
> I hear it in the deep heart's core.[5]

The poet bemoans the loss of the nature of his youth within the confines of a paved civilization; the narrator's arising and going is an attempt to take action in a manner that will bring that nature back, though like Wordsworth's daffodils,[6] this arising and going is more a tapping into memory and imagination of what was than an actual return to building a cabin on a lake and departing the paved way of life. In other words, the paved life will always be there, but it does not need to be. But Yeats's narrator is also conceding that the people around him in his London landscape (and his Dublin landscape for that matter) are too removed from this type of existence to desire it. Indeed, the narrator's "deep heart's core" is, for most in these urban communities, unreachable. The very idea of a pastoral dream has been replaced by a very real preference for the practical, and those who have lost access to this deep heart's core are too integrated into a paved existence to notice what has been lost. The diminishing of desire to hold onto the pastoral dream becomes a lost landscape of childhood memories, and today this lost landscape has spread beyond Ireland's cities to cover the countryside. Places that existed beyond the pale of Dublin's paved roads and neighborhoods are being lost to memories and childhoods forever. Indeed, the lake to which Yeats's narrator wishes to return has become a geographical footnote, a tourist destination, and the one thing that has kept it preserved from urban development. Nature, too, has become a footnote, a lost dream that fades with each subsequent reduction of the natural world. Yeats, in his autobiography, ruminates on this poem: "I grew suddenly oppressed," he said, "at the great weight of stone and thought, 'There are miles and miles of stone and brick all round me. . . . If John the Baptist or his like were to come again, and had his mind set upon it, he would make all these people go out into some wilderness leaving their buildings empty.'"[7]

Just as nature is being ignored in Ireland's rise to the top of the world's economies, so too has nature been ignored in the literature of Ireland's writers. Despite the large body of writing in Irish studies, particularly in the past fifteen years, very little of this writing has focused on Irish authors and their observations of the natural world. As John Wilson Foster notes, "Irish nature writing has been sadly neglected, and there is none represented in the three volumes of *The Field Day Anthology of Irish Writing*."[8] It is important to note here that this anthology, edited by Seamus Deane, has widely been regarded as the most comprehensive anthology of Irish writing ever published. The anthology examines, with appropriate introductions, biographies, and bibliographies, the various traditions of Irish writing in a chronology dating from early Christianity to the present, a thorough compendium of writing. Since Foster's observations about the dearth of nature writing, *The Field Day*, first published in 1991, has been expanded to include two volumes on Irish women's writing, a move that Deane felt was necessary after criticism that the anthology did not effectively represent Irish women writers. Despite the inclusion of these added volumes, however, the anthology has yet to address the plethora of Irish writers whose subject matter resides in the natural world.[9]

A recent collection of essays edited by Helen Thompson, *The Current Debate about the Irish Literary Canon: Essays Reassessing "The Field Day Anthology of Irish Writing,"* examines the Irish canon through previously ignored perspectives, including postcolonial theory, women's writing, the importance of memoirs (especially with Samuel Beckett), modern Irish drama, music, and even eating disorders. Yet even this collection, which primarily questions the selections in Deane's compendium, fails to include even a mention of this vast inattention to Irish nature writing.[10]

Neil Murphy, in an essay that is a part of *The Current Debate*, makes clear that "all texts are political," and "texts constructed in postcolonial nations must somehow reflect the post-coloniality of the subject."[11] In the case of the natural world, however, the subject matter exists outside the realm of traditional political discourse involving human and social history, and so "the post-coloniality of the subject," as Murphy puts it, becomes an irrelevant paradox. Indeed, Murphy concedes this narrow view that has come to embody modern Irish literary studies: "One of the primary consequences of the overwhelming appropriation of Irish studies by political and postcolonial reading strategies has been the marginalizing of a coherent and dominant tradition in Irish writing . . . and the elevation of marginal issues to positions of centrality."[12] Though Murphy's essay was pointed at the rather obvious absence in the study of the creative process in Irish women's writing, he nonetheless makes his point clear. This "coherent and dominant tradition" can certainly trace the importance of nature writing through Irish literary history as well. As he contends, "Politically-motivated analyses are frequently characterized by two specific conditions; fragile theoretical assumptions and selective reading practices."[13] For Murphy, these theoretical assumptions would also presume that any theoretical framework would necessitate a political makeup. That is, the subject matter would need to have some political reference point in order to merit its reading and thus its inclusion in the Irish canon. The "selective reading practices" here would be not only a way to read a specific text but whether certain texts even merit consideration to be read in the first place.

Certainly, any subject matter deemed *exo*political, at least in the sense of literary analysis, would take into account subject matters outside of human interactions within human society. Rather, it would also consider *non*human interactions and *non*human societies. Nature writing falls squarely into this category. Even Irish women's writing, a subject matter virtually ignored in Deane's first three volumes of *The Field Day* anthology, falls within the parameters of politicized writing, marginalized though it had been (so too would postcolonial readings, a reassessment of modern Irish drama and its importance to the canon, and the genre of memoirs and music that are defended in Thomson's *The Current Debate*). Irish nature writing, in essence, is both exopolitical and political in its own right. Analyzing nature writing, especially of early Irish nature poetry, would gather little literary value from a purely political perspective. Thus, most critics assume that nature writing as a body of literature in and of itself would not merit serious criticism, even within the expanding parameters of the canon. Ecocriticism, a quickly blossoming field of literary criticism, brings the natural world, particularly in a twenty-first century filled with environmental concerns, onto the Irish political stage.

With the rise of worldwide ecological concerns, it is important to note that the expanding parameters of the literary canon have, for some time, included ecocritical studies. In the introduction to the wonderful anthology *The Ecocriticism Reader: Landmarks in Literary Ecology*, Cheryll Glotfelty makes this point: "In most literary theory 'the world' is synonymous with society—the social sphere. Ecocriticism expands the notion of 'the world' to include the entire ecosphere."[14] The world includes much more than human society, and literary works have often addressed this place beyond human civilization; but literary criticism needs to see this connection more clearly. "As a critical stance, [ecocriticism] has one foot in literature and the other on land."[15] Through an ecocritical lens, nature takes center stage alongside humanity. In an ecocritical study of Irish literature, the political agendas that were so significant in forming Irish history and culture become subordinate to the larger influence of the natural world. Yet nature, from any other perspective, has too often been cast as a minor character in a drama whose fate is unfolding in Irish nature as a tragedy.

"The most important function of literature today," Glen A. Love argues, "is to redirect human consciousness to a full consideration of its place in a threatened natural world."[16] This redirection should not suppose that humanity is dominant over nature or that human society is more important than nature. As Sueellen Campbell makes clear, "the most important challenge to traditional hierarchies in ecology is the concept of biocentrism—the conviction that humans are neither better nor worse than other creatures but equal to everything else in the natural world."[17]

Woven Shades of Green: An Anthology of Irish Nature Literature is organized in chronological order, beginning with the nature poetry of the Celts and early Christians. These poems were composed at a time when Christianity found God's presence in the forests and groves that populated the landscape of Ireland. Included are the observations of the Irish hermit poets on birds and trees, the changing of the seasons, the sea, and the hermit's place in nature, whereby the natural world is a church and a shrine to God. Part 1 concludes with a translation of *Buile Suibhne*, or *The Frenzy of Sweeney*, a hero who is cursed by a saint and undergoes a series of adventures after he is transformed into a bird at the Battle of Moira and makes his way across the Irish landscape though flight.

Part 2 explores the natural world of a deforested and colonized Ireland, the removal of humanity from nature, and the psychic effect of this disconnection that alters the human-nature relationship. Selections in this part include the poets William Allingham and James Clarence Mangan and the epic (and often overlooked) poem by William Hamilton Drummond "The Giant's Causeway," as well as a selection from William Makepeace Thackeray's *Irish Sketchbook*. Nature literature from a barren landscape and experience of the Great Hunger, or the Irish Famine, includes selections from William Carleton's important novel *Black Prophet* and an excerpt from Emily Lawless's novel *Hurrish*, in which the setting of the harsh natural world of western Ireland becomes the focus of the central plots of each of these novels. The Irish Literary Revival, the focus of part 3, highlights the nature literature of George William Russell (Æ) and includes poetry and selections from his wonderful book *The Candle of Vision*. Also included are excerpts from George Augustus Moore's novel *The Lake*, as well as the poetry of Katharine Tynan, Eva Gore-Booth, Padraic Colum, some of the early nature poetry of W. B. Yeats, the overlooked nature poetry of John Millington Synge, excerpts from Synge's famous memoir *The Aran Islands*, and his one-act play *Riders to the Sea*. Part 4 of the anthology turns to modern Irish nature poetry, including the nature poetry of Patrick Kavanagh, Louis MacNeice, Seamus Heaney, Michael Longley, Eavan Boland, Derek Mahon, Moya Cannon, John Montague, Derek Mahon, Desmond Egan, and Seán Lysaght, all of whom balance a more nuanced relationship to nature that is informed by a balance of both a rational and an emotional approach to Irish nature. In part 5, Ireland's naturalists are highlighted, beginning with the influential Irish scientist John Tyndall and his "Belfast Address," an early nineteenth-century statement for rationalism and natural law, which paved the way for scientific discovery and progress of a more rational and scientific approach to the natural world. Also included in this last part of the anthology are selections from Robert Lloyd Praeger's important scientific travelogue *The Way That I Went*, selections from the current naturalist and journalist Michael

Viney in *A Year's Turning* and selections from his *Irish Times* column "Another Life," and selections from the cartographer Tim Robinson's *Connemara: Listening to the Wind.* The anthology concludes with selections from the writer/philosopher John Moriarty's *Invoking Ireland* and his unique blend of rational, imaginative, emotional, and philosophical observations on the impact of myth and nature in Ireland. An appendix lists environmental organizations in Ireland and highlights ways to get involved in helping to preserve and appreciate the natural beauty of the country that has inspired so many works of literature, through both nonscientific and scientific observation, of the Emerald Isle.

NOTES

1. Mark Lynas, with Iva Pocock, "The Concrete Isle," *Guardian* (London), Guardian Weekend, final ed., December 4, 2004, 16.
2. Ibid.; see also the appendix for more information on the Friends of the Irish Environment.
3. Frank McDonald, quoted ibid.
4. Ibid.
5. W. B. Yeats, "The Lake Isle of Innisfree," in *The Collected Poems of W. B. Yeats* (New York: Simon and Schuster, 1996), 39.
6. See William Wordsworth, "I Wander'd Lonely as a Cloud," in *The Collected Poems of William Wordsworth* (London: Wordsworth Editions, 1998), 219.
7. W. B. Yeats, *Autobiography: Consisting of Reveries over Childhood and Youth, The Trembling of the Veil, and Dramatis Personae* (New York: Macmillan, 1953), 103.
8. John Wilson Foster, "The Culture of Nature," in *Nature in Ireland: A Scientific and Cultural History,* ed. John Wilson Foster and Helena C. G. Cheney (Dublin: Lilliput, 1997), 603.
9. See *The Field Day Anthology of Irish Writing,* gen. ed. Seamus Dean, 3 vols. (Cork: Cork University Press, 2002).
10. Helen Thompson, "Introduction: Field Day, Politics and Irish Writing," in *The Current Debate about the Irish Literary Canon: Essays Reassessing "The Field Day Anthology of Irish Writing,"* ed. Helen Thompson (Lewiston, NY: Edwin Mellen, 2006), 1–37.
11. Neil Murphy, "Political Fantasies: Irish Writing and the Problems of Reading Strategies," ibid., 87.
12. Ibid., 79.
13. Ibid., 66.
14. Cheryll Glotfelty, "Introduction: Literary Studies in an Age of Environmental Crisis," in *The Ecocriticism Reader: Landmarks in Literary Ecology,* ed. Cheryll Glotfelty and Harold Fromm (Athens: University of Georgia Press, 1996), xix.
15. Ibid., xiv.
16. Glen A. Love, "Revaluing Nature: Toward an Ecological Criticism," ibid., 236.
17. Sueellen Campbell, "The Land and Language of Desire: Where Deep Ecology and Post-Structuralism Meet," ibid., 123.

Early Irish Nature Poetry

Introduction to Part I

When you enter a grove peopled with ancient trees, higher than the ordinary, and shutting out the sky with their thickly inter-twined branches, do not the stately shadows of the wood, the stillness of the place, and the awful gloom of this doomed cavern then strike you with the presence of a deity?
—Seneca, *Epistolae morales ad Lucilium*

Simon Schama, in *Landscape and Memory*, states that he wrote his critically acclaimed work "as a way of looking; of rediscovering what we already have, but which somehow eludes our recognition and our appreciation" and that "the cultural habits of humanity have always made room for the sacredness of nature."[1] From the perspective of Ireland and Irish writers, much room has certainly been made, particularly in early Irish writing, when the landscape was composed chiefly of forests.

One of the early names for Ireland was "The Isle of Woods." In "Ireland's Lost Glory," published in *Birds and All Nature* in 1900, the anonymous author makes the observation that many place names in Ireland were derived from the presence of forests, shrubs, groves, and species of trees, most notably the oak. The author's concern stems from the loss of forty-five thousand acres of forest from 1841 to 1881 and that "every landlord cut down, scarcely anyone planted, so that at the present day there is hardly an eightieth part of Ireland's surface under timber."[2] This commentary on the loss of forests parallels modern nature writers who are lamenting the loss of land to urban sprawl and that something important is being lost. As Eoin Neeson points out in "Woodland in History and Culture," the forests remain only in surnames: MacCuill (son of hazel), MacCarthin (son of rowan), MacIbair (son of yew), and MacCuilin (son of holly), among others.[3]

The loss of this forested existence really began in earnest with the rise of British imperialism and their quest for supremacy in Ireland, done chiefly to increase the amount of arable land.[4] In this context, "arable" is really the idea of maximizing land for profit, and of course, this utilitarian approach to land as real estate has immediate relevance to globalization in present-day Ireland. As the author contends, "so anxious were the new landlords to destroy" that, identifying all of the places these landlords did destroy, "if a wood were to spring up in every place bearing a name of this kind the country would become clothed with an almost uninterrupted succession of forests."[5] Despite some of the recent reforesting of Ireland's landscape, "Ireland's Lost Landscape," a text that is over one hundred years old, belies the loss of a country that retains only the memories of place names and the loss of an entire culture whose identity was achieved through this forested landscape.

Ireland, of course, is not unique to this environmental concern. From a world perspective, the loss of forests continues at an astonishing rate. Robert Pogue Harrison, writing in his preface to *Forests: The Shadow of Civilization* in 1991, reflects the same motivations as Schama in *Landscape and Memory*: "What I hope to show is how many untold memories, ancient fears and dreams, popular traditions, and more recent myths and symbols are going up in the fires of deforestation."[6] Within the context of a deforested landscape and living in generations removed from the sight and memories of that landscape, it is sometimes difficult to assess what exactly has been lost. This is especially the case with Irish history, for this history begins with the loss of these forests and focuses instead on the politics that ensue as a result of this changed land. As Harrison contends, "Western civilization literally cleared its space in the midst of forests."[7] For Ireland, this cleared space became the divided and redivided farmland that embodied a human landscape rather than a more natural one. Though Harrison does not reference Ireland in *Forests*, he nonetheless makes this relevant point: "The forest in mythology, religion, and literature appears at a place where the logic of distinction goes astray. Or where our subjective categories are confounded."[8]

The early Irish poets, particularly the hermit poets, were working from such a canvas; the forest itself became a place, from a "deforested" perspective, from which literary analysis would in fact "go astray." This early poetry had its roots in attitudes in a forested culture that was developed and nurtured within druidic traditions to which the natural world was so central. The subject matter of this poetry quite often focused on a particular element within the forest.

Early in Ireland's history, forests covered nearly the entire island. To understand life in this topography, the relationship between the Celtic realm (including the forests of mainland Europe) and the trees requires a closer examination of the early colonizing of Ireland by Celtic tribes. Tacitus (ca. AD 56–ca. 120), a Roman historian, commented on the druidic practices that he had witnessed firsthand within the realm of the forest. "The [forest] grove," he wrote, "is the center of their whole religion. It is regarded as the cradle of the race and the dwelling place of the supreme god to whom all things are subject and obedient."[9] For the Celtic peoples, the grove was the spiritual center of their existence. As James G. Frazer notes in *The Golden Bough*, "For at the dawn of history Europe was covered with immense primaeval forests in which the scattered clearings must have appeared like islets in an ocean of green."[10] These islets served as vantage points from which to observe the forested landscape. Miranda J. Green's *The World of the Druids* references a passage by Lucan, from *Pharsalia*, book 3, that supports this view: "The axe-man came on an ancient and sacred grove. Its interesting branches enclosed a cool central space into which the sun never shone but where an abundance of water sprouted from dark springs."[11] In this passage, the Celtic veneration of forests weaves the aesthetics of the landscape into a vantage point from which the worship of nature can begin, with abundant fresh water on which to survive. Green elaborates on this in her citation of the *Dinnschenchas* (the "History of Places"), a pagan mythic text that traces the mythical geography of ancient Ireland. "Holy trees," Green states, "were particularly associated with sacral kinship and the inauguration rites surrounding the election of a new king."[12]

The sheer size and longevity of these trees and their communal nature in the creation of thick forests were monuments of wisdom and stability for the ancient Celts. In fact, the worship in these groves attained a similar aesthetic experienced in Gothic cathedrals. The Gothic cathedral is a representation of the forest. As Harrison notes, the cathedral "visibly reproduces the ancient scenes of worship in its lofty interior, which rises vertically toward the sky and then curves into a vault from all sides, like so many tree crowns converging into a canopy overhead. Like breaks in the foliage, windows let in light from beyond the enclosure, reflecting an ancient correspondence between forests and the dwelling place of a god."[13] In the Gothic cathedral lie remnants of a civilization that did not worship the Christian God but instead fostered a spiritual connection to the natural world beneath a canopy of leaves.

This grove-worship focused not just on the particular location of breaks in the foliage but also on particular species of trees. This was especially the case for oak, yew, and ash trees. Ash trees, especially, were venerated by the Irish Celts; when the tribes began to arrive in Ireland about 800 BC, they appear to have brought with them a new relationship with trees. When the ancient term *bille* was used, this was generally in reference to the veneration of the ash tree.[14] Certain tree species were also connected to specific human characteristics and emotions. The birch tree, for example, with its peeling bark and light features, became associated with love. This is evinced by birch wreaths, which became a common love token.[15] The hazel tree was associated with wisdom, and it had a special connection to druids and seers. Finn, the hero of the Fenian cycle, received knowledge from contact with the flesh of the salmon of wisdom, and the salmon had gained its own powers of wisdom through consumption of the fruit of the nine sacred hazel trees growing beneath the sea beside a well.[16]

The Mystery

This poem is ascribed to Amergin, a Milesian prince or druid who settled in Ireland hundreds of years before Christ, and is from the *Leabhar Gabhala*, or *Book of Invasions*. The poem is translated by Douglas Hyde.

I am the wind which breathes upon the sea,
I am the wave of the ocean,
I am the murmur of the billows,
I am the ox of the seven combats,
I am the vulture upon the rocks,
I am the beam of the sun,
I am the fairest of plants,
I am the wild boar in valour,
I am a salmon in the water,
I am a lake in the plain,
I am a word of science,
I am the point of the lance of battle,
I am the God who created in the head the fire.
Who is it who throws light into the meeting on the mountain?
Who announces the ages of the moon?
Who teaches the place where couches the sun?
(If not I)[17]

Deer's Cry or St. Patrick's Breastplate

Attributed to St. Patrick (385–461); translation by Kuno Meyer. The coming of Patrick to Ireland about the middle of the fifth century initiated the most peaceful invasion and lasting conquest of all. This hymn is attributed to Patrick and certainly reflects many of the themes found in Patrick's thought. The version we have today was probably written in the late seventh or early eighth century. The hymn is a celebration of the wisdom and power of God both in creation and redemption. It is an excellent example of a lorica, a "breastplate" or corslet of faith recited for the protection of body and soul against all forms of evil—devils, vice, and the evil that humans perpetrate against one another. The name of the hymn derives from a legend of an incident when the high king of Tara, Loeguire, resolved to ambush and kill Patrick and his monks to prevent them from spreading the Christian faith in his kingdom. As Patrick and his followers approached singing this hymn, the king and his men saw only a herd of wild deer and let them pass by. The word "cry" also has the sense of a prayer or petition.

I arise today
Through a mighty strength, the invocation of the Trinity,
Through belief in the threeness,
Through confession of the oneness
Of the Creator of Creation.

I arise today
Through the strength of Christ's birth with His baptism,
Through the strength of His crucifixion with His burial,
Through the strength of His resurrection with His ascension,
Through the strength of His descent for the judgement of Doom.

I arise today
Through the strength of the love of the Cherubim,
In the obedience of angels,
In the service of archangels,
In the hope of the resurrection to meet with reward,
In the prayers of patriarchs,
In prediction of prophets,
In preaching of apostles,
In faith of confessors,
In innocence of holy virgins,
In deeds of righteous men.

I arise today
Through the strength of heaven;
Light of sun,
Radiance of moon,
Splendour of fire,
Speed of lightning,
Swiftness of wind,

Depth of sea,
Stability of earth,
Firmness of rock.

I arise today
Through God's strength to pilot me:
God's might to uphold me,
God's wisdom to guide me,
God's eye to look before me,
God's ear to hear me,
God's word to speak to me,
God's hand to guard me,
God's way to lie before me,
God's shield to protect me,
God's host to save me,

From snares of devils,
From temptation of vices,
From every one who shall wish me ill,
Afar and anear,
Alone and in a multitude.
I summon today all these powers between me and those evils,
Against every cruel merciless power that may oppose my body and soul,
Against incantations of false prophets,
Against black laws of pagandom,
Against false laws of heretics,
Against craft of idolatry,
Against spells of women and smiths and wizards,
Against every knowledge that corrupts man's body and soul.

Christ to shield me today,
Against poising, against burning,
Against drowning, against wounding,
So there come to me abundance of reward.

Christ with me, Christ before me, Christ behind me,
Christ in me, Christ beneath me, Christ above me,
Christ on my right, Christ on my left,
Christ when I lie down, Christ when I sit down,
Christ when I arise, Christ in the heart of every man who thinks of me,
Christ in the mouth of every one who speaks of me,
Christ in the eye of every one who sees me,
Christ in every ear that hears me.

I arise today
Through a mighty strength, the invocation of the Trinity,
Through belief in the threeness,
Through confession of the oneness
Of the Creator of Creation.[18]

St. Columcille of Iona

St. Columcille of Iona (also known as Columba, Colum, Columbus, Combs, and Columkill) was born on December 7, AD 521, in Gartan, County Donegal. He is one of the three patron saints of Ireland, along with Patrick and Brigit. After founding churches in Derry, Swords, Durrow, and Kells, Columcille is said to have made a copy of the Psalter of St. Finnian without permission, found guilty by Domnall the high king, and sentenced to exile. Eventually, Columcille sailed to Iona, an island between Ulster and Gaelic Scotland, where he established a monastery, which became a center of a federation of monastic establishments in Scotland, northern Britain, and Ireland. Numerous legends were connected to Columcille after his death, and many poems were ascribed to him, as was the Cathach, a Latin psalter, probably the oldest surviving manuscript in Ireland. Like Merlin in British tradition, Columcille became the authority for many Irish prophecies, including the Viking invasion. In the poem "Columcille Fecit" (*fecit* meaning "writing"), the verse reflects the beauty of Ireland's natural world from the vantage point of its rugged coast.

Columcille Fecit

[COLUMCILLE WRITING]
Delightful would it be to me to be in Uchd Ailiun

On the pinnacle of a rock,
That I might often see

The face of the ocean;
That I might see its heaving waves

Over the wide ocean,
When they chant music to their Father

Upon the world's course;
That I might see its level sparkling strand,

It would be no cause of sorrow;
That I might hear the song of the wonderful birds,

Source of happiness;
That I might hear the thunder of the crowding waves

Upon the rocks;
That I might hear the roar by the side of the church
Of the surrounding sea;
That I might see its noble flocks

Over the watery ocean;
That I might see the sea-monsters,

The greatest of all wonders;
That I might see its ebb and flood

In their career;
That my mystical name might be, I say,
Cul ri Erin;
That contrition might come upon my heart

Upon looking at her;
That I might bewail my evils all,

Though it were difficult to compute them;
That I might bless the Lord

Who conserves all,
Heaven with its countless bright orders,

Land, strand and flood;
That I might search the books all,

That would be good for my soul;
At times kneeling to beloved Heaven;

At times psalm singing;
At times contemplating the King of Heaven,

Holy the chief;
At times at work without compulsion,

This would be delightful.
At times plucking duilisc from the rocks;

At times at fishing;
At times giving food to the poor;

At times in a carcai:

The best advice in the presence of God
To me has been vouchsafed.
The King whose servant I am will not let
Anything deceive me.[19]

Caelius Sedulius

Caelius Sedulius (ca. 400–454) was a fifth-century Irish bard who composed the first Christian epic, *Carmen Paschale*, or *Easter Song*. The first book contains a summary of the Old Testament, the four others a summary of the New Testament. Dante, Milton, and other poets borrowed from this epic work. He follows usually the Gospel of St. Matthew. His ordinary method of exegesis consists of allegory and symbolism. Thus the four Evangelists correspond to the four seasons, the twelve Apostles to the twelve hours of the day and the twelve months, the four arms of the cross to the four cardinal points. Like most epic poets, Sedulius begins *Carmen Paschale* with an invocation, asking for divine guidance. The invocation also illustrates the early Christian connection to the natural world in the form of a Christian prayer and is at once a creation story of Ireland.

Invocation

ETERNAL God omnipotent! The One
Sole Hope of worlds, Author and Guard alone
Of heaven and earth Thou art, whose high behest
Forbids the tempest's billow-bearing breast
The land to whelm—which fires the orb of noon,
And fills the crescent of the milder moon;
Who'st meted forth alternate day and night
And numbered all the stars—their places bright,
Their signs, times, courses only known to Thee—
Who hast to many forms, most wondrously,
The new earth shaped, and given to dead dust life:
Who hast lost Man restored, for fruit of strife
Forbid, bestown on him a higher food,
And healed the Serpent's sting by sacred blood:

Who hast, when men (save those borne in the Ark)
Were tombed in floods of whelming waters dark
From one sole stock again the race renewed
(A sign that sin-slain man, through noble wood
Once more should be redeemed), and sent to save
One Fount baptismal all the world to lave!

Ope me the way that to the City bright
Leads forth; let thy Word's lamp be light
To guide my footsteps through the narrow gate,
Where the Good Shepherd feeds His sheep elate:
There first the Virgin's white Lamb entered
And all His fair flock followed where He led!

With Thee how smooth the way: for Nature all
Thine empire owns! Thou speak'st, her fetters fall

And all her wonted shows new forms assume:
The frozen fields will into verdue bloom
And winter gild with grain: if Thou but will
'Mid budding Spring the swelling grape shall fill,
And sudden labour tread the bursting vine.
All seasons answer to the call Divine!
So ancient Faith attests, so tell the hours—
No time can change, no age abate Thy powers!

Whereof to sing, in little part, afraid
I seek, as entering a great forest-glade
One strives an over-arching bough to reach.
What were an hundred tongues, an iron speech,
Or what were man an hundredfold to show
Things more than all the lucid stars that glow,
And all the sands where all the oceans flow![20]

Anonymous Early Irish Nature Poetry

Early Irish nature poems were largely anonymous, and the manuscripts of these ancient poems were culled from various monasteries throughout Ireland, existing today largely in translations. Kuno Meyer, a German scholar distinguished in the field of Celtic philology and literature, translated much of these early manuscripts, which have allowed modern readers access to these early poems. In his introduction to *Ancient Irish Poetry*, Meyer comments on the uniqueness of this early Irish verse: "In Nature Poetry the Gaelic muse may vie with that of any other nation. Indeed, these poems occupy a unique position in the literature of the world. To seek out and watch and love Nature, in its tiniest phenomena as in its grandest, was given to no people so early and so fully as to the Celt."[21] The following selections of early Irish poems have been translated by the Irish fiction writer Frank O'Connor, the British Celt scholar Robin Flower, and Kuno Meyer.

The Blackbird by Belfast Lough

ca. 800s; translated by Frank O'Connor

What little throat
Has framed that note?
What gold beak shot
  It far away?
A blackbird on
His leafy throne
Tossed it alone
  Across the bay.[22]

The Scribe

800s; translated by Robin Flower

Over my head the woodland wall
Rises; the ousel sings to me.
Above my booklet lined for words
The woodland birds shake out their glee.

There's the blithe cuckoo chanting clear
In mantle gre from bouth to bough!
God keep me still! for here I write
A scripture bright in great woods now.[23]

The White Lake

Translated by Kuno Meyer

When holy Patrick full of grace
Suffered on Cruach, that blest place,
In grief and gloom enduring then
For Eire's women, Eire's men,

God for his comfort sent a flight
Of birds angelically bright
That sang above the darkling lake
A song of unceasing for his sake.

'Twas thus they chanted, all and some,
'Come hither, Patrick! hither come!
Shield of the Gael, thou light of story,
Appointed star of the golden glory!'

Thus singing all those fair birds smite
The waters with soft wings in flight
Till the dark lake its gloom surrenders
And rolls a tide of silvery splendours.[24]

The Lark

Translated by Kuno Meyer

Learned in music sings the lark,
I leave my cell to listen;
His open beak spills music, hark!
Where Heaven's bright cloudlets glisten.

And so I'll sing my morning psalm
That God bright Heaven may give me
And keep me in eternal calm
And from all sin relieve me.[25]

The Hermit's Song

Translated by Kuno Meyer

I wish, O Son of the living God, O ancient, eternal King,
For a hidden little hut in the wilderness that it may be my dwelling.

An all-grey lithe little lark to be by its side,
A clear pool to wash away sins through the grace of the Holy Spirit.

Quite near, a beautiful wood around it on every side,
To nurse many-voiced birds, hiding it with its shelter.

A southern aspect for warmth, a little brook across its floor,
A choice land with many gracious gifts such as be good for every plant.

A few men of sense—we will tell their number—
Humble and obedient, to pray to the King:—

Four times three, three times four, fit for every need.
Twice six in the church, both north and south:—

Six pairs besides myself.
Praying for ever the King who makes the sun shine.

A pleasant church and with the linen altar-cloth, a dwelling for God from Heaven;
Then, shining candles above the pure white Scriptures.

One house for all to go to for the care of the body,
Without ribaldry, without boasting, without thought of evil.

This is the husbandry I would take, I would choose, and will not hide it:
Fragrant leek, hens, salmon, trout, bees.

Raiment and food enough for me from the King of fair fame,
And I to be sitting for a while praying God in every place.[26]

King and Hermit

Translated by Kuno Meyer

Marvan, brother of King Guare of Connaught in the seventh century, had
renounced the life of a warrior-prince for that of a hermit. The king endeavoured
to persuade his brother to return to his court, when the following colloquy took
place between them.

Guare.
Why, hermit Marvan, sleepest thou not
Upon a feather quilt?
Why rather sleepest thou abroad
Upon a pitchpine floor?

Marvan.
I have a shieling in the wood,
None knows it save my God:
An ash-tree on the hither side, a hazel-bush beyond,
A huge old tree encompasses it.

Two heath-clad doorposts for support,
And a lintel of honeysuckle:
The forest around its narrowness sheds
Its mast upon fat swine.

The size of my shieling tiny, not too tiny,
Many are its familiar paths:
From its gable a sweet strain sings
A she-bird in her cloak of the ousel's hue.

The stags of Oakridge leap
Into the river of clear banks:
Thence red Roiny can be seen.
Glorious Muckraw and Moinmoy.

A hiding mane of green-barked yew
Supports the sky:
Beautiful spot! the large green of an oak
Fronting the storm.

A tree of apples—great its bounty!
Like a hostel, vast!
A pretty bush, thick as a fist, of tiny hazel-nuts,
A green mass of branches.

A choice pure spring and princely water
To drink:
There spring watercresses, yew-berries,
Ivy-bushes thick as a man.

Around it tame swine lie down.
Goats, pigs.
Wild swine, grazing deer,
A badger's brood.

A peaceful troop, a heavy host of denizens of the soil,
A-trysting at my house:
To meet them foxes come.
How delightful!

Fairest princes come to my house,
A ready gathering:
Pure water, perennial bushes,
Salmon, trout.

A bush of rowan, black sloes,
Dusky blackthorns,
Plenty of food, acorns, pure berries,
Bare flags,

A clutch of eggs, honey, delicious mast,
God has sent it:
Sweet apples, red whortleberries.
And blueberries.

Ale with herbs, a dish of strawberries
Of good taste and colour,
Haws, berries of the juniper,
Sloes, nuts.

A cup with mead of hazel-nut, blue-bells,
Quick-growing rushes,
Dun oaklets, manes of briar,
Goodly sweet tangle.

When brilliant summer-time spreads its coloured mantle,
Sweet-tasting fragrance!
Pignuts, wild marjoram, green leeks.
Verdant pureness!

The music of the bright red-breasted men,
A lovely movement!
The strain of the thrush, familiar cuckoos
Above my house.

Swarms of bees and chafers, the little musicians of the world,
A gentle chorus:
Wild geese and ducks, shortly before summer's end,
The music of the dark torrent.

An active songster, a lively wren
From the hazel-bough.
Beautiful hooded birds, woodpeckers,
A vast multitude!

Fair white birds come, herons, seagulls.
The cuckoo sings between—
No mournful music! dun heathpoults
Out of the russet heather.

The lowing of heifers in summer.
Brightest of seasons!
Not bitter, toilsome over the fertile plain.
Delightful, smooth!

The voice of the wind against the branchy wood
Upon the deep-blue sky:
Falls of the river, the note of the swan,
Delicious music!

The bravest band make cheer to me.
Who have not been hired:
In the eyes of Christ the ever-young I am no worse off
Than thou art.

Though thou rejoicest in thy own pleasures,
Greater than any wealth;
I am grateful for what is given me
From my good Christ.

Without an hour of fighting, without the din of strife
In my house,
Grateful to the Prince who giveth every good
To me in my shieling.

Guare.
I would give my glorious kingship
With the share of my father's heritage—
To the hour of my death I would forfeit it
To be in thy company, my Marvan.[27]

Song of the Sea

Translated by Kuno Meyer

A great tempest rages on the Plain of Ler, bold across its high borders
Wind has arisen, fierce winter has slain us; it has come across the sea,
It has pierced us like a spear.

When the wind sets from the east, the spirit of the wave is roused.
It desires to rush past us westward to the land where sets the sun,
To the wild and broad green sea.

When the wind sets from the north, it urges the dark fierce waves
Towards the southern world, surging in strife against the wide sky,
Listening to the witching song.

When the wind sets from the west across the salt sea of swift currents,
It desires to go past us eastward towards the Sun-Tree,
Into the broad long-distant sea.

When the wind sets from the south across the land of Saxons of mighty shields,
The wave strikes the Isle of Scit, it surges up to the summit of Caladnet,
And pounds the grey-green mouth of the Shannon.

The ocean is in flood, the sea is full, delightful is the home of ships,
The wind whirls the sand around the estuary,
Swiftly the rudder cleaves the broad sea.

With mighty force the wave has tumbled across each broad river-mouth,
Wind has come, white winter has slain us, around Cantire, around the land of
    Alba,
Slieve-Dremon pours forth a full stream.

Son of the God the Father, with mighty hosts, save me from the horror of fierce
    tempests!
Righteous Lord of the Feast, only save me from the horrid blast.
From Hell with furious tempest![28]

Summer Has Come

Translated by Kuno Meyer

Summer has come, healthy and free,
Whence the brown wood is aslope;
The slender nimble deer leap.
And the path of seals is smooth.

The cuckoo sings sweet music.
Whence there is smooth restful sleep;
Gentle birds leap upon the hill.
And swift grey stags.

Heat has laid hold of the rest of the deer—
The lovely cry of curly packs!
The white extent of the strand smiles,
There the swift sea is.

A sound of playful breezes in the tops
Of a black oakwood is Drum Daill,
The noble hornless herd runs.
To whom Cuan-wood is a shelter.

Green bursts out on every herb.
The top of the green oakwood is bushy.
Summer has come, winter has gone,
Twisted hollies wound the hound.

The blackbird sings a loud strain.
To him the live wood is a heritage,
The sad angry sea is fallen asleep.
The speckled salmon leaps.

The sun smiles over every land,—
A parting for me from the brood of cares:
Hounds bark, stags tryst.
Ravens flourish, summer has come![29]

Song of Summer

Translated by Kuno Meyer

Summer-time, season supreme!
Splendid is colour then.
Blackbirds sing a full lay
If there be a slender shaft of day.

The dust-coloured cuckoo calls aloud:
Welcome, splendid summer!
The bitterness of bad weather is past.
The boughs of the wood are a thicket.

Panic startles the heart of the deer.
The smooth sea runs apace—
Season when ocean sinks asleep.
Blossom covers the world.

Bees with puny strength carry
A goodly burden, the harvest of blossoms;
Up the mountain-side kine take with them mud,
The ant makes a rich meal.

The harp of the forest sounds music,
The sail gathers—perfect peace;
Colour has settled on every height.
Haze on the lake of full waters.

The corncrake, a strenuous bard, discourses.
The lofty cold waterfall sings
A welcome to the warm pool—
The talk of the rushes has come.

Light swallows dart aloft.
Loud melody encircles the hill,
The soft rich mast buds.
The stuttering quagmire prattles.

The peat-bog is as the raven's coat,
The loud cuckoo bids welcome,
The speckled fish leaps—
Strong is the bound of the swift warrior.

Man flourishes, the maiden buds
In her fair strong pride.
Perfect each forest from top to ground.
Perfect each great stately plain.

Delightful is the season's splendour,
Rough winter has gone:
Every fruitful wood shines white,
A joyous peace is summer.

A flock of birds settles
In the midst of meadows,
The green field rustles.
Wherein is a brawling white stream.

A wild longing is on you to race horses.
The ranked host is ranged around:
A bright shaft has been shot into the land.
So that the water-flag is gold beneath it.

A timorous, tiny, persistent little fellow
Sings at the top of his voice,
The lark sings clear tidings:
Surpassing summer-time of delicate hues![30]

Summer Is Gone

Translated by Kuno Meyer

My tidings for you: the stag bells.
Winter snows, summer is gone.

Wind high and cold, low the sun,
Short his course, sea running high.

Deep-red the bracken, its shape all gone—
The wild-goose has raised his wonted cry.

Cold has caught the wings of birds;
Season of ice—these are my tidings.[31]

A Song of Winter

Translated by Kuno Meyer

Cold, cold!
Cold to-night is broad Moylurg,
Higher the snow than the mountain-range.
The deer cannot get at their food.

Cold till Doom!
The storm has spread over all:
A river is each furrow upon the slope,
Each ford a full pool.

A great tidal sea is each loch,
A full loch is each pool:
Horses cannot get over the ford of Ross,
No more can two feet get there.

The fish of Ireland are a-roaming,
There is no strand which the wave does not pound.
Not a town there is in the land,
Not a bell is heard, no crane talks.

The wolves of Cuan-wood get
Neither rest nor sleep in their lair,
The little wren cannot find
Shelter in her nest on the slope of Lon.

Keen wind and cold ice
Has burst upon the little company of birds,
The blackbird cannot get a lee to her liking.
Shelter for its side in Cuan-wood.

Cosy our pot on its hook.
Crazy the hut on the slope of Lon:
The snow has crushed the wood here.
Toilsome to climb up Ben-bo.

Glenn Rye's ancient bird
From the bitter wind gets grief;
Great her misery and her pain.
The ice will get into her mouth.

From flock and from down to rise—
Take it to heart!—were folly for thee
Ice in heaps on every ford—
That is why I say 'cold'![32]

Arran

Translated by Kuno Meyer

Arran of the many stags,
The sea strikes against its shoulder,
Isle in which companies are fed.
Ridge on which blue spears are reddened.

Skittish deer are on her peaks,
Delicious berries on her manes.
Cool water in her rivers.
Mast upon her dun oaks.

Greyhounds are in it and beagles,
Blackberries and sloes of the dark blackthorn,
Her dwellings close against the woods,
Deer scattered about her oak-woods.

Gleaning of purple upon her rocks.
Faultless grass upon her slopes,
Over her fair shapely crags
Noise of dappled fawns a-skipping.

Smooth is her level land, fat are her swine.
Bright are her fields.
Her nuts upon the tops of her hazel-wood,
Long galleys sailing past her.

Delightful it is when the fair season comes.
Trout under the brinks of her rivers.
Seagulls answer each other round her white cliff,
Delightful at all times is Arran![33]

Buile Suibhne

[FRENZY OF SWEENEY]

Buile Suibhne is considered to be a twelfth-century manuscript. Already in the ninth century, however, there is evidence that Suibhne Geilt (Sweeney the Wild) was a story told and celebrated. Further evidence indicates, from the same period or even earlier, a nature poem attributed to Suibhne is preserved in a fragment of manuscript now in the monastery of St. Paul, Karnten, Austria. Coincidentally, the poem is followed by verses attributed to St. Moling, a character elsewhere associated with Suibhne. Not only does Moling welcome the madman to his church of St. Mullins, Carlow, in the final section of the text, but he is also separately attested as the reputed author of some Middle Irish poems dealing with Suibhne. The poem is a development of an oral tradition that dates back to AD 637 and the Battle of Moira, a battle during which Sweeney (Suibhne) went mad and was transformed, in fulfillment of St. Ronan's curse, into a bird and, by virtue of fright and flight, was relegated to the natural world of Ireland's deep forests. Through the story of his wanderings, both physical and mental, Suibhne became the principal Irish exponent of the legend of the Wild Man, and many of the motifs attached to him are associated with rites of passage and the transition from one state to another. This version, "The Frenzy of Suibhne, being the Adventures of Suibhne-Geilt, a Middle-Irish Romance," was edited by J. G. O'Keeffe and published by the Irish Texts Society in 1913. The most notable version, *Sweeney Astray*, was translated and published by Seamus Heaney in 1983. In all translations, the immersion in Ireland's natural world of deep, abiding forests is a prominent part of the text.

As to Suibhne, son of Colman Cuar, king of Dal Araidhe, we have already told how he went wandering and flying out of battle. Here are set forth the cause and occasion whereby these symptoms and fits of frenzy and flightiness came upon him beyond all others, likewise what befell him thereafter.

There was a certain noble, distinguished holy patron in Ireland, even Ronan Finn, son of Bearach, son of Criodhan, son of Earclugh, son of Ernainne, son of Urene, son of Seachnusach, son of Colum Cuile, son of Mureadhach, son of Laoghaire, son of Niall; a man who fulfilled God's command and bore the yoke of piety, and endured, persecutions for the Lord's sake. He was God's own worthy servant, for it was his wont to crucify his body for love of God and to win a reward for his soul. A sheltering shield against evil attacks of the devil and against vices was that gentle, friendly, active man.

On one occasion he was marking out a church named Cell Luinne in Dal Araidhe. (At that time Suibhne, son of Colman, of whom we have spoken, was king of Dal Araidhe.) Now, in the place where he was, Suibhne heard the sound of Ronan's bell as he was marking out the church, and he asked his people what it was they heard. 'It is Ronan Finn, son of Bearach,' said they, 'who is marking out a church in your territory and land, and it is the sound of his bell you now hear.' Suibhne was greatly angered and enraged, and he set out with the utmost haste to drive the cleric from the church. His wife, Eorann, daughter of Conn of Ciannacht, in order to hold him, seized the wing of the fringed, crimson cloak which was around him, so that the fibula of pure white silver, neatly inlaid with gold, which was on his cloak over his breast, sprang through the house. Therewith, leaving his cloak with the queen, he set out stark-naked in his swift career to expel the cleric from the church, until he reached the place where Ronan was.

He found the cleric at the time glorifying the King of heaven and earth by blithely chanting his psalms with his lined, right-beautiful psalter in front of him. Suibhne took up the psalter and cast it into the depths of the cold-water lake which was near him, so that it was drowned therein. Then he seized Ronan's hand and dragged him out through the church after him, nor did he let go the cleric's hand until he heard a cry of alarm. It was a serving-man of Congai Claon, son of Scannlan, who uttered that cry; he had come from Congal himself to Suibhne in order that he (Suibhne) might engage in battle at Magh Rath. When the serving-man reached the place of parley with Suibhne, he related the news to him from beginning to end. Suibhne then went with the serving-man and left the cleric sad and sorrowful over the loss of his psalter and the contempt and dishonour which had been inflicted on him.

Thereafter, at the end of a day and a night, an otter that was in the lake came to Ronan with the psalter, and neither line nor letter of it was injured. Ronan gave thanks to God for that miracle, and then cursed Suibhne, saying: "Be it my will, together with the will of the mighty Lord, that even as he came stark-naked to expel me, may it be thus that he will ever be, naked, wandering and flying throughout the world; may it be death from a spear-point that will carry him off. My curse once more on Suibhne, and my blessing on Eorann who strove to hold him; and further-more, I bequeath to the race of Colman that destruction and extinction may be their lot the day they shall behold this psalter which was cast into the water by Suibhne"; and he uttered this lay:

Ronan:
Suibhne, son of Colman, has
outraged me, he has dragged me with him by the hand,
to leave Cell Luinne with him,
that I should be for a time absent from it.
He came to me in his swift course
on hearing my bell;
he brought with him vast, awful
wrath to drive me out, to banish me.
Loth was I to be banished here from
the place where I first settled
though loth was I, God has been
able to prevent it.
He let not my hand out of his until
he heard the loud cry which said to
him: 'Come to the battle, Domnall'
has reached famous Magh Rath.
Good has come to me therefrom,
not to him did I give thanks for it
when tidings of the battle came for
him to join the high prince.

From afar he approached the battle
whereby were deranged his sense and reason,
he will roam through Erin as a stark madman,
and it shall be by a spear-point he will die.
He seized my psalter in his hand,
he cast it into the full lake,
Christ brought it to me without a blemish,
so that no worse was the psalter.
A day and a night in the full lake,
nor was the speckled white [book] the worse;
through the will of God's Son
an otter gave it to me again.
As for the psalter that he seized in his hand,
I bequeath to the race of Colman
that it will be bad for the race of fair Colman
the day they shall behold the psalter.
Stark-naked he has come here
to wring my heart, to chase me;
on that account God will cause
that Suibhne shall ever naked be.
Eorann, daughter of Conn of Ciannacht,
strove to hold him by his cloak;
my blessing on Eorann therefor,
and my curse on Suibhne.

Thereupon Ronan came to Magh Rath to make peace between Domnall, son of Aodh, and Congal Claon, son of Scannlan, but he did not succeed. Howbeit, the cleric used to be taken each day as a guarantee between them that nobody would be slain from the time the fighting was stopped until it would be again permitted. Suibhne, however, used to violate the cleric's guarantee of protection inasmuch as every peace and truce which Ronan would make Suibhne would break, for he used to slay a man before the hour fixed for combat each day, and another each evening when the combat ceased. Then on the day fixed for the great battle Suibhne came to battle before the rest.

In this wise did he appear. A filmy shirt of silk was next his white skin, around him was a girdle of royal satin, likewise the tunic which Congal had given him the day he slew Oilill Cedach, king of the Ui Faolain, at Magh Rath; a crimson tunic of one colour was it with a close, well-woven border of beautiful, refined gold set with rows of fair gems of carbuncle from one end to the other of the border, having in it silken loops over beautiful, shining buttons for fastening and opening it, with variegation of pure white silver each way and each path he would go; there was a slender-threaded hard fringe to that tunic. In his hands were two spears very long and (shod) with broad iron, a yellow-speckled, homy shield was on his back, a gold-hilted sword at his left side.

He marched on thus until he encountered Ronan with eight psalmists of his community sprinkling holy water on the hosts, and they sprinkled it on Suibhne as they did on the others. Thinking it was to mock him that the water was sprinkled on him, he placed his finger on the string of the riveted spear that was in his hand, and hurling it at one of Ronan's psalmists slew him with that single cast. He made another cast with the edged, sharp-angled dart at the cleric himself, so that it pierced the bell which was on his breast and the shaft sprang off it up in the air, whereupon the cleric said: 'I pray the mighty Lord that high as went the spear-shaft into the air and among the clouds of Heaven may you go likewise even as any bird, and may the death which you have inflicted on my foster-child be that which will carry you off, to wit, death from a spear-point; and my curse on you, and my blessing on Eorann; (I invoke) Uradhran and Telle on my behalf against your seed and the descendants of Colman Cuar,' and he said:

Ronan:
My curse on Suibhne!
Great is his guilt against me,
his smooth, vigorous
dart he thrust through my holy bell.
That bell which thou hast wounded
will send thee among branches,
so that thou shalt be one with the birds—
the bell of saints before saints.
Even as in an instant went
the spear-shaft on high,
mayst thou go, O Suibhne,
in madness, without respite!
Thou hast slain my foster-child,
thou hast reddened thy spear in him,
thou shalt have in return for it
that with a spear-point thou shalt die.
If there should oppose me
the progeny of Eoghan with stoutness
Uradhran and Telle will send them into decay.
Uradhran and Telle
have sent them into decay,
this is my wish for all time:
my curse with thee!
My blessing on Eorann!
Eorann fair without decay:
through suffering without stint
my curse on Suibhne!

Thereafter, when both battle-hosts had met, the vast army on both sides roared in the manner of a herd of stags so that they raised on high three mighty shouts. Now, when Suibhne heard these great cries together with their sounds and reverberations in the clouds of Heaven and in the vault of the firmament, he looked up, whereupon turbulence, and darkness, and fury, and giddiness, and frenzy, and flight, unsteadiness, restlessness, and unquiet filled him, likewise disgust with every place in which he uséd to be and desire for every place which he had not reached. His fingers were palsied, his feet trembled, his heart beat quick, his senses were overcome, his sight was distorted, his weapons fell naked from his hands, so that through Ronan's curse he went, like any bird of the air, in madness and imbecility.

Now, however, when he arrived out of the battle, it was seldom that his feet would touch the ground because of the swiftness of his course, and when he did touch it he would not shake the dew from the top of the grass for the lightness and the nimbleness of his step. He halted not from that headlong course until he left neither plain, nor field, nor bare mountain, nor bog, nor thicket, nor marsh, nor hill, nor hollow, nor dense-sheltering wood in Ireland that he did not travel that day, until he reached Ros Bearaigh, in Glenn Earcain, where he went into the yew-tree that was in the glen.

Domnall, son of Aedh, won the battle that day, as we have already narrated. Suibhne had a kinsman in the battle, to wit, Aongus the Stout, son of Ardgal, son of Macnia, son of Ninnidh, of the tribes of Ui Ninnedha of Dal Araidhe; he came in flight with a number of his people out of the battle, and the route he took was through Glenn Earcain. Now he and his people were conversing about Suibhne (saying) how strange it was that they had not seen him alive or dead after the battle-hosts had met. Howbeit, they felt certain it was because of Ronan's curse that there were no tidings of his fate. Suibhne in the yew-tree above them heard what they spoke, and he said:

Suibhne:
O warriors, come hither,
O men of Dal Araidhe,
you will find in the tree in which he is
the man whom you seek.
God has vouchsafed me here
life very bare, very narrow,
without music and without restful sleep,
without womenfolk, without a woman-tryst.
Here at Ros Bearaigh am I,
Ronan has put me under disgrace,
God has severed me from my form,
know me no more, O warriors.

When the men heard Suibhne reciting the verses, they recognized him, and urged him to trust them. He said that he would never do so. Then, as they were closing round the tree, Suibhne rose out of it very lightly and nimbly (and went) to Cell Riagain in Tir Conaill where he perched on the old tree of the church. It chanced that it was at that tree Domnall, son of Aedh, and his army were after the battle, and when they saw the madman going into the tree, a portion of the army came and closed in all round it. Thereupon they began describing aloud the madman; one man would say that it was a woman, another that it was a man, until Domnall himself recognized him, whereupon he said: 'It is Suibhne, king of Dal Araidhe, whom Ronan cursed the day the battle was fought. Good in sooth is the man who is there,' said he, 'and if he wished for treasures and wealth he would obtain them from us if only he would trust us. Sad is it to me,' said he, 'that the remnant of Congal's people are thus, for both good and great were the ties that bound me to Congal before undertaking the battle, and good moreover was the counsel of Colum Cille to that youth himself when he went with Congal to ask an army from the king of Alba against me'; whereupon Domnall uttered the lay:

Domhnall:
How is that, O slender Suibhne?
thou wert leader of many hosts;
the day the iniquitous battle was fought
at Magh Rath thou wert most comely.
Like crimson or like beautiful gold
was thy noble countenance after feasting,
like down or like shavings
was the faultless hair of thy head.
Like cold snow of a single night
was the aspect of thy body ever;
blue-hued was thine eye, like crystal,
like smooth, beautiful ice.
Delightful the shape of thy feet,
not powerful methinks was thy chieftainship;
thy fortunate weapons—they could draw blood—
were swift in wounding.
Colum Cille offered thee
Heaven and kingship, O splendid youth,
eagerly (?) thou hast come into the plain
from the chief prophet of Heaven and earth.
Said Colum Cille,
steadfast prophet of truth,
'as many of you as come over the strong flood
will not all return from Erin.'
I offered Congal Claon
when we were together
the blessing of all the men of Erin;
great was the mulct for one egg.
If thou wilt not accept that from me,
O fair Congal, son of Scannal,
what judgment then—deed of great moment—
wilt thou pass upon me?

Congal:
(These) will I accept from thee if thou deemest it well:
give me thy two sons,
thy hand from thee, likewise thy stately wife,
thy daughter and thy eye blue-starred.

Domnall:
Thou shalt not have but spear to spear,
I shall be evermore lying in wait for you,
this is our speech about the bondage;
take thou the full of my curse!
Thy body will be a feast for birds of prey,
ravens will be on thy heavy silence,
a fierce, black spear shall wound thee,
and thou shalt be laid on thy back, destitute.
My bane from land to land
art thou alone beyond each king,
yet I have befriended thee
since the day thy mother brought thee forth.
'Tis there the battle was fought—
at the stead in Magh Rath—
there was a drop on a gleaming sword;
so fell Congal Claon.

Now when Suibhne heard the shout of the multitude and the tumult of the great army, he ascended from the tree towards the rain-clouds of the firmament, over the summits of every place and over the ridge-pole of every land. For a long time thereafter he was (faring) throughout Ireland, visiting and searching in hard, rocky clefts and in bushy branches of tall ivy-trees, in narrow cavities of stones, from estuary to estuary, from peak to peak, and from glen to glen, till he reached ever-delightful Glen Bolcain. It is there the madmen of Ireland used to go when their year in madness was complete, that glen being ever a place of great delight for madmen. For it is thus Glen Bolcain is: it has four gaps to the wind, likewise a wood very beautiful, very pleasant, and clean-banked wells and cool springs, and sandy, clear-water streams, and green-topped watercress and brooklime bent and long on their surface. Many likewise are its sorrels, its wood-sorrels, its lus-bian and its biorragan, its berries, and its wild garlic, its melle, and its miodhbhun, its black sloes and its brown acorns. The madmen moreover used to smite each other for the pick of watercress of that glen and for the choice of its couches.

   Suibhne also remained for a long time in that glen until he happened one night to be on the top of a tall ivy-clad hawthorn tree which was in the glen. It was hard for him to endure that bed, for at every twist and turn he would give, a shower of thorns off the hawthorn would stick in him, so that they were piercing and rubbing his side and wounding his skin. Suibhne thereupon changed from that bed to another place, where there was a dense thicket of great briars with fine thorns and a single protruding branch of blackthorn growing alone up through the thicket. Suibhne settled on the top of that tree, but so slender was it that it bowed and bent under him, so that he fell heavily through the thicket to the ground, and there was not as much as an inch from his hole to the crown of his head that was not wounded and reddened. He then rose up, strengthless and feeble, and came out through the thicket, whereupon he said: 'My conscience!' said he, 'it is hard to endure this life after a pleasant one, and a year to last night I have been leading this life,' whereupon he uttered the lay:

Suibhne:
A year to last night
have I been among the gloom of branches,
between flood and ebb,
without covering around me.
Without a pillow beneath my head,
among the fair children of men;
there is peril to us, O God,
without sword, without spear.
Without the company of women;
save brooklime of warrior-bands—
a pure fresh meal—
watercress is our desire.
Without a foray with a king,
I am alone in my home,
without glorious reavings,
without friends, without music.
Without sleep, alas!
let the truth be told,
without aid for a long time,
hard is my lot.
Without a house right full,
without the converse of generous men,
without the title of king,
without drink, without food.
Alas that I have been parted here
from my mighty, armed host,
a bitter madman in the glen,
bereft of sense and reason.
Without being on a kingly circuit,
but rushing along every path;
that is the great madness,
King of Heaven of saints.
Without accomplished musicians,
without the converse of women,
without bestowing treasures;
it has caused my death, O revered Christ.
Though I be as I am to-night,
there was a time
when my strength was not feeble
over a land that was not bad.
On splendid steeds,
in life without sorrow,
in my auspicious kingship
I was a good, great king.
After that, to be as I am

through selling Thee, O revered Christ!
a poor wretch am I, without power,
in the Glen of bright Bolcan.
The hawthorn that is not soft-topped
has subdued me, has pierced me;
the brown thorn-bush
has nigh caused my death.
The battle of Congal with fame,
to us it was doubly piteous;
on Tuesday was the rout;
more numerous were our dead than our living.
A-wandering in truth,
though I was noble and gentle,
I have been sad and wretched
a year to last night.

In that wise he remained in Glen Bolcain until at a certain time he raised himself up (into the air) and went to Cluain Cille on the border of Tir Conaill and Tir Boghaine. He went then to the brink of the well, where he had for food that night watercress and water. Thereafter he went into the old tree of the church. The erenach of the church was Faibhlen of the family of Brughach, son of Deaghadh. That night there came an exceeding great storm so that the extent of the night's misery affected Suibhne greatly, and he said: 'Sad indeed is it that I was not slain at Magh Rath rather than that I should encounter this hardship'; whereupon he uttered this lay:

Suibhne:
Cold is the snow to-night,
lasting now is my poverty,
there is no strength in me for fight,
famine has wounded me, madman as I am.
All men see that I am not shapely,
bare of thread is my tattered garment,
Suibhne of Ros Earcain is my name,
the crazy madman am I.
I rest not when night comes,
my foot frequents no trodden way,
I bide not here for long,
the bonds of terror come upon me.
My goal lies beyond the teeming main,
voyaging the prow-abounding sea;
fear has laid hold of my poor strength,
I am the crazy one of Glen Bolcain.
Frosty wind tearing me,
already snow has wounded me,
the storm bearing me to death
from the branches of each tree.
Grey branches have wounded me,

they have torn my hands;
the briars have not left
the making of a girdle for my feet.
There is a palsy on my hands,
everywhere there is cause of confusion,
from Sliabh Mis to Sliabh Cuillenn,
from Sliabh Cuillenn to Cuailgne.
Sad forever is my cry
on the summit of Cruachan Aighle,
from Gien Bolcain to Islay,
from Cenn Tire to Boirche.
Small is my portion when day comes,
it comes not as a new day's right (?),
a tuft of watercress of Cluain Cille
with Cell Cua's cuckoo flower.
He who is at Ros Earcach,
neither trouble nor evil shall come to him;
that which makes me strengthless
is being in snow in nakedness.

So Suibhne fared forth until he reached the church at Snamh dha En on the Shannon, which is now called Cluain Boirenn; he arrived there on a Friday, to speak
precisely. The clerics of the church were then fulfilling the office of nones; women
were beating flax, and one was giving birth to a child. 'It is not meet, in sooth,' said
Suibhne, 'for the women to violate the Lord's fast-day; even as the woman beats the
flax,' said he, 'so were my folk beaten in the battle of Magh Rath.' He heard then the
vesper-bell pealing, whereupon he said: 'Sweeter indeed were it to me to hear the
voices of the cuckoos on the banks of the Bann from every side than the grig-graig
of this bell which I hear to-night'; and he uttered the lay:

Suibhne:
Sweeter to me about the waves—
though my talons to-night are feeble—
than the grig-graig of the church-bell,
is the cooing of the cuckoo of the Bann.
O woman, do not bring forth thy son
on a Friday,
the day whereon Suibhne Geilt eats not
out of love for the King of righteousness.
As the women scutch the flax—
'tis true though 'tis I be heard—
even so were beaten my folk
in the battle of Magh Rath.
From Loch Diolair of the cliff
to Derry Coluim Cille
it was not strife that I heard
from splendid, melodious swans.

The belling of the stag of the desert above the cliffs
in Siodhmuine Glinne—
there is no music on earth
in my soul but its sweetness.
O Christ, O Christ, hear me!
O Christ, O Christ, without sin!
O Christ, O Christ, love me!
sever me not from thy sweetness!

On the morrow Suibhne went to Cell Derfile where he fared on watercress of the well and the water which was in the church; there came a great storm in the night, and exceeding sorrow and grief took hold of Suibhne because of the wretchedness of his life; and moreover it was a cause of grief and sorrow to him to be absent from Dal Araidhe, whereupon he uttered these staves:

Suibhne:
My night in Cell Derfile
'tis it has broken my heart;
sad for me, O Son of my God,
is parting from Dal Araidhe.
Ten hundred and ten warriors,
that was my host at Druim Fraoch,
though I am without strength, O Son of God,
'twas I who was their leader in counsel.
Gloomy is my night to-night
without serving-man, without camp;
not so was my night at Druim Damh,
I and Faolchu and Congal.
Alas! that I was detained for the tryst,
O my Prince of the glorious Kingdom!
though I should not get any harm therefrom
forever except this night.

For seven whole years Suibhne wandered over Ireland from one point to another until one night he arrived at Glen Bolcain; for it is there stood his fortress and his dwelling-place, and more delightful was it to him to tarry and abide there than in any other place in Ireland; for thither would he go from every part of Ireland, nor would he leave it except through fear and terror. Suibhne dwelt there that night, and on the morrow morning Loingseachan came seeking him. Some say that Loingseachan was Suibhne's mother's son, others that he was a foster-brother, but, whichever he was, his concern for Suibhne was great, for he (Suibhne) went off three times in madness and thrice he brought him back. This time Loingseachan was seeking him in the glen, and he found the track of his feet by the brink of the stream of which he was wont to eat the watercress. He found also the branches that used to break under his feet as he changed from the top of one to another. That day, however, he did not find the madman, so he went into a deserted house in the glen, and there he fell into deep sleep after the great labour of the pursuit of Suibhne whom he was seeking. Then Suibhne came upon his track so that he reached the house, and there he heard Loingseachan's snore; whereupon he uttered this lay:

Suibhne:
The man by the wall snores,
slumber like that I dare not;
for seven years from the Tuesday at Magh Rath
I have not slept a wink.
O God of Heaven! would that I had not gone
to the fierce battle!
thereafter Suibhne Geilt was my name,
alone in the top of the ivy.
Watercress of the well of Druim Cirb
is my meal at terce;
on my face may be recognized its hue,
'tis true I am Suibhne Geilt.
For certain am I Suibhne Geilt,
one who sleeps under shelter of a rag,
about Sliabh Liag if . . .
these men pursue me.
When I was Suibhne the sage,
I used to dwell in a lonely shieling,
on sedgy land, on a morass, on a mountain-side;
I have bartered my home for a far-off land.
I give thanks to the King above
with whom great harshness is not usual;
'tis the extent of my injustice
that has changed my guise.
Cold, cold for me is it
since my body lives not in the ivy-bushes,
much rain comes upon it
and much thunder.
Though I live from hill to hill
in the mountain above the yew glen;
in the place where Congal Claon was left
alas that I was not left there on my back!
Frequent is my groan,
far from my churchyard is my gaping house;
I am no champion but a needy madman,
God has thrust me in rags, without sense.
'Tis great folly
for me to come out of Glen Bolcain,
there are many apple-trees in Glen Bolcain
for . . . of my head.
Green watercress
and a draft of pure water,

I fare on them, I smile not,
not so the man by the wall.
In summer amid the herons of Cuailgne,
among packs of wolves when winter comes,
at other times under the crown of a wood;
not so the man by the wall.
Happy Glen Bolcain,
fronting the wind, around which madmen of the glen call,
woe is me! I sleep not there;
more wretched am I than the man by the wall.

After that lay he came the next night to Loingseachan's mill which was being
watched over by one old woman, Lonnog, daughter of Dubh Dithribh, mother of
Loingseachan's wife. Suibhne went into the house to her and she gave him small
morsels, and for a long time in that manner he kept visiting the mill. One day Loingseachan set out after him, when he saw him by the mill-stream, and he went to speak
to the old woman, that is, his wife's mother, Lonnog. 'Has Suibhne come to the mill,
woman?' said Loingseachan. 'He was here last night,' said the woman. Loingseachan
then put on the woman's garment and remained in the mill after her; that night
Suibhne came to the mill and he recognised Loingseachan. When he saw his eyes,
he sprang away from him at once out through the skylight of the house, saying:
'Pitiful is your pursuit of me, Loingseachan, chasing me from my place and from
each spot dearest to me in Ireland; and as Ronan does not allow me to trust you, it is
tiresome and importunate of you to be following me'; and he made this lay:

Suibhne:
O Loingseachan, thou art irksome,
I have not leisure to speak with thee,
Ronan does not let me trust thee;
'tis he who has put me in a sorry plight.
I made the luckless cast
from the midst of the battle at Ronan;
it pierced the precious bell
which was on the cleric's breast.
As I hurled the splendid cast
from the midst of the battle at Ronan,
said the fair cleric: 'Thou hast leave
to go with the birds.'
Thereafter I sprang up
into the air above;
in life I have never leaped
a single leap that was lighter.
Were it in the glorious morning,
on the Tuesday following the Monday,
none would be prouder than I am
by the side of a warrior of my folk.

A marvel to me is that which I see,
O Thou that hast shaped this day;
The woman's garment on the floor,
two piercing eyes of Loingseachan.

'Sad is the disgrace you would fain put upon me, Loingseachan,' said he; 'and do not continue annoying me further, but go to your house and I will go on to where Eorann is.'

Now, Eorann at the time was dwelling with Guaire, son of Congal, son of Scann-lan, for it was Eorann who was Suibhne's wife, for there were two kinsmen in the country, and they had equal title to the sovereignty which Suibhne had abandoned, viz.: Guaire, son of Congal, son of Scannlan, and Eochaidh, son of Condlo, son of Scannlan. Suibhne proceeded to the place in which Eorann was. Guaire had gone to the chase that day, and the route he took was to the pass of Sliabh Fuaid and by Sgirig Cinn Glinne and Ettan Tairbh. His camp was beside Glen Bolcain—which is called Glenn Chiach to-day—in the plain of Cinel Ainmirech. Then the madman sat down upon the lintel of the hut in which Eorann was, whereupon he said: 'Do you remember, lady, the great love we gave to each other what time we were together? Easy and pleasant it is for you now, but not so for me'; whereupon Suibhne said, and Eorann answered him (as follows):

Suibhne:
At ease art thou, bright Eorann,
at the bedside with thy lover;
not so with me here,
long have I been restless.
Once thou didst utter, O great Eorann,
a saying pleasing and light,
that thou wouldst not survive
parted one day from Suibhne.
To-day, it is readily manifest,
thou thinkest little of thy old friend;
warm for thee on the down of a pleasant bed,
cold for me abroad till morn.
Welcome to thee, thou guileless mad one!
thou art most welcome of the men of the earth;
though at ease am I, my body is wasted
since the day I heard of thy ruin.
More welcome to thee is the king's son
who takes thee to feast without sorrow;
he is thy chosen wooer;
you seek not your old friend.

Eorann:
Though the king's son were to lead me
to blithe banqueting-halls,

I had liefer sleep in a tree's narrow hollow
beside thee, my husband, could I do so.
If my choice were given me
of the men of Erin and Alba,
I had liefer bide sinless with thee
on water and on watercress.

Suibhne:
No path for a beloved lady
is that of Suibhne here on the track of care;
cold are my beds at Ard Abhla,
my cold dwellings are not few.
More meet for thee to bestow love and affection
on the man with whom thou art alone
than on an uncouth and famished madman,
horrible, fearful, stark-naked.

Eorann:
O toiling madman, 'tis my grief
that thou art uncomely and dejected;
I sorrow that thy skin has lost its colour,
briars and thorns rending thee.

Suibhne:
I blame thee not for it,
thou gentle, radiant woman;
Christ, Son of Mary—great bondage—
He has caused my feebleness.

Eorann:
I would fain that we were together,
and that feathers might grow on our bodies;
in light and darkness I would wander
with thee each day and night.

Suibhne:
One night I was in pleasant Boirche,
I have reached lovely Tuath Inbhir,
I have wandered throughout Magh Fail,
I have happened on Celi Ui Suanaigh.

No sooner had he finished than the army swarmed into the camp from every quarter, whereupon he set off in his headlong flight, as he had often done. He halted not in his career until before the fall of night he arrived at Ros Bearaigh—the first church at which he tarried after the battle of Magh Rath—and he went into the yew-tree which was in the church. Muireadach mac Earca was erenach of the church at the time, and his wife happened to be going past the yew when she saw the madman in it; she recognized that it was Suibhne was there and said to him: 'Come out of the yew, king of Dal Araidhe; there is but one woman before you here.' She said so in order to seize the madman, and to deceive and beguile him. 'I will not go indeed,' said Suibhne, 'lest Loingseachan and his wife come to me, for there was a time when it would have been easier for you to recognize me than it is to-day'; whereupon he uttered these staves:

Suibhne:
O woman, who dost recognize me
with the points of thy blue eyes,
there was a time when my aspect was better
in the assembly of Dal Araidhe.
I have changed in shape and hue
since the hour I came out of the battle;
I was the slender Suibhne
of whom the men of Erin had heard.
Bide thou with thy husband and in thy house,
I shall not tarry in Ros Bearaigh;
until holy Judgment we shall not foregather,
I and thou, O woman.

He emerged then from the tree lightly and nimbly, and went on his way until he reached the old tree at Ros Earcain. (For he had three dwellings in his own country in which he was wont to reside, viz.: Teach mic Ninnedha, Cluain Creamha, and Ros Earcain.) Thereafter for a fortnight and a month he tarried in the yew-tree without being perceived; but at length his place and dwelling were discovered, and the nobles of Dal Araidhe took counsel as to who should go to seize him. Everyone said that it was Loingseachan who should be sent. Loingseachan undertook the task, and he went along until he came to the yew in which Suibhne was, whereupon he beheld the madman on the branch above him. 'Sad is it, Suibhne,' said he, 'that your last plight should be thus, without food, without drink, without raiment, like any bird of the air, after having been in garments of silk and satin on splendid steeds from foreign lands with matchless bridles; with you were women gentle and comely, likewise many youths and hounds and goodly folk of every art; many hosts, many and diverse nobles and chiefs, and young lords, and landholders and hospitallers were at your command. Many cups and goblets and carved buffalo horns for pleasant-flavoured and enjoyable liquors were yours also. Sad is it for you to be in that wise like unto any miserable bird going from wilderness to wilderness.' 'Cease now, Loingseachan,' said Suibhne; 'that is what was destined for us; but have you tidings for me of my country?' 'I have in sooth,' said Loingseachan, 'for your father is dead.' 'That has seized me . . .' said he. 'Your mother is also dead,' said the young man. 'Now all pity for me is at an end,' said he. 'Dead is your brother,' said Loingseachan. 'Gaping is my side on that account,' said Suibhne. 'Dead is your daughter,' said Loingseachan. 'The heart's needle is an only daughter,' said Suibhne. 'Dead is your son who used to call you "daddy,"' said Loingseachan. 'True,' said he, 'that is the drop (?) which brings a man to the ground'; whereupon they, even Loingseachan and Suibhne, uttered this lay between them:

Loingseachan:
O Suibhne from lofty Sliabh na nEach,
thou of the rough blade wert given to wounding;
for Christ's sake, who hath put thee in bondage,
grant converse with thy foster-brother.
Hearken to me if thou hearest me,
O splendid king, O great prince,
so that I may relate gently
to thee tidings of thy good land.
There is life for none in thy land after thee;
it is to tell of it that I have come;
dead is thy renowned brother there,
dead thy father and thy mother.

Suibhne:
If my gentle mother be dead,
harder is it for me to go to my land;
'tis long since she has loved my body;
she has ceased to pity me.
Foolish the counsel of each wild youth
whose elders live not;
like unto a branch bowed under nuts;
whoso is brotherless has a gaping side.

Loingseachan:
There is another calamity there
which is bewailed by the men of Erin,
though uncouth be thy side and thy foot,
dead is thy fair wife of grief for thee.

Suibhne:
For a household to be without a wife
is rowing a rudderless boat,
'tis a garb of feathers to the skin,
'tis kindling a single fire.

Loingseachan:
I have heard a fearful and loud tale
around which was a clear, fierce wail,
'tis a fist round smoke, however,
thou art without sister, O Suibhne.

Suibhne:
A proverb this, bitter the . . .—
it has no delight for me—
the mild sun rests on every ditch,
a sister loves though she be not loved.

Loingseachan:
Calves are not let to cows
amongst us in cold Araidhe
since thy gentle daughter, who has loved thee, died,
likewise thy sister's son.

Suibhne:
My sister's son and my hound,
they would not forsake me for wealth
'tis adding loss to sorrow;
the heart's needle is an only daughter.

Loingseachan:
There is another famous story—
loth am I to tell it—
meetly are the men of the Arada
bewailing thy only son.

Suibhne:
That is the renowned drop (?)
which brings a man to the ground,
that his little son who used to say 'daddy'
should be without life.
It has called me to thee from the tree,
scarce have I caused enmity,
I cannot bear up against the blow
since I heard the tidings of my only son.

Loingseachan:
Since thou hast come, O splendid warrior,
within Loingseachan's hands,
all thy folk are alive,
O scion of Eochu Salbuidhe.
Be still, let thy sense come,
in the east is thy house, not in the west,
far from thy land thou hast come hither,
this is the truth, O Suibhne.
More delightful deemest thou to be amongst deer
in woods and forests
than sleeping in thy stronghold in the east
on a bed of down.
Better deemest thou to be on a holly-branch
beside the swift mill's pond
than to be in choice company
with young fellows about thee.
If thou wert to sleep in the bosom of hills
to the soft strings of lutes,
more sweet wouldst thou deem under the oak-wood

the belling of the brown stag of the herd.
Thou art fleeter than the wind across the valley,
thou art the famous madman of Erin,
brilliant in thy beauty, come hither,
O Suibhne, thou wast a noble champion.

When Suibhne heard tidings of his only son, he fell from the yew, whereupon Loing-seachan closed his arms around him and put manacles on him. He then told him that all his people lived; and he took him to the place in which the nobles of Dal Araidhe were. They brought with them locks and fetters to put on Suibhne, and he was entrusted to Loingseachan to take him with him for a fortnight and a month. He took Suibhne away, and the nobles of the province were coming and going during that time; and at the end of it his sense and memory came to him, likewise his own shape and guise. They took his bonds off him, and his kingship was manifest. Harvest-time came then, and one day Loingseachan went with his people to reap. Suibhne was put in Loingseachan's bed-room after his bonds were taken off him, and his sense had come back to him. The bed-room was shut on him and nobody was left with him but the mill-hag, and she was enjoined not to attempt to speak to him. Nevertheless she spoke to him, asking him to tell some of his adventures while he was in a state of madness. 'A curse on your mouth, hag!' said Suibhne; 'ill is what you say; God will not suffer me to go mad again.' 'I know well,' said the hag, 'that it was the outrage done to Ronan that drove you to madness.' 'O woman,' said he, 'it is hateful that you should be betraying and luring me.' 'It is not betrayal at all but truth'; and Suibhne said:

Suibhne:
O hag of yonder mill,
why shouldst thou set me astray?
is it not deceitful of thee that, through women,
I should be betrayed and lured?

The hag:
'Tis not I who betrayed thee,
O Suibhne, though fair thy fame,
but the miracles of Ronan from Heaven
which drove thee to madness among madmen.

Suibhne:
Were it myself, and would it were I,
that were king of Dal Araidhe
it were a reason for a blow across a chin;
thou shalt not have a feast, O hag.

'O hag,' said he, 'great are the hardships I have encountered if you but knew; many a dreadful leap have I leaped from hill to hill, from fortress to fortress, from land to land, from valley to valley.' 'For God's sake,' said the hag, 'leap for us now one of the leaps you used to leap when you were mad.' Thereupon he bounded over the bed-rail so that he reached the end of the bench. 'My conscience!' said the hag, 'I could leap that myself,' and in the same manner she did so. He took another leap out through the skylight of the hostel. 'I could leap that too,' said the hag, and straightway she leaped. This, however, is a summary of it: Suibhne travelled through five cantreds of Dal Araidhe that day until he arrived at Glenn na nEachtach in Fiodh Gaibhle, and she followed him all that time. When Suibhne rested there on the summit of a tall ivy-branch, the hag rested on another tree beside him. It was then the end of harvest-time precisely. Thereupon Suibhne heard a hunting-call of a multitude in the verge of the wood. 'This,' said he, 'is the cry of a great host, and they are the Ui Faelain coming to kill me to avenge Oilill Cedach, king of the Ui Faelain, whom I slew in the battle of Magh Rath.' He heard the bellowing of the stag, and he made a lay wherein he eulogized aloud the trees of Ireland, and, recalling some of his own hardships and sorrows, he said:

O little stag, thou little bleating one;
O melodious little clamourer,
sweet to us is the music
thou makest in the glen.
Longing for my little home
has come on my senses—
the flocks in the plain,
the deer on the mountain.
Thou oak, bushy, leafy,
thou art high beyond trees;
O hazlet, little branching one,
O fragrance of hazel-nuts.
O alder, thou art not hostile,
delightful is thy hue,
thou art not rending and prickling
in the gap wherein thou art.
O little blackthorn, little thorny one;
O little black sloe-tree;
O watercress, little green-topped one,
from the brink of the ousel (?) spring.
O minen of the pathway,
thou art sweet beyond herbs,
O little green one, very green one,
O herb on which grows the strawberry.
O apple-tree, little apple-tree,
much art thou shaken;
O quicken, little berried one,
delightful is thy bloom.
O briar, little arched one,
thou grantest no fair terms,
thou ceasest not to tear me,
till thou hast thy fill of blood.
O yew-tree, little yew-tree,

in churchyards thou art conspicuous;
o ivy, little ivy,
thou art familiar in the dusky wood.
O holly, little sheltering one,
thou door against the wind;
o ash-tree, thou baleful one,
hand-weapon of a warrior.
O birch, smooth and blessed,
thou melodious, proud one,
delightful each entwining branch
in the top of thy crown.
The aspen a-trembling;
by turns I hear
its leaves a-racing—
meseems 'tis the foray!
My aversion in woods—
I conceal it not from anyone—
is the leafy stirk of an oak
swaying evermore.
Ill-hap by which I outraged
the honour of Ronan Finn,
his miracles have troubled me,
his little bells from the church.
Ill-omened I found
the armour of upright Congai,
his sheltering, bright tunic
with selvages of gold.
It was a saying of each one
of the valiant, active host:
Let not escape from you through the narrow copse
the man of the goodly tunic.
Wound, kill, slaughter,
let all of you take advantage of him;
put him, though it is great guilt,
on spit and on spike.
The horsemen pursuing me
across round Magh Cobha,
no cast from them reaches
me through my back.
Going through the ivy-trees—
I conceal it not, O warrior—
like good cast of a spear
I went with the wind.
O little fawn, O little long-legged one,
I was able to catch thee
riding upon thee

from one peak to another.
From Carn Cornan of the contests
to the summit of Sliabh Niadh,
from the summit of Sliabh Uillinne
I reach Crota Cliach.
From Crota Cliach of assemblies
to Carn Liffi of Leinster,
I arrive before eventide
in bitter Benn Gulbain.
My night before the battle of Congal,
I deemed it fortunate,
before I restlessly
wandered over the mountain-peaks.
Glen Bolcain, my constant abode,
'twas a boon to me,
many a night have I attempted
a stern race against the peak.
If I were to wander alone
the mountains of the brown world,
better would I deem the site of a single hut
in the Glen of mighty Bolcan.
Good its water pure-green,
good its clean, fierce wind,
good its cress-green watercress,
best its tall brooklime.
Good its enduring ivy-trees,
good its bright, cheerful sallow,
good its yewy yews,
best its melodious birch.
If thou shouldst come, O Loingseachan,
to me in every guise,
each night to talk to me,
perchance I would not tarry for thee.
I would not have tarried to speak to thee
were it not for the tale which has wounded me—
father, mother, daughter, son,
brother, strong wife dead.
If thou shouldst come to speak to me,
no better would I deem it;
I would wander before morn
the mountains of Boirche of peaks.
By the mill of the little floury one
thy folk has been ground,
O wretched one, O weary one,
O swift Loingseachan.
O hag of this mill,

why dost thou take advantage of me?
I hear thee revile me
even when thou art out on the mountain.
O hag, O round-headed one,
wilt thou go on a steed?

I would go, O fool-head
if no one were to see me.
O Suibhne, if I go,
may my leap be successful.

If thou shouldst come, O hag,
mayst thou not dismount full of sense!

In sooth, not just is what thou sayest,
thou son of Colman Cas;
is not my riding better without falling back?

Just, in sooth, is what I say,
O hag without sense;
a demon is ruining thee,
thou hast ruined thyself.

Dost thou not deem my arts better,
thou noble, slender madman,
that I should be following thee
from the tops of the mountains?
A proud ivy-bush
which grows through a twisted tree—
if I were right on its summit,
I would fear to come out.
I flee before the skylarks—
'tis a stern, great race—
I leap over the stumps
on the tops of the mountains.
When the proud turtle-dove
rises for us, quickly do I
overtake it
since my feathers have grown.
The silly, foolish woodcock
when it rises for me methinks
'tis a bitter foe, the blackbird
(too) that gives the cry of alarm.
Every time I would bound
till I was on the ground
so that I might see the little fox
below a-gnawing the bones
Beyond every wolf among the ivy-trees

swiftly would he get the advantage of me,
so nimbly would I leap
till I was on the mountain-peak.
Little foxes yelping
to me and from me,
wolves at their rending,
I flee at their sound.
They have striven to reach me,
coming in their swift course,
so that I fled before them
to the tops of the mountains.
My transgression has come
against me whatsoever way I flee;
'tis manifest to me from the pity
shown me that I am a sheep without a fold.
The old tree of Cell Lughaidhe
wherein I sleep a sound sleep;
more delightful in the time of Congal
was the fair of plenteous Line.
There will come the starry frost
which will fall on every pool;
I am wretched, straying
exposed to it on the mountain-peak.
The herons a-calling
in chilly Glenn Aighle,
swift flocks of birds
coming and going.
I love not the merry prattle
that men and women make:
sweeter to me is the warbling
of the *blackbird* in the quarter in which it is.
I love not the trumpeting
I hear at early morn:
sweeter to me the squeal
of the badgers in Benna Broc.
I love not the horn-blowing
so boldly I hear:
sweeter to me the belling of a stag
of twice twenty peaks.
There is the material of a plough-team
from glen to glen:
each stag at rest
on the summit of the peaks.
Though many are my stags
from glen to glen,
not often is a ploughman's hand

closing round their horns.
The stag of lofty Sliabh Eibhlinne,
the stag of sharp Siiabh Fuaid,
the stag of Ealla, the stag of Orrery,
the fierce stag of Loch Lein.
The stag of Seimhne, Larne's stag,
the stag of Line of the mantles,
the stag of Cuailgne, the stag of Conachail,
the stag of Bairenn of two peaks.
O mother of this herd,
thy coat has become grey,
there is no stag after thee
without two score antler-points.
Greater than the material for a little cloak
thy head has turned grey;
if I were on each little point,
there would be a pointlet on every point.
Thou stag that comest lowing
to me across the glen,
pleasant is the place for seats on the top
of thy antler-points.
I am Suibhne, a poor suppliant,
swiftly do I race across the glen;
that is not my lawful name,
rather is it Fer benn.
The springs I found best:
the well of Leithead Lan,
the well most beautiful and cool,
the fountain of Dun Mail.
Though many are my wanderings,
my raiment to-day is scanty;
I myself keep my watch
on the top of the mountains.
O tall, russet fern,
thy mantle has been made red;
there is no bed for an outlaw
in the branches of thy crests.
At ever-angelic Tech Moling,
at puissant Toidhen in the south,
'tis there my eternal resting-place will be,
I shall fall by a [spear]-point.
The curse of Ronan Finn
has thrown me in thy company,
O little stag, little bleating one,
O melodious little clamourer.

After that lay Suibhne came from Fiodh Gaibhle to Benn Boghaine, thence to Benn Faibhne, thence to Rath Murbuilg, but he found no refuge from the hag until he reached Dun Sobairce in Ulster. Suibhne leaped from the summit of the fort sheer down in front of the hag. She leaped quickly after him, but dropped on the cliff of Dun Sobairce, where she was broken to pieces, and fell into the sea. In that manner she found death in the wake of Suibhne.

Thereafter Suibhne said: 'Henceforth I shall not be in Dal Araidhe, for Loingseachan, to avenge his hag, would kill me if I were in his power.' Suibhne then went to Ros Comain in Connacht, and he alighted at the brink of the well, where he fared on watercress and water. A woman came from the erenach's house to the well; Forbhasach, son of Fordhalach, was the erenach. Finnsheng, daughter of Findealach (?), was the name of the woman who came. The madman fled from her and she laid hold of the watercress which was in the stream. Suibhne on the tree in front of her was bemoaning greatly that his portion of watercress was taken away. Whereupon he said: 'O woman,' said he, 'sad is it that you should take my watercress from me, if you but knew the plight in which I am, for neither tribesman nor kinsman pities me, nor do I visit as a guest the house of anyone on the ridge of the world. For kine I have my watercress, my water is my mead, my trees hard and bare or close-sheltering are my friends. And even if you did not take away my watercress,' said he, 'certain is it that you would not be without something else to-night as I am after my watercress has been taken from me': and he made this lay:

O woman who pluckest the watercress
and takest the water,
thou wouldst not be without something to-night
even though thou didst not take my portion.
Alas, O woman!
thou wilt not go the way that I shall go;
I abroad in the tree-tops,
thou yonder in a friend's house.
Alas, O woman!
cold is the wind that has come to me;
nor mother nor son has pity on me,
no cloak is on my breast.
If thou but knewest, O woman,
how Suibhne here is:
he does not get friendship from anyone,
nor does anyone get his friendship.
I go not to a gathering
among warriors of my country,
no safeguard is granted me,
my thought is not on kingship.
I go not as a guest
to the house of any man's son in Erin,
more often am I straying madly

on the pointed mountain-peaks.
None cometh to make music to me
for a while before going to rest,
no pity do I get
from tribesman or kinsman.
When I was Suibhne indeed
and used to go on steeds—
when that comes to my memory
alas that I was detained in life!
I am Suibhne, noble leader,
cold and joyless is my abode,
though I be to-night on wild peaks,
O woman who pluckest my watercress.
My mead is my cold water,
my kine are my cresses,
my friends are my trees,
though I am without mantle or smock.
Cold is the night to-night,
though I am poor as regards watercress,
I have heard the cry of the wild-goose
over bare Imlech Iobhair.
I am without mantle or smock
the evil hour has long clung to me,
I flee at the cry of the heron
as though it were a blow that struck me.
I reach firm Dairbre
in the wondrous days of Spring,
and before night I flee
westward to Benn Boirche.
If thou art learned, O fair, crabbed one,
my field . . .
there is one to whom the burden thou takest
is a grievous matter, O hag.
It is cold they are
at the brink of a clear, pebbly spring—
a bright quaff of pure water
and the watercress you pluck.
My meal is the watercress you pluck,
the meal of a noble, emaciated madman;
cold wind springs around my loins
from the peaks of each mountain.
Chilly is the wind of morn,
It comes between me and my smock,
I am unable to speak to thee,
O woman who pluckest the watercress.

The woman:
Leave my portion to the Lord,
be not harsh to me;
the more wilt thou attain supremacy,
and take a blessing, O Suibhne.

Suibhne:
Let us make a bargain just and fitting
though I am on the top of the yew;
take thou my smock and my tatters,
leave the little bunch of cress.
There is scarce one by whom I am beloved,
I have no house on earth;
since thou takest from me my watercress
my sins to be on thy soul!
Mayest thou not reach him whom thou hast loved,
the worse for him whom thou hast followed;
thou hast left one in poverty
because of the bunch thou hast plucked.
May a raid of the blue-coated Norsemen take thee!
Thine has not been a fortunate meeting for me,
mayest thou get from the Lord the blame
for cutting my portion of watercress.
O woman, if there should come to thee
Loingseachan whose delight is sport,
do thou give him on my behalf
half the watercress thou pluckest.

That night he remained in Ros Comain and went thence on the morrow to delight-ful Sliabh Aughty, thence to smooth, beautiful Sliabh Mis, thence to lofty-peaked Sliabh Bloom, thence to Inis Murray. For a fortnight and a month he tarried in the cave of Donnan of Eig, and went thence to Carrick Alastair where he took up his abode and remained another fortnight and a month. He left it afterwards and bade it farewell, and, proclaiming aloud his own woes, said:

Gloomy this life,
to be without a soft bed,
abode of cold frost,
roughness of wind-driven snow.
Cold, icy wind,
faint shadow of a feeble sun,
shelter of a single tree,
on the summit of a table-land.
Enduring the rain-storm,
stepping over deer-paths,
faring through greensward

on a morn of grey frost.
The bellowing of the stags
throughout the wood,
the climb to the deer-pass,
the voice of white seas.
Yea, O great Lord,
great this weakness,
more grievous this black sorrow,
Suibhne the slender-groined.
Racing over many-hued gaps
of Boirche of hut couches,
the sough of the winter night,
footing it in hailstones.
Lying on a wet bed
on the slopes of Loch Erne,
mind on early departure,
morn of early rising.
Racing over the wave-tops
of Dun Sobairce,
ear to the billows
of Dun Rodairce.
Running from this great wave
to the wave of the rushing Barrow,
sleeping on a hard couch
of fair Dun Cermna.
From fair Dun Cermna
to flowery Benn Boirne,
ear against a stone pillow
of rough Cruachan Oighle.
Restless my wandering
in the plain of the Boroma,
from Benn Iughoine
to Benn Boghaine.
There has come to me
one who has laid hands on me,
she has brought no peace to me,
the woman who has dishonoured me.
She has taken my portion
on account of my sins,
wretched the work—
my watercress has been eaten.
Watercress I pluck,
food in a fair bunch,
four round handfuls
of fair Glen Bolcain.

A meal I seek—
pleasant the bogberry,
a drink of water here
from the well of Ronan Finn.
Bent are my nails,
feeble my loins,
pierced my feet,
bare my thighs.
There will overtake me
a warrior-band stubbornly,
far from Ulster,
faring in Alba.
After this journey—;
sad is my secret song—;
to be in the hard company
of Carraig Alastair.
Carraig Alastair,
abode of sea-gulls,
sad, O Creator,
chilly for its guests.
Carraig Alastair,
bell-shaped rock,
sufficient were it half the height,
nose to the main.
Sad our meeting;
a couple of cranes hard-shanked—
I hard and ragged,
she hard-beaked.
Wet these beds
wherein is my dwelling,
little did I think
it was a rock of holiness.
Bad was it for Congal Claon
that he arrived at the battle;
like an outer yoke
he has earned a curse.
When I fled
from the battle of Magh Rath
before my undoing,
I deserved not harshness.
Sad this expedition;
would that I had not come!
far from my home
is the country I have reached.
Loingseachan will come,

sad his journeys;
though he follow me,
it will not be easy.
Far-stretching woods
are the rampart of this circuit—
the land to which I have come—
not a deed of sadness.
The black lake of fortressed Boirche
greatly has it perturbed me;
the vastness of its depths,
the strength of its wave-crests.
Better found I
pleasant woods,
choice places of wooded Meath,
the vastness of Ossory.
Ulaidh in harvest-time
about quivering Loch Cuan,
a summer visit
to the race of enduring Eoghan.
A journey at Lammastide
to Taillten of fountains,
fishing in springtime
the meandering
Often do I reach
the land I have set in order,
curly-haired hosts,
stern ridges.

Suibhne then left Carraig Alastair and went over the wide-mouthed, storm-swept sea until he reached the land of the Britons. He left the fortress of the king of the Britons on his right hand and came on a great wood. As he passed along the wood he heard lamenting and wailing, a great moan of anguish and feeble sighing. It was another madman who was wandering through the wood. Suibhne went up to him. 'Who are you, my man?' said Suibhne. 'I am a madman,' said he. 'If you are a madman,' said Suibhne, 'come hither so that we may be friends, for I too am a madman.' 'I would,' said the other, 'were it not for fear of the king's house or household seizing me, and I do not know that you are not one of them.' 'I am not indeed,' said Suibhne, 'and since I am not, tell me your family name.' 'Fer Caille (Man of the Wood) is my name,' said the madman; whereupon Suibhne uttered this stave and Fer Caille answered him as follows:

Suibhne:
O Fer Caille, what has befallen thee?
sad is thy voice;
tell me what has marred thee
in sense or form.

Fer Caille:
I would tell thee my story,
likewise my deeds,
were it not for fear of the proud host
of the king's household.
Ealladhan am I
who used to go to many combats,
I am known to all
as the leading madman of the glens.

Suibhne:
Suibhne son of Colman am I
from the pleasant Bush;
the easier for us is converse
here, O man.

After that each confided in the other and they asked tidings of each other. Said Suibhne to the madman: 'Give an account of yourself.' 'I am son of a landholder,' said the madman of Britain, 'and I am a native of this country in which we are, and Ealladhan is my name.' 'Tell me,' said Suibhne, 'what caused your madness.' 'Not difficult to say. Once upon a time two kings were contending for the sovereignty of this country, viz., Eochaidh Aincheas, son of Guaire Mathra, and Cugua, son of Guaire. Of the people of Eochaidh am I,' said he, 'for he was the better of the two. There was then convened a great assembly to give battle to each other concerning the country. I put geasa on each one of my lord's people that none of them should come to the battle except they were clothed in silk, so that they might be conspicuous beyond all for pomp and pride. The hosts gave three shouts of malediction on me, which sent me wandering and fleeing as you see.'

In the same way he asked Suibhne what drove him to madness. 'The words of Ronan,' said Suibhne, 'for he cursed me in front of the battle of Magh Rath, so that I rose on high out of the battle, and I have been wandering and fleeing ever since.' 'O Suibhne,' said Ealladhan, 'let each of us keep good watch over the other since we have placed trust in each other; that is, he who shall soonest hear the cry of a heron from a blue-watered, green-watered lough or the clear note of a cormorant, or the flight of a woodcock from a branch, the whistle or sound of a plover on being woke from its sleep, or the sound of withered branches being broken, or shall see the shadow of a bird above the wood, let him who shall first hear warn and tell the other; let there be the distance of two trees between us; and if one of us should hear any of the before-mentioned things or anything resembling them, let us fly quickly away thereafter.'

They do so, and they were a whole year together. At the end of the year Ealladhan said to Suibhne: 'It is time that we part to-day, for the end of my life has come, and I must go to the place where it has been destined for me to die.' 'What death shall you die?' said Suibhne. 'Not difficult to say,' said Ealladhan; 'I go now to Eas Dubhthaigh, and a blast of wind will get under me and cast me into the waterfall so that I shall be drowned, and I shall be buried afterwards in a churchyard of a saint, and I shall obtain Heaven; and that is the end of my life. And, O Suibhne,' said Ealladhan, 'tell

me what your own fate will be.' Suibhne then told him as the story relates below. At
that they parted and the Briton set out for Eas Dubhthaigh, and when he reached
the waterfall he was drowned in it.

Suibhne then came to Ireland and at the close of day he arrived at Magh Line in
Ulster. When he recognized the plain he said: 'Good in sooth was he with whom I
sojourned on the plain, even Congal Claon, son of Scannlan, and good moreover
was the plain on which we were. One day Congal and I were there and I said to him:
'I would fain go to another master,' because of the meagre recompense I received
from him. Whereat, in order that I might stay with him, he gave me thrice fifty beautiful, foreign steeds together with his own brown steed, and thrice fifty gleaming,
tusk-hilted swords, fifty bondsmen, and fifty bondsmaids, a tunic with gold and a
splendid girdle of chequered silk.' Thereupon Suibhne recited this poem:

Magh Line I am to-night,
my bare breast knows it;
I know too the plain
wherein dwelt my mate Congal.
Once upon a time Congal Claon and I
were here in the plain together;
as we were going to plenteous Druim Lurgain,
we made converse for a while.
Said I to the king—
I am fain to depart
too little do I deem my recompense.
I got from him as a gift
thrice fifty bridled steeds,
thrice fifty strong swords,
fifty foreigners and fifty handmaidens.
I got from him the brown steed,
the best that sped over meadow and sward;
I got his golden tunic
and his girdle of chequered silk.
What plain is a match for Magh Line,
unless it be the plain that is in Meath,
or Magh Femin of many crosses,
or the plain that is in Airgeadros?
Or Magh Feadha, or Magh Luirg,
or Magh Aei with beauty of rank,
or Magh Life, or Magh Li,
or the plain that is in Murthemne?
Of all that I have ever seen
both north and south and west,
I have not yet beheld
the peer of this plain.

After that lay Suibhne came on to Glen Bolcain, and he was wandering through it
when he encountered a mad woman. He fled before her and yet he divined that she

was in a state of madness, and he turned towards her. At that she fled before him. 'Alas, O God!' said Suibhne, 'wretched is this life; here am I fleeing from the crazy woman and she fleeing from me in the midst of Glen Bolcain; dear in sooth is that place'; whereupon he said:

Woe to him who bears enmity,
would that he had not been born or brought forth!
whether it be a woman or a man that bear it,
may the two not reach holy Heaven!
Seldom is there a league of three
without one of them murmuring;
blackthorns and briars have torn me
so that I am the murmurer.
A crazy woman fleeing from her man—
however, it is a strange tale—
a man without clothes, without shoes,
fleeing before the woman.
Our desire when the wild ducks come
at Samhuin, up to May-day,
in each brown wood without scarcity
to be in ivy-branches.
Water of bright Glen Bolcain,
listening to its many birds;
its melodious, rushing streams,
its islands and its rivers.
Its sheltering holly and its hazels,
its leaves, its brambles, its acorns,
its delicious, fresh berries,
its nuts, its refreshing sloes.
The number of its packs of hounds in woods,
the bellowing of its stags,
its pure water without prohibition;
'tis not I that hated it.

Thereafter Suibhne went to the place where Eorann was and stood at the outer door of the house wherein were the queen and her womenfolk, and then he said: 'At ease art thou, Eorann, though ease is not for me.' 'True,' said Eorann, 'but come in,' said she. 'In sooth I will not,' said Suibhne, 'lest the army pen me in the house.' 'Methinks,' said the woman, 'no better is your reason from day to day, and since you do not wish to stay with us,' said she, 'go away and do not visit us at all, for we are ashamed that you should be seen in that guise by people who have seen you in your true guise.' 'Wretched in sooth is that,' said Suibhne, 'woe to him who trusts a woman after these words. For great was my kindness to the woman who dismisses me thus, seeing that on one day I gave her thrice fifty cows and fifty steeds; and if it were the day I slew Oilill Cedach, king of the Ui Faolain, she would have been glad to see me'; whereupon he said:

Woe to those who strike women's fancy,
however excellent their form,
since Suibhne Geilt
has got no sympathy from his first love.
And woe to him who trusts in women
whether by night or by day,
whatever be in their minds,
after the treachery of Eorann.
Good was my kindness to the woman—
without guile, without deceit—
she got from me thrice fifty cows
and fifty steeds in one day.
When I was in the conflict
I would not avoid an armed band;
where there was a fight or a tussle
I was a match for thirty.
Rightly did Congal ask
of us Ulster warriors:
which of you will repel in battle
Oilill Cedach the combative?
Wild and angry the man,
huge his shield and his spear,
he stilled for a time the host,
the matchless, huge man.
Said I at Congal's side—
it was not the response of a timid man—
I will ward off mighty Oilill,
though hard beyond all is it to encounter him.
Headless I left Oilill,
and right glad was I thereat;
by me also there fell
five sons of the king of Magh Mairge.

Thereupon Suibhne rose lightly, stealthily, airily, from the point of every height and from the summit of one hill to another until he reached Benn Boirche in the south. In that place he rested saying: 'This is a spot for a madman, but yet no place is it for corn or milk or food; it is an uncomfortable, unquiet place, nor has it shelter against storm or shower, though it is a lofty, beautiful place,' whereupon he uttered these words:

Cold to-night is Benn Boirche,
'tis the abode of a blighted man;
no place is it for food or milk,
nor in storm and endless snow.
Cold is my bed at night
on the summit of Benn Boirche;

I am weak, no raiment covers me
on a sharp-branching holly-tree.
When cold has gripped me in the ice
I move sharply against it,
I give fire to the glinting wind
blowing over the plain of Laoghaire's Leinster.
Glen Bolcain of the clear spring,
it is my dwelling to abide in;
when Samhuin comes, when summer goes,
it is my dwelling where I abide.
Wheresoever I might wander west and east
throughout Glanamhrach's glens
the biting snowstorm is in my face,
for shelter of the chilly madman of Erin.
That is my beloved glen,
my land of foregathering,
my royal fortress that has fallen to my share,
my shelter against storm.
For my sustenance at night
I have all that my hands glean
in dark oak-woods
of herbs and plenteous fruit.
I love the precious bog-berries,
they are sweeter than . . .
brooklime, sea-weed, they are my desire,
the lus bian and the watercress.
Apples, berries, beautiful hazel-nuts,
blackberries, acorns from the oak-tree,
raspberries, they are the due of generosity,
haws of the prickly-sharp hawthorn.
wood-sorrels, goodly wild garlic,
and clean-topped cress,
together they drive hunger from me,
mountain acorns, melle root.
I in a green land that is not a glen,
O Christ, may I never reach it!
it is not my due to be there;
but though I am cold, it also is cold.

On the morning of the morrow Suibhne came on to Magh Femhin, thence he fared
to the limpid, green-streamed Shannon, thence to lofty, beautiful Aughty, thence
to the smooth-green, bright land of Maenmagh, thence to the noble and delightful
river Suck, thence to the shores of spreading Lough Ree. That night he made his
resting-place in the fork of Bile Tiobradain in Crich Gaille in the east of Connaught.
That was one of his beloved places in Ireland. Great sorrow and misery came upon
him, whereupon he said: 'Great in sooth is the trouble and anxiety I have suffered

hitherto; cold was my dwelling-place last night on the summit of Benn Boirche, *no less* cold is my dwelling-place to-night in the fork of Bile Tiobradain.'

For it was snowing that night and as fast as the snow fell it was frozen, whereupon he said: 'My conscience! Great is the suffering I have endured from the time my feathers have grown until to-night. I know,' said he, 'that though I might meet my death therefrom, it were better that I should trust people than suffer these woes forever.' Thereupon he recited the poem proclaiming aloud his woes:

Suibhne:
I am in great grief to-night,
the pure wind has pierced my body;
wounded are my feet, my cheek is wan,
O great God! it is my due.
Last night I was in Benn Boirche,
the rain of chilly Aughty beat on me;
to-night my limbs are racked
in the fork of a tree in pleasant Gaille.
I have borne many a fight without cowardice
since feathers have grown on my body;
each night and each day
more and more do I endure ill.
Frost and foul storm have wrung my heart,
snow has beaten on me on Sliabh mic Sin;
to-night the wind has wounded me,
without the heather of happy Glen Bolcain.
Unsettled is my faring through each land,
it has befallen me that I am without sense or reason,
from Magh Line to Magh Li,
from Magh Li to the impetuous Liffey.
I pass over the wooded brow of Sliabh Fuaid,
in my flight I reach Rathmor,
across Magh Aoi, across bright Magh Luirg,
I reach the border of fair Cruachan.
From Sliabh Cua—no easy expedition—
I reach pleasant Glais Gaille;
from Glais Gaille, though a long step,
I arrive at sweet Sliabh Breagh to the east.
Wretched is the life of one homeless,
sad is the life, O fair Christ!
a meal of fresh, green-tufted watercress,
a drink of cold water from a clear stream.
Stumbling from withered tree-tops,
faring through furze—deed without falsehood—
shunning mankind, keeping company with wolves,
racing with the red stag over the field.
Sleeping of nights without covering in a wood

in the top of a thick, bushy tree,
without hearing voice or speech;
O Son of God, great is the misery!
Foolishly I race up a mountain-peak
alone, exhausted by dint of vigour;
I have parted from my faultless shape;
O Son of God, great is the misery!

'Howbeit,' said he, 'even if Domhnall, son of Aodh, were to slay me, I will go to Dal Araidhe and I will entrust myself to my own people, and if the mill-hag had not invoked Christ against me so that I might perform leaps for her awhile, I would not have gone again into madness.'

A gleam of reason came to him then, and he set out towards his country to entrust himself to his people and abide with them. At that time it was revealed to Ronan that Suibhne had recovered his reason and that he was going to his country to abide among his folk; whereupon Ronan said: 'I entreat the noble, almighty King that that persecutor may not be able to approach the church to persecute it again as he once did, and, until his soul has parted from his body, may there be no help or relief to him from the vengeance which God inflicted on him in revenge for the dishonour done to His people, so that no other like tyrant after him may inflict outrage or dishonour on the Lord or on His people.'

God heard Ronan's prayer, for when Suibhne came to the centre of Sliabh Fuaid he stopped still there, and a strange apparition appeared to him at midnight; seven trunks, headless and red, and heads without bodies, and five bristling, rough-grey heads without body or trunk among them, screaming and leaping this way and that about the road. When he came among them he heard them talking to each other, and this is what they were saying: 'He is a madman,' said the first head; 'a madman of Ulster,' said the second head; 'follow him well,' said the third head; 'may the pursuit be long,' said the fourth head; 'until he reaches the sea,' said the fifth head. They rose forth together towards him. He soared aloft in front of them (passing) from thicket to thicket, and no matter how vast was the glen before him he would not touch it, but would leap from one edge of it to another, and from the summit of one hill to the summit of another.

Great in sooth was the terror, the crying and wailing, the screaming and crying aloud, the din and tumult of the heads after him as they were clutching and eagerly pursuing him. Such were the force and swiftness of that pursuit that the heads leaped on his calves, his houghs, his thighs, his shoulders, and the nape of his neck, so that the impact of head against head, and the clashing of all against the sides of trees and the heads of rocks, against the surface and the earth, seemed to him like the rush of a wild torrent from the breast of a high mountain; nor did they cease until he escaped from them into the filmy clouds of the sky.

Then they parted from him, both goat-heads and dog-heads—for it seemed to him that these were all intermingled with the other heads pursuing him. The wandering and flying which he had ever before done were as nothing in comparison with this, for he would not rest long enough to take a drink to the end of three fortnights after that until he came one night to the summit of Sliabh Eidhneach; that night he rested there on the top of a tree until morning. He then began lamenting grievously; whereupon he said: 'Wretched indeed is it with me to-night after the hag and the heads on Sliabh Fuaid, and yet it is right that I should be as I am, because of the many to whom I myself have done harm'; whereupon he said:

Mournful am I to-night,
I am sad and wretched, my side is naked,
if folk but knew me
I have cause for lament.
Frost, ice, snow, and storm,
forever scourging me,
I without fire, without house,
on the summit of Sliabh Eidhneach.
I have a mansion and a good wife,
everyone would say that I was a prince;
'tis He who is Lord and King
has wrought my downfall.
Wherefore did God rescue me from the battle
that no one was found there to slay me,
rather than that I should go step by step
with the hag of the mill?
The hag of the mill at her house,
Christ's curse on her soul!
woe whosoever has trusted the hag!
woe to whom she has given his dog's portion!
Loingseachan was on my track
throughout every wilderness in Erin,
until he lured me from the tree
what time he related my son's death.
He carried me into the great house
wherein the host was feasting,
and bound me behind in the house
face to face with my first love.
The people of the house without reproach
playing games and laughing;
I and my folk in the house
leaping and jumping.
Were it not for the hag of the house,
I would not have gone again into madness;
she besought me by Christ of Heaven
to leap for her a little while.
I leaped a leap or two
for the sake of the Heavenly Father Himself;
the hag at her house said
that even so could she herself leap.
Once more I leaped out

over the top of the fortress;
swifter than smoke through a house
was the flight of the hag.
We wandered through all Erin,
from Teach Duinn to Traigh Ruire,
from Traigh Ruire to Benna Brain,
but the hag I did not elude.
Through plain and bog and hillside
I escaped not from the slattern
until she leaped with me the famous leap
to the summit of Dun Sobairce.
Thereafter I leaped down the dun,
nor did I step back,
I went out into the sea,
yonder I left the hag.
There came then to the strand
the devil's crew to meet her,
and they bore away her body;
woe to the land of Erin in which it was buried!
Once as I passed over Sliabh Fuaid
on a dark, black, gloomy night,
on the hill I beheld five heads,
having been cut off in one place.
Said one of them of a sudden—
harsh was the voice to me—
a madman of Ulster, follow him
so that you drive him before you to the sea.
I sped before them along the path
and I set not foot on ground;
both goat-head and dog-head
then began to curse.
'Tis right that I should get harm;
many a night have I leaped a lake,
many eyes of fond women
have I made weep.

On a certain occasion Suibhne happened to be in Luachair Deaghaidh on his wild career of folly; he went thence in his course of madness until he reached Fiodh Gaibhle of clear streams and beautiful branches. In that place he remained a year and during that year his food consisted of blood-red, saffron holly-berries and dark-brown acorns, and a drink of water from the Gabhal, that is, the river from which the wood is named. At the end of that time deep grief and heavy sorrow took hold of Suibhne there because of the wretchedness of his life; whereupon he uttered this little poem:

I am Suibhne, alas!
my wretched body is utterly dead,

evermore without music, without sleep,
save the soughing of the rude gale.
I have come from Luachair Deaghaidh
to the border of Fiodh Gaibhle,
this is my fare—I hide it not—
ivy-berries, oak-mast.
A year have I been on the mountain
in this form in which I am,
without food going into my body
save crimson holly-berries.
The madman of Glen Bolcain am I,
I shall not hide my gnawing grief;
to-night my vigour has come to an end,
not to me is there no cause for grief.

One day it happened that he went to Druim Iarainn in Connacht where he *ate* green-topped watercress of the church by the brink of the green-flecked well and he drank some of its water after. A cleric came out of the church and he was indignant and resentful towards the madman for eating the food which he himself used to eat, and he said that it was happy and contented Suibhne was in the yew-tree after taking his meal from himself. 'Sad in sooth is that (saying), o cleric,' said Suibhne, 'for I am the most discontented and unhappy creature in the world, for neither rest nor slumber comes on my eyes for fear of my being slain. That is natural, because I would equally go into madness at seeing the united hosts of the universe threatening me as at the flight of a single wren; and, O God of Heaven! cleric,' said Suibhne, 'that you are not in my place and I in the state of devotion in which you are, so that your mind and understanding might recognise that it is not usual for the like of me or for my counterpart to be happy as you say'; whereupon the cleric recited the beginning of the poem and Suibhne responded (by reciting) the end, as follows:

The Cleric:
Thou art at ease, madman,
on the top of the yew-branch
beside my little abode,
thou hast eaten my watercress.

Suibhne:
My life is not one of ease,
O cleric of Druim Iarainn,
such is my fear
that I do not close an eye.
If I were to see the men of the world
coming to me, O man of the bell,
I would flee from them as fast
as at the flight of a wren.
Alas! that thou art not in my place
and I a devout cleric,

so that thy mind might grasp
that it is not the accomplishment of a madman to be at ease.

One day as Suibhne was wandering aimlessly and restlessly through Connacht he came at last to All Fharannain in Tir Fhiachrach Mhuaide; a delightful valley with a beautiful green-streamed river dropping swiftly down the cliff and a blessed place there wherein was a synod of saints and multitudes of righteous folk. Numerous too on that cliff were the beautiful trees, heavy and rich with fruits numerous also the well-sheltered ivy-trees and heavy-topped apple-trees bending to the ground with the weight of their fruit; wild deer and hares and great, heavy swine were there also, likewise many fat seals that used to sleep on that cliff after coming from the main beyond. Suibhne greatly coveted that place and he began praising and describing it aloud; whereupon he uttered this lay:

Cliff of Farannan, abode of saints,
with many fair hazels and nuts,
swift cold water
rushing down its side.
Many green ivy-trees are there
and mast such as is prized,
and fair, heavy-topped apple-trees
bending their branches.
Many badgers going under its shelter
and fleet hares too,
and . . . brows of seals
coming hither from the main.
I am Suibhne, son of upright Colman,
many a frosty night have I been feeble;
Ronan of Druim Gess has outraged me,
I sleep 'neath a tree at yonder waterfall.

At length Suibhne came along to the place where Moling was, even Teach Moling. The psalter of Kevin was at the time in front of Moling as he was reading it to the students. In the cleric's presence Suibhne then came to the brink of the fountain and began to eat watercress. 'O mad one, that is eating early,' Moling spoke and Suibhne answered him:

Moling: An early hour is it, thou madman,
for due celebration.

Suibhne: Though to thee, cleric, it may seem early,
terce has come in Rome.

Moling: How dost thou know, mad one,
when terce comes in Rome?

Suibhne: Knowledge comes to me from my Lord
each morn and each eve.

Moling: Relate through the mystery of speech
tidings of the fair Lord.

Suibhne: With thee is the (gift of) prophecy
if thou art Moling.

Moling: How dost thou know me,
thou toiling, cunning madman?

Suibhne: Often have I been upon this green
since my reason was overthrown.

Moling: Why dost thou not settle in one place,
thou son of Colman Cuar?

Suibhne: I had rather be in one seat
in life everlasting.

Moling: Miserable one, will thy soul reach
hell with vastness of slime?

Suibhne: God inflicts no pain on me
save being without rest.

Moling: Move hither that thou mayest eat
what thou deemest sweet.

Suibhne: If you but knew, cleric,
more grievous is it to be without a cloak.

Moling: Thou shalt take my cowl
or thou shalt take my smock.

Suibhne: Though to-day I am ghastly,
there was a time when it was better.

Moling: Art thou the dreaded Suibhne
who came from the battle of Rath?

Suibhne: If I am, 'tis not to be guaranteed
what I might eat at early morn.

Moling: Whence has come my recognition,
cunning madman, to thee?

Suibhne: Often am I upon this green
watching thee from afar.

Moling: Delightful is the leaf of this book,
the psalter of holy Kevin.

Suibhne: More delightful is a leaf of my yew
in happy Glen Bolcain.

Moling: Dost thou not deem this churchyard pleasant
with its school of beautiful colours?

Suibhne: Not more unpleasant was my muster
the morning at Magh Rath.

Moling: I will go for celebration
to Glais Cille Cro.

Suibhne: I will leap a fresh ivy-bush
a high leap, and it will be a greater feat.

Moling: Wearisome is it to me in this church
waiting on the strong and weak.

Suibhne: More wearisome is my couch
in chilly Benn Faibhni.

Moling: Where comes thy life's end,
in church or lake?

Suibhne: A herd of thine
will slay me at early morn.

'Welcome in sooth is your coming here, Suibhne,' said Moling, 'for it is destined for you to be here and to end your life here; to leave here your history and adventures, and to be buried in a churchyard of righteous folk; and I bind you,' said Moling, 'that however much of Ireland you may travel each day, you will come to me each evening so that I may write your history.'

Thereafter during that year the madman was visiting Moling. One day he would go to Innis Bo Finne in west Connacht, another day to delightful Eas Ruaidh, another day to smooth, beautiful Sliabh Mis, another day to ever-chilly Benn Boirche, but go where he would each day, he would attend at vespers each night at Teach Moling. Moling ordered a collation for him for that hour, for he told his cook to give him some of each day's milking. Muirghil was her name; she was wife of Mongan, swine-herd to Moling. This was the extent of the meal the woman used to give him: she used to thrust her heel up to her ankle in the cowdung nearest her and leave the full of it of new milk there for Suibhne. He used to come cautiously and carefully into the vacant portion of the milking yard to drink the milk.

One night a dispute arose between Muirgil and another woman in the milking enclosure, whereupon the latter said: 'the worse is it for you,' said she, 'that another man is not more welcome to you, and yet that you do not prefer your own husband to come to you than the madman who is visiting you for the past year.' The herd's sister hearkened to that; nevertheless she mentioned nothing about it until she saw Muirgil on the morrow morning going to leave the milk for Suibhne in the cow-dung near the hedge at which he was. The herd's sister, seeing that, came in and said to her brother: 'You cowardly creature, your wife is in yonder hedge with another man,' said she. The herd hearing that became jealous, and he rose suddenly and angrily and seized a spear that was within on a rack and made for the madman.

The madman's side was towards him as he was lying down eating his meal out of the cowdung. The herd made a thrust of the spear out of his hand at Suibhne and wounded him in the nipple of his left breast, so that the point went through him, breaking his back in two. (Some say that it is the point of a deer's horn the herd had placed under him in the spot where he used to take his drink out of the cowdung, that he fell on it and so met his death.)

Enna Mac Bracain was then sounding the bell for prime at the door of the church-yard and he saw the deed that was done there; whereupon he uttered the lay:

Sad is that, O swineherd of Moling,
thou hast wrought a wilful, sorry deed,
woe to him who has slain by dint of his strength
the king, the saint, the saintly madman.
Evil to thee will be the outcome therefrom—
going at last without repentance—
thy soul will be in the devils keeping,
thy body will be . . .
In Heaven the same will be the place
for me and for him, O man,
psalms will be sung by fasting folk
for the soul of the true guest.
He was a king, he was a madman,
a man illustrious, noble, was he;
there is his grave—bright festival—
pity for him has rent my heart.

Enna turned back and told Moling that Suibhne had been slain by his swineherd Mongan. Moling at once set out accompanied by his clerics to the place where Suibhne was, and Suibhne acknowledged his faults and (made) his confession to Moling and he partook of Christ's body and thanked God for having received it, and he was anointed afterwards by the clerics.

The herd came up to him. 'Dour is the deed you have done, O herd,' said Suibhne, 'even to slay me, guiltless, for henceforth I cannot escape through the hedge because of the wound you have dealt me.' 'If I had known that it was you were there,' said the herd, 'I would not have wounded you however much you may have injured me.' 'By Christ, man!' said he, 'I have done you no injury whatever as you think, nor injury to anyone else on the ridge of the world since God sent me to madness; and of small account should be the harm to you through my being in the hedge here and getting a little milk for God's sake from yonder woman. And I would not trust myself with your wife nor with any other woman for the earth and its fruits.' 'Christ's curse on you, O herd!' said Moling. 'Evil is the deed you have done, short be your span of life here and hell beyond, because of the deed you have done.' 'There is no good to me therefrom,' said Suibhne, 'for your wiles have compassed me and I shall be dead from the wound that has been dealt me.' 'You will get an eric for it,' said Moling, 'even that you be in Heaven as long as I shall be'; and the three uttered this lay between them, that is, Suibhne, Mongan, and Moling:

Suibhne: Not pleasant is the deed thou hast done,
O herd of Moling Luachair,
I cannot go through the hedge
for the wound thy black hand has dealt me.

Mongan: Speak to me if thou hearest,
who art thou in truth, man?

Suibhne: Suibhne Geilt without reproach am I,
O herd of Moling Luachair.

Mongan: If I but knew, O slender Suibhne,
O man, if I could have recognised thee,
I would not have thrust a spear against thy skin
though I had seen thee harm me.

Suibhne: East or west I have not done
harm to one on the world's ridge
Since Christ has brought me from my valiant land
in madness throughout Erin.

Mongan: The daughter of my father and my mother
related—'twas no trifle to me—
how she found thee in yonder hedge
with my own wife at morn.

Suibhne: It was not right of thee to credit that
until thou hadst learnt its certainty,
alas that thou shouldst come hither to slay me
until thine eyes had seen!
Though I should be from hedge to hedge,
its harm were a trifle to thee,
though a woman should give me to drink
a little milk as alms.

Mongan: If I but knew what comes of it,
from wounding thee through breast and heart,
till Doom my hand would not wound thee,
O Suibhne of Glen Bolcain.

Suibhne: Though thou hast wounded me in the hedge,
I have not done thee ill;
I would not trust in thine own wife
for the earth and its fruits.
Alas for him who has come for a while from home
to thee, O Moling Luachair,
the wound thy herd has dealt me
stays me from wandering through the woods.

Moling: The curse of Christ who hath created everyone
on thee, said Moling to his herd,
sorry is the deed thou hast done
through envy in thine heart.
Since thou hast done a dread deed,
said Moling to his herd,
thou wilt get in return for it
a short span of life and hell.

Suibhne: Though thou mayest avenge it, O Moling,
I shall be no more;
no relief for me is it,
your treachery has compassed me.

Moling: Thou shalt get an eric for it,
said Moling Luachair, I avow;
thou shalt be in Heaven as long as I shall be
by the will of the great Lord, O Suibhne.

Mongan: It will be well with thee, O slender Suibhne,
thou in Heaven, said the herd,
not so with me here,
without Heaven, without my lifes span.

Suibhne: There was a time when I deemed more melodious
than the quiet converse of people,
the cooing of the turtle-dove
flitting about a pool.
There was a time when I deemed more melodious
than the sound of a little bell beside me
the warbling of the blackbird to the mountain
and the belling of the stag in a storm.
There was a time when I deemed more melodious
than the voice of a beautiful woman beside me,
to hear at dawn
the cry of the mountain-grouse.
There was a time when I deemed more melodious
the yelping of the wolves
than the voice of a cleric within
a-baaing and a-bleating.
Though goodly you deem in taverns
your ale-feasts with honour,
I had liefer drink a quaff of water in theft
from the palm of my hand out of a well.
Though yonder in your church you deem melodious
the soft converse of your students,
more melodious to me is the splendid chant
of the hounds of Glen Bolcain.

Though goodly ye deem the salt meat and the *flesh*
that are eaten in banqueting-houses,
I had liefer eat a tuft of fresh watercress
in some place without sorrow.
The herd's sharp spear has wounded me,
so that it has passed clean through my body;
alas, O Christ, who hast launched every judgment,
that I was not slain at Magh Rath!
Though goodly each bed without guile
I have made throughout Erin,
I had liefer a couch above the lake
in Benn Boirche, without concealment.
Though goodly each bed without guile
I have made throughout Erin,
I had liefer the couch above the wood
I have made in Glen Bolcain.
To Thee, O Christ, I give thanks
for partaking of Thy Body;
sincere repentance in this world
for each evil I have ever done.

A death-swoon came on Suibhne then, and Moling, attended by his clerics, rose, and each man placed a stone on Suibhne's tomb. 'Dear in sooth is he whose tomb this is,' said Moling; 'often were we two—happy time!—conversing one with the other along this pathway. Delightful to me was it to behold Suibhne—he whose tomb this is—at yonder well. The Madman's Well is its name, for often would he eat of its watercress and drink its water, and (so) the well is named after him. Dear, too, every other place that Suibhne used to frequent'; whereupon Moling said:

The tomb of Suibhne here!
remembrance of him has wrung my heart!
dear to me too, out of love for him,
each place in which the holy madman used to be.
Dear to me is fair Glen Bolcain
because of perfect Suibhne's love of it;
dear each stream that flows out of it,
dear its green-topped watercress.
Yonder is the Well of the Madman,
dear was he to whom it gave food,
dear to me its clear sand,
dear its pure water.
On me was imposed his preparation,
it seemed long until I should see him,
he asked that he be taken to my house,
dear was the lying in wait.
Dear each cool stream
wherein the green-topped watercress grew,

each well of bright water too,
because Suibhne used to visit it.
If it be the will of the King of the stars,
arise and come with me,
give me, O heart, thy hand
from the grave and from the tomb!
Melodious to me was the converse of Suibhne,
long shall I keep his memory in my breast:
I entreat my noble King of Heaven
above his grave and on his tomb!

Thereafter, Suibhne rose out of his swoon and Moling taking him by the hand the two proceeded to the door of the church. When Suibhne placed his shoulders against the door-post he breathed a loud sigh and his spirit fled to Heaven, and he was buried honourably by Moling.

So far, some of the tales and adventures of Suibhne son of Colman Cuar, king of Dal Araidhe.[34]

NOTES TO PART I

Introduction epigraph: Lucius Annae Seneca, *Epistolae morales ad Lucilium* 4.41 (64 CE).
1. Simon Schama, *Landscape and Memory* (New York: Vintage Books, 1995), 18.
2. "Ireland's Lost Glory," *Birds and All Nature* 7, no. 4, ed. C. C. Marble (Chicago: A. W. Mumford, 1900), 188.
3. Eoin Neeson, "Woodland in History and Culture," in *Nature in Ireland: A Scientific and Cultural History*, ed. John Wilson Foster and Helena C. G. Cheney (Dublin: Lilliput, 1997), 135.
4. "Ireland's Lost Glory," 188.
5. Ibid.
6. Robert Pogue Harrison, *Forests: The Shadow of Civilization* (Chicago: University of Chicago Press, 1992), ix. See also Schama, *Landscape and Memory*.
7. Harrison, *Forests*, ix.
8. Ibid., x.
9. Tacitus, *The Sacred Grove*, in *Tacitus*, trans. M. Hutton, rev. E. H. Warmington (Cambridge, MA: Harvard University Press, 1980); see also *The Works of Tacitus*, trans. Alfred John Church and William Jackson Brodribb, http://www.sacred-texts.com/cla/tac/.
10. James G. Frazer, *The Golden Bough: The Roots of Religion and Folklore* (New York: Gramercy Books, 1993), 56.
11. Miranda J. Green, *The World of the Druids* (London: Thames and Hudson, 1997), 107.
12. Ibid., 109.
13. Harrison, *Forests*, 178.
14. Neeson, "Woodland in History and Culture," 134.
15. Ibid.
16. Green, *World of the Druids*, 109.
17. Amergin, *The Mystery*, trans. Douglas Hyde, in *Voices and Poetry of Ireland* (London: Harper-Collins, 2003), 3.
18. "Deer's Cry or St. Patrick's Breastplate," in "A Taste of Ireland's Poets," Servants of the Word, accessed October 8, 2017, http://dailyscripture.servantsoftheword.org/ireland/early7.htm; see also "Deer's Cry," in *Selections from Ancient Irish Poetry*, trans. Kuno Meyer (London: Constable, 1911; Project Gutenberg, 2010), 25–27, http://www.gutenberg.org/files/32030/32030-h/32030-h.htm.

19. St. Columcille of Iona, "Columcille Fecit," in *The Oxford Companion to Irish Literature*, ed. Robert Welch (Oxford, UK: Clarendon, 1996), 108–9.

20. *Catholic Encyclopedia*, s.v. "Sedulius," accessed March 11, 2018, http://www.newadvent.org/cathen/13680a.htm; Caelius Sedulius, "Invocation," in *Carmen Paschale* [*Easter Song*], Inspirational Stories, accessed October 8, 2017, http://www.inspirationalstories.com/poems/invocation-caelius-sedulius-poems/.

21. Kuno Meyer, introduction to *Selections from Ancient Irish Poetry*, xii.

22. "The Blackbird by Belfast Lough," trans. Frank O'Connor, in *The Oxford Handbook of Modern Irish Poetry*, ed. Fran Brearton and Alan Gillis (Oxford: Oxford University Press, 2012), 325.

23. "The Scribe," trans. Robin Flower, in "A Taste of Ireland's Poets," Servants of the Word, accessed March 11, 2018, http://dailyscripture.servantsoftheword.org/ireland/early6.htm. The poem is found in the margins of a ninth-century Irish treatise on Latin grammar, which now resides in the monastery of St. Gall in Switzerland.

24. "The White Lake," trans. Robin Flower, in *A Taste of Ireland's Poets*, Servants of the Word, accessed March 11, 2018, http://dailyscripture.servantsoftheword.org/ireland/early6.htm.

25. "The Lark," trans. Robin Flower in *A Taste of Ireland's Poets*, Servants of the Word, accessed March 11, 2018, http://dailyscripture.servantsoftheword.org/ireland/early6.htm.

26. "The Hermit's Song," in Meyer, *Selections from Ancient Irish Poetry*, 30–31.

27. "King and Hermit," ibid., 47–50.

28. "Song of the Sea," ibid., 51–52.

29. "Summer Has Come," ibid., 53.

30. "Song of Summer," ibid., 54–55.

31. "Summer Is Gone," ibid., 56.

32. "A Song of Winter," ibid., 57–58.

33. "Arran," ibid., 59.

34. *Buile Suibhne*, ca. 1100, ed. J. G. O'Keeffe (Dublin: Dublin Institute for Advanced Studies, 1931), compiled by Beatrix Färber, proof corrections by Vibeke Dijkman and Maxim Fomin (CELT: Corpus of Electronic Texts; Cork: University College Cork 2001, 2008, 2013), 3–159, http://www.ucc.ie/celt/published/G302018/index.html. See also *Sweeney Astray*, trans. Seamus Heaney (London: Faber and Faber, 1983).

Nature Writing and the Changing Irish Landscape

Introduction to Part II

I would have been glad to have lived under my woodside, and to have kept a flock of sheep, rather than to have undertaken this government.
—Oliver Cromwell, to Parliament, 1658

For most of Ireland's inhabited history, its landscape has benefited from wet climactic conditions and a favorable climate in which to grow wheat. A major climate change occurred between the eleventh and fifteenth centuries that allowed wheat to thrive, making Ireland an attractive home for Norman knights and farmers who valued land that could produce this highly valued crop. This plentiful period changed when the Great Plague occurred from 1348 to 1350, and these three years of misery affected all of Europe. Preceded by the wettest and coldest summers of the millennium, this period became known as the Little Ice Age.[1] The long, harsh winters and short summers that followed this ice age became the death knell for the growing of wheat in Ireland. As John Feehan notes, "the colony collapsed, and the growing of wheat was abandoned in northern Europe. This miserable climactic epoch lasted until the middle of the nineteenth century, the devastating potato famine of the late 1840s marking its end with human misery, as the plague marked the beginning."[2]

Part of the difficulty in understanding the Irish and their relationship to nature, and indeed why many critics have not looked to nature writing for an answer, is because of nature's lack of importance as a subject matter when weighed against the heavy volume of literature devoted to Irish civilization. Simply put, the natural history of Ireland was always perceived as background information, even when natural events conspired to make nature the enemy. As Ireland's forests gave way to its farmland, Irish peasants, living in this rural existence, viewed nature as an affront in their struggle for survival, while the Irish subsequently lost touch with the land. As Terry Eagleton's *Heathcliff and the Great Hunger* points out, "Nature in Ireland is too stubbornly social and material a category, too much a matter of rent, conacre, pigs, and potatoes for it to be distanced, stylized, and subjectivated."[3] So, instead of being understood and valued as an important component of existence, nature became subservient to the needs and desires of a rapidly expanding population. The wild, uncultivated land was something to be vanquished; it became property and potential profit, and its cultivation became the primary desire of British landholders. Sir John Davies's treatise *A Discovery of the True Causes Why Ireland Was Never Entirely Subdued* made a distinct observation of Ireland's uncultivated lands. According to Davies, the Irish lacked any serious interest in building and landscaping in order to utilize the land for economic gain. As Oona Frawley notes about this treatise, "The uncivilized state that the Irish were believed to live in closely aligned with the uncultivated state of the land; the implication is, of course, that if the landscape were tamed so too would the people be. Such an attitude provided justification for policies aiming to reform."[4]

As Simon Schama notes in his *Landscape and Memory*, "Landscapes are culture before they are nature; constructs of the imagination projected onto wood and water and rock."[5] The beauty or function of a landscape is then predetermined by man, and his choice is either an artistic representation of nature or an agricultural one that becomes part of the social fabric of the community. From an economic perspective, if the needs of the people must be met, then the natural world will need to be subservient to these means.

After the fall of the forests, the landscape of early Ireland was transformed predominantly into open land to raise herds of cattle. The *wilderness* of this open land changed in the sixteenth century with the imposition of a new model of agriculture that favored personal tenure, introduced systematic enclosure, and segmented the entire Irish landscape into small enclosures. Just as the forests had disappeared, so too had the large, open meadows. As Feehan notes, "Ireland did not have a poet to chronicle the passing of the Irish open field but the bards of the old school bemoaned, 'the open fields crossed by girdles of twisting fences' and 'fairs held in the places of the chase.'"[6]

Foster's Corn Law of 1784, a law that was enacted to protect Ireland's domestic market, was chiefly responsible for altering the country's topography.[7] The Corn Law eliminated the use of foreign grain and turned Ireland, as William Trevor puts it in his *A Writer's Ireland*, "into a land of tillage and wheat fields."[8] This subculture of Ireland's food production essentially drove humanity and nature apart; now the whole point of planting and growing was tied to production and profit, and this tillage began to take its toll on nutrients in the soil. As the environmentalist William Howarth notes, "The dogma that culture will always master nature has long directed Western progress, inspiring the wars, invasions, and other forms of conquest that have crowded the earth and strained its carrying capacity."[9] For Ireland, Western progress begins and ends in its soil. The political conflicts with the British Empire, the conversion from forest to farmland, and the elimination of the variety of crops that grew out of the soil all contributed to the illusion that nature was being controlled for the benefit of human progress.

Much of the selections in part 2 of this work involve humanity and nature in conflict or disconnect, including Thomas Gainsford's *A Description of Ireland*, which illustrates an Irish landscape under cultivation and control of humanity, a countryside that fosters a very different relationship to the Irish than its forested past. William Allingham's poetry and the poems of James Clarence Mangan reflect a paradox of a beautiful and sublime landscape, where at once the natural world contains both a peacefulness and terror, and it is a landscape from which the failure of the potato crop will be revealed. Through the disconnect between the Irish and nature within this shifted landscape, famine ensues. William Carlton's important famine novel *The Black Prophet* details the foreshadowing of the disaster especially in the first chapter, included here, in which the setting of a poor, rural western Ireland serves not only as a backdrop, with humanity and nature utterly disconnected, but also as a major cause of the starvation that will take the lives of a million Irish. This selection is followed by a selection from *Hurrish*, a novel by Emily Lawless, set in the Burren of County Clare, where the emptiness and the harsh living conditions in a place devoid of agriculture becomes the ultimate and ironic stage on which the Land Wars, the building of conflict, and the ultimate violence between Irish peasants and English landowners play out. In both novels, the setting of a rural Ireland, where the natural world maintains control, becomes the crucial starting point from which their tragic stories are told.

Thomas Gainsford

Thomas Gainsford was an author and news editor and belonged to the Surrey family of Gainsford. He is known to have served in Ireland under Richard de Burgh, fourth earl of Clanricarde, as "third officer" of the "earl's regiment" when the Spaniards were dislodged from Kinsale on December 24, 1601. He was also engaged in the war against Tyrone in Ulster. As captain, Gainsford undertook to occupy land in Ulster at the plantation of 1610. Following his military career, Gainsford began a career as an editor and is reputed to have been the first London periodical news editor. Ben Jonson dubbed Gainsford "Captain Pamphlet" as Gainsford became associated with the publications of the news syndicate formed in 1622 by Nathaniel Butter, Thomas Archer, Nicholas Bourne, William Sheffard, and Bartholomew Downes and was responsible for taking control of the style, organization, and presentation of the news. He helped readers to understand news from many cities, armies, and battle scenes that could otherwise have been confusing to readers unfamiliar with European dynasties and armies but concerned by news of Catholic advances in the Counter-Reformation. Gainsford also wrote many editorials "To the Reader," establishing a relationship with readers and addressing them and their anxieties directly. Gainsford's most popular book was *The Glory of England* (1618), because it compares England favorably with the empires and kingdoms of Tartaria, China, India, Persia, the Turks, Ethiopia, Russia and the northern kingdoms, Germany, Spain, Italy, France, and the Low Country. *The Glory of England* also included a glorifying view of Ireland. In *A Description of Ireland: A.D. 1618*, Gainsford captures the natural beauty of the Irish landscape along with the Irish people who inhabit that landscape.[10]

A Description of Ireland: A.D. 1618

The country and kingdom of Ireland is generally for natural air and, commodity of blessings, sufficient to satisfy a covetous or curious appetite: but withal divided into such fastness of mountain, bogg, and wood, that it hath emboldened the inhabitants to presume on hereditary *securitie* as if disobedience had a protection. For the mountains deny any carriages but by great industry and strength of men (so have we drawn the canon over the deepest bogs and stoniest hills) and the passages are every way dangerous, both for unfirmness of ground, and the lurking rebel, who will plash down whole trees over the passes and so intricately wind them, or lay them, that they shall be a strong barricade, and then lurk in ambush amongst the standing wood, playing upon all comers, as they intend to go along. On the bog they likewise presume with a naked celerity to come as near our foot and horse, as is possible, and then fly off again, knowing we cannot, or indeed dare not follow them: and thus they serve us in the narrow entrances into their glens; and stony paths, or if you will, dangerous quagmires of their mountains, where 100 shot shall rebate the hasty approach of 500; and a few muskets (if they durst carry any) well placed, will stagger a pretty army; not acquainted with the terror, or unpreventing the mischief.

The province of Leinster is more orderly than the rest, as being reasonable well inhabited, and having some form of a Commonwealth; so that I find no mistake either for delight or profit, but that the want of wood abridgeth their computation of happiness; yet questionless was the principal cause of our reducing them to civility, and the place wherein we first settled many English families. Some unite, and some divide the Kingdom of Meth from Leinster, and make it a province of itself, containing East Meth; West Meth and Longford, wherein O Roorck is resident, supposing himself the greatest Gentleman in the world; yea contesting many times with O Neal, however with much ado he afforded him precedency: The country is very fruitful and pleasant, not so mountainous, but ill inhabited; For the wars, and their own bestiality, have not only made a separation of all good order, but even terrified both beast and fowl from commorance among them in many places.

The province Munster hath some Towns well advanced by the sea coasts, and many excellent harbours, wherein Ireland may boast over all countries of Europe: The grounds adjacent are very fertile, and in many places affords cause of ostentation but more inward they are very barren and mountainous, full of bogs, woods, and other remote places, whose fastness hath incited the people to over great presumption: yet because of the spaciousness with men desiring good order, it might be reduced and reformed, as enjoying plentiful and sweet rivers, full of fish, and some of sufficient depth to transport reasonable boats into the land.

The province of Conach is divided from the rest by a goodly river called the Shannon being as I take it the greatest of any island in the world: For it stretches a course of 200 miles, and filleth his channel along the shores of Longford, Meths, Ormond, Limerick and Kerry, yet serveth them in no great stead: For their shipping cometh no further, than Limerick where it is five mile broad fresh water, and 60 mile from the main sea, from thence small cotts, as they term their boats, carry their wood, turf, fish and other commodities: but for fish, as Salmon, Bream, Pike and divers other sorts, I shall not be believed to relate their numbers, and hugeness by such as are enemies to observation, or the belief of the blessings of other countries. Within 20 miles of Limerick, as I take it a little beyond, the precinct of Caher-castle, a strange rock hath taken her lodging even cross the river and filleth the room in such a manner that almost the navigation is hindered thereby but what cannot men and money do? And why should not the idle people be industriously employed to remove the same, and so free the passage to Athlone: As for an objection of impossibility; the judgement of men hath yielded to survey, and many examples have confirmed the effects of more laborious attempts. The fourth part, namely Tomond (for by reason of the rivers interposing itself I see no reason why it should be disjointed from Conach) with Galway and Clanricard is very stony, full of marble, alabaster, and iett, and hath better order both for number and good buildings in their castles, than in other parts of Ireland: The north from Athlone, to the Abbey of Aboile, and so beyond the Curlews as far as Sligo, is of excellent temperature and goodness: These Curlews are mountains full of dangerous passages, especially when the Kern take a stomach and pride to enter into action, as they term their rebellion and tumultuary insurrection. On the other side of the County of Mayo consorteth with the pleasingest place in the Kingdom, by whose beaten banks lie those famous islands of Life, of whom a ridiculous tale is fathered, that nothing dies in them, so that when the inhabitants grow old, they are carried elsewhere, which custom they have of late superstitiously observed both in these islands of Aran, and some other adjoining of the same condition, as they suppose.

The province of Ulster, and called the North is very large, and withal mountains; full of great loughs of freshwater, except Lough Cone, which ebbeth and floweth, as the sea shouldeth aside the straight at Strangford, and with that violence at the ebb, that a ship under sail with a reasonable gale of wind cannot enter against the tide. These lake's nature hath appointed in steed of rivers, and stored with fish, especially Trout, and Pike, of such strange proportion, that if I should tell you of a Trout taken up in Tyrone 46 inches long, and presented to the Lord Mountjoy, then Deputy: you would demand, whether I was oculatus testis; and I answer, I eat my part of it, and I take it both my Lord Danvers and Sir William Goodolphin were at the table, and worthy Sir Iosias Bodley hath the portraiture depicted in plano. Here are no towns, or at least very few, but divers Castles dispersed, and the inhabitants remove their cabins, as their cattle change pasture, somewhat like the Tartarians, except in times of war, and troubles, then do they retire under the couett [cover?] of castles, and order their houses wound with rods, and covered with turfs, as well as they can, bringing their cattle even within their houses, lying altogether in one room both to prevent robberies of Kern, and spoiled by wolves. Amongst these every country is subject to the Law Tanist which is, he which is best able to maintain the reputation of their families, is the great O, and commander.

Through the Kingdom generally the winter is neither so cold, nor the summer so hot as in England, by reason whereof harvest is very late, and in the north wheat will not quickly ripen, nor have they acorns once in a dozen year: their principal corn is oates, which are commonly burnt out of the straw, and they then trod from the husks with men's feet; of this they made their bread in cakes, being first ground by calliots and drudges very naked, and beastly sitting on the ground, with the mill like our mustard quernes between their legs, and then upon broad iron press they bake the meal when it is needed; which custom they best observe in Munster with their chiefest corn. The continual showers and mists make the country more dangerous to our nation, debarring the absolute assurance of wholesome air; and the consequent health: seldom any frost continues or snow, lieth long, but on the mountains; in which are great store of deer both red and sallow. The abundance of wolves compels them to house their cattle in the bawns of their castles, where all the winter nights they stand up to the bellies in dirt: another reason is to prevent thieves, and false-hearted brethren, who have spies abroad, and will come 30 mile out of one province into another to practice a cunning robbery; the people are generally haters of bondage, and beyond measure proud: so that the younger brothers, and bastards, who are dear as the other, scorn all endeavours, but liberty and war. The gentlewomen stomach, and in truth vilipend others, who get their living by trade, merchandise, or mechanically; yet are divers [en]gravers in gold and silver, called plain tinkers, who make their chalices, harps, buttons for their sleeves, crucifixes, and such like, in estimation amongst them. Their noblemen, or Lords called Dynastas, are known by O and Mac, and every family hath such minister of justice to the people, famoused by the title of Breahans, and yet the exactions over their tenants by way of cuttings, and other terrible impositions, have caused divers rebellions and insurrections amongst themselves, which when the State hath attempted to reform, then have they stood on their guard, and taken indirect occasions to condemn our usurpation, whereby their odious and hateful repinings, like a monstrous cloth, have made their disobedience loathsome, and brought upon them such miseries, as a calamitous war and angry prince inflicted turbulent people withal. These families have also such, as by way of history elate them to exorbitant actions, joining withal abuse of Poetry, and deceit of Physic, known by the name of Bardes, on whom depend certain harpers, rhymers, and whom Priests, which live in a kindred, the father instructing the son, or brother, and he his cousin or friend. The name Galliglass is in a manner extinct, but of Kerne in great reputation as serving them in their revolts, and proving sufficient soldiers, but excellent for skirmish. They have strong and able bodies, proud hearts, pestilent wits, liberal of life, subject to incontinency, amorous, wherein their women are extraordinarily pleased, patient to endure, lovers of music and hospitality, constant to their maintainers, whether men or women, implacable in their hatred, light of belief, covetous of glory, impatient of reproach, or contumely not thinking it yet any disgrace to receive a nickname at their christening, as Con O Neale Banco, because he was lame. Besides, they are all extremely superstitious, as indeed barbarous people are best observers of ceremonies, and when any of them enters into religion, it is admirable with what austerity they reform themselves: Their children are nursed abroad, and their foster fathers and foster mothers are as dear to them as their own kindred: They use incantations and spells, wearing girdles of women's hair and locks of your lovers; they suppose idleness a glory of nature, and by their sluttish, or rather savage customs, strive to scorn (as they say) our superfluity: they are ready upon any enforcement by the impostering Art of their Bardes to innovation, as envying our first conquest, and stomaching they were never able to expel us: They are desperate in revenge, and their Kerne think no man dead, until his head be off. They suppose theft no great offence, as imitating the Lacedemonians; for they pray to prosper in their attempts: but these be commonly the bastards of Priests, who prove nitrous villains, and daughters either beg or became strumpets, or if you will, beggarly strumpets. They commonly intermix oaths with their speeches, as by the Trinity, God, his saints, St Patrick, St Bridget, faith and truth, the temple, your hand, O Neales hand, and such like. Their marriages are strange; for they are made sometimes so conditionally, that upon a slight occasion the man taketh another wife, the wife another husband. They are easily delivered of their children (I have known of them delivered in the morning and march along with us the same day) and if they have any by divers men, at their deaths they resign them to the right father; the new married and conceived with child giveth the Barde her best clothes. They have soft and excellent skins and hands; but the small of their legs hangeth in a manner over their brogs: Their apparel is a mantle to sleep in, and that on the ground or some rushes or flags: a thick gathered smock with wide sleeves graced with bracelets and crucifixes about their necks: They wear linen rowels about their heads of divers fashions: in Ulster carelessly wound about: In Conach like Bishop's mitres, a very stately attire, and once prohibited by statute: in Munster resembling a thick Cheshire Cheese. Their smocks are saffroned against vermin; for they wear them three months together: but to be lowsie is hereditary with the best of them, and no disgrace. But men and women not long since accustomed a savage manner of diet, which was raw flesh, drinking the blood, now they seeth it, and quaff up the liquor, and then take Vsquebath: not having flesh they feed on watercresses and shamrocks and bonniclaboch, which is milk strangely put into a tub a souring, till it be clotted, and curdled together: When the cow will not let her milk down they blow her behind very strangely, and sometimes thrust up their arms to their elbows, speaking words of gentleness and intreaty by way of bemoaning. The men wear trousers, mantle, and a cap of steel; they are curious about their horses tending to witchcraft; they have not saddles but strange fashioned pads, their horses are for the most part unshod behind: they use axes, staves, broad swords and darts: In Terconnell the hair of their heads grows so long and curled, that they go bear-headed, and are called Glibs, the women Glibbins. These and many other do the mere Irish observe with resolution and our wonderment not to be diverted, as if the Poet should find fault with: "*Quo semel est imbuta recens seruabit odorem Testa diu.*"

Horace, epist. 1.2. 69–70.

And thus much for Topography or superficial view of the kingdoms of the world.[11]

William Allingham

William Allingham (1824–1889) was an Irish poet who became most famous after his death with the publication of his diaries in 1907, edited by his wife. His entries elaborate on his friendships with the significant literary authors of the day, including Dante Gabriel Rossetti, Alfred Lord Tennyson, and Thomas Carlyle. In 1855, Allingham's *Day and Night Songs* was published with nine illustrations by Arthur Hughes, D. G. Rossetti, and John E. Millais. His poetry, influenced by the tradition of Border Ballads, often address Irish social problems and psychological conflicts presented within Irish communities. However, a large body of his poems address the beauty of the Irish landscape and focus on the importance of local places and indeed offer a sanctuary from the perils of everyday Irish life. His poem "The Faeries" is widely anthologized; many of his lesser-known nature poems attain the same lyrical enjoyment and illustrate the richness of Ireland's natural world. His poems about local places and fairies had a lasting effect on W. B. Yeats and helped influence his early nature poetry and the beginnings of the Irish Literary Revival.

Wishing

Ring-ting! I wish I were a Primrose,
A bright yellow Primrose blowing in the Spring!
   The stooping boughs above me,
   The wandering bee to love me,
The fern and moss to creep across
     And the Elm-tree for our King!

Nay—stay! I wish I were an Elm-tree,
A great lofty Elm-tree, with green leaves gay!
   The winds would set them dancing,
   The sun and moonshine glance in,
The birds would house among the boughs,
     And sweetly sing!

O—no! I wish I were a Robin,
A Robin or a little Wren, everywhere to go;
   Through forest, field, or garden,
   And ask no leave or pardon,
Till Winter comes with icy thumbs
     To ruffle up our wing!

Well—tell! Where should I fly to,
Where go to sleep in the dark wood or dell?
   Before a day was over,
   Home comes the rover,
For Mother's kiss,—sweeter this
     Than any other thing![12]

The Fairies

Up the airy mountain,
Down the rushy glen,
We daren't go a-hunting
For fear of little men;
Wee folk, good folk,
Trooping all together;
Green jacket, red cap,
And white owl's feather!
Down along the rocky shore
Some make their home,
They live on crispy pancakes
Of yellow tide-foam;
Some in the reeds
Of the black mountain lake,
With frogs for their watch-dogs,
All night awake.

High on the hill-top
The old King sits;
He is now so old and gray
He's nigh lost his wits.
With a bridge of white mist
Columbkill he crosses,
On his stately journeys
From Slieveleague to Rosses;
Or going up with music
On cold starry nights,
To sup with the Queen
Of the gay Northern Lights.

They stole little Bridget
For seven years long;
When she came down again
Her friends were all gone.
They took her lightly back,
Between the night and morrow,
They thought that she was fast asleep,
But she was dead with sorrow.
They have kept her ever since
Deep within the lake,
On a bed of flag-leaves,
Watching till she wake.

By the craggy hill-side,
Through the mosses bare,
They have planted thorn-trees

For pleasure here and there.
Is any man so daring
As dig them up in spite,
He shall find their sharpest thorns
In his bed at night.

Up the airy mountain,
Down the rushy glen,
We daren't go a-hunting
For fear of little men;
Wee folk, good folk,
Trooping all together;
Green jacket, red cap,
And white owl's feather![13]

The Lover and Birds

    Within a budding grove,
In April's ear sang every bird his best,
But not a song to pleasure my unrest,
Or touch the tears unwept of bitter love;
Some spake, methought, with pity, some as if in jest.
      To every word
      Of every bird
    I listen'd, and replied as it behove.

    Scream'd Chaffinch, 'Sweet, sweet, sweet!
Pretty lovey, come and meet me here!'
'Chaffinch,' quoth I, 'be dumb awhile, in fear
Thy darling prove no better than a cheat,
And never come, or fly when wintry days appear.'
      Yet from a twig,
      With voice so big,
    The little fowl his utterance did repeat.

    Then I, 'The man forlorn
Hears Earth send up a foolish noise aloft.'
'And what'll he do? What'll he do?' scoff'd
The Blackbird, standing, in an ancient thorn,
Then spread his sooty wings and flitted to the croft
      With cackling laugh;
      Whom I, being half
    Enraged, called after, giving back his scorn.

    Worse mock'd the Thrush, 'Die! die!
Oh, could he do it? could he do it? Nay!
Be quick! be quick! Here, here, here!' (went his lay.)
'Take heed! take heed!' then 'Why? why? why? why? why?

See-ee now! see-ee now!' (he drawl'd) 'Back! back! back! R-r-r-run away!'
    O Thrush, be still!
    Or at thy will,
Seek some less sad interpreter than I.

  'Air, air! blue air and white!
Whither I flee, whither, O whither, O whither I flee!'
(Thus the Lark hurried, mounting from the lea)
'Hills, countries, many waters glittering bright,
Whither I see, whither I see! deeper, deeper, deeper, whither I see, see, see!'
    'Gay Lark,' I said,
    'The song that's bred
In happy nest may well to heaven make flight.'

  'There's something, something sad,
I half remember'—piped a broken strain.
Well sung, sweet Robin! Robin sung again.
'Spring's opening cheerily, cheerily! be we glad!'
Which moved, I wist not why, me melancholy mad,
    Till now, grown meek,
    With wetted cheek,
Most comforting and gentle thoughts I had.[14]

Among the Heather

One evening, walking out, I o'ertook a modest colleen,
When the wind was blowing cool and the harvest leaves were falling.
'Is our road perchance the same? Might we travel on together?'
'Oh, I keep the mountainside,' she replied, 'among the heather.'

'Your mountain air is sweet when the days are long and sunny,
When the grass grows round the rocks, and the whin-bloom smells like honey;
But the winter's coming fast with its foggy, snowy weather,
And you'll find it bleak and chill on your hill among the heather.'

She praised her mountain home, and I'll praise it too with reason,
For where Molly is there's sunshine and flowers at every season.
Be the moorland black or white, does it signify a feather?
Now I know the way by heart, every part among the heather.

The sun goes down in haste, and the night falls thick and stormy,
Yet I'd travel twenty miles for the welcome that's before me.
Singing hi for Eskydun, in the teeth of wind and weather.
Love'll warm me as I go through the snow, among the heather.[15]

In a Spring Grove

Here the white-ray'd anemone is born,
    Wood-sorrel, and the varnish'd buttercup;
    And primrose in its purfled green swathed up,
Pallid and sweet round every budding thorn,
Gray ash, and beech with rusty leaves outworn.
    Here, too, the darting linnet hath her nest
In the blue-lustered holly, never shorn,
    Whose partner cheers her little brooding breast,
Piping from some near bough. O simple song!
O cistern deep of that harmonious rillet,
And these fair juicy stems that climb and throng
    The vernal world, and unexhausted seas
Of flowing life, and soul that asks to fill it,
    Each and all these,—and more, and more than these![16]

The Ruined Chapel

By the shore, a plot of ground
Clips a ruin'd chapel round,
Buttress'd with a grassy mound;
Where Day and Night and Day go by,
And bring no touch of human sound.

Washing of the lonely seas,
Shaking of the guardian trees,
Piping of the salted breeze;
Day and Night and Day go by
To the endless tune of these.

Or when, as winds and waters keep
A hush more dead than any sleep,
Still morns to stiller evenings creep,
And Day and Night and Day go by;
Here the silence is most deep.

The empty ruins, lapsed again
Into Nature's wide domain,
Sow themselves with seed and grain
As Day and Night and Day go by;
And hoard June's sun and April's rain.

Here fresh funeral tears were shed;
Now the graves are also dead;
And suckers from the ash-tree spread,
While Day and Night and Day go by;
And stars move calmly overhead.[17]

William Hamilton Drummond

William Hamilton Drummond (1778–1865) was a poet and theological writer. In addition to being a Presbyterian minister and Unitarian Christian theologian, he was also an honored poet, an educationalist, and an early advocate of the rights of animals. He declared that animal rights came out of a respect for and an obligation to God. Further, this obligation pertained to the entirety of the natural world. Drummond's 1800 epic poem *The Giant's Causeway* is a product of the poet's fascination with natural history and more specifically with the natural wonder on the Northern Irish coast. Giant's Causeway consists of about forty thousand interlocking basalt columns and was formed by an ancient volcanic eruption. Much of the knowledge on which the poem is based comes from the concept of Neptunism, a scientific theory of geology formulated in the late eighteenth century, which proposed that rocks formed from the crystallization of minerals in Earth's early oceans. Though the theory has since been discounted, Drummond nevertheless creates a poem filled with imagery that records the geology and the erosion of this famous natural wonder, while at the same time evoking its power and mystery as a gateway to Ireland's natural world. Drummond was a clergyman, but he was also a topographical poet. As a naturalist, Drummond was able to observe firsthand the unique basalt stones that composed the causeway, giving him the inspiration for his epic.[18] Though epic poetry is generally reserved for extended narrative involving human conflict, this poem focuses squarely on one natural wonder. In book 1 of the epic, Drummond's verse explores the history and mythology of the Giant's Causeway. In book 2, he draws attention to the various folk legends that relate to the origins of these rocks.

The Giant's Causeway, Book First

Come lonely Genius of my natal shore,
From cave or bower, wild glen, or mountain hoar;
And while by ocean's rugged bounds I muse,
Thy solemn influence o'er my soul diffuse:
Whether thou wanderest o'er the craggy steep.
Where the lore spirits of the tempest weep,
Or rov'st with trackless footsteps o'er the waves,
Or wak'st the echoes of thy hundred caves;
With joy I hail thy visionary form,
Rough, dark, august, and clad in night and storm:
To me more dear thy rocky realm by far,
The cliff, the whirlwind, and the billowy war,
Than e'en the loveliest scenes which Flora yields,
Her myrtle bowers, or incense-breathing fields.

Yet mid thy rocks might some wild flowrets bloom,
And first for me exhale their sweet perfume,
Yielding a chaplet to my vagrant muse,
Blooming and pearled with fresh Parnassian dews;
Though tempests roared in every dark-browed cave,

And wild beneath me burst the yawning wave,
O'er the high steep how ardent would I rise,
Elate with hope to seize the glorious prize!

How sweet to wander here when orient day
Tinges with roseate hue the milky spray!
What time the Spring from Winter's bondage clear,
Wakes into life and joy the infant year;
When smile the cloudless heavens, and western gales
Sport in the tumbling billows' glassy vales.
See! where exulting o'er the azure field,
The day's bright regent lifts his golden shield,
Round, dazzling, vast, ethereal world of Same,
That warms, illumes, sustains this beauteous frame.
Roll on bright orb, in peerless splendour roll;
To worlds on worlds the life-diffusing soul:
Around thy path what nameless glories stream,
Fire the blue vault, and o'er the billows gleam,
As if the heavens revealed to mortal sight,
Their topaz pavements in a blaze of light;
And through the morn's red portals poured abroad,
Life, love, and rapture, from the throne of God.
Burnished with gold, the cliffs resplendent shine,
And cast their shadows in the glancing brine,
Trembling and soft, as though the magic hand
of some cerulean nymph, in colours bland,
Had traced the scene, and back to nature gave
Her beauteous image from the pictured wave.
Light flit the vapours o'er the distant hill,
The prospect opens wide and wider still;
Cantire's blue heights with purple radiance glow,
And Jura's paps yet white with winter snow;
Bright o'er the billows shine the sparkling isles,
And heaven on earth with boundless beauty smiles.

O thou whose soul the muses' lore inspires,
Whose bosom science warms, or genius fires,
If nature charm thee in her wildest forms,
Throned on the cliff 'midst cataracts and storms;
Or with surpassing harmony arrayed,
In pillared mole, or towering colonnade,
Seek Dalriada's wild romantic shore—
Wind through her vallies, and her capes explore.
Let folly's sons to lands far distant roam,
And praise the charms of every clime but home:
Yet sure such scenes can Dalriada boast,
As please the painter and the poet most;

Swift torrents foaming down the mountain side,
Rocks that in clouds grotesque their summits hide,
Gigantic pyramids, embattled steeps,
Bastions and temples nodding o'er the deeps,
Aerial bridges o'er vast fissures thrown,
Triumphal arches, gods of living stone,
Eolian antres, thunder-rifted spires,
And all the wonders of volcanic fires.
Here broken, shattered, in confusion dread,
Towers, bridges, arches, gods and temples spread:
Stupendous wrecks, where awful wildness reigns!
While all th' ideal forms which fancy feigns
Sweep the dun rack, and to the poet's eyes,
In many a strange embodied shape arise.
In scenes like these did Collins first behold
Pale Fear, and Danger's limbs of Giant mould;
Gray poured the sorrows of his Cambrian lyre,
And mighty Shakespeare breathed heaven's pure ethereal fire.

Ye cliffs and grots where boding tempests wail,
Ye terraced capes, ye rocks, ye billows hail:
Amazing scene, how wild, how wondrous grand,
In circuit vast, the pillared shores expand!
Great fane of God! where nature sits enshrined,
Pouring her inspiration o'er the mind.—
Mid pointed obelisks, and rocky bowers,
And tessellated moles, and giant towers,
She reigns sublime; while round her throne repair
The fleet-winged spirits of the sea and air,
And through yon pillars, organ of the blast,
When sounding Boreas bends the groaning mast,
Bid the long deep majestic anthem rise,
In mighty concert to the echoing skies,
And warring floods——

Dark o'er the foam-white waves,
The giants' pier the war of tempests braves,
A far projecting, firm, basaltic way
Of clustering columns wedged in dense array;
With skill so like, yet so surpassing art,
With such design, so just in every part,
That reason pauses, doubtful if it stand
The work of mortal, or immortal hand.

Ye favoured few, whom nature's partial care
Leads through the realms of ocean, earth and air;
Who read with piercing eye her various laws,

Mark each effect, and trace the latent cause;
But chief do thou Mac Donnell, taught to scan
Each form and feature of the beauteous plan,
Declare did ocean, in his secret bed,
When erst his waves the shoreless world o'erspread,
Or central fires, or fierce volcanic flame,
In sulphurous gulf profound, the wonder frame?

The sportive fancy of th' untutored swain,
To wonder prone, and slave to error's reign,
Unskilled to search how nature's plastic hand
Moulds the rough rock, and forms the solid land;
To Fion, ruler of the giant line,
Ascribes the glory of the strange design;
And fondly deems, though reason spurn the thought,
That human power the massy fabric wrought.
Nor let the sage, in lettered pride severe,
The simple legend with impatience hear.

From Albin oft, when darkness veiled the pole,
Swift o'er the surge the tartaned plunderers stole,
And Erin's vales with purple torrents ran,
Beneath the claymores of the murd'rous clan;
Till Cumhal's son, to Dalriada's coast,
Led the tall squadrons of his Finnian host,
Where his bold thought the wondrous plan designed,
The proud conception of a giant mind,
To bridge the ocean for the march of war,
And wheel round Albin's shores his conquering car.

For many a league along the quarried shore,
Each storm-swept cape the race gigantic tors;
And though untaught by Grecian lore to trace
The Doric grandeur, or Corinthian grace;
Not void of skill in geometric rules,
With art disdaining all the pride of schools,
Each mighty artist, from the yielding rock,
Hewed many a polished, dark, prismatic block;
One end was modelled like the rounded bone,
One formed a socket for its convex stone;
Then side to side and joint to joint they bound,
Columns on columns locked, and mound on mound:
Close as the golden cells which bees compose,
So close they ranged them in compacted rows,
Till rolling time beheld the fabric rise,
Span the horizon, and invade the skies,
And, curved concentric to the starry sphere,

Mount o'er the thunder's path, and storm's career:
To Staffa's rock th' enormous arch they threw,
And Albin trembled, as the wonder grew.

Thus Death and Sin, when from the realms of night,
They traced through chaos the archangel's flight,
Chained to hell's beach a mole of wondrous length,
And raised a bridge of adamantine strength,
Connecting earth and hell; a spacious road,
Smooth, sloping downward to th' accurs'd abode.

When first to Staffa's cavern'd shores they came,
They reared a palace of stupendous frame,
Worthy their chief, and honoured by his name:
Deep in the surge, the broad dense base they spread, ·
And raised to heaven the massy columns' head;
High rose the rock-wove arch, and o'er the flood,
Like Neptune's fane the pillared structure stood,
Solemn, and grand beyond the laboured pile
Of Gothic fane, or minster's vaulted aisle.
Oft has its wild harmonious echoes rung,
As minstrels sweet to deeds of glory strung
Their deep-toned harps, or warrior chieftains strong
Raised the loud chorus of the martial song.
Now the lone sea-bird's melancholy wail
Sounds through the vault, and loads the murmuring gale;
While thundering Ocean all his billows calls,
And rolls in foam along the fluted walls,
That back return such harmony of sound,
As if an hundred bards were ranged around,
Bowed o'er the columns, striving to disarm
The tempest's rage by music's sweetest charm;
Or Ossian's thrilling harp, suspended high,
Trilled by Æolian minstrels' pensive sigh,
Awoke such notes as saints delighted hear,
Or angel spirits pour on mortal ear.

Now armed for war, along their iron road,
Stern in their ire, the giant warriors strode;
As files on files advanced in serried might,
How flashed their arms' intolerable light;
Casques, shields and spears, and banners floating gay,
And mail-clad steeds, and chariots' proud array,
Bright glancing as the fires which heaven adorn,
When fair Aurora brings the boreal morn!
Thus monstrous forms o'er heaven's nocturnal arch,
Seen by the sage, in pomp celestial march;

See Aries there his glittering brow unfold,
And raging Taurus toss his horns of gold;
With bended bow the sullen Archer lowers,
Aid there Aquarius comes with all his showers;
Lions and Centaurs, Gorgons, Hydras rise,
And Gods and Heroes blaze along the skies.

   Then mighty deeds that giant race had wrought,
And bold beyond the muse's boldest thought;
Had dared, perchance, with unresisted sway,
To force to Scandia's shores their onward way;
Or like their earth-born sires, infuriate driven,
Had matched their arms against the might of heaven:
But deep dismay spread Albin's shores around,
When crouding frequent to each sacred mound
Of rocks, or crags that ne'er felt chisel's stroke.
By hill or glen, or wood of hallowed oak;
Bards, Druids, Warriors, as their altars blaze,
For aid, for vengeance loud petitions raise;
Three days thrice told, on Odin loud they call,
Each day sees thrice three human victims fall.

   "Rise mighty Odin, rise in power divine,
And sink to Hela's gulf our foes and thine,
These sons of Frost, whom mad ambition goads
To brave thy power, and scale thy blest abodes."

   Throned on dark clouds, dread Odin beard from far,
In icy realms beneath the northern star,
Where in Valhalla's courts his warlike train
Quaff the brown draught from skulls of heroes slain:
Deep-moved he rose, and soon with loud alarms
Heaven's pavements rang, as Odin rushed to arms.
Swift down the bow of many a fulgent dye,
Bridge of the Gods, th' immortal footsteps hie;
Hail, sleet and darkness o'er his bosom spread,
The rush of waters roared around his head,
While wrapt in light'ning and devouring storm,
He swept the winds, a dim terrific form;
Aloft in wrath his brandished arm he raised,
Bright in his hand the hissing thunder blazed,
While on the centre of the arch he stood,
And sent his potent mandate o'er the flood.

   "Arise," he cried, " ye ministers of ire,
Ye hurricanes, ye floods, and red-winged fire;
Arise, go forth in congregated might,
And whelm these impious toils in lasting night."

Then livid fires the vault of heaven o'ercast,
High rose the floods, and furious howled the blast;
Then Lochlin's Gods in might resistless came;
Thor's mace impetuous smote the trembling frame;
The sister fates, twelve dark tremendous shades,
Sang their dire spells, and waved their shining blades,
While Loke and Hela, from their chains unbound,
Shook to its rooted base the yawning ground
Then tossed each isle, and cliff, and rugged steep,
Wild rolled the mountains like a stormy deep,
And crashing, roaring, thundering loud to heaven,
Down rushed the arch, in shattered fragments riven,
With horrid din, as if th' exploding ball,
And heaven's rent pillars mingled in their fall.

Deep in the dreary caves of ocean lie
The ponderous ruins far from mortal eye:
Yet each abutment of the structure stands
A proud memorial of the giant bands,
Through earth's extended realms renowned afar,
As great in peace, and terrible in war.
And then, if earth to heaven in arms opposed,
Might aught avail, in conflict had they closed
With Lochlin's gods, and Odin, felt
Had rued the dint of Fion's better steel.
But by enchanted spells unnerv'd they mood.
Fixed to the beach, till horror chilled their blood,
And total change pervading nerve and bone,
Hard grew their limbs, and all were turned to stone.
Now oft their shadowy spectres, flitting light,
Croud to their favourite mole at noon of night.
In fancy's eye, the curious toil pursue,
And all the tasks that pleased in life renew.
One, huge of stature, dark beneath the gloom,
Grasps in his brawny hand the mimic loom;
One rides the lion rock; in cadence low,
One bids the organ's beauteous structure blow;
While far aloof on yon lone column's height,
Their Lord and Hero glories in the sight.

Thus grey Tradition tells the wondrous tale,
And Fancy's visions thus for truth prevail.

What forms august of kings and heroes bold
Bear my rapt spirit to the times of old?
Genius of Ossian! say what rocky dell
Hears the wild inspiration of thy shell?

What mighty spirits of thy sires renowned,
Bow from their airy halls to hear the sound?

Ah me! no more these whispering rocks among
Floats the sweet voice of minstrelsy and song;
Around the blazing oak, no Finnian train
Hear their loved Ossian's soul-subduing strain;
No more they mingle in the war's alarms,
Nor hail the glorious din of death in arms:
The wild heath blossoms o'er their mountain bed,
Dark in the house of breathless slumber spread;
A high-heaped cairn of grey unsculptured stones,
Raised to the storm, protects the heroes' bones;
There dumb oblivion spreads her Stygian wings,
And the shrill blast their sullen requiem sings.

But still the heaven-rapt bard, whose glowing mind
Not Death can hold, nor Hell's strong limits bind,
Around these capes beholds their spirits roam,
Sees their light corraghs ride the northern foam:
Shields, spears, and crested helms around him start,
And sounds celestial vibrate to his heart.

Oft he recals those mournful days of yore,
When blazed the baleful war-torch round the shoat,
As through the rampired cliffs the battle-horn
Pealed its shrill echoes on the ear of morn;
When rival clans, with fell ambition strove,
Inspired by glory, dire revenge, or love.
And now he cons how Deirdre's fatal charms
Roused all the valour of the isle to arms:
How great Tirowen; on the Saxon horde
Proved the keen temper of Ultonia's sword;
Or Sourlebuoy, from lonely glen or hill,
Poured through the martial pipe his pibrock shrill:
'Till Aura, tinged with many a crimson spring,
Heard Erin's steel on Albin's target ring,
And saw the wily Gäel, turned from flight,
Roll on his scattered foes the storm of fight.
—Now—to the heughs of black polluted shade,
He sees the fierce Monro, with gory blade
Sweep like a driving flame before the wind,
And headlong hurl the poor defenceless hind.—
Anon he hears, round Derry's castled walls,
Dire Famine howling as the warrior falls.[19]

James Clarence Mangan

James Clarence Mangan (1803–1849), like Allingham, is known primarily for his political poems. Mangan was both a poet and a translator, and he helped greatly in preserving the literature of Ireland's past. When Mangan died of cholera in 1849, he had experienced one of the darkest periods in Irish history. The last two decades of his life, when most of his poems were published, saw Catholic Ireland get the vote, saw the revolution of 1848, and saw, most traumatic of all, the Great Famine. In 1846, during the height of the Famine, Mangan wrote some of his finest poems, including the brooding poem "Dark Rosaleen." In Mangan's poems, and in the worsening conditions of the country while he wrote them, the roots of the Celtic revival and the modern Irish state can be traced. While Mangan's poetry and criticism of British power in Ireland and of the country's economic and psychological poverty were prominent themes during this time, the lasting power of Mangan's poetry lies in his attention to Ireland's natural world. Like the poets of the Revival who followed him, Mangan's observations of the beauty of Ireland's natural world was paramount to his vision of a future Ireland. The enduring power of nature would be tied back into a Celtic past and a simplicity of life drawn from the spiritual power of nature.[20]

The Dawning of the Day*

'Twas a balmy summer morning
Warm and early,
Such as only June bestows;
Everywhere, the earth adorning,
Dews lay pearly
In the lily-bell and rose.
Up from each green leafy bosk and hollow
Rose the blackbird's pleasant lay,
And the soft cuckoo was sure to follow.
'Twas the dawning of the Day!

Through the perfumed air the golden
Bees flew round me:
Bright fish dazzled from the sea,
'Till medreamt some faëry olden
World-spell bound me
In a trance of witcherie!
Steeds pranced round anon with stateliest housings,
Bearing riders pranked in rich array,
Like flushed revellers after wine-carousings:
'Twas the dawning of the Day!

---

* The following song, translated from the Irish of O'Doran, refers to a singular atmospherical phenomenon said to be sometimes observed at Blackrock, near Dundalk, at daybreak, by the fishermen of that locality. Many similar narratives are to be met with in the poetry of almost all countries; but O'Doran has endeavored to give the legend a political coloring, of which, I apprehend, readers in general will hardly deem it susceptible.

Then a strain of song was chanted,
And the lightly
Floating sea-nymphs drew anear.
Then again the shore seemed haunted
By hosts brightly
Clad, and wielding shield and spear!
Then came battle-shouts, an onward rushing,
Swords and chariots, and a phantom fray.
Then all vanished. The warm skies were blushing
In the dawning of the Day!

Cities girt with glorious gardens
(Whose immortal
Habitants, in robes of light
Stood, methought, as angel-wardens
Nigh each portal,)
Now arose to daze my sight.
Eden spread around, revived and blooming;
When . . . lo! as I gazed, all passed away.
I saw but black rocks and billows looming
In the dim chill dawn of day.[21]

The Fair Hills of Eiré, O!

Take a blessing from my heart to the land of my birth,
And the fair hills of Eiré, O!
And to all that yet survive of Eibhear's tribe on earth,
On the fair hills of Eiré, O!
In that land so delightful the wild thrush's lay
Seems to pour a lament forth for Eiré's decay.
Alas, alas, why pine I a thousand miles away
From the fair hills of Eiré, O!

The soil is rich and soft, the air is mild and bland,
On the fair hills of Eiré, O!
Her barest rock is greener to me than this rude land;
O the fair hills of Eiré, O!
Her woods are tall and straight, grove rising over grove;
Trees flourish in her glens below and on her heights above;
Ah, in heart and in soul I shall ever, ever love
The fair hills of Eiré, O!

A noble tribe, moreover, are the now hapless Gael,
On the fair hills of Eiré, O!
A tribe in battle's hour unused to shrink or fail
On the fair hills of Eiré, O!
For this is my lament in bitterness outpoured

To see them slain or scattered by the Saxon sword:
O woe of woes to see a foreign spoiler horde ·
On the fair hills of Eiré, O!

Broad and tall rise the *cruachs* in the golden morning glow
On the fair hills of Eiré, O!
O'er her smooth grass for ever sweet cream and honey flow
On the fair hills of Eiré, O!
Oh, I long, I am pining, again to behold
The land that belongs to the brave Gael of old.
Far dearer to my heart than a gift of gems or gold
Are the fair hills of Eiré, O!

The dewdrops lie bright mid the grass and yellow corn
On the fair hills of Eiré, O!
The sweet-scented apples blush redly in the morn
On the fair hills of Eiré, O!
The water-cress and sorrel fill the vales below,
The streamlets are hushed till the evening breezes blow,
While the waves of the Suir, noble river! ever flow
Neath the fair hills of Eiré, O!

A fruitful clime is Eiré's, through valley, meadow, plain,
And the fair hills of Eiré, O!
The very bread of life is in the yellow grain
On the fair hills of Eiré, O!
Far dearer unto me than the tones music yields
Is the lowing of the kine and the calves in her fields,
In the sunlight that shone long ago on the shields
Of the Gaels, on the fair hills of Eiré, O!²²

The Lovely Land: On a Landscape Painted by Maclise

Glorious birth of mind and color!
Gazing on thy radiant face,
The most lorn of Adam's race
Might forget all dolor!

What divinest light is beaming
Over mountain, mead, and grove!
That blue noontide sky above,
Seems asleep and dreaming.

Rich Italia's wild-birds warble
In the foliage of those trees:
I can trace thee, Veronese,
In these rocks of marble!

Yet, no! Mark I not where quiver
The sun's rays on yonder stream?
Only a Poussin could dream
Such a sun and river.

What bold imaging! Stony valley,
And fair bower of eglantine;
Here I see the black ravine,
There the lilied alley.

This is some rare climate olden,
Peopled, not by men, but fays;
Some lone land of genii days,
Storyful and golden!

O for magic power to wander
One bright year through such a land!
Might I even one hour stand
On the blest hills yonder!

But—what spy I? . . . Here by noonlight
'Tis the same! the pillar-tower
I have oft passed thrice an hour,
Twilight, sunlight, moonlight.

Shame to me, my own, my sireland,
Not to know thy soil and skies!
Shame, that through Maclise's eyes
I first see thee, Ireland!

Nay, no land doth rank above thee
Or for loveliness or worth:
So shall I, from this day forth,
Ever sing and love thee.[23]

William Makepeace Thackeray

Though William Makepeace Thackeray (1811–1863) was an English novelist and essay writer, he was also a successful travel writer. He visited Ireland in both 1840 and 1842 to do research for *Irish Sketchbook* (his 1840 sojourn was cut short because his wife's attempted suicide). *Irish Sketchbook* focuses on "the manners and scenery of the country."[24] The text of this work has become more generally associated with "the manners" of Ireland by illustrating the political and economic state of the country in the years immediately before the Great Famine. For Thackeray, this involved acute observations of shabby homes, utter poverty, and lack of work; everywhere in the country, including Dublin, Thackeray records artifacts of neglect and ruin that were all ultimately warning signs of the devastation to come. However, Thackeray also observes, alongside of this, "the scenery of the country," as this excerpt illustrates. Like Gainsford, he sees a unique and beautiful landscape that identifies Ireland as a separate sphere from the natural world of England, a country similar in geography that coexists with a poor and suffering Irish people.

From Irish Sketchbook

THE PATTERN AT CROAGHPATRICK

On the Pattern day, however, the washerwomen and children had all disappeared—nay, the stream, too, seemed to be gone out of town. There was a report current also, that on the occasion of the Pattern, six hundred teetotallers had sworn to revolt; and I fear that it was the hope of witnessing this awful rebellion which induced me to stay a couple of days at Westport. The Pattern was commenced on the Sunday, and the priests going up to the mountain took care that there should be no sports nor dancing on that day but that the people should only content themselves with the performance of what are called religious duties. Religious duties! Heaven help us! If these reverend gentlemen were worshippers of Moloch or Baal, or any deity whose honour demanded bloodshed, and savage rites, and degradation, and torture, one might fancy them encouraging the people to the disgusting penances the poor things here perform. But it's too hard to think that in our days any priests of any religion should be found superintending such a hideous series of self-sacrifices as are, it appears, performed on this hill.

A friend who ascended the hill brought down the following account of it. The ascent is a very steep and hard one, he says; but it was performed in company of thousands of people who were making their way barefoot to the several "stations" upon the hill.

"The first station consists of one heap of stones, round which they must walk seven times, casting a stone on the heap each time, and before and after every stone's throw saying a prayer.

"The second station is on the top of the mountain. Here there is a great altar—a shapeless heap of stones. The poor wretches crawl *on their knees* into this place, say fifteen prayers, and after going round the entire top of the mountain fifteen times, say fifteen prayers again.

"The third station is near the bottom of the mountain at the further side from Westport. It consists of three heaps. The penitents must go seven times round these collectively, and seven times afterwards round each individually, saying a prayer before and after each progress."

My informant describes the people as coming away from this "frightful exhibition suffering severe pain, wounded and bleeding in the knees and feet, and some of the women shrieking with the pain of their wounds." Fancy thousands of these bent upon their work, and priests standing by to encourage them!—For shame, for shame! If all the popes, cardinals, bishops, hermits, priests, and deacons that ever lived were to come forward and preach this as a truth—that to please God you must macerate your body, that the sight of your agonies is welcome to Him, and that your blood, groans, and degradation find favour in His eyes, I would not believe them. Better have over a company of Fakeers at once, and set the Suttee going.

Of these tortures, however, I had not the fortune to witness a sight: for going towards the mountain for the first four miles, the only conveyance I could find was half the pony of an honest sailor, who said, when applied to, "I tell you what I do wid you: I give you a spell about." But, as it turned out we were going different ways, this help was but a small one. A car with a spare seat, however (there were hundreds of others quite full, and scores of rattling country-carts covered with people, and thousands of bare legs trudging along the road)—a car with a spare seat passed by at two miles from the Pattern, and that just in time to get comfortably wet through on arriving there. The whole mountain was enveloped in mist; and we could nowhere see thirty yards before us. The women walked forward, with their gowns over their heads; the men sauntered on in the rain, with the utmost indifference to it. The car presently came to a cottage, the court in front of which was black with two hundred horses, and where as many drivers were jangling and bawling; and here we were told to descend. You had to go over a wall and across a brook, and behold the Pattern.

The pleasures of the poor people—for after the business on the mountain came the dancing and love-making at its foot—were wofully spoiled by the rain, which rendered dancing on the grass impossible; nor were the tents big enough for that exercise. Indeed, the whole sight was as dismal and half-savage a one as I have seen. There may have been fifty of these tents squatted round a plain of the most brilliant green grass, behind which the mist-curtains seemed to rise immediately; for you could not even see the mountain-side beyond them. Here was a great crowd of men and women, all ugly, as the fortune of the day would have it (for the sagacious reader has, no doubt, remarked that there are ugly and pretty days in life). Stalls were spread about, whereof the owners were shrieking out the praises of their wares—great coarse damp-looking bannocks of bread for the most part, or, mayhap, a dirty collection of pigs-feet and such refreshments. Several of the booths professed to belong to "confectioners" from Westport or Castlebar, the confectionery consisting of huge biscuits and doubtful-looking ginger-beer—ginger-ale or gingeretta it is called in this country, by a fanciful people who love the finest titles. Add to these, cauldrons containing water for "tay" at the doors of the booths, other pots full of masses of pale legs of mutton (the owner "prodding," every now and then, for a bit, and holding it up and asking the passenger to buy). In the booths it was impossible to stand upright or to see much, on account of smoke. Men and women were crowded in these rude tents, huddled together, and disappearing in the darkness. Owners came bustling out to replenish the empty water-jugs: and landladies stood outside in the rain calling strenuously upon all passers-by to enter.

Meanwhile, high up on the invisible mountain, the people were dragging their bleeding knees from altar to altar, flinging stones, and muttering some endless litanies, with the priests standing by. I think I was not sorry that the rain, and the care of my precious health, prevented me from mounting a severe hill to witness a sight that could only have caused one to be shocked and ashamed that servants of God should encourage it. The road home was very pleasant; everybody was wet through, but everybody was happy, and by some miracle we were seven on the car. There was the honest Englishman in the military cap, who sang, "The sea, the hopen sea's my 'ome," although not any one of the company called upon him for that air. Then the music was taken up by a good-natured lass from Castlebar; then the Englishman again, "With burnished brand and musketoon;" and there was no end of pushing, pinching, squeezing, and laughing. The Englishman, especially, had a favourite yell, with which he saluted and astonished all cottagers, passengers, cars, that we met or overtook. Presently came prancing by two dandies, who were especially frightened by the noise. "Thim's two tailors from Westport," said the carman, grinning with all his might. "Come, gat out of the way there, gat along!" piped a small English voice from above somewhere. I looked up, and saw a little creature perched on the top of a tandem, which he was driving with the most knowing air—a dreadful young hero, with a white hat, and a white face, and a blue bird's-eye neckcloth. He was five feet high, if an inch, an ensign, and sixteen; and it was a great comfort to think, in case of danger or riot, that one of his years and personal strength was at hand to give help.

"Thim's the afficers," said the carman, as the tandem wheeled by, a small groom quivering on behind—and the carman spoke with the greatest respect this time. Two days before, on arriving at Westport, I had seen the same equipage at the door of the inn—where for a moment there happened to be no waiter to receive me. So, shouldering a carpet-bag, I walked into the inn-hall, and asked a gentleman standing there where was the coffee-room? It was the military tandem-driving youth, who with much grace looked up in my face, and said calmly, "*I dawnt know.*" I believe the little creature had just been dining in the very room—and so present my best compliments to him.

The Guide-book will inform the traveller of many a beautiful spot which lies in the neighbourhood of Westport, and which I had not time to visit; but I must not take leave of the excellent little inn without speaking once more of its extreme comfort; nor of the place itself, without another parting word regarding its beauty. It forms an event in one's life to have seen that place, so beautiful is it, and so unlike all other beauties that I know of. Were such beauties lying upon English shores it would be a world's wonder: perhaps, if it were on the Mediterranean, or the Baltic, English travellers would flock to it by hundreds; why not come and see it in Ireland? Remote as the spot is, Westport is only two days' journey from London now, and lies in a country far more strange to most travellers than France or Germany can be.[25]

William Carleton

William Carleton (1794–1869) was the most prominent Irish novelist to write during the Famine years. Though he converted from Catholic to Protestant, much of his writing focused on the practices of the rural poor, including the customs of wakes, weddings, and dances. He ultimately saw the ignorance of the poor as their undoing, for the poor did nothing to help their rural economies by understanding their relationship to the natural world more effectively. This inability led to a crisis with the potato blight, which could have been avoided, or at least diminished, with more attention to education in the science of land management. If the land was maintained and utilized using educated scientific principles, the Famine would have been avoided. This excerpt, from Carleton's novel *The Black Prophet*, sets the stage for famine by weighing in on these very concerns, including the heavy imagery of a dark and imposing natural world that prophesizes doom.

From **The Black Prophet**

CHAPTER 1

Some twenty and odd years ago there stood a little cabin at the foot of a round hill, that very much resembled a cupola in shape, and which, from its position and height, commanded a prospect of singular beauty. This hill was one of a range that ran from north to southwest; but in consequence of its standing, as it were, somewhat out of the ranks, its whole appearance and character as a distinct feature of the country were invested with considerable interest to a scientific eye, especially to that of a geologist. An intersection or abrupt glen divided it from those which constituted the range or group alluded to; through this, as a pass in the country, and the only one for miles, wound a road into an open district on the western side, which road, about half a mile after its entering the glen, was met by a rapid torrent that came down from the gloomy mountains that rose to the left. The foot of this hill, which on the southern side was green and fertile to the top, stretched off and was lost in the rich land that formed the great and magnificent valley it helped to bound, and to which the chasm we have described was but an entrance; the one bearing to the other, in size and position, much the same relation that a small bye-lane in a country town bears to the great leading street which constitutes its principal feature.

Noon had long passed, and the dim sun of a wet autumnal day was sloping down towards the west through clouds and gloom, when a young girl of about twenty-one or twenty-two years of age came out of the cabin we have mentioned, and running up to the top of a little miniature hill or knob that rose beside it, looked round in every direction, as if anxious to catch a glimpse of some one whom she expected. It appeared, however, that she watched in vain; for after having examined the country in every direction with an eye in which might be read a combined expression of eagerness, anger and disappointment, she once more returned to the cabin with a slow and meditating step. This she continued to do from time to time for about an hour and a half, when at length a female appeared approaching, whom she at once recognized.

The situation of this hovel, for such, in fact, it must be termed, was not only strikingly desolate, but connected also with wild and supernatural terrors. From the position of the glen itself, a little within which it stood, it enjoyed only a very limited portion of the sun's cheering beams. As the glen was deep and precipitous, so was the morning light excluded from it by the northeastern hills, as was that of evening by those which rose between it and the west. Indeed, it would be difficult to find a spot marked by a character of such utter solitude and gloom. Naturally barren, it bore not a single shrub on which a bird could sit or a beast browse, and little, of course, was to be seen in it but the bare gigantic projections of rock which shot out of its steep sides in wild and uncouth shapes, or the grey, rugged expanses of which it was principally composed. Indeed, we feel it difficult to say whether the gloom of winter or the summer's heat fell upon it with an air of lonelier desolation. It mattered not what change of season came, the place presented no appearance of man or his works. Neither bird or beast was seen or heard, except rarely, within its dreary bosom, the only sounds it knew being the monotonous murmurs of the mountain torrent, or the wild echoes of the thunder storms that pealed among the hills about it. Silence and solitude were the characteristics which predominated in it and it would not be easy to say whether they were felt more during the gloom of November or the glare of June.

In the mouth of this glen, not far from the cabin we have described, two murders had been committed about twenty years before the period of our narrative, within the lapse of a month. The one was that of a carman, and the other of a man named Sullivan, who also had been robbed, as it was supposed the carman had been, for the bodies of both had been made way with and were never found. This was evident—in the one case by the horse and cart of the carman remaining by the grey stone in question, on which the traces of blood were long visible; and in the other by the circumstance of Sullivan's hat and part of his coat having been found near the cabin in question on the following day, in a field through which his path home lay, and in which was a pool of blood, where his foot-marks were deeply imprinted, as if in a struggle for life and death. For this latter murder a man named Dalton had been taken up, under circumstances of great suspicion, he having been the last person seen in the man's company. Both had been drinking together in the market, a quarrel had originated between them about money matters, blows had been exchanged, and Dalton was heard to threaten him in very strong language. Nor was this all. He had been observed following or rather dogging him on his way home, and although the same road certainly led to the residence of both, yet when his words and manner were taken into consideration, added to the more positive proof that the foot-marks left on the place of struggle exactly corresponded with his shoes, there could be little doubt that he was privy to Sullivan's murder and disappearance, as well probably as to his robbery. At all events the glen was said to be haunted by Sullivan's spirit, which was in the habit, according to report, of appearing near the place of murder, from whence he was seen to enter this chasm—a circumstance which, when taken in connection with its dark and lonely aspect, was calculated to impress upon the place the reputation of being accursed, as the scene of crime and supernatural appearances. We remember having played in it when young, and the feeling we experienced was one of awe and terror, to which might be added, on contemplating the "dread repose" and solitude around us, an impression that we were removed hundreds of miles from the busy ongoings and noisy tumults of life, to which, as if seeking protection, we generally hastened with a strong sense of relief, after having tremblingly gratified our boyish curiosity.

The young girl in question gave the female she had been expecting any thing but a cordial or dutiful reception. In personal appearance there was not a point of resemblance between them, although the *tout ensemble* of each was singularly striking and remarkable. The girl's locks were black as the raven's wing: her figure was tall and slender, but elastic and full of symmetry. The ivory itself was not more white nor glossy than her skin; her teeth were bright and beautiful, and her mouth a perfect rosebud. It is unnecessary to say that her eyes were black and brilliant, for such ever belong to her complexion and temperament; but it *is* necessary to add, that they were piercing and unsettled, and you felt that they looked into you rather than at you or upon you. In fact, her features were all perfect, yet it often happened that their general expression was productive of no agreeable feeling on the beholder. Sometimes her smile was sweet as that of an angel, but let a single impulse or whim be checked, and her face assumed a character of malignity that made her beauty appear like that which we dream of in an evil spirit.

The other woman, who stood to her in the relation of step-mother, was above the middle size. Her hair was sandy, or approaching to a pale red; her features were coarse, but regular; and her whole figure that of a well-made and powerful woman. In her countenance might be read a peculiar blending of sternness and benignity, each evidently softened down by an expression of melancholy—perhaps of suffering—as if some secret care lay brooding at her heart. The inside of the hovel itself had every mark of poverty and destitution about it. Two or three stools, a pot or two, one miserable standing bed, and a smaller one gathered up under a rug in the corner, were almost all that met the eye on entering it; and simple as these meagre portions of furniture were, they bore no marks of cleanliness or care. On the contrary, everything appeared to be neglected, squalid and filthy—such, precisely, as led one to see at a glance that the inmates of this miserable hut were contented with their wretched state of life, and had no notion whatsoever that any moral or domestic duty existed, by which they might be taught useful notions of personal comfort and self-respect.

"So," said the young woman, addressing her step-mother, as she entered, "you're come back at last, an' a purty time you tuck to stay away!"

"Well," replied the other, calmly, "I'm here now at any rate; but I see you're in one of your tantrums, Sally, my lady. What's wrong, I say? In the mean time don't look as if you'd ait us widout salt."

"An' a bitter morsel you'd be," replied the younger, with a flashing glance—"divil a more so. Here am I, sittin', or running out an' in, these two hours, when I ought to be at the dance in Kilnahushogue, before I go to Barny Gormly's wake; for I promised to be at both. Why didn't you come home in time?"

"Bekaise, achora, it wasn't agreeable to me to do so. I'm beginnin' to got ould an' stiff, an' its time for me to take care of myself."

"Stiffer may you be, then, soon, an' oulder may you never be, an' that's the best I wish you!"

"Aren't you afeard to talk to me in that way?" said the elder of the two.

"No—not a bit. You won't flake me now as you used to do. I am able an' willin' to give blow for blow at last, thank goodness; an' will, too, if ever you thry that thrick."

The old woman gazed at her angrily, and appeared for a moment to meditate an assault. After a pause, however, during which the brief but vehement expression of rising fury passed from her countenance, and her face assumed an expression more of compassion than of anger, she simply said, in a calm tone of voice—

"I don't know that I ought to blame you so much for your temper, Sarah. The darkness of your father's sowl is upon yours; his wicked spirit is in you, an' may Heaven above grant that you'll never carry about with you, through this unhappy life, the black an' heavy burden that weighs down his heart! If God hasn't said it, you have his coorse, or something nearly as bad, before you. Oh! Go to the wake as soon as you like, an' to the dance, too. Find some one that'll take you off of my hands; that'll put a house over your head—give you a bit to ait, an' a rag to put on you; an' may God pity him that's doomed to get you! If the woeful state of the country, an' the hunger an' sickness that's abroad, an' that's comin' harder an' faster on us every day, can't tame you or keep you down, I dunna what will. I'm sure the black an' terrible summer we've had ought to make you think of how we'll get over all that's before us! God pity you, I say again, an' whatever poor man is to be cursed wid you!"

"Keep your pity for them that wants it," replied the other, "an' that's not me. As for God's pity, it isn't yours to give, and even if it was, you stand in need of it yourself more than I do. You're beginning to praich to us now that you're not able to bait us; but for your praichments an' your baitins, may the divil pay you for all alike!—as he will—an' that's my prayer."

A momentary gush of the step-mother's habitual passion overcame her; she darted at her step-daughter, who sprung to her limbs, and flew at her in return. The conflict at first was brief, for the powerful strength of the elder female soon told. Sarah, however, quickly disengaged herself, and seizing an old knife which lay on a shell that served as a dresser, she made a stab at the very heart of her step-mother, panting as she did it with an exulting vehemence of vengeance that resembled the growlings which a savage beast makes when springing on its prey.

"Ha!" she exclaimed, "you have it now—you have it! Call on God's pity now, for you'll soon want it. Ha! Ha!"

The knife, however, owing to the thick layers of cloth with which the dress of the other was patched, as well as to the weakness of the thin and worn blade, did not penetrate her clothes, nor render her any injury whatsoever. The contest was again resumed. Sarah, perceiving that she had missed her aim, once more put herself into a posture to renew the deadly attempt; and the consequence was, that a struggle now took place between them which might almost be termed one for life and death. It was indeed a frightful and unnatural struggle. The old woman, whose object was, if possible, to disarm her antagonist, found all her strength—and it was great—scarcely a match for the murderous ferocity which was now awakened in her. The grapple between them consequently became furious; and such was the terrible impress of diabolical malignity which passion stamped upon the features of this young tigress, that her step-mother's heart, for a moment quailed on beholding it, especially when associated with the surprising activity and strength which she put forth. Her dark and finely-pencilled eye-brows were fiercely knit, as it were, into one dark line; her lips were drawn back, displaying her beautiful teeth, that were now ground together into what resembled the lock of death: her face was pale with over-wrought resentment, and her deep-set eyes glowed with a wild and flashing fire that was fearful, while her lips were encircled with the white foam of revengeful and deadly determination; and what added most to the terrible expression on her whole face was the exulting smile of cruelty which shed its baleful light over it, resolving the whole contest, as it were, and its object—the murder of her step-mother—into the fierce play of some beautiful vampire that was ravening for the blood of its awakened victim.

After a struggle of some two or three minutes, the strength and coolness of the step-mother at length prevailed, she wrested the knife out of Sarah's hands and, almost at the same moment, stumbled and fell. The other, however, was far from relaxing her hold. On the contrary, she clung to her fiercely, shouting out—

"I won't give you up yet—I love you too well for that—no, no, it's fond of you I'm gettin'. I'll hug you, mother, dear; ay will I, and kiss you too, an' lave my mark behind me!" and, as she spoke, her step-mother felt her face coming in savage proximity to her own.

"If you don't keep away, Sarah," said the other, "I'll stab you. What do you mane, you bloody devil? It is going to tear my flesh with your teeth you are? Hould off! Or, as heaven's above us, I'll stab you with the knife."

"You can't," shouted the other; "the knife's bent, or you'd be done for before this. I'll taste your blood for all that!" and, as the words were uttered, the step-mother gave a sudden scream, making at the same time a violent effort to disentangle herself, which she did.

Sarah started to her feet, and flying towards the door, exclaimed with shouts of wild triumphant laughter—

"Ha, ha, ha! Do you feel anything? I was near havin' the best part of one of your ears—ha, ha, ha!—but unfortunately I missed it; an' now look to yourself. *Your* day is gone, an' mine is come. I've tasted your blood, an' I like it—ha, ha, ha!—an' if as *you* say it's kind father for me to be fond o' blood, I say you had better take care of yourself. And I tell you more: we'll take care of your fair-haired beauty for you—my father and myself will—an' I'm told to act against her, an' I will too; an' you'll see what we'll bring your pet, *Gra Gal* Sullivan, to yet! There's news for you!"

She then went down to the river which flowed past, in whose yellow and turbid waters—for it was now swollen with rain—she washed the blood from her hands and face with an apparently light heart. Having meditated for some time, she fell a laughing at the fierce conflict that had just taken place, exclaiming to herself—

"Ha, ha, ha! Well now if I had killed her—got the ould knife into her heart—I might lave the counthry. If I had killed her now, throth it 'ud be a good joke, an' all in a fit of passion, bekase she didn't come home in time to let me meet *him*. Well, I'll go back an' spake soft to her, for, afther all, she'll give me a hard life of it."

She returned; and, having entered the hut, perceived that the ear and cheek of her step-mother were still bleeding.

"I'm sorry for what I did," she said, with the utmost frankness and good nature. "Forgive me, mother; you know I'm a hasty devil—for a devil's limb I am, no doubt of it. Forgive me, I say—do now—here, I'll get something to stop the blood."

She sprang at the moment, with the agility of a wild cat, upon an old chest that stood in the corner of the hut, exhibiting as she did it, a leg and foot of surpassing symmetry and beauty. By stretching herself up to her full length, she succeeded in pulling down several old cobwebs that had been for years in the corner of the wall; and in the act of doing so, disturbed some metallic substance, which fell first upon the chest, from which it tumbled off to the ground, where it made two or three narrowing circles, and then lay at rest.

"Murdher alive, mother!" she exclaimed, "what is this? Hallo! A tobaccy-box—a fine round tobaccy-box of iron, bedad—an what's this on it!—let me see; two letthers. Wait till I rub the rust off; or stay, the rust shows them as well. Let me see—P. an' what's the other? Ay, an' M. P. M.—arra, what can that be for? Well, devil may care! Let it lie on the shelf there. Here now—none of your cross looks, I say—put these cobwebs to your face, an' they'll stop the bleedin'. Ha, ha, ha!—well—ha, ha, ha!—but you are a sight to fall in love wid this minute!" she exclaimed, laughing heartily at the blood-stained visage of the other. "You won't spake, I see. Divil may care then, if you don't you'll do the other thing—let it alone: but, at any rate, there's the cobwebs for you, if you like to put them on; an' so *bannatht latht*, an' let that be a warnin' to you not to raise your hand to me again.

'A sailor courted a farmer's daughter
That lived on the isle of Man.'" &c.

She then directed her steps to the dance in Kilnahushogue, where one would actually suppose, if mirth, laughter, and extraordinary buoyancy of spirits could be depended on, that she was gifted, in addition to her remarkable beauty, with the innocent and delightful disposition of an angel.

The step-mother having dressed the wound as well as she could, sat down by the fire and began to ruminate on the violent contest which had just taken place, and in which she had borne such an unfortunate part. This was the first open and determined act of personal resistance which she had ever, until that moment, experienced at her step-daughter's hands; but now she feared that, if they were to live, as heretofore, under the same roof, their life would be one of perpetual strife—perhaps of ultimate bloodshed—and that these domestic brawls might unhappily terminate in the death of either. She felt that her own temper was none of the best, and knew that so long as she was incapable of restraining it, or maintaining her coolness under the provocations to which the violent passions of Sarah would necessarily expose her, so long must such conflicts as that which had just occurred take place between them. She began now to fear Sarah, with whose remorseless disposition she was too well acquainted, and came to the natural conclusion, that a residence under the same roof was by no means compatible with her own safety.

"She has been a curse to me!" she went on, unconsciously speaking aloud; "for when she wasn't able to bate me herself, her father did it for her. The divil is said to be fond of his own; an' so does he dote on her, bekase she's his image in everything that's bad. A hard life I'll lead between them from this out, espeshially now that she's got the upper hand of me. Yet what else can I expect or desarve? This load that is on my conscience is worse. Night and day I'm sufferin' in the sight of God, an' actin' as if I wasn't to be brought in judgment afore him. What am I to do? I wish I was in my grave! But then, agin', how am I to face death?—and that same's not the worst; for afther death comes judgment! May the Lord prepare me for it, and guide and direct me how to act! One thing, I know, must be done—either she or I will lave this house; for live undher the same roof wid her I will not."

She then rose up, looked out of the door a moment, and, resuming her seat, went on with her soliloquy—

"No; he said it was likely he wouldn't be home to-night. Wanst he gets upon his ould prophecies, he doesn't care how long he stays away; an' why he can take the delight he does in prophesyin' and foretellin' good or evil, accordin' as it sarves his purpose, I'm sure I don't know—espeshially when he only laughs in his sleeve at the people for believin' him; but what's that about poor *Gra Gal* Sullivan? She threatened her, and spoke of her father, too, as bein' in it. Ah, ah! I must watch him there; an' you, too, my lady divil—for it 'ill go hard wid me if either of you injure a hair of her head. No, no, plaise God!—none of your evil doins or unlucks prophecies for her, so long, any way, as I can presarve her from them. How black the evenin' is gatherin', but God knows that it's the awful saison all out for the harvest—it is that—it is that!"

Having given utterance to these sentiments, she took up the tobacco-box which Sarah had, in such an accidental manner, tumbled out of the wall, and surveying it for some moments, laid it hastily on the chest, and, clasping her hands exclaimed—

"Saviour of life! it's the same! Oh, merciful God, it's thrue! it's thrue!—the very same I seen wid *him* that evenin': I know it by the broken hinge and the two letthers. The Lord forgive me my sins!—for I see now that do what we may, or hide it as we like, God is above all! Saviour of life, how will this end? An' what will I do?—or how am I to act? But any way, I must hide this, and put it out of *his* reach."

She accordingly went out, and having ascertained that no person saw her, thrust the box up under the thatch of the roof, in such a way that it was impossible to suspect, by any apparent disturbance of the roof, that it was there; after which, she sat down with sensations of dread that were new to her, and that mingled themselves as strongly with her affections as it was possible for a woman of a naturally firm and undaunted character to feel them.[26]

Emily Lawless

Emily Lawless (1845–1913) was both a poet and a novelist who was raised in both England and western Ireland. Much of her writing, in both her poems and novels, reflects her Unionist political views and portrays a balanced collection of peasant heroes and heroines, with a sympathetic view of British landowners. In her first novel, *Hurrish*, the setting of Ireland's rugged west becomes central to the rural strife that leads to agrarian crime and neighbor conflicts during the Irish Land Wars of the 1880s. The title of the novel is drawn from its hero, Horatio O'Brien, known to his family and friends as "Hurrish." He is a large, passive man with a small farm in the Burren district of County Clare. Lawless, writing always from a loyalist perspective, offers a violent tale of local rivalries about land, resulting in brutal confrontations and, finally, in murder. The protagonists of the Burren are seen as victims of a disorderly society and whose mistrust of the law leads inevitably to brutality and chaos. The author's own antagonism to the Land League, established to better the lot of impoverished smallholders, is clear, yet she does not exonerate the colonial authority from blame either. More importantly, Lawless emphasizes the presence of the natural world of the Burren, a limestone, moon-like landscape that stretches for about one hundred square miles across County Clare and is a place from which making a living off the land is a formidable task. Like William Carleton's *The Black Prophet*, *Hurrish* provides an appropriate backdrop of the sublime natural world of Ireland's rural west, against which the story plays out, to emphasize the plight between landowners and tenants amid the harsh topography of this limestone landscape.

From Hurrish: A Study

AN IRON LAND

Wilder regions there are few to be found, even in the wildest west of Ireland, than that portion of north Clare known to its inhabitants as "The Burren." Seen from the Atlantic, which washes its western base, it presents to the eye a succession of low hills, singularly grey in tone,—deepening often, towards evening, into violet or dull reddish plum colour—sometimes, after sunset, to a pale ghostly iridescence. They are quite low these hills—not above a thousand feet at their highest point, and for the most part considerably less. Hills of this height, whatever their other merits, seldom attain to the distinction of being spoken of as "grand." Their character is essentially "mutton-suggesting." You picture them dotted over with flocks of sheep, which nibble the short sweet grass, and frisk in their idle youth over the little declivities. If here and there a rib or so of rock protrudes, they merely seem to be foils to the general smoothness. But these Burren hills are literally not clothed at all. They are startlingly, I may say scandalously, naked. From their base up to the battered turret of rock which serves as a summit, not a patch, not a streak, not an indication even, of green is often to be found in the whole extent. On others a thin sprinkling of grass struggles upward for a few hundred feet, and in valleys and hollows, where the washings of the rocks have accumulated, a grass grows, famous all over cattle-feeding Ireland for its powers of fattening. So, too, in the long vertical rifts or fissures which everywhere cross and recross its surface, maiden-hair ferns and small tenderpetalled flowers unfurl, out of reach of the cruel blasts. These do not, however, affect the general impression, which is that of nakedness personified—not comparative, but absolute. The rocks are not scattered over the surface, as in other stony tracts, but the whole surface is rock. They are not hills, in fact, but skeletons—rain-worn, time-worn, wind-worn,—starvation made visible, and embodied in a landscape.

And these strange little hills have had an equally strange history. They were the last home and the last standing-ground of a race whose very names have become a matter of more or less ingenious guesswork. Formorians? Firbolgs? Tuatha da Danaans? Who were they, and what were they? We know nothing, and apparently are not destined to know anything. They came—we know not whence, and they vanished—to all appearance into the Atlantic; pushed westward, like the Norwegian lemming, until, like that most unaccountable of little animals, they, too, sprang into the waves and were lost. Little change has taken place in the aspect of the region since those unknown races passed away. Their great stone-duns are even still in many places the largest buildings to be seen,—the little oratories and churches which succeeded them having become in their turn, with hardly an exception, ruins like themselves, their very sites forgotten, melted into the surrounding stoniness. The Burren is not—in all probability never will be—a tourist-haunt, but for the few who know it, it has a place apart, a distinct personality—strange, remote, indescribable. Everything that the eye rests on tells us that we are on one of the last standpoints of an old world, worn out with its own profusion, and reduced here to the barest elements. Mother Earth, once young, buxom, frolicsome, is here a wrinkled woman, sitting alone in the evening of her days, and looking with melancholy eyes at the sunset.

The valley of Gortnacoppin is a sort of embodiment of the Burren. Standing in it you might fairly believe yourself in the heart of some alpine region, high above the haunts of men, where only the eagle or the marmot make their homes. All the suggestions are alpine, some of them almost arctic. The white stream cutting its way through the heaped-up drift; the water churning and frothing hither and thither in its impatience, and leaving a white deposit upon all the reeds and stones; the pallid greyish-green vegetation, with here and there a bit of dazzling red or orange; the chips and flakes of rock which lie strewn about; the larger stones and boulders toppled down from the cliff above, and lying heaped one over the other in the bed of the stream,—many of the latter, you may perceive, have not long fallen, for their edges are still unweathered. Here and there over the top and sides of the drift a little thin grass has spread itself, through which trenches have been torn, showing the earth and stones below. Truly a grim scene!—suggestive of nothing so much as one of those ugly little early German prints, where every stick and stone seems to be grimacing with unpleasant intention. Only look hard enough at any of the rocks, and you will assuredly see a gnome appear!

Towards the bottom, where it approaches the sea, this valley, however, expands, and becomes an irregular lake-like circle, mapped out into small fields, separated from one another by tottering lace-work walls. After following the downward course of the upper valley, you would have been surprised at the sudden fertility of this little space, the greenness of the grass, the promising look of the small crops of bottle-green potatoes. If something of a geologist, however, you would have suspected that the mass of detritus, borne down from the hills, and spread abroad here at their feet, had something to say to that satisfactory result.

Between five and six years ago the greater part of this little fertile oasis was rented by Horatio, or, as he was less classically called by his neighbours, Hurrish O'Brien, one of the countless O'Briens of Clare. His cabin—a rather large one, built of stone and thatched—stood upon the summit of a little ridge, conspicuous, like a small fly upon a large windowpane, in the absence of any other building; rendered still more so by a good-sized ash-tree, which stood upon the ridge beside it—a noticeable distinction in so leafless a district.

It was a warm morning late in May, and even the stony Barren had begun to feel a touch of spring, its ferns and little delicate-petalled blossoms to reach out inquiring heads over their stony prisons. Hurrish had just returned to breakfast. He had been down early to the sea, to set some fishing-lines—for, like most of the inhabitants of that amphibious part of the island, he was part farmer and part fisherman,—perhaps it would be more accurate in his case to say three-parts farmer to one-part fisherman, the latter vocation being, in fact, rather a matter of "intertainment" than profit.

The door of the cabin was open, and the window unshuttered (the latter for an excellent reason, there were no shutters), yet the cabin itself was lit by its fire. The light, spreading from the blazing turf, broke in red flakes upon the bare rafters of the roof, upon the roughly plastered walls, upon a quantity of highly coloured pious prints upon the walls, upon others of a less pious character pinned beside them, upon a rough white terrier, two solemn black pigs, and three children scattered over the mud floor, upon an *omnium gatherum* of tags and rags, stray fragments of furniture, tools, clothing, straw, bedding, sacks, heaps of potatoes,—an indescribable and incalculable collection of long accumulated rubbish, huddled, in more or less picturesque confusion, one on top of another—the sort of picturesqueness which fastidious people prefer in its painted rather than in its actual form! Hurrish sat upon a low "creepy" stool, with a huge mug of stirabout (known to the ignorant as porridge) upon his knees, which he was shovelling down his throat by the aid of a large iron spoon. A broad-shouldered, loose-limbed, genial-faced giant was Hurrish, such as these western Irish counties occasionally breed. Irish in every feature, look, and gesture, there was yet a smack of something foreign about him, to be accounted for possibly by that oft-quoted admixture of Spanish blood, the result of bygone centuries of more or less continuous intercourse. His hair was black as a cormorant's wing, and curly under the old felt hat, half of whose brim had vanished in some distant engagement; his beard was curly too, and black, yet his eyes were grey, his skin evidently originally fair, and his expression open, good-humoured, irresolute, with a spice of native fun and jollity about it. Despite the jollity which was its prevailing expression, he did not seem to be altogether a contented giant. There were lines of perplexity and disturbance here and there discernible. Yet Hurrish O'Brien was a well-to-do man. He had a good stock of cows and calves; he held his farm on a moderate rental; his wife had brought him fifty gold sovereigns tied up in a pocket-handkerchief; his children were strong and healthy; and he was regarded by his neighbours generally as one of the "warmest" men between Blackhead and the mouth of the Shannon.

Opposite, upon another low creepy-stool, sat his mother, Bridget O'Brien, engaged in stirring a steaming black pot—an employment which would have given a sensitive looker-on a delightful thrill, so appropriate was the operation to the operator. In Bridget O'Brien the Southern type was also strongly visible. Women like her—as gaunt, as wrinkled, as black-browed, as witch-like—may be seen seated upon thousands of doorsteps all over the Spanish peninsula. It is not a very comfortable type, one would think, for everyday domestic use; too suggestive of an elderly bird of prey—a vulture, old, yet with claws ever upon the watch to tear, and a beak which yearns to plunge itself into the still palpitating flesh. Her eyes were black—a wicked black—and bright still amid the multiplicity of wrinkles which surrounded them, as cracks a half-dried pool. Her hair, too, was dark, and hung in heavy hanks about her forehead, reaching nearly to the grizzled eyebrows, projecting like undipped eaves over her eyes.

Bridget O'Brien was an ardent patriot! The latest tide of revolutionary sentiment had begun to spread its waves even to the heart of remotest Burren, and she was the chief recipient of it in the O'Brien household. It was she who knew when, where, how, and why the latest agrarian outrage had been committed, and was the first to raise the war-cry of triumph and exultation upon these joyful occasions. Not that the rest of the family were backward in their degree. Hurrish had called himself a Fenian almost ever since he could remember, and nothing but his distance from the seat of war had prevented him from striking a blow when that ill-starred apology for a rebellion came to its final and melancholy close Animosity against England was a creed with him, a sort of shibboleth—something like the middle-class English hatred of France some three-quarters of a century ago. His belief in its wickedness and atrocities was a belief that knew absolutely no misgivings. Had he been assured that, like Herod of old, an order had just been issued by its Government for all infants under two years of age to be slaughtered, I doubt if it would have struck him as at all incredible, or even out of character with what he supposed to be the normal nature of its proceedings.

Hurrish's patriotic potations, however, were mild and diluted compared with those quaffed to the very dregs by his mother. He was not a man easily roused to bitterness, and would hardly, I think, have cared to kill even an Englishman, unless some very good purpose could have been served by so doing. When Bridget brought back tales of vengeance, executed upon the latest enemies of their country, he listened, but rarely found himself warmed to the point of emulation; the details of those gallant achievements being apt, in fact, to have rather a chilling and discouraging effect upon his imagination. What he enjoyed was what may be called the frivolous side of patriotism,—the mere noise, the crowd, the excitement, the waving flags, the new tin-pikes, the thrilling, delightful, inexhaustible oratory of his chosen leaders. All this was meat, drink, and clothing to him, and he would have walked thirty miles any day of his life to enjoy it. On the other hand, the detailed projects of vengeance were apt to pass over his head. He admitted their necessity, but blinked the details. When Clancy, for instance, with his wife and four small children were turned out of their cabin in the dead of a January night, because Clancy had taken Lynch's farm, contrary to well-known if unwritten local laws, Hurrish had been disposed to feel sorry for the more juvenile of the criminals. Not so his mother. "What

ailed he to be pityin' of thim? wasn't it known they wouldn't have been sarved so if
they hadn't been desarvin'?" that thorough-going woman asked fiercely. Hideous
prints, of still more hideous significance, disfigured a considerable portion of the
cabin walls. There was one cheerful design in particular, representing the roasting
alive of men in swallow-tail coats, tall hats, and white neck-cloths, presumably landlords and their myrmidons. The intention was allegorical, probably, but to Bridget it
was literal enough, and it was upon such pabulum she feasted her eyes with all the
relish of a petticoated vampire.

Poor little Alley Sheehan, Hurrish's niece by marriage, could not so much as bear
to look at the side of the wall where these prints hung, and averted her eyes whenever she happened to approach them. They made her feel cold and sick. She was too
much afraid of old Bridget, however, to show this repugnance openly, for Bridget
was a domestic despot, and not by any means one of the benevolent variety. There
was no blood tie between them, either, to soften the yoke. When Alley's mother
died, Hurrish and his wife had taken her to live with them out of sheer charity and
kindness of heart. When poor Mary O'Brien in her turn died, old Bridget would
willingly have turned Alley out upon the cold highroad to beg. There were points,
however, where Hurrish, yielding as he was, could hold his own, and this was one of
them. He had a very tender spot in his heart for little Alley, whose great grey eyes it
was hard to meet without softening. They were wonderful eyes, such as are only to
be seen in their perfection west of the Shannon,—violet grey, with lashes which fell
in a straight black drift upon the cheek below,—eyes with a rippling light and shade
in the irises, such as streams show when flowing clear over a pebbly bottom. The
face, too, which went with them suited the eyes, which is by no means invariably the
case, more especially in Ireland.

For all her eyes, Alley counted for very little in the estimation of her contemporaries. The average young Irish male is not perhaps a particularly discriminating
animal, and the finer points are apt to be undiscernible by him. Hers was the sort
of beauty which needs indeed some eye-culture to appreciate, a beauty which clings
with peculiar tenacity to the inward vision after the outward presentment has faded,
which no rags, no dirt, no circumstances, however repellent, avail to spoil—nay,
which seem to bloom the brighter for such accessories, as the peculiar blue of a
speedwell shines best on that discarded heap of refuse where we grudge yet delight
to see it. There was a touch of ascetic dreaminess about her which suited her stony
environment, and remotely suggested the cloister—a sort of nun-like fragility and
separateness. Yet Alley was not really delicate. She could carry her creel of turf or her
can of butter-milk as long and as lightly as any girl in the Burren. Her small shapely
brown feet could tramp unwearily a long summer's day over the stones. Those beautiful pathetic eyes of hers had never known the shelter of a hat or a bonnet in all
their days. Strange flower of humanity, a very young girl's beauty! Springing, we
hardly know whence; dropped often where it seems least to tell; with something
pathetic about it always, and most of all where so few years seem bound, as in a case
like this, to bring it to an end.[27]

NOTES TO PART II

Introduction epigraph: Oliver Cromwell, "Speech XVII, 1658," in *Oliver Cromwell's Letters and Speeches: Including Supplements to the First Edition*, with contributions by Thomas Carlyle, vol. 2 (New York: Harper and Brothers, 1860), 391.

1. John Feehan, "The Heritage of the Rocks," in *Nature in Ireland: A Scientific and Cultural History*, ed. John Wilson Foster and Helena C. G. Cheney (Dublin: Lilliput, 1997), 20.
2. Ibid.
3. Terry Eagleton, *Heathcliff and the Great Hunger: Studies in Irish Culture* (London: Verso, 1995), 7.
4. Oona Frawley, *Irish Pastoral: Nostalgia in Twentieth-Century Irish Literature* (Dublin: Irish Academic Press, 2005), 26.
5. Simon Schama, *Landscape and Memory* (New York: Vintage Books, 1995), 61.
6. John Feehan, "Threat and Conservation: Attitudes to Nature in Ireland," in Foster and Cheney, *Nature in Ireland*, 580, quoting E. McLysaght, *Irish Life in the Seventeenth Century: After Cromwell* (Dublin and Cork: Talbot, 1939).
7. See "Foster's Corn Law of 1784," in *Encyclopaedia of Ireland* (Dublin: Allen Figgis, 1968), 91.
8. William Trevor, *A Writer's Ireland: Landscape in Literature* (New York: Viking, 1984), 96.
9. William Howarth, "Some Principles of Ecocriticism," in *The Ecocriticism Reader: Landmarks in Literary Ecology*, ed. Cheryll Glotfelty and Harold Fromm (Athens: University of Georgia Press, 1996), 77.
10. Mark Eccles, "Thomas Gainsford, 'Captain Pamphlet,'" *Huntington Library Quarterly* 45, no. 4 (1982): 259–70.
11. Thomas Gainsford, *A Description of Ireland: A.D. 1618, The Other Clare* 36 (2012): 33–37, modernized by Luke McInerney (CELT: Corpus of Electronic Texts, Cork: University College Cork, 2013), 35–37, http://www.ucc.ie/celt/published/E610006.html.
12. William Allingham, "Wishing," *Saturday Evening Post*, December 22, 1860, 4.
13. Allingham, "The Fairies," in *Sixteen Poems by William Allingham: Selected by William Butler Yeats* (Dundrum, Ireland: Dun Emer, 1905; Project Gutenberg, 2005), 12–14, http://www.gutenberg.org/files/16839/16839.txt.
14. Allingham, "The Lover and Birds," ibid., 29–30.
15. William Allingham, "Among the Heather," in *Selected Poems from the Works of William Allingham*, ed. Helen Paterson Allingham (London: Macmillan, 1912), 54–55, https://babel.hathitrust.org/cgi/pt?id=njp.32101067627305.
16. Allingham, "In a Spring Grove," ibid., 75.
17. Allingham, "The Ruined Chapel," in *Sixteen Poems*, 34–35.
18. John Wilson Foster, "Encountering Traditions," in Foster and Cheney, *Nature in Ireland*, 65.
19. William Hamilton Drummond, *The Giants' Causeway: A Poem* (Belfast: Joseph Smyth for Longman et al., 1811), 3–19, http://babel.hathitrust.org/cgi/pt?id=loc.ark:/13960/t6ww8rk3p;view=1up;seq=11.
20. See "James Clarence Mangan," in *The Oxford Companion to Irish Literature*, ed. Robert Welch (Oxford, UK: Clarendon, 1996), 355.
21. James Clarence Mangan, "The Dawning of the Day," in *James Clarence Mangan: His Selected Poems* (Boston: Lamson, Wolffe, 1897), 188–89, https://archive.org/stream/jamesclarencemani897mang/jamesclarencemani897mang_djvu.txt.
22. Mangan, "The Fair Hills of Eiré, O!," ibid., 129–31.
23. Mangan, "The Lovely Land: On a Landscape Painted by Maclise," ibid., 330–32.
24. William Makepeace Thackeray, *Irish Sketchbook*, ed. Walter Jerrold (London: J. M. Dent, 1903), 413, https://books.google.com/books/about/The_Irish_sketch_book.html?id=5ecMAAAAYAAJ.
25. Thackeray, "The Pattern at Croaghpatrick," ibid., 264–69.
26. William Carleton, "Glendhu, or the Black Glen; Scene of Domestic Affection," in *The Black Prophet: A Tale of Irish Famine*, in *Traits and Stories of the Irish Peasantry*, vol. 3 of *The Works of William Carleton* (New York: P. F. Collier, 1881; Project Gutenberg, 2004), 777–81, http://www.gutenberg.org/files/16018/16018-h/16018-h.htm.
27. Emily Lawless, "An Iron Land," in *Hurrish: A Study* (Edinburgh and London: William Blackwood and Sons, 1886), 1–11, https://archive.org/details/hurrishastudy01lawlgoog.

PART III

Nature and the Irish Literary Revival

Introduction to Part III

Our "natural magic" is but the ancient religion of the world, the ancient worship of Nature and that troubled ecstasy before her, that certainty of all beautiful places being haunted, which it brought into men's minds.
                                        —Yeats, "The Celtic Element in Literature"

The upheaval of the Irish landscape through the Famine and post-Famine years of the nineteenth century manifested itself with a deep disconnection between the Irish and the natural world. Poets took refuge in the safe havens of Ireland's cities and focused their energies on social matters and the political frictions with the British. The disorder of the social system, of family and community, laid its blame on the political consequences that paved the way for these Famine and post-Famine periods to unfold. In short, politics and history took their hold on the Irish culture. As Catherine Maignant points out, "In the nineteenth century, the reign of almighty History began, irrevocably putting an end to the traditional Irish social mode based on the reproductions of patterns of behavior within a dull and uniform temporal frame."[1] This temporal frame, which had supplied a mode of consistency for generations and which had allowed for a strong connection between Ireland and the natural world, had now been severed by economic, social, and cultural changes that were happening not just in nineteenth-century Ireland but throughout the Western world.[2] In other words, humanity was becoming systematically detached from nature by the onslaught of politics and of written history. Humanity no longer saw its place within patterns of behavior that had their allegiances ground firmly in the landscape.

William Allingham (1824–1889), whose poetry remained deeply rooted in the natural world, lamented the loss of this humanity in nature in "The Ruined Chapel," where

> The empty ruins, lapsed again
> Into Nature's wide domain,
> Sow themselves with seed and grain
> As Day and Night and Day go by;
> And hoard June's sun and April's rain.[3]

Like the ruins of Trollope's Ballycloran estate, the church itself personifies Ireland, as days and nights pass without the slightest hope that humanity and nature will again be reunited. This fully dehumanized landscape is, as Allingham writes, "a hush more dead than any sleep."[4] This deadness, however, is not the Burren of Emily Lawless's *Hurrish* novel, for this structure was once a church where peasants prayed, in a place once connected both to God and to Nature. Detachment from the natural world is implicit in the abandoned house of God; the Irish peasants have gone off to better pastures, to places of history and economy, where the threat of an ever-encroaching nature will never again create Famine.

119

As Paula Gunn Allen notes in her study of non-English Native American cultures, "In English, one can divide the universe into two parts: the natural and the supernatural. Humanity has no real part in either, being neither animal nor spirit." This creates conflict because "this necessarily forces English-speaking people into a position of alienation from the world they live in."[5] For the Irish, this alienation is most notable in the removal from their Celtic past and in a separation from an ancient language and a culture woven into both natural and supernatural realms.

Therefore, part 3 includes works that reflect an esoteric natural world in which the writers of the Irish Literary Revival find a profound emotional connection through a merging of mythology, nature, and poetry, including versions of "The Children of Lir" by Katharine Tynan and Æ (George William Russell), Tynan's version of "St. Francis and the Birds," which will be revisited by Seamus Heaney in "St. Francis and the Blackbird" in part 4, and the mythology of Connla's Well in Æ's "The Nuts of Knowledge" and the secret waters of Ireland in poems by Æ and Eva Gore-Booth. Also included in this part are several early Yeats poems, including the myth of Aengus, Fergus, and King Goll, as well as some of his lesser-known works, followed by the nature poetry of J. M. Synge, as well as an excerpt from Synge's nonfiction masterpiece *The Aran Islands*, along with his famous one-act play *Riders to the Sea*. Also included in this section are a selection of nature poems from the often overlooked poet Padraic Colum and the preface and chapter 1 from George Moore's important novel *The Lake*, in which a priest's relationship to the natural world of Ireland is explored in beautiful depth.

Katharine Tynan

Katharine Tynan (1859–1931) was an integral part of the Irish Literary Revival. As an Irish nationalist, she produced poetry, novels, and nonfiction that spanned the late nineteenth and early twentieth centuries; her wealth of published writing was driven partly by the need to support her family, so her topics were wide, including about a hundred romance and gothic novels for women, twenty-three collections of short stories, six volumes of autobiography, three volumes of sketches, a religious play, a book of axioms, and three biographies.[6] Her nonfiction work covers Irish history, books about raising children (including a religious text and a book on etiquette), and a collaboratively written book on flowers. As a journalist, she researched and wrote articles and sketches on social, political, and gender issues, but her enduring legacy lies in her eighteen volumes of poetry. While many of the poems in these collections center on the themes of nationalism and of being an Irish Catholic, the subjects of Tynan's poems are drawn primarily from the natural world. Her early poems, chiefly from *The Wind in the Trees* (1898), best illustrate her success as a nature poet, and her rendition of "The Children of Lir" is especially powerful in its heavy imagery drawn from the marshes and lakes of Ireland's west.

The Children of Lir

Out upon the sand-dunes thrive the coarse long grasses;
Herons standing knee-deep in the brackish pool;
Overhead the sunset fire and flame amasses
And the moon to eastward rises pale and cool.
Rose and green around her, silver-gray and pearly,
Chequered with the black rooks flying home to bed;
For, to wake at daybreak, birds must couch them early:
And the day's a long one since the dawn was red.

On the chilly lakelet, in that pleasant gloaming,
See the sad swans sailing: they shall have no rest:
Never a voice to greet them save the bittern's booming
Where the ghostly sallows sway against the West.
'Sister,' saith the gray swan, 'Sister, I am weary,'
Turning to the white swan wet, despairing eyes;
'O' she saith, 'my young one! O' she saith, 'my dearie!'
Casts her wings about him with a storm of cries.

Woe for Lir's sweet children whom their vile stepmother
Glamoured with her witch-spells for a thousand years;
Died their father raving, on his throne another,
Blind before the end came from the burning tears.
Long the swans have wandered over lake and river;
Gone is all the glory of the race of Lir:
Gone and long forgotten like a dream of fever:
But the swans remember the sweet days that were.

Hugh, the black and white swan with the beauteous feathers,
Fiachra, the black swan with the emerald breast,
Conn, the youngest, dearest, sheltered in all weathers,
Him his snow-white sister loves the tenderest.
These her mother gave her as she lay a-dying;
To her faithful keeping; faithful hath she been,
With her wings spread o'er them when the tempest's crying,
And her songs so hopeful when the sky's serene.

Other swans have nests made 'mid the reeds and rushes,
Lined with downy feathers where the cygnets sleep
Dreaming, if a bird dreams, till the daylight blushes,
Then they sail out swiftly on the current deep.
With the proud swan-father, tall, and strong, and stately,
And the mild swan-mother, grave with household cares,
All well-born and comely, all rejoicing greatly:
Full of honest pleasure is a life like theirs.

But alas! for my swans with the human nature,
Sick with human longings, starved for human ties,
With their hearts all human cramped to a bird's stature.
And the human weeping in the bird's soft eyes.
Never shall my swans build nests in some green river,
Never fly to Southward in the autumn gray,
Rear no tender children, love no mates for ever;
Robbed alike of bird's joys and of man's are they.

Babbles Conn the youngest, 'Sister, I remember
At my father's palace how I went in silk,
Ate the juicy deer-flesh roasted from the ember,
Drank from golden goblets my child's draught of milk.
Once I rode a-hunting, laughed to see the hurry,
Shouted at the ball-play, on the lake did row;
You had for your beauty gauds that shone so rarely.'
'Peace' saith Fionnuala, 'that was long ago.'

'Sister,' saith Fiachra, 'well do I remember
How the flaming torches lit the banquet-hall,
And the fire leapt skyward in the mid-December,
And among the rushes slept our staghounds tall.
By our father's right hand you sat shyly gazing,
Smiling half and sighing, with your eyes a-glow,
As the bards sang loudly all your beauty praising.'
'Peace,' saith Fionnuala, 'that was long ago.'

'Sister,' then saith Hugh 'most do I remember
One I called my brother, one, earth's goodliest man,
Strong as forest oaks are where the wild vines clamber,
First at feast or hunting, in the battle's van.

Angus, you were handsome, wise, and true, and tender,
Loved by every comrade, feared by every foe:
Low, low, lies your beauty, all forgot your splendour.'
'Peace,' saith Fionnuala, 'that was long ago.'

Dews are in the clear air and the roselight paling;
Over sands and sedges shines the evening star;
And the moon's disc lonely high in heaven is sailing;
Silvered all the spear-heads of the rushes are.
Housed warm are all things as the night grows colder,
Water-fowl and sky-fowl dreamless in the nest;
But the swans go drifting, drooping wing and shoulder
Cleaving the still water where the fishes rest.[7]

High Summer

Pinks and syringa in the garden closes,
And the sweet privet hedge and golden roses,
The pines hot in the sun, the drone of the bee,
They die in Flanders to keep these for me.

The long sunny days and the still weather,
The cuckoo and the blackbird shouting together,
The lambs calling their mothers out on the lea,
They die in Flanders to keep these for me.

All doors and windows open: the South wind blowing
Warm through the clean sweet rooms on tiptoe going,
Where many sanctities, dear and delightsome, be,
They die in Flanders to keep these for me.

Daisies leaping in foam on the green grasses,
The dappled sky and the stream that sings as it passes;
These are bought with a price, a bitter fee,
They die in Flanders to keep these for me.[8]

Indian Summer

   This is the sign!
This flooding splendour, golden and hyaline,
This sun a golden sea on hill and plain,—
That God forgets not, that He walks with men.
His smile is on the mountain and the pool
And all the fairy lakes are beautiful.

   This is the word!
That makes a thing of flame the water-bird.
This mercy of His fulfilled in the magical
Clear glow of skies from dawn to evenfall,

Telling His Hand is over us, that we
Are not delivered to the insatiable sea.

This is the pledge!
The promise writ in gold to the water's edge:
His bow's in Heaven and the great floods are over.
Oh, broken hearts, lift up! The Immortal Lover
Embraces, comforts with the enlivening sun,
The sun He bids stand still till the day is won.[9]

Nymphs

Where are ye now, O beautiful girls of the mountain,
   Oreads all?
Nothing at all stirs here save the drip of the fountain;
   Answers our call
Only the heart-glad thrush, in the Vale of Thrushes;
   Stirs in the brake
But the dew-bright ear of the hare in his couch of rushes
   Listening, awake.[10]

St. Francis to the Birds

Little sisters, the birds:
We must praise God, you and I—
You, with songs that fill the sky,
I, with halting words.

All things tell His praise,
Woods and waters thereof sing,
Summer, Winter, Autumn, Spring,
And the night and days.

Yea, and cold and heat,
And the sun and stars and moon,
Sea with her monotonous tune,
Rain and hail and sleet,

And the winds of heaven,
And the solemn hills of blue,
And the brown earth and the dew,
And the thunder even,

And the flowers' sweet breath.
All things make one glorious voice;
Life with fleeting pains and joys,
And our brother, Death.

Little flowers of air,
With your feathers soft and sleek,
And your bright brown eyes and meek,
He hath made you fair.

He hath taught to you
Skill to weave in tree and thatch
Nests where happy mothers hatch
Speckled eggs of blue.

And hath children given:
When the soft heads overbrim
The brown nests, then thank ye Him
In the clouds of heaven.

Also in your lives
Live His laws Who loveth you.
Husbands, be ye kind and true;
Be home-keeping, wives:

Love not gossiping;
Stay at home and keep the nest;
Fly not here and there in quest
Of the newest thing.

Live as brethren live:
Love be in each heart and mouth;
Be not envious, be not wroth,
Be not slow to give.

When ye build the nest,
Quarrel not o'er straw or wool;
He who hath be bountiful
To the neediest.

Be not puffed nor vain
Of your beauty or your worth,
Of your children or your birth,
Or the praise ye gain.

Eat not greedily:
Sometimes for sweet mercy's sake,
Worm or insect spare to take;
Let it crawl or fly.

See ye sing not near
To our church on holy day,
Lest the human-folk should stray
From their prayers to hear.

Now depart in peace:
In God's name I bless each one;
May your days be long i' the sun
And your joys increase.

And remember me,
Your poor brother Francis, who
Loves you and gives thanks to you
For this courtesy.

Sometimes when ye sing,
Name my name, that He may take
Pity for the dear song's sake
On my shortcoming.[11]

The Birds' Bargain

'O spare my cherries in the net,'
Brother Benignus prayed; 'and I
Summer and winter, shine and wet,
Will pile the blackbirds' table high.'

'O spare my youngling peas,' he prayed,
'That for the Abbot's table be;
And every blackbird shall be fed;
Yea, they shall have their fill,' said he.

His prayer, his vow, the blackbirds heard,
And spared his shining garden-plot.
In abstinence went every bird,
All the old thieving ways forgot.

He kept his promise to his friends,
And daily set them finest fare
Of corn and meal and manchet-ends,
With marrowy bones for winter bare.

Brother Benignus died in grace:
The brethren keep his trust, and feed
The blackbirds in this pleasant place,
Purged, as dear heaven, from strife and greed.

The blackbirds sing the whole year long,
Here where they keep their promise given,
And do the mellowing fruit no wrong.
Brother Benignus smiles in heaven.[12]

The Garden

I know a garden like a child,
Clean and new-washed and reconciled.
It grows its own sweet way, yet still
Has guidance of some tender will
That clips, confines, its wilder mood
And makes it happy, being good.

Around the lordly mountains stand,
For this is an enchanted land,
As though their splendours stood to grace
This little lovely garden place,
Looking with wise and keeping eyes
Upon the garden sanctities.

Box borders edge each little bed,
Paths narrow for a child to tread
Divide the kitchen garden, dear
And sweet with musk and lavender,
And water-mints and beans in bloom.
Be sure the honey-bee's at home.

How should I tell in a sweet list
Of beauties, rose and amethyst;
The little water-garden cool
On sultry days, and beautiful
The wall-garden, the shade, the sun,
Since they are lovely, every one.

Hot honey of the pines is sweet,
And when the day's at three o'clock heat
A winding walk will you invite
To a new garden out of sight.
And a green seat is set so near
The sluggish, stealing backwater.

The Spirit of the garden plays
At hide-and-seek an hundred ways
And when you've captured her, she will
Elude you, calling backward still,
A silver echo—a sweet child,
Demure and lovesome, gay and wild.[13]

The Wind That Shakes the Barley

There's music in my heart all day,
    I hear it late and early,
It comes from fields are far away,
    The wind that shakes the barley.
        Ochone!

Above the uplands drenched with dew
    The sky hangs soft and pearly,
An emerald world is listening to
    The wind that shakes the barley.
        Ochone!

Above the bluest mountain crest
    The lark is singing rarely,
It rocks the singer into rest,
    The wind that shakes the barley.
        Ochone!

Oh, still through summers and through springs
    It calls me late and early.
Come home, come home, come home, it sings,
    The wind that shakes the barley.[14]
        Ochone!

Æ (George William Russell)

Æ (George William Russell; 1867–1935) was an Irish nationalist and organizer, an essayist, a poet, a painter, and a mystic. Russell worked for many years with the Irish Agricultural Organization Society (IAOS), a farm and land co-op. He became an important organizer and spokesman for the group, helping to establish local credit unions that would work for the people they served, build local communities, and help those communities understand their relationship with the land and the natural world. Russell was a close friend of W. B. Yeats and an integral contributor to the Revival. As with many spiritually minded people of his era, he was a theosophist, interested in clairvoyance and Eastern mysticism.[15] This interest in mysticism is evident in the imagery and lyricism of his poetry. For Æ, this movement from Christianity to theosophy allowed him a more fluid esoteric connection to the natural world of Ireland. For Æ, this set of beliefs embodied a universal truth drawn from a pre-Christian Ireland that led to his involvement in the Literary Revival; the principles of theosophy would resonate through all of his nature poetry. These beliefs are further illuminated in *The Candle of Vision*, a memoir of his visions, which he published in 1918. The esoteric current that runs through the work, though, like his poetry, is his awareness of the spiritual forces drawn from an acute perception and observation of Ireland's natural world. Æ was also a painter, and as a visual artist, his sensibilities were tied to an emulation of the colors of the earth. As a careful observer of all of the intrinsic differences in nature, he was able to make a more natural transition to poetry and to painting the landscape with words. For Æ, as with Ralph Waldo Emerson and the Transcendentalists, the religious experience that could be drawn into his creativity was not to be found within the walls of a church but in the boundlessness of nature. The woods, the fields, and the birds all became a source of spiritual energy for Æ.

By the Margin of the Great Deep

When the breath of twilight blows to flame the misty skies,
All its vaporous sapphire, violet glow and silver gleam
With their magic flood me through the gateway of the eyes;
   I am one with the twilight's dream.

When the trees and skies and fields are one in dusky mood,
Every heart of man is rapt within the mother's breast:
Full of peace and sleep and dreams in the vasty quietude,
   I am one with their hearts at rest.

From our immemorial joys of hearth and home and love
Strayed away along the margin of the unknown tide,
All its reach of soundless calm can thrill me far above
   Word or touch from the lips beside.

Aye, and deep and deep and deeper let me drink and draw
From the olden fountain more than light or peace or dream,
Such primeval being as o'erfills the heart with awe,
   Growing one with its silent stream.[16]

Oversoul

I am Beauty itself among beautiful things.
                              —Bhagavad-Gita.
The East was crowned with snow-cold bloom
And hung with veils of pearly fleece:
They died away into the gloom,
Vistas of peace—and deeper peace.

And earth and air and wave and fire
In awe and breathless silence stood;
For One who passed into their choir
Linked them in mystic brotherhood.

Twilight of amethyst, amid
Thy few strange stars that lit the heights,
Where was the secret spirit hid?
Where was Thy place, O Light of Lights?

The flame of Beauty far in space—
Where rose the fire: in Thee? in Me?
Which bowed the elemental race
To adoration silently?[17]

The Great Breath

Its edges foamed with amethyst and rose,
Withers once more the old blue flower of day:
There where the ether like a diamond glows
    Its petals fade away.

A shadowy tumult stirs the dusky air;
Sparkle the delicate dews, the distant snows;
The great deep thrills, for through it everywhere
    The breath of Beauty blows.

I saw how all the trembling ages past,
Moulded to her by deep and deeper breath,
Neared to the hour when Beauty breathes her last
    And knows herself in death.[18]

The Voice of the Waters

Where the Greyhound River windeth through a loneliness so deep,
Scarce a wild fowl shakes the quiet that the purple boglands keep,
Only God exults in silence over fields no man may reap.

Where the silver wave with sweetness fed the tiny lives of grass
I was bent above, my image mirrored in the fleeting glass,
And a voice from out the water through my being seemed to pass.

"Still above the waters brooding, spirit, in thy timeless quest;
Was the glory of thine image trembling over east and west
Not divine enough when mirrored in the morning water's breast?"

With the sighing voice that murmured I was borne to ages dim
Ere the void was lit with beauty breathed upon by seraphim,
We were cradled there together folded in the peace in Him.

One to be the master spirit, one to be the slave awoke,
One to shape itself obedient to the fiery words we spoke,
Flame and flood and stars and mountains from the primal waters broke.

I was huddled in the heather when the vision failed its light,
Still and blue and vast above me towered aloft the solemn height,
Where the stars like dewdrops glistened on the mountain slope of night.[19]

A New World

I who had sought afar from earth
    The faery land to meet,
Now find content within its girth
    And wonder nigh my feet.

To-day a nearer love I choose
    And seek no distant sphere;
For aureoled by faery dews
    The dear brown breasts appear.

With rainbow radiance come and go
    The airy breaths of day;
And eve is all a pearly glow
    With moonlit winds a-play.

The lips of twilight burn my brow,
    The arms of night caress:
Glimmer her white eyes drooping now
    With grave old tenderness.

I close mine eyes from dream to be
    The diamond-rayed again,
As in the ancient hours ere we
    Forgot ourselves to men.

And all I thought of heaven before
    I find in earth below:
A sunlight in the hidden core
    To dim the noonday glow.

And with the earth my heart is glad,
    I move as one of old;
With mists of silver I am clad
    And bright with burning gold.[20]

A Vision of Beauty

Where we sat at dawn together, while the star-rich heavens shifted,
We were weaving dreams in silence, suddenly the veil was lifted.
By a hand of fire awakened, in a moment caught and led
Upward to the heaven of heavens—through the star-mists overhead
Flare and flaunt the monstrous highlands; on the sapphire coast of night
Fall the ghostly froth and fringes of the ocean of the light.
Many coloured shine the vapours: to the moon-eye far away
'Tis the fairy ring of twilight, mid the spheres of night and day,
Girdling with a rainbow cincture round the planet where we go,
We and it together fleeting, poised upon the pearly glow;
We and it and all together flashing through the starry spaces
In a tempest dream of beauty lighting up the face of faces.
Half our eyes behold the glory; half within the spirit's glow
Echoes of the noiseless revels and the will of Beauty go.
By a hand of fire uplifted—to her star-strewn palace brought,
To the mystic heart of beauty and the secret of her thought:
Here of yore the ancient Mother in the fire mists sank to rest,
And she built her dreams about her, rayed from out her burning breast:
Here the wild will woke within her lighting up her flying dreams,
Round and round the planets whirling break in woods and flowers and streams,
And the winds are shaken from them as the leaves from off the rose,
And the feet of earth go dancing in the way that beauty goes,
And the souls of earth are kindled by the incense of her breath
As her light alternate lures them through the gates of birth and death.
O'er the fields of space together following her flying traces,
In a radiant tumult thronging, suns and stars and myriad races
Mount the spirit spires of beauty, reaching onward to the day
When the Shepherd of the Ages draws his misty hordes away
Through the glimmering deeps to silence, and within the awful fold
Life and joy and love forever vanish as a tale is told,
Lost within the Mother's being. So the vision flamed and fled,
And before the glory fallen every other dream lay dead.[21]

Carrowmore

It's a lonely road through bogland to the lake at Carrowmore,
And a sleeper there lies dreaming where the water laps the shore;
Though the moth-wings of the twilight in their purples are unfurled,
Yet his sleep is filled with music by the masters of the world.

There's a hand is white as silver that is fondling with his hair.
There are glimmering feet of sunshine that are dancing by him there:
And half-open lips of faery that were dyed a faery red
In their revels where the Hazel Tree its holy clusters shed.

"Come away," the red lips whisper, "all the world is weary now;
'Tis the twilight of the ages and it's time to quit the plough.
Oh, the very sunlight's weary ere it lightens up the dew,
And its gold is changed and faded before it falls to you.

"Though your colleen's heart be tender, a tenderer heart is near.
What's the starlight in her glances when the stars are shining clear?
Who would kiss the fading shadow when the flower-face glows above?
'Tis the beauty of all Beauty that is calling for your love."

Oh, the great gates of the mountain have opened once again,
And the sound of song and dancing falls upon the ears of men,
And the Land of Youth lies gleaming, flushed with rainbow light and mirth,
And the old enchantment lingers in the honey-heart of earth.[22]

Creation

As one by one the veils took flight,
The day withdrew, the stars came up.
The spirit issued pale and bright
Filling thy beauty like a cup.

Sacred thy laughter on the air,
Holy thy lightest word that fell,
Proud the innumerable hair
That waved at the enchanter's spell.

O, Master of the Beautiful,
Creating us from hour to hour,
Give me this vision to the full
To see in lightest things thy power.

This vision give, no heaven afar,
No throne, and yet I will rejoice
Knowing beneath my feet a star
Thy word in every wandering voice.[23]

The Winds of Angus

The grey road whereupon we trod became as holy ground:
The eve was all one voice that breathed its message with no sound:
And burning multitudes pour through my heart, too bright, too blind,
Too swift and hurried in their flight to leave their tale behind.
Twin gates unto that living world, dark honey-coloured eyes,
The lifting of whose lashes flushed the face with Paradise,
Beloved, there I saw within their ardent rays unfold
The likeness of enraptured birds that flew from deeps of gold

To deeps of gold within my breast to rest, or there to be
Transfigured in the light, or find a death to life in me.
So love, a burning multitude, a seraph wind that blows
From out the deep of being to the deep of being goes.
And sun and moon and starry fires and earth and air and sea
Are creatures from the deep let loose, who pause in ecstasy,
Or wing their wild and heavenly way until again they find
The ancient deep, and fade therein, enraptured, bright, and blind.[24]

The Nuts of Knowledge

A cabin on the mountain side hid in a grassy nook
Where door and windows open wide that friendly stars may look.
The rabbit shy can patter in, the winds may enter free,
Who throng around the mountain throne in living ecstasy.

And when the sun sets dimmed in eve and purple fills the air,
I think the sacred Hazel Tree is dropping berries there
From starry fruitage waved aloft where Connla's Well o'erflows;
For sure the enchanted waters run through every wind that blows.

I think when night towers up aloft and shakes the trembling dew,
How every high and lonely thought that thrills my being through
Is but a ruddy berry dropped down through the purple air,
And from the magic tree of life the fruit falls everywhere.[25]

Children of Lir

We woke from our sleep in the bosom where cradled together we lay:
The love of the dark hidden Father went with us upon our way.
And gay was the breath in our being, and never a sorrow or fear
Was on us as, singing together, we flew from the infinite Lir.

Through nights lit with diamond and sapphire we raced with the children of dawn,
A chain that was silver and golden linked spirit to spirit, my swan,
Till day in the heavens passed over, and still grew the beat of our wings,
And the breath of the darkness enfolded to teach us unspeakable things.

Yet lower we fell and for comfort our pinionless spirits had now
The leaning of bosom to bosom, the lifting of lip unto brow.
Though chained to the earth yet we mourned not the loss of our heaven above,
But passed from the vision of beauty to the fathomless being of love.

Still gay is the breath in our being, we wait for the bell branch to ring
To call us away to the Father, and then we will rise on the wing,
And fly through the twilights of time till the home lights of heaven appear;
Our spirits through love and through longing made one in the infinite Lir.[26]

From **The Candle of Vision**

THE EARTH BREATH

After that awakening earth began more and more to bewitch me, and to lure me to her heart with honied entreaty. I could not escape from it even in that busy office where I sat during week-days with little heaps of paper mounting up before me moment by frenzied moment. An interval of inactivity and I would be aware of that sweet eternal presence overshadowing me. I was an exile from living nature but she yet visited me. Her ambassadors were visions that made me part of themselves. Through the hot foetid air of the gaslit room I could see the feverish faces, the quick people flitting about, and hear the voices; and then room, faces and voices would be gone, and I would be living in the Mother's being in some pure, remote elemental region of hers. Instead of the dingy office there would be a sky of rarest amethyst; a snow-cold bloom of cloud; high up in the divine wilderness, solitary, a star; all rapt, breathless and still; rapt the seraph princes of wind and wave and fire, for it was the hour when the King, an invisible presence, moved through His dominions and Nature knew and was hushed at the presence of her Lord. Once, suddenly, I found myself on some remote plain or steppe, and heard unearthly chimes pealing passionately from I know not what far steeples. The earth-breath streamed from the furrows to the glowing heavens. Overhead the birds flew round and round crying their incomprehensible cries, as if they were maddened, and knew not where to nestle, and had dreams of some more enraptured rest in a diviner home. I could see a ploughman lifting himself from his obscure toil and stand with lit eyes as if he too had been fire-smitten and was caught into heaven as I was, and knew for that moment he was a god. And then I would lapse out of vision and ecstasy, and hear the voices, and see again through the quivering of the hot air the feverish faces, and seem to myself to be cast out of the spirit. I could hardly bear after thinking of these things, for I felt I was trapped in some obscure hell. You, too, trapped with me, dear kindly people, who never said a harsh word to the forgetful boy. You, too, I knew, had your revelations. I remember one day how that clerk with wrinkled face, blinking eyes and grizzly beard, who never seemed apart from his work, to have interests other than his pipe and paper, surprised me by telling me that the previous midnight he waked in his sleep, and some self of him was striding to and fro in the moonlight in an avenue mighty with gigantic images; and that dream self he had surprised had seemed to himself unearthly in wisdom and power. What had he done to be so high in one sphere and so petty in another? Others I could tell of, too, who had their moment of awe when the spirit made its ancient claim on them. But none were so happy or so unhappy as I was. I was happy at times because the divine world which had meant nothing to my childhood was becoming a reality to manhood: and I knew it was not a dream, for comrades in vision soon came to me, they who could see as I saw, and hear as I heard, and there were some who had gone deeper into that being than I have ever travelled. I was more miserable than my work-a-day companions, because the very intensity of vision made the recoil more unendurable. It was an agony of darkness and oblivion, wherein I seemed like those who in nightmare are buried in caverns so deep beneath the roots of the world that there is no hope of escape, for the way out is unknown, and the way to them is forgotten by those who walk in light. In those black hours the universe, a gigantic presence, seemed at war with me. I was condemned, I thought, to be this speck of minute life because of some sin committed in remote ages, I and those with me. We were all lost children of the stars. Everything that suggested our high original being, a shaft of glory from the far fire in the heavens spearing the gloom of the office, the blue twilight deepening through the panes until it was rich with starry dust, the sunny clouds careering high over the city, these things would stir pangs of painful remembrance and my eyes would suddenly grow blind and wet. Sometimes, too, I would rebel and plot in my obscurity, and remember moments when the will in me seemed to be a titanic power, and my spirit would brood upon ways of escape and ascent to its native regions, as those fallen angels in Milton's tremendous narrative rose up from torture, and conspired to tear the throne from Him. And then all that would appear to me to be futile as a speck of dust trying to stay itself against the typhoon, and the last door would close upon me and leave me more hopeless than before.

THE SLAVE OF THE LAMP

Because I was a creature of many imaginings and of rapid alternations of mood out of all that there came to me assurance of a truth, of all truths most inspiring to one in despair in the Iron Age and lost amid the undergrowths of being. I became aware of a swift echo or response to my own moods in circumstance which had seemed hitherto immutable in its indifference. I found every intense imagination, every new adventure of the intellect endowed with magnetic power to attract to it its own kin. Will and desire were as the enchanter's wand of fable, and they drew to themselves their own affinities. Around a pure atom of crystal all the atoms of the element in solution gather, and in like manner one person after another emerged out of the mass, betraying their close affinity to my moods as they were engendered. I met these people seemingly by accident along is country roads, or I entered into conversation with strangers and found they were intimates of the spirit. I could prophesy from the uprising of new moods in myself that I, without search, would soon meet people of a certain character, and so I met them. Even inanimate things were under the sway of these affinities. They yielded up to me what they had specially for my eyes. I have glanced in passing at a book left open by some one in a library, and the words first seen thrilled me, for they confirmed a knowledge lately attained in vision. At another time a book taken down idly from a shelf opened at a sentence quoted from Upanishad, scriptures then to me unknown, and this sent my heart flying eastwards because it was the answer to a spiritual problem I had been brooding over an hour before. It was hardly a week after my first awakening that I began to meet those who were to be my lifelong comrades on the quest, and who were, like myself, in a boyhood troubled by the spirit. I had just attempted to write in verse when I met a boy whose voice was soon to be the most beautiful voice in Irish literature. I sought none of these out because I had heard of them and surmised a kinship. The concurrence of our personalities seemed mysterious and controlled by some law of spiritual gravitation, like that which in the chemistry of nature makes one molecule fly to another. I remember the exultation with which I realised about life that, as Heraclitus has said, it was in a flux, and that in all its flowings there was meaning and law; that I could not lose what was my own; I need not seek, for what was my own would come to me; if any passed it was because they were no longer mine. One buried in a dungeon for many years could not have hailed sunshine, the sweet-smelling earth, and the long hidden infinitude of the skies more joyously than I the melting of that which had seemed immutable. It is those who live and grow swiftly, and who continually compare what is without with what is within, who have this certainty. Those who do not change see no change and recognise no law. He who has followed even in secrecy many lights of the spirit can see one by one the answering torches gleam. When I was made certain about this I accepted what befell with resignation. I knew that all I met was part of myself and that what I could not comprehend was related by affinity to some yet unrealised forces in my being. We have within us the Lamp of the World; and Nature, the genie, is Slave of the Lamp, and must fashion life about us as we fashion it within ourselves. What we are alone has power. We may give up the outward personal struggle and ambition, and if we leave all to the Law all that is rightly ours will be paid. Man becomes truly the Super-man when he has this proud consciousness. No matter where he may be, in what seeming obscurity, he is still the King, still master of his fate, and circumstance reels about him or is still as he, in the solitude of his spirit, is mighty or is humble. We are indeed most miserable when we dream we have no power over circumstance, and I account it the highest wisdom to know this of the living universe that there is no destiny in it other than that we make for ourselves. How the spirit is kindled, how it feels its power, when, outwardly quiet, it can see the coming and going of life, as it dilates within itself or is still! Then do we move in miracle and wonder. Then does the universe appear to us as it did to the Indian sage who said that to him who was perfect in meditation all rivers were sacred as the Ganges and all speech was holy.

THE MANY-COLOURED LAND

I have always been curious about the psychology of my own vision as desirous of imparting it, and I wish in this book to relate the efforts of an artist and poet to discover what truth lay in his own imaginations. I have brooded longer over the nature of imagination than I have lingered over the canvas where I tried to rebuild my vision. Spiritual moods are difficult to express and cannot be argued over, but the workings of imagination may well be spoken of, and need precise and minute investigation. I surmise from my reading of the psychologists who treat of this that they themselves were without this faculty and spoke of it as blind men who would fain draw although without vision. We are overcome when we read *Prometheus Unbound*, but who, as he reads, flings off the enchantment to ponder in what state was the soul of Shelley in that ecstasy of swift creation. Who has questioned the artist to whom the forms of his thought are vivid as the forms of nature? Artist and poet have rarely been curious about the processes of their own minds. Yet it is reasonable to assume that the highest ecstasy and vision are conditioned by law and attainable by all, and this might be argued as of more importance even than the message of the seers. I attribute to that unwavering meditation and fiery concentration of will a growing luminousness in my brain as if I had unsealed in the body a fountain of interior light. Normally we close our eyes on a cloudy gloom through which vague forms struggle sometimes into definiteness. But the luminous quality gradually became normal in me, and at times in meditation there broke in on me an almost intolerable lustre of light, pure and shining faces, dazzling processions of figures, most ancient, ancient places and peoples, and landscapes lovely as the lost Eden. These appeared at first to have no more relation to myself than images from a street without one sees reflected in a glass; but at times meditation prolonged itself into spheres which were radiant with actuality. Once, drawn by some inner impulse to meditate at an unusual hour, I found quick oblivion of the body. The blood and heat of the brain ebbed from me as an island fades in the mists behind a swift vessel fleeting into light. The ways were open within. I rose through myself and suddenly felt as if I had awakened from dream. Where was I? In what city? Here were hills crowned with glittering temples, and the ways, so far as I could see, were thronged with most beautiful people, swaying as if shaken by some ecstasy running through all as if the Dark Hidden Father was breathing rapturous life within His children. Did I wear to them an aspect like their own? Was I visible to them as a new-comer in their land of lovely light? I could not know, but those nigh me flowed towards me with outstretched hands. I saw eyes with a beautiful flame of love in them looking into mine. But I could stay no longer for something below drew me down and I was again an exile from light. There came through meditation a more powerful orientation of my being as if to a hidden sun, and my thoughts turned more and more to the spiritual life of Earth. All the needles of being pointed to it. I felt instinctively that all I saw in vision was part of the life of Earth which is a court where there are many starry palaces. There the Planetary Spirit was King, and that Spirit manifesting through the substance of Earth, the Mighty Mother, was, I felt, the being I groped after as God. The love I had for nature as garment of that deity grew deeper. That which was my own came to me as it comes to all men. That which claimed me drew me to itself. I had my days and nights of freedom. How often did I start in the sunshine of a Sabbath morning, setting my face to the hills, feeling somewhat uncertain as a lover who draws nigh to a beauty he adores, who sometimes will yield everything to him and sometimes is silent and will only endure his presence. I did not know what would happen to me, but I was always expectant, and walked up to the mountains as to the throne of God. Step by step there fell from me the passions and fears of the week-day, until, as I reached the hillside and lay on the grassy slope with shut eyes, I was bare of all but desire for the Eternal. I was once more the child close to the Mother. She rewarded me by lifting for me a little the veil which hides her true face. To those high souls who know their kinship the veil is lifted, her face is revealed, and her face is like a bride's. Petty as was my everyday life, with the fears and timidities which abnormal sensitiveness begets, in those moments of vision I understood instinctively the high mood they must keep who would walk with the highest; and who with that divine face glimmering before him could do aught but adore!

There is an instinct which stills the lips which would speak of mysteries whose day for revelation has not drawn nigh. The little I know of these I shall not speak of. It is always lawful to speak of that higher wisdom which relates our spiritual being to that multitudinous unity which is God and Nature and Man. The only justification for speech from me, rather than from others whose knowledge is more profound, is that the matching of words to thoughts is an art I have practised more. What I say may convey more of truth, as the skilled artist, painting a scene which he views for the first time, may yet suggest more beauty and enchantment than the habitual dweller, unskilled in art, who may yet know the valley he loves so intimately that he could walk blindfold from end to end.

I do not wish to write a book of wonders, but rather to bring thought back to that Being whom the ancient seers worshipped as Deity. I believe that most of what was said of God was in reality said of that Spirit whose body is Earth. I must in some fashion indicate the nature of the visions which led me to believe with Plato that the earth is not at all what the geographers suppose it to be, and that we live like frogs at the bottom of a marsh knowing nothing of that Many-Coloured Earth which is superior to this we know, yet related to it as soul to body. On that Many-Coloured Earth, he tells us, live a divine folk, and there are temples wherein the gods do truly dwell, and I wish to convey, so far as words may, how some apparitions of that ancient beauty came to me in wood or on hillside or by the shores of the western sea.

Sometimes lying on the hillside with the eyes of the body shut as in sleep I could see valleys and hills, lustrous as a jewel, where all was self-shining, the colours brighter and purer, yet making a softer harmony together than the colours of the world I know. The winds sparkled as they blew hither and thither, yet far distances were clear through that glowing air. What was far off was precise as what was near, and the will to see hurried me to what I desired. There, too, in that land I saw fountains as of luminous mist jetting from some hidden heart of power, and shining folk who passed into those fountains inhaled them and drew life from the magical air. They were, I believe, those who in the ancient world gave birth to legends of nymph and dryad. Their perfectness was like the perfectness of a flower, a beauty which had never, it seemed, been broken by act of the individualised will which with us makes possible a choice between good and evil, and the marring of the mould of natural beauty. More beautiful than we they yet seemed less than human, and I surmised I had more thoughts in a moment than they through many of their days. Sometimes I wondered had they individualised life at all, for they moved as if in some orchestration of their being. If one looked up, all looked up. If one moved to breathe the magical airs from the fountains, many bent in rhythm. I wondered were their thoughts all another's, one who lived within them, guardian or oversoul to their tribe?

Like these were my first visions of supernature, not spiritual nor of any high import, not in any way so high as those transcendental moments of awe, when almost without vision the Divine Darkness seemed to breathe within the spirit. But I was curious about these forms, and often lured away by them from the highest meditation; for I was dazzled like a child who escapes from a dark alley in one of our cities of great sorrow where its life has been spent, and who comes for the first time upon some rich garden beyond the city where the air is weighted with scent of lilac or rose, and the eyes are made gay with colour. Such a beauty begins to glow on us as we journey towards Deity, even as earth grows brighter as we journey from the gloomy pole to lands of the sun; and I would cry out to our humanity, sinking deeper into the Iron Age, that the Golden World is all about us and that beauty is open to all, and none are shut out from it who will turn to it and seek for it.

As the will grew more intense, the longing for the ancestral self more passionate, there came glimpses of more rapturous life in the being of Earth. Once I lay on the sand dunes by the western sea. The air seemed filled with melody. The motion of the wind made a continuous musical vibration. Now and then the silvery sound of bells broke on my ear. I saw nothing for a time. Then there was an intensity of light before my eyes like the flashing of sunlight through a crystal. It widened like the opening of a gate and I saw the light was streaming from the heart of a glowing figure. Its body was pervaded with light as if sunfire rather than blood ran through its limbs. Light streams flowed from it. It moved over me along the winds, carrying a harp, and there was a circling of golden hair that swept across the strings. Birds flew about it, and over the brows was a fiery plumage as of wings of outspread flame. On the face was an ecstasy of beauty and immortal youth. There were others, a lordly folk, and they passed by on the wind as if they knew me not or the earth I lived on. When I came back to myself my own world seemed grey and devoid of light though the summer sun was hot upon the sands.

One other vision I will tell because it bears on things the ancients taught us, and on what I have to write in later pages. Where I saw this I will not say. There was a hall vaster than any cathedral, with pillars that seemed built out of living and trembling opal, or from some starry substances which shone with every colour, the colours of eve and dawn. A golden air glowed in this place, and high between the pillars were thrones which faded, glow by glow, to the end of the vast hall. On them sat the Divine Kings. They were fire-crested. I saw the crest of the dragon on one, and there was another plumed with brilliant fires that jetted forth like feathers of flame. They sat shining and starlike, mute as statues, more colossal than Egyptian images of their gods, and at the end of the hall was a higher throne on which sat one greater than the rest. A light like the sun glowed behind him. Below on the floor of the hall lay a dark figure as if in trance, and two of the Divine Kings made motions with their hands about it over head and body. I saw where their hands waved how sparkles of fire like the flashing of jewels broke out. There rose out of that dark body a figure as tall, as glorious, as shining as those seated on the thrones. As he woke to the hall he became aware of his divine kin, and he lifted up his hands in greeting. He had returned from his pilgrimage through darkness, but now an initiate, a master in the heavenly guild. While he gazed on them the tall golden figures from their thrones leaped up, they too with hands uplifted in greeting, and they passed from me and faded swiftly in the great glory behind the throne.

THE MEMORY OF EARTH

We experience the romance and delight of voyaging upon uncharted seas when the imagination is released from the foolish notion that the images seen in reverie and dream are merely the images of memory refashioned; and in tracking to their originals the forms seen in vision we discover for them a varied ancestry, as that some come from the minds of others, and of some we cannot surmise another origin than that they are portions of the memory of Earth which is accessible to us. We soon grow to think our memory but a portion of that eternal memory and that we in our lives are gathering an innumerable experience for a mightier being than our own. The more vividly we see with the inner eye the more swiftly do we come to this conviction. Those who see vaguely are satisfied with vague explanations which those who see vividly at once reject as inadequate. How are we to explain what has happened to many, and oftentimes to myself, that when we sit amid ancient ruins or in old houses they renew their life for us? I waited for a friend inside a ruined chapel and while there a phantasm of its ancient uses came vividly before me. In front of the altar I saw a little crowd kneeling, most prominent a woman in a red robe, all pious and emotionally intent. A man stood behind these leaning by the wall as if too proud to kneel. An old man in ecclesiastical robes, abbot or bishop, stood, a crozier in one hand, while the other was uplifted in blessing or in emphasis of his words. Behind the cleric a boy carried a vessel, and the lad's face was vain with self-importance. I saw all this suddenly as if I was contemporary and was elder in the world by many centuries. I could surmise the emotional abandon of the red-robed lady, the proud indifference of the man who stood with his head but slightly bent, the vanity of the young boy as servitor in the ceremony, just as in a church to-day we feel the varied mood of those present. Anything may cause such pictures to rise in vivid illumination before us, a sentence in a book, a word, or contact with some object. I have brooded over the grassy mounds which are all that remain of the duns in which our Gaelic ancestors lived, and they builded themselves up again for me so that I looked on what seemed an earlier civilisation, saw the people, noted their dresses, the colours of natural wool, saffron or blue, how rough like our own home-spuns they were; even such details were visible as that the men cut meat at table with knives and passed it to the lips with their fingers. This is not, I am convinced, what people call imagination, an interior creation in response to a natural curiosity about past ages. It is an act of vision. a perception of images already existing breathed on some ethereal medium which in no way differs from the medium which holds for us our memories; and the reperception of an image in memory which is personal to us in no way differs as a psychical act from the perception of images in the memory of Earth. The same power of seeing is turned upon things of the same character and substance. It is not only rocks and ruins which infect us with such visions. A word in a book when one is sensitive may do this also. I sought in a classical dictionary for information about some myth. What else on the page my eye caught I could not say, but something there made two thousand years to vanish. I was looking at the garden of a house in some ancient city. From the house into the garden fluttered two girls, one in purple and the other in a green robe, and they, in a dance of excitement, ran to the garden wall and looked beyond it to the right. There a street rose high to a hill where there was a pillared building. I could see through blinding sunlight a crowd swaying down the street drawing nigh the house, and the two girls were as excited as girls might be to-day if king or queen were entering their city. This instant upris-ing of images following a glance at a page cannot be explained as the refashioning of the pictures of memory. The time which elapsed after the page was closed and the apparition in the brain was a quarter of a minute or less. One can only surmise that pictures so vividly coloured, so full of motion and sparkle as are moving pictures in the theatres were not an instantaneous creation by some magical artist within us, but were evoked out of a vaster memory than the personal, that the Grecian names my eye had caught had the power of symbols which evoke their affinities, and the picture of the excited girls and the shining procession was in some fashion, I know not how, connected with what I had read. We cannot pass by the uprising of these images with some vague phrase about suggestion or imagination and shirk further inquiry. If with the physical eye twenty-five years ago a man had seen a winged aeroplane amid the clouds it had roused him to a tumult of speculation and inquiry. But if the same picture had been seen in the mind it would speedily have been buried as mere fancy. There would have been no speculation, though what appears within us might well be deemed more important than what appears without us. Every tint, tone, shape, light or shade in an interior image must have intelligible cause as the wires, planes, engines and propellers of the aeroplane have. We must infer, when the image is clear and precise, an original of which this is the reflection. Whence or when were the originals of the pictures we see in dream or reverie? There must be originals; and, if we are forced to dismiss as unthinkable any process by which the pictures of our personal memory could unconsciously be reshaped into new pictures which appear in themselves authentic copies of originals, which move, have light, colour, form, shade such as nature would bestow, then we are led to believe that memory is an attribute of all living creatures and of Earth also, the greatest living creature we know, and that she carries with her, and it is accessible to us, all her long history, cities far gone behind time, empires which are dust, or are buried with sunken continents beneath the waters. The beauty for which men perished is still shining; Helen is there in her Troy, and Deirdre wears the beauty which blasted the Red Branch. No ancient lore has perished. Earth retains for herself and her children what her children might in passion have destroyed, and it is still in the realm of the Ever Living to be seen by the mystic adventurer. We argue that this memory must be universal, for there is nowhere we go where Earth does not breathe fragments from her ancient story to the meditative spirit. These memories gild the desert air where once the proud and golden races had been and had passed away, and they haunt the rocks and mountains where the Druids evoked their skiey and subterrene deities. The laws by which this history is made accessible to us seem to be the same as those which make our own learning swift to our service. When we begin thought or discussion on some subject we soon find ourselves thronged with memories ready for use. Everything in us related by affinity to the central thought seems to be mobilised; and in meditation those alien pictures we see, not the pictures of memory, but strange scenes, cities, beings and happenings, are, if we study them, all found to be in some relation to our mood. If our will is powerful enough and if by concentration and aspiration we have made the gloom in the brain to glow, we can evoke out of the memory of earth images of whatsoever we desire. These earth memories come to us in various ways. When we are passive, and the ethereal medium which is the keeper of such images, not broken up by thought, is like clear glass or calm water, then there is often a glowing of colour and form upon it, and there is what may be a reflection from some earth memory connected with the place we move in or it may be we have direct vision of that memory. Meditation again evokes images and pictures which are akin to its subject and our mood and serve in illustration of it. Once, when I was considering the play of arcane forces in the body, a book appeared before me, a coloured symbol on each page. I saw the book was magical, for while I looked on one of these the symbol vanished from the page, and the outline of a human body appeared, and then there came an interior revelation of that, and there was a shining of forces and a flashing of fires, rose, gold, azure and silver along the spinal column, and these flowed up into the brain where they struck upon a little ball that was like white sunfire for brilliancy, and they flashed out of that again in a pulsation as of wings on each side of the head; and then the page darkened, and the changing series closed with the Caduceus of Mercury and contained only a symbol once more.

Such pictures come without conscious effort of will, but are clearly evoked by it. Lastly, but more rarely with me, because the electric intensity of will required was hard to attain, I was able at times to evoke deliberately out of the memory of nature pictures of persons or things long past in time, but of which I desired knowledge. I regret now, while I was young and my energies yet uncoiled, that I did not practise this art of evocation more in regard to matters where knowledge might be regarded as of spiritual value; but I was like a child who discovers a whole set of fresh toys, and plays with one after the other, and I was interested in all that came to me, and was too often content to be the servant of my vision and not its master. It was an excitement of spirit for one born in a little country town in Ireland to find the circle of being widened so that life seemed to dilate into a paradise of beautiful memories, and to reach to past ages and to mix with the eternal consciousness of Earth, and when we come on what is new we pause to contemplate it, and do not hurry to the end of our journey. The instances of earth memories given here are trivial in themselves, and they are chosen, not because they are in any way wonderful, but rather because they are like things many people see, and so they may more readily follow my argument. The fact that Earth holds such memories is itself important, for once we discover this imperishable tablet, we are led to speculate whether in the future a training in seership might not lead to a revolution in human knowledge. It is a world where we may easily get lost, and spend hours in futile vision with no more gain than if one looked for long hours at the dust. For those to whom in their spiritual evolution these apparitions arise I would say: try to become the master of your vision, and seek for and evoke the greatest of earth memories, not those things which only satisfy curiosity, but those which uplift and inspire, and give us a vision of our own greatness; and the noblest of all Earth's memories is the august ritual of the ancient mysteries, where the mortal, amid scenes of unimaginable grandeur, was disrobed of his mortality and made of the company of the gods.[27]

William Butler Yeats

William Butler (W. B.) Yeats (1865–1939), a poet, a playwright, and the founder of the Abbey Theatre, was the driving force behind the Irish Literary Revival and a contributor to the nationalist cause of Irish independence.[28] His legacy as perhaps Ireland's greatest poet comes from the themes of nationalism in his plays and later in his poetry. But Yeats's early work was ground more firmly in its attention to nature. Like Æ, Yeats was drawn to the mystical realm; he became involved with the Hermetic Order of the Golden Dawn, a mystical order that believed that technology and urban living had separated humankind from this mystical realm. Yeats researched folk memory to discover tales and legends from Ireland's past that were otherwise long forgotten, tales that were drawn from the supernatural realm by the Irish peasantry. In his research, he includes his own opinions and commentary and alleges that the ancient pagan spirits and the Catholicism of modern Ireland live together in harmony. Consequently, his early poetry reflects these mystical beliefs. Impressed by the tales and myths of the Celtic past, Yeats devoted much of his early poetry to Irish mythology and wove many of these myths into his verse, including his epic poem *The Wanderings of Oisin*.[29] More importantly, however, Yeats also recognized the strong relationship that existed between the ancient Celts, the modern Irish peasantry, and the natural world—so while he devoted attention to forgotten Irish myths in some of his early work, most of his early poems draw their inspiration from Ireland's natural world. Collected here in this anthology are some of Yeats's lesser-known works, alongside some familiar ones, that posit their focus on Ireland's natural world.

Coole Park, 1929

I meditate upon a swallow's flight,
Upon an aged woman and her house,
A sycamore and lime-tree lost in night
Although that western cloud is luminous,
Great works constructed there in nature's spite
For scholars and for poets after us,
Thoughts long knitted into a single thought,
A dance-like glory that those walls begot.

There Hyde before he had beaten into prose
That noble blade the Muses buckled on,
There one that ruffled in a manly pose
For all his timid heart, there that slow man,
That meditative man, John Synge, and those
Impetuous men, Shawe-Taylor and Hugh Lane,
Found pride established in humility,
A scene well set and excellent company.

They came like swallows and like swallows went,
And yet a woman's powerful character
Could keep a swallow to its first intent;
And half a dozen in formation there,

That seemed to whirl upon a compass-point,
Found certainty upon the dreaming air,
The intellectual sweetness of those lines
That cut through time or cross it withershins.

Here, traveller, scholar, poet, take your stand
When all those rooms and passages are gone,
When nettles wave upon a shapeless mound
And saplings root among the broken stone,
And dedicate—eyes bent upon the ground,
Back turned upon the brightness of the sun
And all the sensuality of the shade—
A moment's memory to that laurelled head.[30]

Coole Park and Ballylee, 1931

Under my window-ledge the waters race,
Otters below and moor-hens on the top,
Run for a mile undimmed in Heaven's face
Then darkening through 'dark' Raftery's 'cellar' drop,
Run underground, rise in a rocky place
In Coole demesne, and there to finish up
Spread to a lake and drop into a hole.
What's water but the generated soul?

Upon the border of that lake's a wood
Now all dry sticks under a wintry sun,
And in a copse of beeches there I stood,
For Nature's pulled her tragic buskin on
And all the rant's a mirror of my mood:
At sudden thunder of the mounting swan
I turned about and looked where branches break
The glittering reaches of the flooded lake.

Another emblem there! That stormy white
But seems a concentration of the sky;
And, like the soul, it sails into the sight
And in the morning's gone, no man knows why;
And is so lovely that it sets to right
What knowledge or its lack had set awry,
So arrogantly pure, a child might think
It can be murdered with a spot of ink.

Sound of a stick upon the floor, a sound
From somebody that toils from chair to chair;
Beloved books that famous hands have bound,
Old marble heads, old pictures everywhere;
Great rooms where travelled men and children found

Content or joy; a last inheritor
Where none has reigned that lacked a name and fame
Or out of folly into folly came.

A spot whereon the founders lived and died
Seemed once more dear than life; ancestral trees,
Or gardens rich in memory glorified
Marriages, alliances and families,
And every bride's ambition satisfied.
Where fashion or mere fantasy decrees
We shift about—all that great glory spent—
Like some poor Arab tribesman and his tent.

We were the last romantics—chose for theme
Traditional sanctity and loveliness;
Whatever's written in what poets name
The book of the people; whatever most can bless
The mind of man or elevate a rhyme;
But all is changed, that high horse riderless,
Though mounted in that saddle Homer rode
Where the swan drifts upon a darkening flood.[31]

Who Goes with Fergus?

Who will go drive with Fergus now,
And pierce the deep wood's woven shade,
And dance upon the level shore?
Young man, lift up your russet brow,
And lift your tender eyelids, maid,
And brood on hopes and fear no more.

And no more turn aside and brood
Upon love's bitter mystery;
For Fergus rules the brazen cars,
And rules the shadows of the wood,
And the white breast of the dim sea
And all dishevelled wandering stars.[32]

Down by the Salley Gardens

Down by the salley gardens my love and I did meet;
She passed the salley gardens with little snow-white feet.
She bid me take love easy, as the leaves grow on the tree;
But I, being young and foolish, with her would not agree.

In a field by the river my love and I did stand,
And on my leaning shoulder she laid her snow-white hand.
She bid me take life easy, as the grass grows on the weirs;
But I was young and foolish, and now am full of tears.[33]

In the Seven Woods

I have heard the pigeons of the Seven Woods
Make their faint thunder, and the garden bees
Hum in the lime-tree flowers; and put away
The unavailing outcries and the old bitterness
That empty the heart. I have forgot awhile
Tara uprooted, and new commonness
Upon the throne and crying about the streets
And hanging its paper flowers from post to post,
Because it is alone of all things happy.
I am contented, for I know that Quiet
Wanders laughing and eating her wild heart
Among pigeons and bees, while that Great Archer,
Who but awaits His hour to shoot, still hangs
A cloudy quiver over Pairc-na-lee.[34]

The Shadowy Waters (Introductory Lines)

I walked among the seven woods of Coole:
Shan-walla, where a willow-bordered pond
Gathers the wild duck from the winter dawn;
Shady Kyle-dortha; sunnier Kyle-na-gno,
Where many hundred squirrels are as happy
As though they had been hidden by green boughs
Where old age cannot find them; Pairc-na-lea,
Where hazel and ash and privet blind the paths:
Dim Pairc-na-carraig, where the wild bees fling
Their sudden fragrances on the green air;
Dim Pairc-na-tarav, where enchanted eyes
Have seen immortal, mild, proud shadows walk;
Dim Inchy wood, that hides badger and fox
And marten-cat, and borders that old wood
Wise Biddy Early called the wicked wood:
Seven odours, seven murmurs, seven woods.
I had not eyes like those enchanted eyes,
Yet dreamed that beings happier than men
Moved round me in the shadows, and at night
My dreams were cloven by voices and by fires;
And the images I have woven in this story
Of Forgael and Dectora and the empty waters
Moved round me in the voices and the fires,
And more I may not write of, for they that cleave
The waters of sleep can make a chattering tongue
Heavy like stone, their wisdom being half silence.
How shall I name you, immortal, mild, proud shadows?
I only know that all we know comes from you,

And that you come from Eden on flying feet.
Is Eden far away, or do you hide
From human thought, as hares and mice and coneys
That run before the reaping-hook and lie
In the last ridge of the barley? Do our woods
And winds and ponds cover more quiet woods,
More shining winds, more star-glimmering ponds?
Is Eden out of time and out of space?
And do you gather about us when pale light
Shining on water and fallen among leaves,
And winds blowing from flowers, and whirr of feathers
And the green quiet, have uplifted the heart?

I have made this poem for you, that men may read it
Before they read of Forgael and Dectora,
As men in the old times, before the harps began,
Poured out wine for the high invisible ones.[35]

The Cat and the Moon

The cat went here and there
And the moon spun round like a top,
And the nearest kin of the moon,
The creeping cat, looked up.
Black Minnaloushe stared at the moon,
For, wander and wail as he would,
The pure cold light in the sky
Troubled his animal blood.
Minnaloushe runs in the grass
Lifting his delicate feet.
Do you dance, Minnaloushe, do you dance?
When two close kindred meet,
What better than call a dance?
Maybe the moon may learn,
Tired of that courtly fashion,
A new dance turn.
Minnaloushe creeps through the grass
From moonlit place to place,
The sacred moon overhead
Has taken a new phase.
Does Minnaloushe know that his pupils
Will pass from change to change,
And that from round to crescent,
From crescent to round they range?
Minnaloushe creeps through the grass
Alone, important and wise,
And lifts to the changing moon
His changing eyes.[36]

The Fairy Pedant

Scene: A circle of Druidic stones

FIRST FAIRY. Afar from our lawn and our levee,
O sister of sorrowful gaze!
Where the roses in scarlet are heavy
And dream of the end of their days,
You move in another dominion
And hang o'er the historied stone:
Unpruned in your beautiful pinion
Who wander and whisper alone.

ALL. Come away while the moon's in the woodland,
We'll dance and then feast in a dairy.
Though youngest of all in our good band,
You are wasting away, little fairy.

SECOND FAIRY. Ah! cruel ones, leave me alone now
While I murmur a little and ponder
The history here in the stone now;
Then away and away I will wander,
And measure the minds of the flowers,
And gaze on the meadow-mice wary,
And number their days and their hours—

ALL. You're wasting away, little fairy.

SECOND FAIRY. O shining ones, lightly with song pass,
Ah! leave me, I pray you and beg.
My mother drew forth from the long grass
A piece of a nightingale's egg,
And cradled me here where are sung,
Of birds even, longings for aery
Wild wisdoms of spirit and tongue.

ALL. You're wasting away, little fairy.

FIRST FAIRY [*turning away*]. Though the tenderest roses were round you,
The soul of this pitiless place
With pitiless magic has bound you—
Ah! woe for the loss of your face,
And the loss of your laugh with its lightness—
Ah! woe for your wings and your head—
Ah! woe for your eyes and their brightness—
Ah! woe for your slippers of red.

ALL. Come away while the moon's in the woodland,
We'll dance and then feast in a dairy.
Though youngest of all in our good band,
She's wasting away, little fairy.[37]

The Lake Isle of Innisfree

I will arise and go now, and go to Innisfree,
And a small cabin build there, of clay and wattles made:
Nine bean-rows will I have there, a hive for the honey-bee,
And live alone in the bee-loud glade.

And I shall have some peace there, for peace comes dropping slow,
Dropping from the veils of the morning to where the cricket sings;
There midnight's all a glimmer, and noon a purple glow,
And evening full of the linnet's wings.

I will arise and go now, for always night and day
I hear lake water lapping with low sounds by the shore;
While I stand on the roadway, or on the pavements grey,
I hear it in the deep heart's core.[38]

The Madness of King Goll

I sat on cushioned otter-skin:
My word was law from Ith to Emain,
And shook at Invar Amergin
The hearts of the world-troubling seamen,
And drove tumult and war away
From girl and boy and man and beast;
The fields grew fatter day by day,
The wild fowl of the air increased;
And every ancient Ollave said,
While he bent down his fading head.
'He drives away the Northern cold.'
They will not hush, the leaves a-flutter round me, the beech leaves old.

I sat and mused and drank sweet wine;
A herdsman came from inland valleys,
Crying, the pirates drove his swine
To fill their dark-beaked hollow galleys.
I called my battle-breaking men
And my loud brazen battle-cars
From rolling vale and rivery glen;
And under the blinking of the stars
Fell on the pirates by the deep,
And hurled them in the gulph of sleep:
These hands won many a torque of gold.
They will not hush, the leaves a-flutter round me, the beech leaves old.

But slowly, as I shouting slew
And trampled in the bubbling mire,
In my most secret spirit grew
A whirling and a wandering fire:

I stood: keen stars above me shone,
Around me shone keen eyes of men:
I laughed aloud and hurried on
By rocky shore and rushy fen;
I laughed because birds fluttered by,
And starlight gleamed, and clouds flew high,
And rushes waved and waters rolled.
They will not hush, the leaves a-flutter round me, the beech leaves old.

And now I wander in the woods
When summer gluts the golden bees,
Or in autumnal solitudes
Arise the leopard-coloured trees;
Or when along the wintry strands
The cormorants shiver on their rocks;
I wander on, and wave my hands,
And sing, and shake my heavy locks.
The grey wolf knows me; by one ear
I lead along the woodland deer;
The hares run by me growing bold.
They will not hush, the leaves a-flutter round me, the beech leaves old.

I came upon a little town
That slumbered in the harvest moon,
And passed a-tiptoe up and down,
Murmuring, to a fitful tune,
How I have followed, night and day,
A tramping of tremendous feet,
And saw where this old tympan lay
Deserted on a doorway seat,
And bore it to the woods with me;
Of some inhuman misery
Our married voices wildly trolled.
They will not hush, the leaves a-flutter round me, the beech leaves old.

I sang how, when day's toil is done,
Orchil shakes out her long dark hair
That hides away the dying sun
And sheds faint odours through the air:
When my hand passed from wire to wire
It quenched, with sound like falling dew
The whirling and the wandering fire;
But lift a mournful ulalu,
For the kind wires are torn and still,
And I must wander wood and hill
Through summer's heat and winter's cold.
They will not hush, the leaves a-flutter round me, the beech leaves old.[39]

The Song of Wandering Aengus

I went out to the hazel wood,
Because a fire was in my head,
And cut and peeled a hazel wand,
And hooked a berry to a thread;
And when white moths were on the wing,
And moth-like stars were flickering out,
I dropped the berry in a stream
And caught a little silver trout.

When I had laid it on the floor
I went to blow the fire aflame,
But something rustled on the floor,
And some one called me by my name:
It had become a glimmering girl
With apple blossom in her hair
Who called me by my name and ran
And faded through the brightening air.

Though I am old with wandering
Through hollow lands and hilly lands.
I will find out where she has gone,
And kiss her lips and take her hands;
And walk among long dappled grass,
And pluck till time and times are done
The silver apples of the moon,
The golden apples of the sun.[40]

The Stolen Child

Where dips the rocky highland
Of Sleuth Wood in the lake,
There lies a leafy island
Where flapping herons wake
The drowsy water rats;
There we've hid our faery vats,
Full of berries
And of reddest stolen cherries.
Come away, O human child!
To the waters and the wild
With a faery, hand in hand,
For the world's more full of weeping than you can understand.

Where the wave of moonlight glosses
The dim gray sands with light,
Far off by furthest Rosses
We foot it all the night,

Weaving olden dances
Mingling hands and mingling glances
Till the moon has taken flight;
To and fro we leap
And chase the frothy bubbles,
While the world is full of troubles
And anxious in its sleep.
Come away, O human child!
To the waters and the wild
With a faery, hand in hand,
For the world's more full of weeping than you can understand.

Where the wandering water gushes
From the hills above Glen-Car,
In pools among the rushes
That scarce could bathe a star,
We seek for slumbering trout
And whispering in their ears
Give them unquiet dreams;
Leaning softly out
From ferns that drop their tears
Over the young streams.
Come away, O human child!
To the waters and the wild
With a faery, hand in hand,
For the world's more full of weeping than you can understand.

Away with us he's going,
The solemn-eyed:
He'll hear no more the lowing
Of the calves on the warm hillside
Or the kettle on the hob
Sing peace into his breast,
Or see the brown mice bob
Round and round the oatmeal chest.
For he comes, the human child,
To the waters and the wild
With a faery, hand in hand,
For the world's more full of weeping than he can understand.[41]

The Two Trees

Beloved, gaze in thine own heart,
The holy tree is growing there;
From joy the holy branches start,
And all the trembling flowers they bear.
The changing colours of its fruit

Have dowered the stars with merry light;
The surety of its hidden root
Has planted quiet in the night;
The shaking of its leafy head
Has given the waves their melody,
And made my lips and music wed,
Murmuring a wizard song for thee.
There the Loves a circle go,
The flaming circle of our days,
Gyring, spiring to and fro
In those great ignorant leafy ways;
Remembering all that shaken hair
And how the winged sandals dart,
Thine eyes grow full of tender care:
Beloved, gaze in thine own heart.

Gaze no more in the bitter glass
The demons, with their subtle guile.
Lift up before us when they pass,
Or only gaze a little while;
For there a fatal image grows
That the stormy night receives,
Roots half hidden under snows,
Broken boughs and blackened leaves.
For all things turn to barrenness
In the dim glass the demons hold,
The glass of outer weariness,
Made when God slept in times of old.
There, through the broken branches, go
The ravens of unresting thought;
Flying, crying, to and fro,
Cruel claw and hungry throat,
Or else they stand and sniff the wind,
And shake their ragged wings; alas!
Thy tender eyes grow all unkind:
Gaze no more in the bitter glass.[42]

The White Birds

I would that we were, my beloved, white birds on the foam of the sea!
We tire of the flame of the meteor, before it can fade and flee;
And the flame of the blue star of twilight, hung low on the rim of the sky,
Has awaked in our hearts, my beloved, a sadness that may not die.

A weariness comes from those dreamers, dew-dabbled, the lily and rose;
Ah, dream not of them, my beloved, the flame of the meteor that goes,
Or the flame of the blue star that lingers hung low in the fall of the dew:
For I would we were changed to white birds on the wandering foam: I and you!

I am haunted by numberless islands, and many a Danaan shore,
Where Time would surely forget us, and Sorrow come near us no more;
Soon far from the rose and the lily and fret of the flames would we be,
Were we only white birds, my beloved, buoyed out on the foam of the sea![43]

The Wild Swans at Coole

The trees are in their autumn beauty,
The woodland paths are dry,
Under the October twilight the water
Mirrors a still sky;
Upon the brimming water among the stones
Are nine and fifty swans.

The nineteenth Autumn has come upon me
Since I first made my count;
I saw, before I had well finished,
All suddenly mount
And scatter wheeling in great broken rings
Upon their clamorous wings.

I have looked upon those brilliant creatures,
And now my heart is sore.
All's changed since I, hearing at twilight,
The first time on this shore,
The bell-beat of their wings above my head,
Trod with a lighter tread.

Unwearied still, lover by lover,
They paddle in the cold
Companionable streams or climb the air;
Their hearts have not grown old;
Passion or conquest, wander where they will,
Attend upon them still.

But now they drift on the still water,
Mysterious, beautiful;
Among what rushes will they build,
By what lake's edge or pool
Delight men's eyes, when I awake some day
To find they have flown away?[44]

Eva Gore-Booth

Eva Gore-Booth (1870–1926) was the author of nine books of poetry, seven plays, and several books of spiritual essays and Gospel studies. She was a major contributor to the Revival and a close friend of W. B. Yeats. Gore-Booth worked strenuously in the women's trade-union movement, sharing a lifelong commitment to feminism, socialism, and pacifism with the English suffragist Esther Roper. Gore-Booth was also a political activist and one of the first female suffragists to advocate extending the vote to both female property owners and women in the working class. While living in England, Gore-Booth published a number of pamphlets and essays that dealt with these political issues. She edited the *Women's Labour News* and published *Women Workers and Parliamentary Representation* (1904) and *Women's Right to Work* (1908). Gore-Booth's poetry, especially her early works, fit into the themes embodied by the Irish Literary Revival, especially with its attention to the natural world. Admired by W. B. Yeats, Gore-Booth's poems were anthologized by George Russell; one poem in particular, "The Little Waves of Breffny," attained wide popularity and is included in this volume.[45]

The Dreamer

All night I stumble through the fields of light,
And chase in dreams the starry rays divine
That shine through soft folds of the robe of night,
Hung like a curtain round a sacred shrine.

When daylight dawns I leave the meadows sweet
And come back to the dark house built of clay,
Over the threshold pass with lagging feet,
Open the shutters and let in the day.

The gray lit day heavy with griefs and cares,
And many a dull desire and foolish whim,
Leans o'er my shoulder as I spread my wares
On dusty counters and at windows dim.

She gazes at me with her sunken eyes,
That never yet have looked on moonlit flowers,
And amid glaring deeds and noisy cries
Counts out her golden tale of lagging hours.

Over the shrine of life no curtain falls,
All men may enter at the open gate,
The very rats find refuge in her walls—
Her tedious prison walls of love and hate.

Yet when the twilight vails that dim abode
I bar the door and make the shutters fast,
And hurry down the shadowy western road,
To seek in dreams my starlit home and vast.[46]

Re-Incarnation

The darkness draws me, kindly angels weep
Forlorn beyond receding rings of light,
The torrents of the earth's desires sweep
My soul through twilight downward into night.

Once more the light grows dim, the vision fades,
Myself seems to myself a distant goal,
I grope among the bodies' drowsy shades,
Once more the Old Illusion rocks my soul.

Once more the Manifold in shadowy streams
Of falling waters murmurs in my ears,
The One Voice drowns amid the roar of dreams
That crowd the narrow pathway of the years.

I go to seek the starshine on the waves,
To count the dewdrops on the grassy hill,
I go to gather flowers that grow on graves,
The world's wall closes round my prisoned will.

Yea, for the sake of the wild western wind
The sphered spirit scorns her flame-built throne,
Because of primroses, time out of mind,
The Lonely turns away from the Alone.

Who once has loved the cornfield's rustling sheaves,
Who once has heard the gentle Irish rain
Murmur low music in the growing leaves,
Though he were god, comes back to earth again.

Oh Earth! green wind-swept Eirinn, I would break
The tower of my soul's initiate pride
For a gray field and a star-haunted lake,
And those wet winds that roam the country side.

I who have seen am glad to close my eyes,
I who have soared am weary of my wings,
I seek no more the secret of the wise,
Safe among shadowy, unreal human things.

Blind to the gleam of those wild violet rays
That burn beyond the rainbow's circle dim,
Bound by dark nights and driven by pale days,
The sightless slave of Time's imperious whim;

Deaf to the flowing tide of dreams divine
That surge outside the closed gates of birth,
The rhythms of eternity, too fine
To touch with music the dull ears of earth—

I go to seek with humble care and toil
The dreams I left undreamed, the deeds undone,
To sow the seed and break the stubborn soil,
Knowing no brightness whiter than the sun.

Content in winter if the fire burns clear
And cottage walls keep out the creeping damp,
Hugging the Old Illusion warm and dear,
The Silence and the Wise Book and the Lamp.[47]

Secret Waters

Lo, in my soul there lies a hidden lake,
High in the mountains, fed by rain and snow,
The sudden thundering avalanche divine,
And the bright waters' everlasting flow,
Far from the highways' dusty glare and heat.
Dearer it is and holier, for Christ's sake,
Than his own windy lake in Palestine,
For there the little boats put out to sea
Without him, and no fisher hears his call,
Yea, on the desolate shores of Galilee
No man again shall see his shadow fall.
Yet here the very voice of the one Light
Haunts with sharp ecstasy each little wind
That stirs still waters on a moonlit night,
And sings through high trees growing in the mind,
And makes a gentle rustling in the wheat. . . .
Yea, in the white dawn on this happy shore,
With the lake water washing at his feet,
He stands alive and radiant evermore,
Whose presence makes the very East wind kind,
And turns to heaven the soul's green-lit retreat.[48]

The Little Waves of Breffny

The grand road from the mountain goes shining to the sea,
And there is traffic in it and many a horse and cart,
But the little roads of Cloonagh are dearer far to me,
And the little roads of Cloonagh go rambling through my heart.

A great storm from the ocean goes shouting o'er the hill,
And there is glory in it and terror on the wind,
But the haunted air of twilight is very strange and still,
And the little winds of twilight are dearer to my mind.

The great waves of the Atlantic sweep storming on their way,
Shining green and silver with the hidden herring shoal,
But the Little Waves of Breffny have drenched my heart in spray,
And the Little Waves of Breffny go stumbling through my soul.[49]

The Weaver

I was the child that passed long hours away
Chopping red beetroot in the hay-piled barn;
Now must I spend the wind-blown April day
Minding great looms and tying knots in yarn.

Once long ago I tramped through rain and slush
In brown waves breaking up the stubborn soil,
I wove and wove the twilight's purple hush
To fold about the furrowed heart of toil.

Strange fires and frosts burnt out the seasons' dross,
I watched slow Powers the woven cloth reveal,
While God stood counting out His gain and loss,
And Day and Night pushed on the heavy wheel.

Held close against the breast of living Powers
A little pulse, yet near the heart of strife,
I followed the slow plough for hours and hours
Minding through sun and shower the loom of life.

The big winds, harsh and clear and strong and salt,
Blew through my soul and all the world rang true,
In all things born I knew no stain or fault,
My heart was soft to every flower that grew.

The cabbages in my small garden patch
Were rooted in the earth's heart; wings unseen
Throbbed in the silence under the dark thatch,
And brave birds sang long ere the boughs were green.[50]

John Millington Synge

John Millington (J. M.) Synge (1871–1909) was another key contributor to the Irish Literary Revival. After traveling throughout Europe and playing violin for peasants in the Black Forest of Italy and Germany in the hope of becoming a musician, Synge gave up the music life and settled down to become a writer in Paris. There he met Yeats, who was advised to visit the "poor Irish writer staying at the top of the house." Synge was struggling as a writer at the time and needed inspiration, so Yeats reportedly told him, "Go to the Aran Islands and find a life that has never been expressed in literature."[51] Synge took Yeats's advice and visited the Aran Islands for several weeks each year from 1898 to 1902. Living among the villagers of Inishmaan, Synge was able to observe a place where man and nature interacted to create a simple life for the inhabitants and live in an isolated place removed for the more political concerns of the mainland. Through his writing, Synge would be able to explore a way of life totally unique, a way of life that interacted more closely with nature than any place in Ireland. His observations of the struggle between the inhabitants of the Aran Islands and the unforgiving forces of the Atlantic Ocean inspired him to write his famous one-act play *Riders to the Sea*.[52]

In Kerry

We heard the thrushes by the shore and sea,
And saw the golden stars' nativity,
Then round we went the lane by Thomas Flynn,
Across the church where bones lie out and in;
And there I asked beneath a lonely cloud
Of strange delight, with one bird singing loud,
What change you'd wrought in graveyard, rock and sea,
This new wild paradise to wake for me. . . .
Yet knew no more than knew those merry sins
Had built this stack of thigh-bones, jaws and shins.[53]

To the Oaks of Glencree

My arms are round you, and I lean
Against you, while the lark
Sings over us, and golden lights, and green
Shadows are on your bark.

There'll come a season when you'll stretch
Black boards to cover me:
Then in Mount Jerome I will lie, poor wretch,
With worms eternally.[54]

Prelude

Still south I went and west and south again,
Through Wicklow from the morning till the night,
And far from cities, and the sights of men,
Lived with the sunshine, and the moon's delight.

I knew the stars, the flowers, and the birds,
The grey and wintry sides of many glens,
And did but half remember human words,
In converse with the mountains, moors, and fens.[55]

In Glencullen

Thrush, linnet, stare and wren,
Brown lark beside the sun,
Take thought of kestril, sparrow-hawk,
Birdlime and roving gun.

You great-great-grand-children
Of birds I've listened to,
I think I robbed your ancestors
When I was young as you.[56]

On an Island

You've plucked a curlew, drawn a hen,
Washed the shirts of seven men,
You've stuffed my pillow, stretched my sheet,
And filled the pan to wash your feet,
You've cooped the pullets, wound the clock,
And rinsed the young men's drinking crock;
And now we'll dance to jigs and reels,
Nailed boots chasing girls' naked heels,
Until your father'll start to snore,
And Jude, now you're married, will stretch on the floor.[57]

From The Aran Islands

Late this evening I saw a three-oared curagh with two old women in her besides the rowers, landing at the slip through a heavy roll. They were coming from Inishere, and they rowed up quickly enough till they were within a few yards of the surf-line, where they spun round and waited with the prow towards the sea, while wave after wave passed underneath them and broke on the remains of the slip. Five minutes passed; ten minutes; and still they waited with the oars just paddling in the water, and their heads turned over their shoulders.

I was beginning to think that they would have to give up and row round to the lee side of the island, when the curagh seemed suddenly to turn into a living thing. The prow was again towards the slip, leaping and hurling itself through the spray. Before it touched, the man in the bow wheeled round, two white legs came out over the prow like the flash of a sword, and before the next wave arrived he had dragged the curagh out of danger.

This sudden and united action in men without discipline shows well the education that the waves have given them. When the curagh was in safety the two old women were carried up through the surf and slippery seaweed on the backs of their sons.

In this broken weather a curagh cannot go out without danger, yet accidents are rare and seem to be nearly always caused by drink. Since I was here last year four men have been drowned on their way home from the large island. First a curagh belonging to the south island which put off with two men in her heavy with drink, came to shore here the next evening dry and uninjured, with the sail half set, and no one in her.

More recently a curagh from this island with three men, who were the worse for drink, was upset on its way home. The steamer was not far off, and saved two of the men, but could not reach the third.

Now a man has been washed ashore in Donegal with one pampooty on him, and a striped shirt with a purse in one of the pockets, and a box for tobacco.

For three days the people have been trying to fix his identity. Some think it is the man from this island, others think that the man from the south answers the description more exactly. To-night as we were returning from the slip we met the mother of the man who was drowned from this island, still weeping and looking out over the sea. She stopped the people who had come over from the south island to ask them with a terrified whisper what is thought over there.

Later in the evening, when I was sitting in one of the cottages, the sister of the dead man came in through the rain with her infant, and there was a long talk about the rumours that had come in. She pieced together all she could remember about his clothes, and what his purse was like, and where he had got it, and the same for his tobacco box, and his stockings. In the end there seemed little doubt that it was her brother.

"Ah!" she said, "It's Mike sure enough, and please God they'll give him a decent burial."

Then she began to keen slowly to herself. She had loose yellow hair plastered round her head with the rain, and as she sat by the door sucking her infant, she seemed like a type of the women's life upon the islands.

For a while the people sat silent, and one could hear nothing but the lips of the infant, the rain hissing in the yard, and the breathing of four pigs that lay sleeping in one corner. Then one of the men began to talk about the new boats that have been sent to the south island, and the conversation went back to its usual round of topics.

The loss of one man seems a slight catastrophe to all except the immediate relatives. Often when an accident happens a father is lost with his two eldest sons, or in some other way all the active men of a household die together.

A few years ago three men of a family that used to make the wooden vessels—like tiny barrels—that are still used among the people, went to the big island together.

They were drowned on their way home, and the art of making these little barrels died with them, at least on Inishmaan, though it still lingers in the north and south islands.

Another catastrophe that took place last winter gave a curious zest to the observance of holy days. It seems that it is not the custom for the men to go out fishing on the evening of a holy day, but one night last December some men, who wished to begin fishing early the next morning, rowed out to sleep in their hookers.

Towards morning a terrible storm rose, and several hookers with their crews on board were blown from their moorings and wrecked. The sea was so high that no attempt at rescue could be made, and the men were drowned.

"Ah!" said the man who told me the story, "I'm thinking it will be a long time before men will go out again on a holy day. That storm was the only storm that reached into the harbour the whole winter, and I'm thinking there was something in it."

Today when I went down to the slip I found a pig-jobber from Kilronan with about twenty pigs that were to be shipped for the English market.

When the steamer was getting near, the whole drove was moved down on the slip and the curaghs were carried out close to the sea. Then each beast was caught in its turn and thrown on its side, while its legs were hitched together in a single knot, with a tag of rope remaining, by which it could be carried.

Probably the pain inflicted was not great, yet the animals shut their eyes and shrieked with almost human intonations, till the suggestion of the noise became so intense that the men and women who were merely looking on grew wild with excitement, and the pigs waiting their turn foamed at the mouth and tore each other with their teeth.

After a while there was a pause. The whole slip was covered with a mass of sobbing animals, with here and there a terrified woman crouching among the bodies, and patting some special favourite to keep it quiet while the curaghs were being launched.

Then the screaming began again while the pigs were carried out and laid in their places, with a waistcoat tied round their feet to keep them from damaging the canvas. They seemed to know where they were going, and looked up at me over the gunnel with an ignoble desperation that made me shudder to think that I had eaten of this whimpering flesh. When the last curagh went out I was left on the slip with a band of women and children, and one old boar who sat looking out over the sea.

The women were over-excited, and when I tried to talk to them they crowded round me and began jeering and shrieking at me because I am not married. A dozen screamed at a time, and so rapidly that I could not understand all that they were saying, yet I was able to make out that they were taking advantage of the absence of their husbands to give me the full volume of their contempt. Some little boys who were listening threw themselves down, writhing with laughter among the seaweed, and the young girls grew red with embarrassment and stared down into the surf.

For a moment I was in confusion. I tried to speak to them, but I could not make myself heard, so I sat down on the slip and drew out my wallet of photographs. In an instant I had the whole band clambering round me, in their ordinary mood.

When the curaghs came back—one of them towing a large kitchen table that stood itself up on the waves and then turned somersaults in an extraordinary manner—word went round that the ceannuighe (pedlar) was arriving.

He opened his wares on the slip as soon as he landed, and sold a quantity of cheap knives and jewellery to the girls and the younger women. He spoke no Irish, and the bargaining gave immense amusement to the crowd that collected round him.

I was surprised to notice that several women who professed to know no English could make themselves understood without difficulty when it pleased them.

"The rings is too dear at you, sir," said one girl using the Gaelic construction; "let you put less money on them and all the girls will be buying."

After the jewellery he displayed some cheap religious pictures—abominable oleographs—but I did not see many buyers.

I am told that most of the pedlars who come here are Germans or Poles, but I did not have occasion to speak with this man by himself.

I have come over for a few days to the south island, and, as usual, my voyage was not favourable.

The morning was fine, and seemed to promise one of the peculiarly hushed, pellucid days that occur sometimes before rain in early winter. From the first gleam of dawn the sky was covered with white cloud, and the tranquillity was so complete that every sound seemed to float away by itself across the silence of the bay. Lines of blue smoke were going up in spirals over the village, and further off heavy fragments of rain-cloud were lying on the horizon. We started early in the day, and, although the sea looked calm from a distance, we met a considerable roll coming from the south-west when we got out from the shore.

Near the middle of the sound the man who was rowing in the bow broke his oar-pin, and the proper management of the canoe became a matter of some difficulty. We had only a three-oared curagh, and if the sea had gone much higher we should have run a good deal of danger. Our progress was so slow that clouds came up with a rise in the wind before we reached the shore, and rain began to fall in large single drops. The black curagh working slowly through this world of grey, and the soft hissing of the rain gave me one of the moods in which we realise with immense distress the short moment we have left us to experience all the wonder and beauty of the world.

The approach to the south island is made at a fine sandy beach on the north-west. This interval in the rocks is of great service to the people, but the tract of wet sand with a few hideous fishermen's houses, lately built on it, looks singularly desolate in broken weather.

The tide was going out when we landed, so we merely stranded the curagh and went up to the little hotel. The cess-collector was at work in one of the rooms, and there were a number of men and boys waiting about, who stared at us while we stood at the door and talked to the proprietor.

When we had had our drink I went down to the sea with my men, who were in a hurry to be off. Some time was spent in replacing the oar-pin, and then they set out, though the wind was still increasing. A good many fishermen came down to see the start, and long after the curagh was out of sight I stood and talked with them in Irish, as I was anxious to compare their language and temperament with what I knew of the other island.

The language seems to be identical, though some of these men speak rather more distinctly than any Irish speakers I have yet heard. In physical type, dress, and general character, however, there seems to be a considerable difference. The people on this island are more advanced than their neighbours, and the families here are gradually forming into different ranks, made up of the well-to-do, the struggling, and the quite poor and thriftless. These distinctions are present in the middle island also, but over there they have had no effect on the people, among whom there is still absolute equality.

A little later the steamer came in sight and lay to in the offing. While the curaghs were being put out I noticed in the crowd several men of the ragged, humorous type that was once thought to represent the real peasant of Ireland. Rain was now falling heavily, and as we looked out through the fog there was something nearly appalling in the shrieks of laughter kept up by one of these individuals, a man of extraordinary ugliness and wit.

At last he moved off toward the houses, wiping his eyes with the tail of his coat and moaning to himself "Tá mé marbh," ("I'm killed"), till some one stopped him and he began again pouring out a medley of rude puns and jokes that meant more than they said.

There is quaint humour, and sometimes wild humour, on the middle island, but never this half-sensual ecstasy of laughter. Perhaps a man must have a sense of intimate misery, not known there, before he can set himself to jeer and mock at the world. These strange men with receding foreheads, high cheekbones, and ungovernable eyes seem to represent some old type found on these few acres at the extreme border of Europe, where it is only in wild jests and laughter that they can express their loneliness and desolation.

The mode of reciting ballads in this island is singularly harsh. I fell in with a curious man to-day beyond the east village, and we wandered out on the rocks towards the sea. A wintry shower came on while we were together, and we crouched down in the bracken, under a loose wall. When we had gone through the usual topics he asked me if I was fond of songs, and began singing to show what he could do.

The music was much like what I have heard before on the islands—a monotonous chant with pauses on the high and low notes to mark the rhythm; but the harsh nasal tone in which he sang was almost intolerable. His performance reminded me in general effect of a chant I once heard from a party of Orientals I was travelling with in a third-class carriage from Paris to Dieppe, but the islander ran his voice over a much wider range.

His pronunciation was lost in the rasping of his throat, and, though he shrieked into my ear to make sure that I understood him above the howling of the wind, I could only make out that it was an endless ballad telling the fortune of a young man who went to sea, and had many adventures. The English nautical terms were employed continually in describing his life on the ship, but the man seemed to feel that they were not in their place, and stopped short when one of them occurred to give me a poke with his finger and explain gib, topsail, and bowsprit, which were for me the most intelligible features of the poem. Again, when the scene changed to Dublin, "glass of whiskey," "public-house," and such things were in English.

When the shower was over he showed me a curious cave hidden among the cliffs, a short distance from the sea. On our way back he asked me the three questions I am met with on every side—whether I am a rich man, whether I am married, and whether I have ever seen a poorer place than these islands.

When he heard that I was not married he urged me to come back in the summer so that he might take me over in a curagh to the Spa in County Glare, where there is "spree mor agus go leor ladies" ("a big spree and plenty of ladies").

Something about the man repelled me while I was with him, and though I was cordial and liberal he seemed to feel that I abhorred him. We arranged to meet again in the evening, but when I dragged myself with an inexplicable loathing to the place of meeting, there was no trace of him.

It is characteristic that this man, who is probably a drunkard and shebeener and certainly in penury, refused the chance of a shilling because he felt that I did not like him. He had a curiously mixed expression of hardness and melancholy. Probably his character has given him a bad reputation on the island, and he lives here with the restlessness of a man who has no sympathy with his companions.

I have come over again to Inishmaan, and this time I had fine weather for my passage. The air was full of luminous sunshine from the early morning, and it was almost a summer's day when I set sail at noon with Michael and two other men who had come over for me in a curagh.

The wind was in our favour, so the sail was put up and Michael sat in the stem to steer with an oar while I rowed with the others.

We had had a good dinner and drink and were wrought up by this sudden revival of summer to a dreamy voluptuous gaiety, that made us shout with exultation to hear our voices passing out across the blue twinkling of the sea.

Even after the people of the south island, these men of Inishmaan seemed to be moved by strange archaic sympathies with the world. Their mood accorded itself with wonderful fineness to the suggestions of the day, and their ancient Gaelic seemed so full of divine simplicity that I would have liked to turn the prow to the west and row with them for ever.[58]

Riders to the Sea

SCENE. *An Island off the West of Ireland.*

(*Cottage kitchen, with nets, oil-skins, spinning wheel, some new boards standing by the wall, etc. Cathleen, a girl of about twenty, finishes kneading cake, and puts it down in the pot-oven by the fire; then wipes her hands, and begins to spin at the wheel. Nora, a young girl, puts her head in at the door.*)

NORA (*in a low voice*). Where is she?

CATHLEEN. She's lying down, God help her, and may be sleeping, if she's able.

[*Nora comes in softly, and takes a bundle from under her shawl.*]

CATHLEEN (*spinning the wheel rapidly*). What is it you have?

NORA. The young priest is after bringing them. It's a shirt and a plain stocking were got off a drowned man in Donegal.

[*Cathleen stops her wheel with a sudden movement, and leans out to listen.*]

NORA. We're to find out if it's Michael's they are, some time herself will be down looking by the sea.

CATHLEEN. How would they be Michael's, Nora. How would he go the length of that way to the far north?

NORA. The young priest says he's known the like of it. "If it's Michael's they are," says he, "you can tell herself he's got a clean burial by the grace of God, and if they're not his, let no one say a word about them, for she'll be getting her death," says he, "with crying and lamenting."

[*The door which Nora half closed is blown open by a gust of wind.*]

CATHLEEN (*looking out anxiously*). Did you ask him would he stop Bartley going this day with the horses to the Galway fair?

NORA. "I won't stop him," says he, "but let you not be afraid. Herself does be saying prayers half through the night, and the Almighty God won't leave her destitute," says he, "with no son living."

CATHLEEN. Is the sea bad by the white rocks, Nora?

NORA. Middling bad, God help us. There's a great roaring in the west, and it's worse it'll be getting when the tide's turned to the wind.

[*She goes over to the table with the bundle.*]

Shall I open it now?

CATHLEEN. Maybe she'd wake up on us, and come in before we'd done. (*Coming to the table.*) It's a long time we'll be, and the two of us crying.

NORA (*goes to the inner door and listens*). She's moving about on the bed. She'll be coming in a minute.

CATHLEEN. Give me the ladder, and I'll put them up in the turf-loft, the way she won't know of them at all, and maybe when the tide turns she'll be going down to see would he be floating from the east.

[*They put the ladder against the gable of the chimney; Cathleen goes up a few steps and hides the bundle in the turf-loft. Maurya comes from the inner room.*]

MAURYA (*looking up at Cathleen and speaking querulously*). Isn't it turf enough you have for this day and evening?

CATHLEEN. There's a cake baking at the fire for a short space (*throwing down the turf*) and Bartley will want it when the tide turns if he goes to Connemara.

[*Nora picks up the turf and puts it round the pot-oven.*]

MAURYA (*sitting down on a stool at the fire*). He won't go this day with the wind rising from the south and west. He won't go this day, for the young priest will stop him surely.

NORA. He'll not stop him, mother, and I heard Eamon Simon and Stephen Pheety and Colum Shawn saying he would go.

MAURYA. Where is he itself?

NORA. He went down to see would there be another boat sailing in the week, and I'm thinking it won't be long till he's here now, for the tide's turning at the green head, and the hooker's tacking from the east.

CATHLEEN. I hear some one passing the big stones.

NORA (*Looking out*). He's coming now, and he in a hurry.

BARTLEY (*comes in and looks round the room. Speaking sadly and quietly*). Where is the bit of new rope, Cathleen, was bought in Connemara?

CATHLEEN (*coming down*). Give it to him, Nora; it's on a nail by the white boards. I hung it up this morning, for the pig with the black feet was eating it.

NORA (*giving him a rope*). Is that it, Bartley?

MAURYA. You'd do right to leave that rope, Bartley, hanging by the boards. (*Bartley takes the rope.*) It will be wanting in this place, I'm telling you, if Michael is washed up to-morrow morning, or the next morning, or any morning in the week, for it's a deep grave we'll make him by the grace of God.

BARTLEY (*beginning to work with the rope*). I've no halter the way I can ride down on the mare, and I must go now quickly. This is the one boat going for two weeks or beyond it, and the fair will be a good fair for horses I heard them saying below.

MAURYA. It's a hard thing they'll be saying below if the body is washed up and there's no man in it to make the coffin, and I after giving a big price for the finest white boards you'd find in Connemara.

[*She looks round at the boards.*]

BARTLEY. How would it be washed up, and we after looking each day for nine days, and a strong wind blowing a while back from the west and south?

MAURYA. If it wasn't found itself, that wind is raising the sea, and there was a star up against the moon, and it rising in the night. If it was a hundred horses, or a thousand horses you had itself, what is the price of a thousand horses against a son where there is one son only?

BARTLEY (*working at the halter, to Cathleen*). Let you go down each day, and see the sheep aren't jumping in on the rye, and if the jobber comes you can sell the pig with the black feet if there is a good price going.

MAURYA. How would the like of her get a good price for a pig?

BARTLEY (*to Cathleen*). If the west wind holds with the last bit of the moon let you and Nora get up weed enough for another cock for the kelp. It's hard set we'll be from this day with no one in it but one man to work.

MAURYA. It's hard set we'll be surely the day you're drownd'd with the rest. What way will I live and the girls with me, and I an old woman looking for the grave?

[*Bartley lays down the halter, takes off his old coat, and puts on a newer one of the same flannel.*]

BARTLEY (*to Nora*). Is she coming to the pier?

NORA (*looking out*). She's passing the green head and letting fall her sails.

BARTLEY (*getting his purse and tobacco*). I'll have half an hour to go down, and you'll see me coming again in two days, or in three days, or maybe in four days if the wind is bad.

MAURYA (*turning round to the fire, and putting her shawl over her head*). Isn't it a hard and cruel man won't hear a word from an old woman, and she holding him from the sea?

CATHLEEN. It's the life of a young man to be going on the sea, and who would listen to an old woman with one thing and she saying it over?

BARTLEY (*taking the halter*). I must go now quickly. I'll ride down on the red mare, and the gray pony 'll run behind me. . . . The blessing of God on you.

[*He goes out.*]

MAURYA (*crying out as he is in the door*). He's gone now, God spare us, and we'll not see him again. He's gone now, and when the black night is falling I'll have no son left me in the world.

CATHLEEN. Why wouldn't you give him your blessing and he looking round in the door? Isn't it sorrow enough is on every one in this house without your sending him out with an unlucky word behind him, and a hard word in his ear?

[*Maurya takes up the tongs and begins raking the fire aimlessly without looking round.*]

NORA (*turning towards her*). You're taking away the turf from the cake.

CATHLEEN (*crying out*). The Son of God forgive us, Nora, we're after forgetting his bit of bread.

[*She comes over to the fire.*]

NORA. And it's destroyed he'll be going till dark night, and he after eating nothing since the sun went up.

CATHLEEN (*turning the cake out of the oven*). It's destroyed he'll be, surely. There's no sense left on any person in a house where an old woman will be talking for ever.

[*Maurya sways herself on her stool.*]

CATHLEEN (*cutting off some of the bread and rolling it in a cloth; to Maurya*). Let you go down now to the spring well and give him this and he passing. You'll see him then and the dark word will be broken, and you can say "God speed you," the way he'll be easy in his mind.

MAURYA (*taking the bread*). Will I be in it as soon as himself?

CATHLEEN. If you go now quickly.

MAURYA (*standing up unsteadily*). It's hard set I am to walk.

CATHLEEN (*looking at her anxiously*). Give her the stick, Nora, or maybe she'll slip on the big stones.

NORA. What stick?

CATHLEEN. The stick Michael brought from Connemara.

MAURYA (*taking a stick Nora gives her*). In the big world the old people do be leaving things after them for their sons and children, but in this place it is the young men do be leaving things behind for them that do be old.

[*She goes out slowly. Nora goes over to the ladder.*]

CATHLEEN. Wait, Nora, maybe she'd turn back quickly. She's that sorry, God help her, you wouldn't know the thing she'd do.

NORA. Is she gone round by the bush?

CATHLEEN (*looking out*). She's gone now. Throw it down quickly, for the Lord knows when she'll be out of it again.

NORA (*getting the bundle from the loft*). The young priest said he'd be passing to-morrow, and we might go down and speak to him below if it's Michael's they are surely.

CATHLEEN (*taking the bundle*). Did he say what way they were found?

NORA (*coming down*). "There were two men," says he, "and they rowing round with poteen before the cocks crowed, and the oar of one of them caught the body, and they passing the black cliffs of the north."

CATHLEEN (*trying to open the bundle*). Give me a knife, Nora, the string's perished with the salt water, and there's a black knot on it you wouldn't loosen in a week.

NORA (*giving her a knife*). I've heard tell it was a long way to Donegal.

CATHLEEN (*cutting the string*). It is surely. There was a man in here a while ago—the man sold us that knife—and he said if you set off walking from the rocks beyond, it would be seven days you'd be in Donegal.

NORA. And what time would a man take, and he floating?

[*Cathleen opens the bundle and takes out a bit of a stocking. They look at them eagerly.*]

CATHLEEN (*in a low voice*). The Lord spare us, Nora! isn't it a queer hard thing to say if it's his they are surely?

NORA. I'll get his shirt off the hook the way we can put the one flannel on the other. (*She looks through some clothes hanging in the corner.*) It's not with them, Cathleen, and where will it be?

CATHLEEN. I'm thinking Bartley put it on him in the morning, for his own shirt was heavy with the salt in it (*pointing to the corner*). There's a bit of a sleeve was of the same stuff. Give me that and it will do.

[*Nora brings it to her and they compare the flannel.*]

CATHLEEN. It's the same stuff, Nora; but if it is itself aren't there great rolls of it in the shops of Galway, and isn't it many another man may have a shirt of it as well as Michael himself?

NORA (*who has taken up the stocking and counted the stitches, crying out*). It's Michael, Cathleen, it's Michael; God spare his soul, and what will herself say when she hears this story, and Bartley on the sea?

CATHLEEN (*taking the stocking*). It's a plain stocking.

NORA. It's the second one of the third pair I knitted, and I put up three score stitches, and I dropped four of them.

CATHLEEN (*counts the stitches*). It's that number is in it (*crying out*). Ah, Nora, isn't it a bitter thing to think of him floating that way to the far north, and no one to keen him but the black hags that do be flying on the sea?

NORA (*swinging herself round, and throwing out her arms on the clothes*). And isn't it a pitiful thing when is nothing left of a man who was a great rower and fisher, but a bit of an old shirt and a plain stocking?

CATHLEEN (*after an instant*). Tell me is herself coming, Nora? I hear a little sound on the path.

NORA (*looking out*). She is, Cathleen. She's coming up to the door.

CATHLEEN. Put these things away before she'll come in. Maybe it's easier she'll be after giving her blessing to Bartley, and we won't let on we've heard anything the time he's on the sea.

NORA (*helping Cathleen to close the bundle*). We'll put them here in the corner.

[*They put them into a hole in the chimney corner. Cathleen goes back to the spinning-wheel.*]

NORA. Will she see it was crying I was?

CATHLEEN. Keep your back to the door the way the light'll not be on you.

[*Nora sits down at the chimney corner, with her back to the door. Maurya comes in very slowly, without looking at the girls, and goes over to her stool at the other side of the fire. The cloth with the bread is still in her hand. The girls look at each other, and Nora points to the bundle of bread.*]

CATHLEEN (*after spinning for a moment*). You didn't give him his bit of bread?

[*Maurya begins to keen softly, without turning round.*]

CATHLEEN. Did you see him riding down?

[*Maurya goes on keening.*]

CATHLEEN (*a little impatiently*). God forgive you; isn't it a better thing to raise your voice and tell what you seen, than to be making lamentation for a thing that's done? Did you see Bartley, I'm saying to you.

MAURYA (*with a weak voice*). My heart's broken from this day.

CATHLEEN (*as before*). Did you see Bartley?

MAURYA. I seen the fearfulest thing.

CATHLEEN (*leaves her wheel and looks out*). God forgive you; he's riding the mare now over the green head, and the gray pony behind him.

MAURYA (*starts, so that her shawl falls back from her head and shows her white tossed hair. With a frightened voice*). The gray pony behind him.

CATHLEEN (*coming to the fire*). What is it ails you, at all?

MAURYA (*speaking very slowly*). I've seen the fearfulest thing any person has seen, since the day Bride Dara seen the dead man with the child in his arms.

CATHLEEN AND NORA. Uah.

[*They crouch down in front of the old woman at the fire.*]

NORA. Tell us what it is you seen.

MAURYA. I went down to the spring well, and I stood there saying a prayer to myself. Then Bartley came along, and he riding on the red mare with the gray pony behind him. (*She puts up her hands, as if to hide something from her eyes.*) The Son of God spare us, Nora!

CATHLEEN. What is it you seen.

MAURYA. I seen Michael himself.

CATHLEEN (*speaking softly*). You did not, mother; It wasn't Michael you seen, for his body is after being found in the far north, and he's got a clean burial by the grace of God.

MAURYA (*a little defiantly*). I'm after seeing him this day, and he riding and galloping. Bartley came first on the red mare; and I tried to say "God speed you," but something choked the words in my throat. He went by quickly; and "the blessing of God on you," says he, and I could say nothing. I looked up then, and I crying, at the gray pony, and there was Michael upon it—with fine clothes on him, and new shoes on his feet.

CATHLEEN (*begins to keen*). It's destroyed we are from this day. It's destroyed, surely.

NORA. Didn't the young priest say the Almighty God wouldn't leave her destitute with no son living?

MAURYA (*in a low voice, but clearly*). It's little the like of him knows of the sea. . . . Bartley will be lost now, and let you call in Eamon and make me a good coffin out of the white boards, for I won't live after them. I've had a husband, and a husband's father, and six sons in this house—six fine men, though it was a hard birth I had with every one of them and they coming to the world—and some of them were found and some of them were not found, but they're gone now the lot of them. . . . There were Stephen, and Shawn, were lost in the great wind, and found after in the Bay of Gregory of the Golden Mouth, and carried up the two of them on the one plank, and in by that door.

[*She pauses for a moment, the girls start as if they heard something through the door that is half open behind them.*]

NORA (*in a whisper*). Did you hear that, Cathleen? Did you hear a noise in the north-east?

CATHLEEN (*in a whisper*). There's some one after crying out by the seashore.

MAURYA (*continues without hearing anything*). There was Sheamus and his father, and his own father again, were lost in a dark night, and not a stick or sign was seen of them when the sun went up. There was Patch after was drowned out of a curagh that turned over. I was sitting here with Bartley, and he a baby, lying on my two knees, and I seen two women, and three women, and four women coming in, and they crossing themselves, and not saying a word. I looked out then, and there were men coming after them, and they holding a thing in the half of a red sail, and water dripping out of it—it was a dry day, Nora—and leaving a track to the door.

[*She pauses again with her hand stretched out towards the door. It opens softly and old women begin to come in, crossing themselves on the threshold, and kneeling down in front of the stage with red petticoats over their heads.*]

MAURYA (*half in a dream, to Cathleen*). Is it Patch, or Michael, or what is it at all?

CATHLEEN. Michael is after being found in the far north, and when he is found there how could he be here in this place?

MAURYA. There does be a power of young men floating round in the sea, and what way would they know if it was Michael they had, or another man like him, for when a man is nine days in the sea, and the wind blowing, it's hard set his own mother would be to say what man was it.

CATHLEEN. It's Michael, God spare him, for they're after sending us a bit of his clothes from the far north.

[*She reaches out and hands Maurya the clothes that belonged to Michael. Maurya stands up slowly and takes them in her hands. Nora looks out.*]

NORA. They're carrying a thing among them and there's water dripping out of it and leaving a track by the big stones.

CATHLEEN (*in a whisper to the women who have come in*). Is it Bartley it is?

ONE OF THE WOMEN. It is surely, God rest his soul.

[*Two younger women come in and pull out the table. Then men carry in the body of Bartley, laid on a plank, with a bit of a sail over it, and lay it on the table.*]

CATHLEEN (*to the women, as they are doing so*). What way was he drowned?

ONE OF THE WOMEN. The gray pony knocked him into the sea, and he was washed out where there is a great surf on the white rocks.

[*Maurya has gone over and knelt down at the head of the table. The women are keening softly and swaying themselves with a slow movement. Cathleen and Nora kneel at the other end of the table. The men kneel near the door.*]

MAURYA (*raising her head and speaking as if she did not see the people around her*). They're all gone now, and there isn't anything more the sea can do to me. . . . I'll have no call now to be up crying and praying when the wind breaks from the south, and you can hear the surf is in the east, and the surf is in the west, making a great stir with the two noises, and they hitting one on the other. I'll have no call now to be going down and getting Holy Water in the dark nights after Samhain, and I won't care what way the sea is when the other women will be keening. (*To Nora.*) Give me the Holy Water, Nora, there's a small sup still on the dresser.

[*Nora gives it to her.*]

MAURYA (*drops Michael's clothes across Bartley's feet, and sprinkles the Holy Water over him*). It isn't that I haven't prayed for you, Bartley, to the Almighty God. It isn't that I haven't said prayers in the dark night till you wouldn't know what I'ld be saying; but it's a great rest I'll have now, and it's time surely. It's a great rest I'll have now, and great sleeping in the long nights after Samhain, if it's only a bit of wet flour we do have to eat, and maybe a fish that would be stinking.

[*She kneels down again, crossing herself, and saying prayers under her breath.*]

CATHLEEN (*to an old man*). Maybe yourself and Eamon would make a coffin when the sun rises. We have fine white boards herself bought, God help her, thinking Michael would be found, and I have a new cake you can eat while you'll be working.

THE OLD MAN (*looking at the boards*). Are there nails with them?

CATHLEEN. There are not, Colum; we didn't think of the nails.

ANOTHER MAN. It's a great wonder she wouldn't think of the nails, and all the coffins she's seen made already.

CATHLEEN. It's getting old she is, and broken.

[*Maurya stands up again very slowly and spreads out the pieces of Michael's clothes beside the body, sprinkling them with the last of the Holy Water.*]

NORA (*in a whisper to Cathleen*). She's quiet now and easy; but the day Michael was drowned you could hear her crying out from this to the spring well. It's fonder she was of Michael, and would any one have thought that?

CATHLEEN (*slowly and clearly*). An old woman will be soon tired with anything she will do, and isn't it nine days herself is after crying and keening, and making great sorrow in the house?

MAURYA (*puts the empty cup mouth downwards on the table, and lays her hands together on Bartley's feet*). They're all together this time, and the end is come. May the Almighty God have mercy on Bartley's soul, and on Michael's soul, and on the souls of Sheamus and Patch, and Stephen and Shawn (*bending her head*); and may He have mercy on my soul, Nora, and on the soul of every one is left living in the world.

[*She pauses, and the keen rises a little more loudly from the women, then sinks away.*]

MAURYA (*continuing*). Michael has a clean burial in the far north, by the grace of the Almighty God. Bartley will have a fine coffin out of the white boards, and a deep grave surely. What more can we want than that? No man at all can be living for ever, and we must be satisfied.

[*She kneels down again and the curtain falls slowly.*][59]

George Augustus Moore

George Augustus Moore (1852–1933) was a novelist and contributor to the Irish Literary Revival. However, his relationship with Yeats and the Abbey Theatre became strained regarding its direction; Moore was not interested in the heroic dramas in which Yeats was interested. Instead, Moore became involved with the revival of the Gaelic language, though he was not an Irish speaker himself. His failure to find any good modern Gaelic literature led him to his writing *The Untilled Field* (1903), which was translated into Gaelic and used by the Gaelic League. His most successful novel was *The Lake* (1905). In writing the novel, Moore developed what he termed the "melodic line," a fluid and rhythmic prose based on oral speech patterns in which the impressions working on the narrator's consciousness are integrated with his flow of thought, not unlike the stream-of-consciousness that James Joyce employed in *Ulysses*. *The Lake* concerns Father Oliver Gogarty, a priest who has grown up and lived his life around Lake Carra, a large body of water outside Westport in County Mayo. Father Oliver, imbued with the beauty of the woods and lake of his childhood, enters the priesthood out of obligation; it is, like many who enter the priesthood, he believes, a calling from God, and the church for him becomes an extension of the natural world and his childhood aspiration. For Father Oliver, the woods and nature, and by extension the giving of his life to God, had always been a part of him. A conflict arises when a member of his congregation bears his child. Though the plot deals chiefly with a priest losing his Catholic faith (as Moore himself had done, much like Æ), Moore has created a unique stream-of-consciousness in Father Gogarty, whose mind is woven into the ancient presence of Ireland's forests and the memory of a Celtic, pre-Christian past ground firmly in a relationship with the trees. The preface and chapter 1 establish the imagery and foreground the conflicts that will cause Father Gogarty to reject the modern church and turn instead to the spiritual force of Ireland's natural world.[60]

From **The Lake**

PREFACE

The concern of this preface is with the mistake that was made when "The Lake" was excluded from the volume entitled "The Untilled Field," reducing it to too slight dimensions, for bulk counts; and "The Lake," too, in being published in a separate volume lost a great deal in range and power, and criticism was baffled by the division of stories written at the same time and coming out of the same happy inspiration, one that could hardly fail to beget stories in the mind of anybody prone to narrative—the return of a man to his native land, to its people, to memories hidden for years, forgotten, but which rose suddenly out of the darkness, like water out of the earth when a spring is tapped.

Some chance words passing between John Eglinton and me as we returned home one evening from Professor Dowden's were enough. He spoke, or I spoke, of a volume of Irish stories; Tourguéniev's name was mentioned, and next morning—if not the next morning, certainly not later than a few mornings after—I was writing "Homesickness," while the story of "The Exile" was taking shape in my mind. "The Exile" was followed by a series of four stories, a sort of village odyssey. "A Letter to

Rome" is as good as these and as typical of my country. "So on He Fares" is the one that, perhaps, out of the whole volume I like the best, always excepting "The Lake," which, alas, was not included, but which belongs so strictly to the aforesaid stories that my memory includes it in the volume.

In expressing preferences I am transgressing an established rule of literary conduct, which ordains that an author must always speak of his own work with downcast eyes, excusing its existence on the ground of his own incapacity. All the same an author's preferences interest his readers, and having transgressed by telling that these Irish stories lie very near to my heart, I will proceed a little further into literary sin, confessing that my reason for liking "The Lake" is related to the very great difficulty of the telling, for the one vital event in the priest's life befell him before the story opens, and to keep the story in the key in which it was conceived, it was necessary to recount the priest's life during the course of his walk by the shores of a lake, weaving his memories continually, without losing sight, however, of the long, winding, mere-like lake, wooded to its shores, with hills appearing and disappearing into mist and distance. The difficulty overcome is a joy to the artist, for in his conquest over the material he draws nigh to his idea, and in this book mine was the essential rather than the daily life of the priest, and as I read for this edition I seemed to hear it. The drama passes within the priest's soul; it is tied and untied by the flux and reflux of sentiments, inherent in and proper to his nature, and the weaving of a story out of the soul substance without ever seeking the aid of external circumstance seems to me a little triumph. It may be that I heard what none other will hear, not through his own fault but through mine, and it may be that all ears are not tuned, or are too indifferent or indolent to listen; it is easier to hear "Esther Waters" and to watch her struggles for her child's life than to hear the mysterious warble, soft as lake water, that abides in the heart. But I think there will always be a few who will agree with me that there is as much life in "The Lake," as there is in "Esther Waters"—a different kind of life, not so wide a life, perhaps, but what counts in art is not width but depth.

Artists, it is said, are not good judges of their own works, and for that reason, and other reasons, maybe, it is considered to be unbecoming for a writer to praise himself. So to make atonement for the sins I have committed in this preface, I will confess to very little admiration for "Evelyn Innes" and "Sister Teresa." The writing of "Evelyn Innes" and "Sister Teresa" was useful to me inasmuch that if I had not written them I could not have written "The Lake" or "The Brook Kerith." It seems ungrateful, therefore, to refuse to allow two of my most successful books into the canon merely because they do not correspond with my æstheticism. But a writer's æstheticism is his all; he cannot surrender it, for his art is dependent upon it, and the single concession he can make is that if an overwhelming demand should arise for these books when he is among the gone—a storm before which the reed must bend—the publisher shall be permitted to print "Evelyn Innes" and "Sister Teresa" from the original editions, it being, however, clearly understood that they are offered to the public only as apocrypha. But this permission must not be understood to extend to certain books on which my name appears—viz., "Mike Fletcher," "Vain Fortune," "Parnell and His Island"; to some plays, "Martin Luther," "The Strike at Arlingford," "The Bending of the Boughs"; to a couple of volumes of verse entitled

"Pagan Poems" and "Flowers of Passion"—all these books, if they are ever reprinted again, should be issued as the work of a disciple—Amico Moorini I put forward as a suggestion.

G.M.

CHAPTER 1

It was one of those enticing days at the beginning of May when white clouds are drawn about the earth like curtains. The lake lay like a mirror that somebody had breathed upon, the brown islands showing through the mist faintly, with gray shadows falling into the water, blurred at the edges. The ducks were talking in the reeds, the reeds themselves were talking, and the water lapping softly about the smooth limestone shingle. But there was an impulse in the gentle day, and, turning from the sandy spit, Father Oliver walked to and fro along the disused cart-track about the edge of the wood, asking himself if he were going home, knowing very well that he could not bring himself to interview his parishioners that morning.

On a sudden resolve to escape from anyone that might be seeking him, he went into the wood and lay down on the warm grass, and admired the thickly-tasselled branches of the tall larches swinging above him. At a little distance among the juniper-bushes, between the lake and the wood, a bird uttered a cry like two stones clinked sharply together, and getting up he followed the bird, trying to catch sight of it, but always failing to do so; it seemed to range in a circle about certain trees, and he hadn't gone very far when he heard it behind him. A stonechat he was sure it must be, and he wandered on till he came to a great silver fir, and thought that he spied a pigeon's nest among the multitudinous branches. The nest, if it were one, was about sixty feet from the ground, perhaps more than that; and, remembering that the great fir had grown out of a single seed, it seemed to him not at all wonderful that people had once worshipped trees, so mysterious is their life, so remote from ours. And he stood a long time looking up, hardly able to resist the temptation to climb the tree—not to rob the nest like a boy, but to admire the two gray eggs which he would find lying on some bare twigs.

At the edge of the wood there were some chestnuts and sycamores. He noticed that the large-patterned leaf of the sycamores, hanging out from a longer stem, was darker than the chestnut leaf. There were some elms close by, and their half-opened leaves, dainty and frail, reminded him of clouds of butterflies. He could think of nothing else. White, cotton-like clouds unfolded above the blossoming trees; patches of blue appeared and disappeared; and he wandered on again, beguiled this time by many errant scents and wilful little breezes.

Very soon he came upon some fields, and as he walked through the ferns the young rabbits ran from under his feet, and he thought of the delicious meals that the fox would snap up. He had to pick his way, for thorn-bushes and hazels were springing up everywhere. Derrinrush, the great headland stretching nearly a mile into the lake, said to be one of the original forests, was extending inland. He remembered it as a deep, religious wood, with its own particular smell of reeds and rushes. It went further back than the island castles, further back than the Druids; and was among Father Oliver's earliest recollections. Himself and his brother James used to go there when they were boys to cut hazel stems, to make fishing-rods; and one had only to turn over the dead leaves to discover the chips scattered circlewise in the open spaces where the coopers sat in the days gone by making hoops for barrels. But iron hoops were now used instead of hazel, and the coopers worked there no more. In the old days he and his brother James used to follow the wood-ranger, asking him questions about the wild creatures of the wood—badgers, marten cats, and otters. And one day they took home a nest of young hawks. He did not neglect to feed them, but they had eaten each other, nevertheless. He forgot what became of the last one.

A thick yellow smell hung on the still air. "A fox," he said, and he trailed the animal through the hazel-bushes till he came to a rough shore, covered with juniper-bushes and tussocked grass, the extreme point of the headland, whence he could see the mountains—the pale southern mountains mingling with the white sky, and the western mountains, much nearer, showing in bold relief. The beautiful motion and variety of the hills delighted him, and there was as much various colour as there were many dips and curves, for the hills were not far enough away to dwindle to one blue tint; they were blue, but the pink heather showed through the blue, and the clouds continued to fold and unfold, so that neither the colour nor the lines were ever the same. The retreating and advancing of the great masses and the delicate illumination of the crests could be watched without weariness. It was like listening to music. Slieve Cairn showing straight as a bull's back against the white sky, a cloud filling the gap between Slieve Cairn and Slieve Louan, a quaint little hill like a hunchback going down a road. Slieve Louan was followed by a great boulder-like hill turned sideways, the top indented like a crater, and the priest likened the long, low profile of the next hill to a reptile raising itself on its forepaws.

He stood at gaze, bewitched by the play of light and shadow among the slopes; and when he turned towards the lake again, he was surprised to see a yacht by Castle Island. A random breeze just sprung up had borne her so far, and now she lay becalmed, carrying, without doubt, a pleasure-party, inspired by some vague interest in ruins, and a very real interest in lunch; or the yacht's destination might be Kilronan Abbey, and the priest wondered if there were water enough in the strait to let her through in this season of the year. The sails flapped in the puffing breeze, and he began to calculate her tonnage, certain that if he had such a boat he would not be sailing her on a lake, but on the bright sea, out of sight of land, in the middle of a great circle of water. As if stung by a sudden sense of the sea, of its perfume and its freedom, he imagined the filling of the sails and the rattle of the ropes, and how a fair wind would carry him as far as the cove of Cork before morning. The run from Cork to Liverpool would be slower, but the wind might veer a little, and in four-and-twenty hours the Welsh mountains would begin to show above the horizon. But he would not land anywhere on the Welsh coast. There was nothing to see in Wales but castles, and he was weary of castles, and longed to see the cathedrals of York and Salisbury; for he had often seen them in pictures, and had more than once thought of a walking tour through England. Better still if the yacht were to land him somewhere on the French coast. England was, after all, only an island like Ireland—a little larger, but still an island—and he thought he would like a continent to roam in. The French cathedrals were more beautiful than the English, and it would be pleasant to wander in the French country in happy-go-lucky fashion,

resting when he was tired, walking when it pleased him, taking an interest in whatever might strike his fancy.

It seemed to him that his desire was to be freed for a while from everything
he had ever seen, and from everything he had ever heard. He merely wanted to
wander, admiring everything there was to admire as he went. He didn't want to
learn anything, only to admire. He was weary of argument, religious and political.
It wasn't that he was indifferent to his country's welfare, but every mind requires
rest, and he wished himself away in a foreign country, distracted every moment by
new things, learning the language out of a volume of songs, and hearing music, any
music, French or German—any music but Irish music. He sighed, and wondered
why he sighed. Was it because he feared that if he once went away he might never
come back?

This lake was beautiful, but he was tired of its low gray shores; he was tired of
those mountains, melancholy as Irish melodies, and as beautiful. He felt suddenly
that he didn't want to see a lake or a mountain for two months at least, and that his
longing for a change was legitimate and most natural. It pleased him to remember
that everyone likes to get out of his native country for a while, and he had only
been out of sight of this lake in the years he spent in Maynooth. On leaving he had
pleaded that he might be sent to live among the mountains by Kilronan Abbey, at
the north end of the lake, but when Father Conway died he was moved round to the
western shore; and every day since he walked by the lake, for there was nowhere else
to walk, unless up and down the lawn under the sycamores, imitating Father Peter,
whose wont it was to walk there, reading his breviary, stopping from time to time
to speak to a parishioner in the road below; he too used to read his breviary under
the sycamores; but for one reason or another he walked there no longer, and every
afternoon now found him standing at the end of this sandy spit, looking across the
lake towards Tinnick, where he was born, and where his sisters lived.

He couldn't see the walls of the convent to-day, there was too much mist about;
and he liked to see them; for whenever he saw them he began to think of his sister
Eliza, and he liked to think of her—she was his favourite sister. They were nearly the
same age, and had played together; and his eyes dwelt in memory on the dark corner
under the stairs where they used to play. He could even see their toys through the
years, and the tall clock which used to tell them that it was time to put them aside.
Eliza was only eighteen months older than he; they were the red-haired ones, and
though they were as different in mind as it was possible to be, he seemed nearer
Eliza than anyone else. In what this affinity consisted he couldn't say, but he had
always felt himself of the same flesh and blood. Neither his father nor mother had
inspired this sense of affinity; and his sister Mary and his brothers seemed to him
merely people whom he had known always—not more than that; whereas Eliza was
quite different, and perhaps it was this very mutuality, which he could not define,
that had decided their vocations.

No doubt there is a moment in every man's life when something happens to turn
him into the road which he is destined to follow; for all that it would be superficial
to think that the fate of one's life is dependent upon accident. The accident that turns
one into the road is only the means which Providence takes to procure the working
out of certain ends. Accidents are many: life is as full of accidents as a fire is full of

sparks, and any spark is enough to set fire to the train. The train escapes a thousand, but at last a spark lights it, and this spark always seems to us the only one that could have done it. We cannot imagine how the same result could have been obtained otherwise. But other ways would have been found; for Nature is full of resource, and if Eliza had not been by to fire the idea hidden in him, something else would. She was the means, but only the means, for no man escapes his vocation, and the priesthood was his. A vocation always finds a way out. But was he sure if it hadn't been for Eliza that he wouldn't have married Annie McGrath? He didn't think he would have married Annie, but he might have married another. All the same, Annie was a good, comfortable girl, a girl that everybody was sure would make a good wife for any man, and at that time many people were thinking that he should marry Annie. On looking back he couldn't honestly say that a stray thought of Annie hadn't found its way into his mind; but not into his heart—there is a difference.

At that time he was what is known as a growing lad; he was seventeen. His father was then dead two years, and his mother looked to him, he being the eldest, to take charge of the shop, for at that time it was almost settled that James was to go to America. They had two or three nice grass farms just beyond the town: Patsy was going to have them; and his sisters' fortunes were in the bank, and very good fortunes they were. They had a hundred pounds apiece and should have married well. Eliza could have married whomever she pleased. Mary could have married, too, and to this day he couldn't tell why she hadn't married.

The chances his sister Mary had missed rose up in his mind—why, he did not know; and a little bored by these memories, he suddenly became absorbed in the little bleat of a blackcap perched on a bush, the only one amid a bed of flags and rushes; "an alder-bush," he said. "His mate is sitting on her eggs, and there are some wood-gatherers about; that's what's worrying the little fellow." The bird continued to utter its troubled bleat, and the priest walked on, thinking how different was its evensong. He meditated an excursion to hear it, and then, without his being aware of any transition, his thoughts returned to his sister Mary, and to the time when he had once indulged in hopes that the mills along the river-side might be rebuilt and Tinnick restored to its former commercial prosperity. He was not certain if he had ever really believed that he might set these mills going, or if he had, he encouraged an illusion, knowing it to be one. He was only certain of this, that when he was a boy and saw no life ahead of him except that of a Tinnick shopman, he used to feel that if he remained at home he must have the excitement of adventure. The beautiful river, with its lime-trees, appealed to his imagination; the rebuilding of the mills and the reorganization of trade, if he succeeded in reorganizing trade, would mean spending his mornings on the wharves by the river-side, and in those days his one desire was to escape from the shop. He looked upon the shop as a prison. In those days he liked dreaming, and it was pleasant to dream of giving back to Tinnick its trade of former days; but when his mother asked him what steps he intended to take to get the necessary capital, he lost his temper with her. He must have known that he could never make enough money in the shop to set the mills working! He must have known that he would never take his father's place at the desk by the dusty window! But if he shrank from an avowal it was because he had no other proposal to make. His mother understood him, though the others didn't, and seeing his inability to say what kind of work he would put his hand to, she had spoken of Annie McGrath. She didn't say he should marry Annie—she was a clever woman in her way—she merely said that Annie's relations in America could afford to supply sufficient capital to start one of the mills. But he never wanted to marry Annie, and couldn't do else but snap when the subject was mentioned, and many's the time he told his mother that if the mills were to pay it would be necessary to start business on a large scale. He was an impracticable lad and even now he couldn't help smiling when he thought of the abruptness with which he would go down to the river-side to seek a new argument wherewith to confute his mother, to return happy when he had found one, and sit watching for an opportunity to raise the question again.

No, it wasn't because Annie's relations weren't rich enough that he hadn't wanted to marry her. And to account for his prejudice against marriage, he must suppose that some notion of the priesthood was stirring in him at the time, for one day, as he sat looking at Annie across the tea-table, he couldn't help thinking that it would be hard to live alongside of her year in and year out. Although a good and a pleasant girl, Annie was a bit tiresome to listen to, and she wasn't one of those who improve with age. As he sat looking at her, he seemed to understand, as he had never understood before, that if he married her all that had happened in the years back would happen again—more children scrambling about the counter, with a shopman (himself) by the dusty window putting his pen behind his ear, just as his father did when he came forward to serve some country woman with half a pound of tea or a hank of onions.

And as these thoughts were passing through his mind, he remembered hearing his mother say that Annie's sister was thinking of starting dressmaking in the High Street. "It would be nice if Eliza were to join her," his mother added casually. Eliza laid aside the skirt she was turning, raised her eyes and stared at mother, as if she were surprised mother could say anything so stupid. "I'm going to be a nun," she said, and, just as if she didn't wish to answer any questions, went on sewing. Well might they be surprised, for not one of them suspected Eliza of religious inclinations. She wasn't more pious than another, and when they asked her if she were joking, she looked at them as if she thought the question very stupid, and they didn't ask her any more.

She wasn't more than fifteen at the time, yet she spoke out of her own mind. At the time they thought she had been thinking on the matter—considering her future. A child of fifteen doesn't consider, but a child of fifteen may *know*, and after he had seen the look which greeted his mother's remarks, and heard Eliza's simple answer, "I've decided to be a nun," he never doubted that what she said was true. From that day she became for him a different being; and when she told him, feeling, perhaps, that he sympathized with her more than the others did, that one day she would be Reverend Mother of the Tinnick Convent, he felt convinced that she knew what she was saying—how she knew he could not say.

His childhood had been a slumber, with occasional awakenings or half awakenings, and Eliza's announcement that she intended to enter the religious life was the first real awakening; and this awakening first took the form of an acute interest in Eliza's character, and, persuaded that she or her prototype had already existed, he searched the lives of the saints for an account of her, finding many partial portraits of her; certain typical traits in the lives of three or four saints reminded him of Eliza, but there was no complete portrait. The strangest part of the business was that he traced his vocation to his search for Eliza in the lives of the saints. Everything that happened afterwards was the emotional sequence of taking down the books from the shelf. He didn't exaggerate; it was possible his life might have taken a different turn, for up to that time he had only read books of adventure—stories about robbers and pirates. As if by magic, his interest in such stories passed clean out of his mind, or was exchanged for an extraordinary enthusiasm for saints, who by renouncement of animal life had contrived to steal up to the last bounds, whence they could see into the eternal life that lies beyond the grave. Once this power was admitted, what interest could we find in the feeble ambitions of temporal life, whose scope is limited to three score and ten years? And who could doubt that saints attained the eternal life, which is God, while still living in the temporal flesh? For did not the miracles of the saints prove that they were no longer subject to natural laws? Ancient Ireland, perhaps, more than any other country, understood the supremacy of spirit over matter, and strove to escape through mortifications from the prison of the flesh. Without doubt great numbers in Ireland had fled from the torment of actual life into the wilderness. If the shore and the islands on this lake were dotted with fortress castles, it was the Welsh and the Normans who built them, and the priest remembered how his mind took fire when he first heard of the hermit who lived in Church Island, and how disappointed he was when he heard that Church Island was ten miles away, at the other end of the lake.

For he could not row himself so far; distance and danger compelled him to consider the islands facing Tinnick—two large islands covered with brushwood, ugly brown patches—ugly as their names, Horse Island and Hog Island, whereas Castle Island had always seemed to him a suitable island for a hermitage, far more so than Castle Hag. Castle Hag was too small and bleak to engage the attention of a sixth-century hermit. But there were trees on Castle Island, and out of the ruins of the castle a comfortable sheiling could be built, and the ground thus freed from the ruins of the Welshman's castle might be cultivated. He remembered commandeering the fisherman's boat, and rowing himself out, taking a tape to measure, and how, after much application of the tape, he had satisfied himself that there was enough arable land in the island for a garden; he had walked down the island certain that a quarter of an acre could grow enough vegetables to support a hermit, and that a goat would be able to pick a living among the bushes and the tussocked grass: even a hermit might have a goat, and he didn't think he could live without milk. He must have been a long time measuring out his garden, for when he returned to his boat the appearance of the lake frightened him; it was full of blustering waves, and it wasn't likely he'd ever forget his struggle to get the boat back to Tinnick. He left it where he had found it, at the mouth of the river by the fisherman's hut, and returned home thinking how he would have to import a little hay occasionally for the goat. Nor would this be all; he would have to go on shore every Sunday to hear Mass, unless he built a chapel. The hermit of Church Island had an oratory in which he said Mass! But if he left his island every Sunday his hermitage would be a mockery. For the moment he couldn't see how he was to build a chapel—a sheiling, perhaps; a chapel was out of the question, he feared.

He would have to have vestments and a chalice, and, immersed in the difficulty of obtaining these, he walked home, taking the path along the river from habit, not because he wished to consider afresh the problems of the ruined mills. The dream of restoring Tinnick to its commerce of former days was forgotten, and he walked on, thinking of his chalice, until he heard somebody call him. It was Eliza, and as they leaned over the parapet of the bridge, he could not keep himself from telling her that he had rowed out to Castle Island, never thinking that she would reprove him, and sternly, for taking the fisherman's boat without asking leave. It was no use to argue with Eliza that the fisherman didn't want his boat, the day being too rough for fishing. What did she know about fishing? She had asked very sharply what brought him out to Castle Island on such a day. There was no use saying he didn't know; he never was able to keep a secret from Eliza, and feeling that he must confide in somebody, he told her he was tired of living at home, and was thinking of building a sheiling on the island.

Eliza didn't understand, and she understood still less when he spoke of a bee-hive hut, such as the ancient hermits of Ireland lived in. She was entirely without imagination; but what surprised him still more than her lack of sympathy with his dream-project was her inability to understand an idea so inherent in Christianity as the hermitage, for at that time Eliza's mind was made up to enter the religious life. He waited a long time for her answer, but the only answer she made was that in the early centuries a man was either a bandit or a hermit. This wasn't true: life was peaceful in Ireland in the sixth and seventh centuries; even if it weren't, she ought to have understood that change of circumstance cannot alter an idea so inherent in man as the hermitage, and when he asked her if she intended to found a new Order, or to go out to Patagonia to teach the Indians, she laughed, saying she was much more interested in a laundry than in the Indians. Her plea that the Tinnick Convent was always in straits for money did not appeal to him then any more than it did to-day.

"The officers in Tinnick have to send their washing to Dublin. A fine reason for entering a convent," he answered.

But quite unmoved by the sarcasm, she replied that a woman can do nothing unless she be a member of a congregation. He shrank from Eliza's mind as from the touch of something coarse, and his suggestion that the object of the religious life is meditation did not embarrass her in the very least, and he remembered well how she had said:

"Putting aside for the moment the important question whether there may or may not be hermits in the twentieth century, tell me, Oliver, are you thinking of marrying Annie McGrath? You know she has rich relations in America, and you might get them to supply the capital to set the mills going. The mills would be a great advantage. Annie has a good headpiece, and would be able to take the shop off your hands, leaving you free to look after the mills."

"The mills, Eliza! there are other things in the world beside those mills!"

"A hermitage on Castle Island?"

Eliza could be very impertinent when she liked. If she had no concern in what was being said, she looked round, displaying an irritating curiosity in every passer-by, and true to herself she had drawn his attention to the ducks on the river while he was telling her of the great change that had come over him. He had felt like boxing her ears. But the moment he began to speak of taking Orders she forgot all about the ducks; her eyes were fixed upon him, she listened to his every word, and when he finished speaking, she reminded him there had always been a priest in the family. All her wits were awake. He was the one of the family who had shown most aptitude for learning, and their cousin the Bishop would be able to help him. What she would like would be to see him parish priest of Tinnick. The parish was one of the best in the diocese. Not a doubt of it, she was thinking at that moment of the advantage this arrangement would be to her when she was directing the affairs of the convent.

If there was no other, there was at least one woman in Ireland who was interested in things. He had never met anybody less interested in opinions or in ideas than Eliza. They had walked home together in silence, at all events not saying much, and that very evening she left the room immediately after supper. And soon after they heard sounds of trunks being dragged along the passage; furniture was being moved, and when she came downstairs she just said she was going to sleep with Mary.

"Oliver is going to have my room. He must have a room to himself on account of his studies."

On that she gathered up her sewing, and left him to explain. He felt that it was rather sly of her to go away like that, leaving all the explanation to him. She wanted him to be a priest, and was full of little tricks. There was no time for thinking it over. There was only just time to prepare for the examination. He worked hard, for his work interested him, especially the Latin language; but what interested him far more than his aptitude for learning whatever he made up his mind to learn was the discovery of a religious vocation in himself. Eliza feared that his interest in hermits sprang from a boyish taste for adventure rather than from religious feeling, but no sooner had he begun his studies for the priesthood, than he found himself over-taken and overpowered by an extraordinary religious fervour and by a desire for prayer and discipline. Never had a boy left home more zealous, more desirous to excel in piety and to strive for the honour and glory of the Church.

An expression of anger, almost of hatred, passed over Father Oliver's face, and he turned from the lake and walked a few yards rapidly, hoping to escape from memories of his folly; for he had made a great fool of himself, no doubt. But, after all, he preferred his enthusiasms, however exaggerated they might seem to him now, to the commonplace—he could not call it wisdom—of those whom he had taken into his confidence. It was foolish of him, no doubt, to have told how he used to go out in a boat and measure the ground about Castle Island, thinking to build himself a beehive hut out of the ruins. He knew too little of the world at that time; he had no idea how incapable the students were of understanding anything outside the narrow interests of an ecclesiastical career. Anyhow, he had had the satisfaction of having beaten them in all the examinations; and if he had cared to go in for advancement, he could have easily got ahead of them all, for he had better brains and better inter-est than any of them. When he last saw that ignorant brute Peter Fahy, Fahy asked him if he still put pebbles in his shoes. It was to Fahy he had confided the cause of his lameness, and Fahy had told on him; he was ridiculously innocent in those days, and he could still see them gathered about him, pretending not to believe that he kept a cat-o'-nine-tails in his room, and scourged himself at night. It was Tom Bryan who said that he wouldn't mind betting a couple of shillings that Gogarty's whip wouldn't draw a squeal from a pig on the roadside. The answer to that was: "A touch will make a pig squeal: you should have said an ass!" But at the moment he couldn't think of an answer.

No doubt everyone looked on him as a ninny, and they persuaded him to prove to them that his whip was a real whip by letting Tom Bryan do the whipping for him. Tom Bryan was a rough fellow, who ought to have been driving a plough; a ploughman's life was too peaceful an occupation for him—a drover's life would have suited him best, prodding his cattle along the road with a goad; it was said that was how he maintained his authority in the parish. The remembrance of the day he bared his back to that fellow was still a bitter one. With a gentle smile he had handed the whip to Tom Bryan, the very smile which he imagined the hermits of old time used to wear. The first blow had so stunned him that he couldn't cry out, and this blow was followed by a second which sent the blood flaming through his veins, and then by another which brought all the blood into one point in his body. He seemed to lose consciousness of everything but three inches of back. Nine blows he bore without wincing; the tenth overcame his fortitude, and he had reeled away from Tom Bryan.

Tom had exchanged the whip he had given him for a great leather belt; that was why he had been hurt so grievously—hurt till the pain seemed to reach his very heart. Tom had belted him with all his strength; and half a dozen of Tom's pals were waiting outside the door, and they came into the room, their wide mouths agrin, asking him how he liked it. But they were unready for the pain his face expressed, and in the midst of his agony he noticed that already they foresaw consequences, and he heard them reprove Tom Bryan, their intention being to dissociate themselves from him. Cowards! cowards! cowards!

They tried to help him on with his shirt, but he had been too badly beaten, and Tom Bryan came up in the evening to ask him not to tell on him. He promised, and he wouldn't have told if he could have helped it. But some explanation had to be forthcoming—he couldn't lie on his back. The doctor was sent for. . . .

And next day he was told the President wished to see him. The President was Eliza over again; hermits and hermitages were all very well in the early centuries, but religion had advanced, and nowadays a steadfast piety was more suited to modern requirements than pebbles in the shoes. If it had been possible to leave for America that day he thought he would have gone. But he couldn't leave Maynooth because he had been fool enough to bare his back to Tom Bryan. He couldn't return home to tell such a story as that. All Tinnick would be laughing at him, and Eliza, what would she think of him? He wasn't such a fool as the Maynooth students thought him, and he realized at once that he must stay in Maynooth and live down remembrance of his folly. So, as the saying goes, he took the bit between his teeth.

The necessity of living down his first folly, of creating a new idea of himself in the minds of the students, forced him to apply all his intelligence to his studies, and he made extraordinary progress in the first years. The recollection of the ease with which he outdistanced his fellow-students was as pleasant as the breezes about the lake, and his thoughts dwelt on the opinion which he knew was entertained, that for many years no one at Maynooth had shown such aptitude for scholarship. He only had to look at a book to know more about it than his fellow-students would know if they were to spend days over it. He won honours. He could have won greater honours, but his conscience reminded him that the gifts he received from God were not bestowed upon him for the mere purpose of humiliating his fellow-students. He often felt then that if certain talents had been given to him, they were given to him to use for the greater glory of God rather than for his own glorification; and his feeling was that there was nothing more hateful in God's sight than intellectual, unless perhaps spiritual, pride, and his object during his last years at Maynooth was to exhibit himself to the least advantage.

It is strange how an idea enters the soul and remakes it, and when he left Maynooth he used his influence with his cousin, the Bishop, to get himself appointed to the poorest parish in Connaught. Eliza had to dissemble, but he knew that in her heart she was furious with him. We are all extraordinarily different one from another, and if we seem most different from those whom we are most like, it is because we know nothing at all about strangers. He had gone to Kilronan in spite of Eliza, in spite of everyone, their cousin the Bishop included. He had been very happy in Bridget Clery's cottage, so happy that he didn't know himself why he ever consented to leave Kilronan.

No, it was not because he was too happy there. He had to a certain extent out-grown his very delicate conscience.[61]

Padraic Colum

Padraic Colum (1881–1972) was a playwright, novelist, poet, and folklorist. Colum is known for his part in establishing the Abbey Theatre during the Revival, where his realistic peasant drama *The Land* (1905) gave him early literary success in its depiction of rural Irish life. However, another play, *Thomas Muskerry* (1910), was also staged by the Abbey and not well received, and Colum failed to follow through on his early promise as a dramatist. Colum married in 1912 and in 1914 moved to New York, where he began to write children's stories for the *Sunday Tribune*, which led to a collection, *The King of Ireland's Son* (1916), followed by many children's books, for which he became more known. In 1922, the Hawaiian legislature commissioned Colum to write about the folklore of the islands for a three-volume collection for children. A book of verse, *Dramatic Legends* (1922), was followed by his first novel, *Castle Conquer* (1923), set in an impoverished nineteenth century, as was *The Flying Swans* (1937). But his early poetry, especially his nature poetry, is often overlooked in his large body of work. Included here are select poems from his first collection, *Wild Earth*, published in 1907.[62]

A Drover

To Meath of the pastures,
From wet hills by the sea,
Through Leitrim and Longford
Go my cattle and me.

I hear in the darkness
Their slipping and breathing—
I name them the bye-ways
They're to pass without heeding.

Then the wet, winding roads,
Brown bogs with black water;
And my thoughts on white ships
And the King o' Spain's daughter.

O! farmer, strong farmer!
You can spend at the fair;
But your face you must turn
To your crops and your care.

And soldiers—red soldiers!
You've seen many lands;
But you walk two by two,
And by captain's commands.

O! the smell of the beasts,
The wet wind in the morn;
And the proud and hard earth
Never broken for corn;

And the crowds at the fair,
The herds loosened and blind,
Loud words and dark faces
And the wild blood behind.

(O! strong men with your best
I would strive breast to breast,
I could quiet your herds
With my words, with my words.)

I will bring you, my kine,
Where there's grass to the knee;
But you'll think of scant croppings
Harsh with salt of the sea.[63]

A Cradle Song

O, men from the fields!
Come gently within.
Tread softly, softly,
O! men coming in.

Mavourneen is going
From me and from you,
Where Mary will fold him
With mantle of blue!

From reek of the smoke
And cold of the floor,
And the peering of things
Across the half-door.

O, men from the fields!
Soft, softly come thro'.
Mary puts round him
Her mantle of blue.[64]

Across the Door

The fiddles were playing and playing,
    The couples were out on the floor;
From converse and dancing he drew me,
    And across the door.

Ah! strange were the dim, wide meadows,
    And strange was the cloud-strewn sky,
And strange in the meadows the corncrakes,
    And they making cry!

The hawthorn bloom was by us,
    Around us the breath of the south.
White hawthorn, strange in the night-time—
    His kiss on my mouth![65]

The Crane

I know you, Crane:
I, too, have waited,
Waited until my heart
Melted to little pools around my feet!

Comer in the morning ere the crows,
Shunner,
Searcher ——
Something find for me!
The pennies that were laid upon the eyes
Of old, wise men I knew.[66]

Dublin Roads

When you were a lad that lacked a trade,
Oh, many's the thing you'd see on the way
From Kill-o'-the-Grange to Ballybrack,
And from Cabinteely down into Bray,
When you walked these roads the whole of a day.

High walls there would be to the left and right,
With ivies growing across the top,
And a briary ditch on the other side,
And a place where a quiet goat might crop,
And a wayside bench where a man could stop.

A hen that had found a thing in her sleep,
One would think, the way she went craw-craw-cree,
You would hear as you sat on the bench was there,
And a cock that thought he crew mightily,
And all the stir of the world would be

A cart that went creaking along the road,
And another cart that kept coming a-near;
A man breaking stones; for bits of the day
One stroke and another would come to you clear,
And then no more from that stone-breaker.

And his day went by as the clouds went by,
As hammer in hand he sat alone,
Breaking the mendings of the road;

The dazzles up from the stones were thrown
When, after the rain, the sun down-shone.

And you'd leave him there, that stone-breaker,
And you'd wonder who came to see what was done
By him in a day, or a month, or a week:
He broke a stone and another one,
And you left him there and you travelled on.

A quiet road! You would get to know
The briars and stones along by the way;
A dozen times you'd see last year's nest;
A peacock's cry, a pigeon astray
Would be marks enough to set on a day;

Or the basket-carriers you would meet
A man and a woman—they were a pair!
The woman going beside his heel:
A straight-walking man with a streak of him bare,
And eyes that would give you a crafty stare.

Coming down from the hills they'd have ferns to sell,
Going up from the strand, they'd have cockles in stock:
Sand in their baskets from the sea,
Or clay that was stripped from a hillside rock—
A pair that had often stood in the dock!

Or a man that played on a tin-whistle:
He looked as he'd taken a scarecrow's rig;
Playing and playing as though his mind
Could do nothing else but go to a jig,
And no one around him, little or big.

And you'd meet no man else until you came
Where you could look down upon the sedge,
And watch the Dargle water flow,
And men smoke pipes on the bridge's ledge,
While a robin sang by the haws in a hedge.

Or no bird sang, and the bird-catchers
Would have talk enough for a battle gained,
When they came from the field and stood by the bridge,
Taking shelter beside it while it rained,
While the bird new-caught huddled and strained

In this cage or that, a linnet or finch,
And the points it had were declared and surmised:
And this one's tail was spread out, and there
Two little half-moons, the marks that were prized;
And you looked well on the bird assized!

Then men would go by with a rick of hay
Piled on a cart; with them you would be
Walking beside the piled-up load:
It would seem as it left the horses free,
They went with such stride and so heartily

And so you'd go back along the road.[67]

River Mates

I'll be an otter, and I'll let you swim
A mate beside me; we will venture down
A deep, full river when the sky above
Is shut of the sun; spoilers are we:—
Thick-coated: no dog's tooth can bite at our veins,
With eyes and ears of poachers: deep-earthed ones
Turned hunters; let him slip past,—
The little vole; my teeth are on an edge
For the King-Fish of the River!
    I hold him up,
The glittering salmon that smells of the sea:
I hold him high and whistle!
      Now we go
Back to our earths: we will tear and eat
Sea-smelling salmon: you will tell the cubs
I am the Booty-bringer, I am the Lord
Of the River—the deep, dark, full and flowing River.[68]

NOTES TO PART III

Introduction epigraph: W. B. Yeats, "The Celtic Element in Literature," in *Ideas of Good and Evil,* in *The Collected Works of W. B. Yeats,* vol. 4, *Early Essays,* ed. Richard J. Finneran and George Bornstein (New York: Scribner, 2007), 130.
1. Catherine Maignant, "Rural Ireland in the Nineteenth Century and the Advent of the Modern World," in *Rural Ireland, Real Ireland?,* ed. Jacqueline Genet (Gerrards Cross, UK: Smythe, 1996), 29.
2. Ibid.
3. William Allingham, "The Ruined Chapel," in *Selected Poems from the Works of William Allingham,* ed. Helen Paterson Allingham (London: Macmillan, 1912), 33, https://babel.hathitrust.org/cgi/pt?id=njp.32101067627305.
4. Ibid.
5. Paula Gunn Allen, "The Sacred Hoop: A Contemporary Perspective," in *The Ecocriticism Reader: Landmarks in Literary Ecology,* ed. Cheryll Glotfelty and Harold Fromm (Athens: University of Georgia Press, 1996), 247.
6. See "Katharine Tynan," in *The Oxford Companion to Irish Literature,* ed. Robert Welch (Oxford, UK: Clarendon, 1996), 573.
7. Katharine Tynan, "Children of Lir," in *Twenty One Poems by Katharine Tynan: Selected by W. B. Yeats (1861–1931)* (Dundrum, Ireland: Dun Emer, 1907), 22–25, http://www.digital.library.upenn.edu/women/tynan/poems/poems.html.

8. Tynan, "High Summer," in *A Treasury of War Poetry: British and American Poems of the World War, 1914–1919, Second Series*, ed. George Herbert Clarke (Boston: Houghton Mifflin, 1919), 166.

9. Tynan, "Indian Summer," in *Flower of Youth: Poems in War Time* (London: Sidgwick and Jackson, 1915), 43, https://en.wikisource.org/wiki/Flower_of_youth,_poems_in_war_time.

10. Tynan, "Nymphs," in *Twenty One Poems*, 29.

11. Tynan, "St. Francis to the Birds," ibid., 19–22.

12. Tynan, "The Birds' Bargain," ibid., 26–27.

13. Tynan, "The Garden," in *Herb o' Grace: Poems of War-Time* (London: Sidgwick and Jackson, 1918), 84–85, https://babel.hathitrust.org/cgi/pt?id=njp.32101067645703.

14. Tynan, "The Wind That Shakes the Barley," in *The Wind in the Trees: A Book of Country Verse* (London: Grant Richards, 1898), 57–58, https://archive.org/details/windintreesbookooootynarich.

15. See "George (William) Russell," in Welch, *Oxford Companion to Irish Literature*, 503.

16. Æ, "By the Margin of the Great Deep," in *Collected Poems by A.E.* (London: Macmillan, 1913), 3–4, http://www.bartleby.com/253/3.html.

17. Æ, "Oversoul," ibid., 8, http://www.bartleby.com/253/6.html.

18. Æ, "The Great Breath," ibid., 9, http://www.bartleby.com/253/7.html.

19. Æ, "The Voice of the Waters," ibid., 59–60, http://www.bartleby.com/253/42.html.

20. Æ, "A New World," ibid., 52, http://www.bartleby.com/253/38.html.

21. Æ, "A Vision of Beauty," ibid., 86–88, http://www.bartleby.com/253/60.html.

22. Æ, "Carrowmore," ibid., 106–7, http://www.bartleby.com/253/74.html.

23. Æ, "Creation," ibid., 119, http://www.bartleby.com/253/81.html.

24. Æ, "The Winds of Angus," ibid., 120–21, http://www.bartleby.com/253/82.html.

25. Æ, "The Nuts of Knowledge," ibid., 158–59, http://www.bartleby.com/253/109.html.

26. Æ, "Children of Lir," ibid., 160–61, http://www.bartleby.com/253/110.html.

27. Æ (George William Russell), *The Candle of Vision* (London: Macmillan, 1918), 9–18, 26–37, 56–65, http://www.archive.org/stream/candleofvisionooae18/candleofvisionooae18_djvu.txt.

28. See "William Butler Yeats," in Welch, *Oxford Companion to Irish Literature*, 609–11.

29. W. B. Yeats, *The Wanderings of Oisin, and Other Poems* (London: Kegan Paul, Trench, 1889).

30. Yeats, "Coole Park, 1929," in *The Collected Poems of W. B. Yeats* (London: Wordsworth Editions, 1994), 205–6.

31. Yeats, "Coole Park and Ballylee, 1931," ibid., 206–7.

32. Yeats, "Who Goes with Fergus?," ibid., 34.

33. Yeats, "Down by the Salley Gardens," ibid., 16.

34. Yeats, "In the Seven Woods," ibid., 61.

35. Yeats, "The Shadowy Waters (Introductory Lines)," ibid., 347–48.

36. Yeats, "The Cat and the Moon," ibid., 141–42.

37. Yeats, "The Fairy Pedant," in *The Collected Works of W. B. Yeats*, vol. 1, *The Poems*, 2nd ed., ed. Richard J. Finneran (New York: Simon and Schuster, 1997), 509–10.

38. Yeats, "The Lake Isle of Innisfree," in *Collected Poems*, 31.

39. Yeats, "The Madness of King Goll," ibid., 12–13.

40. Yeats, "The Song of Wandering Aengus," ibid., 47.

41. Yeats, "The Stolen Child," ibid., 14–15; emphasis in the original.

42. Yeats, "The Two Trees," ibid., 39–40.

43. Yeats, "The White Birds," ibid., 33.

44. Yeats, "The Wild Swans at Coole," in *The Wild Swans at Coole* (New York: Macmillan, 1919), http://www.bartleby.com/148/1.html.

45. See "Eva Gore-Booth," in Welch, *Oxford Companion to Irish Literature*, 222.

46. Eva Gore-Booth, "The Dreamer," in *Poems of Eva Gore-Booth* (London: Longmans, Green, 1929), https://www.poetryfoundation.org/poems/46533/the-dreamer-56d226720a908.

47. Gore-Booth, "Re-Incarnation," ibid., https://www.poetryfoundation.org/poems/46532/re-incarnation.

48. Gore-Booth, "Secret Waters," ibid., https://www.poetryfoundation.org/poems/46537/secret-waters.

49. Gore-Booth, "The Little Waves of Breffny," ibid., https://www.poetryfoundation.org/poems/46529/the-little-waves-of-breffny.

50. Gore-Booth, "The Weaver," ibid., https://www.poetryfoundation.org/poems/46528/the-weaver.

51. The Aran Islands, "Island Writers," accessed March 14, 2018, http://www.aranislands.ie/island-writers/.

52. See "Edmund John Millington Synge," in Welch, *Oxford Companion to Irish Literature*, 548.

53. J. M. Synge, "In Kerry," in *Poems and Translations* (Dublin: Maunsel, 1911), 3, https://archive.org/stream/translationoopoemssyngrich/translationoopoemssyngrich_djvu.txt.

54. Synge, "To the Oaks of Glencree," ibid., 15.

55. Synge, "Prelude," ibid., 21.

56. Synge, "In Glencullen," ibid., 18.

57. Synge, "On an Island," ibid., 10.

58. Synge, *The Aran Islands*, in *The Complete Works of John M. Synge* (New York: Random House, 1904), 414–24.

59. Synge, *Riders to the Sea*, ibid., 81–97.

60. See "George Augustus Moore," in Welch, *Oxford Companion to Irish Literature*, 373–75.

61. George Augustus Moore, *The Lake* (London: William Heinemann, 1921; Project Gutenberg, 2004), https://www.gutenberg.org/files/11304/11304-h/11304-h.htm.

62. See "Padraic Colum," in Welch, *Oxford Companion to Irish Literature*, 108.

63. Padraic Colum, "The Drover," in *Wild Earth and Other Poems* (New York: Henry Holt, 1916), 5–6, https://archive.org/details/wildearthandoth01colugoog.

64. Colum, "A Cradle Song," ibid., 28.

65. Colum, "Across the Door," ibid., 27.

66. Colum, "The Crane," in *The Collected Poems of Padraic Colum* (New York: Devin-Adair, 1916), 166.

67. Colum, "Dublin Roads," in *Selected Poems of Padraic Colum* (Syracuse, NY: Syracuse University Press, 1989), 50.

68. Colum, "River Mates," in *Wild Earth and Other Poems*, 69.

Modern Irish Nature Poetry

Introduction to Part IV

When the Industrial Revolution finally arrived in Ireland full force during the twentieth century, a burgeoning part of the Irish population began to recognize nature as enemy, or at the very least, the people began to see the natural world not only as a threat but also as an unnecessary threat. The choices of larger, more developed communities became preferable, and the untamed wilderness became a place that robbed the spirit. Nature had become synonymous with agriculture and landscape, human constructions where tending to the land and knowing about the land were requisite for survival. Nature was beautiful, and it was a way to connect spiritually with God; but nature was also too difficult a burden on the human condition. Nature drained the individual; it took the physical life out, and the immersion in it was simply not worth the price. No, the way to becoming more human was with a fuller, more developed society rife with conveniences that made nature an unnecessary component of everyday life. A civilized lifestyle in the early twentieth century denied the ideals espoused by the Literary Revival. This became evident when poets began to assess the changes occurring in Irish society as the result of industry and a turning away from the threat that the natural world posed to a comfortable and more materialistic lifestyle, and these themes resonated in their writing.

The modern Irish nature poets, however, respond with a return to nature that puts particular attention to each facet of the natural world: its divergent species, its uniqueness of geography and landscape, and the places that make Ireland Irish. The journey itself into nature from the urban landscape, for the modern poets that include Michael Longley, Patrick Kavanagh, Louis MacNeice, Eavan Boland, Mary O'Malley, Moya Cannon, Derek Mahon, John Montague, Seán Lysaght, and Seamus Heaney, will take on the particular forms, through attention to the plants, animals, and geography of the country, that make up Ireland's natural world. It is the journey outside the world of industry and humanity that begins and ends in a rural existence. It is the road that

> leads on towards
> That incandescent palace
> Where from one room to the next
> There is no one to be seen.[1]

For Longley and Ireland's modern nature poets, their respective sojourns across Ireland's landscape become the unique manner through which each can write about nature and its enduring power. They are travelers who return from nature, renewed by what they have found there. As Edward O. Wilson appropriately wrote of these journeys into nature in *The Diversity of Life*, a work from one of America's most important nature writers that explores the ways to preserve diversity in nature, "Into wilderness people travel in search of new life and wonder, and from wilderness they return to the parts of the earth that have been humanized and made physically secure. Wilderness settles peace on the soul because it needs no help; it is beyond human contrivance."[2]

For each of the poets in part 4, nature becomes a psychological necessity, an act of restoration that reveals itself in verse through close observations of nature. Modern Irish nature poets are really better categorized as naturalist poets, examining the nuances of species and environment more meticulously than their predecessors, examining especially the distinct qualities of Irelands' animals, including hedgehogs and badgers and the many species of Ireland's birds, including the osprey, the kingfisher, the golden eagle, and the goldcrest.

Patrick Kavanagh

Patrick Kavanagh (1904–1967) was both a poet and a novelist. Kavanagh was born in Innis-keen, County Monaghan, Ireland, to the son of a father who was both a cobbler and a sub-sistence farmer in the parish of Inniskeen. Life on this small plot of land and the struggle of rural farm life would be integral to his poetry. At the age of thirteen, Kavanagh became an apprentice shoemaker. He gave it up fifteen months later, admitting that he did not make one wearable pair of boots. For the next twenty years, Kavanagh worked on the family farm before moving to Dublin in 1939 to establish himself as a writer. Because of his newfound urban experience, Kavanagh was critical of Romanticism and the Irish Revival in their admi-ration for nature and the rustic life, as illustrated by his epic poem *The Great Hunger* (1942), an antipastoral poem that centers on the everyday strife of a poor Irish farmer that both celebrates and condemns the harshness of the natural world. Kavanagh moved to Dublin permanently in 1939. There he flourished as a poet. His years living a harsh rural Irish life inspired him to produce a remarkable body of nature poems from an urban perspective, and the themes of these poems often wavered between a praise of rural life in nature and an attack on this way of life.

Poplars

I walked under the tall poplars that my father planted
On a day in April when I was a boy
Running beside the heap of saplingso
From which he picked the straightest spears of sky.
The sun was shining that day
As he shone for the Truatha de Danann
And no one was old or sad
For life was just beginning.[3]

Lilacs in the City

There are lilacs in the city
I saw them looking over
Black walls like pretty
Nuns of an enclosed Order
Curious to know
How the earth-wheels go.
I said to them: close down
Your eye-lids on the town
And do not heed
The streeted ghosts of speed
And do not imagine that
God is excited at
The wonder machines
For Death will reap them all

But for you the eternal queens
Blow kisses.
Do not look beyond your wall.[4]

October

O yellow leafiness you create for me
A world that was and now is poised above time,
I do not need to puzzle out Eternity
As I walk this arboreal street on the edge of a town.
The breeze too, even the temperature
And pattern of movement is precisely the same
as broke my heart for youth passing. Now I am sure
Of something. Something will be mine wherever I am.
I want to throw myself on the public street without caring
for anything but the prayering that the earth offers.
It is October over all my life and the light is staring
As it caught me once in a plantation by the fox coverts.
A man is ploughing ground for winter wheat
And my nineteen years weigh heavily on my feet.[5]

Canal Bank Walk

Leafy-with-love banks and the green waters of the canal
Pouring redemption for me, that I do
The will of God, wallow in the habitual, the banal,
Grow with nature again as before I grew.
The bright stick trapped, the breeze adding a third
Party to the couple kissing on an old seat,
And a bird gathering materials for the nest for the Word
Eloquently new and abandoned to its delirious beat.
O unworn world enrapture me, encapture me in a web
Of fabulous grass and eternal voices by a beech,
Feed the gaping need of my senses, give me ad lib
To pray unselfconsciously with overflowing speech
For this soul needs to be honoured with a new dress woven
From green and blue things and arguments that cannot be proven.[6]

Having to Live in the Country

Back once again in wild, wet Monaghan
Exiled from thought and feeling,
A mean brutality reigns:
It is really a horrible position to be in
And I equate myself with Dante
And all who have lived outside civilization.

It isn't a question of place but of people;
Wordsworth and Coleridge lived apart from the common man,
Their friends called on them regularly.
Swift is in a somewhat different category
He was a genuine exile and his heavy heart
Weighed him down in Dublin.
Yet even he had compensations for in the Deanery
He received many interesting friends
And it was the eighteenth century.

I suppose that having to live
Among men whose rages
Are for small wet hills full of stones
When one man buys a patch and pays a high price for it
That is not the end of his paying.
"Go home and have another bastard" shout the children,
Cousin of the underbidder, to the young wife of the purchaser.
The first child was born after six months of marriage,
Desperate people, desperate animals.
What must happen the poor priest
Somewhat educated who has to believe that these people have souls
As bright as a poet's—though I don't, mind, speak for myself.[7]

Inniskeen Road: July Evening

The bicycles go by in twos and threes—
There's a dance in Billy Brennan's barn to-night,
And there's the half-talk code of mysteries
And the wink-and-elbow language of delight.
Half-past eight and there is not a spot
Upon a mile of road, no shadow thrown
That might turn out a man or woman, not
A footfall tapping secrecies of stone.
I have what every poet hates in spite
Of all the solemn talk of contemplation.
Oh, Alexander Selkirk knew the plight
Of being king and government and nation.
A road, a mile of kingdom, I am king
Of banks and stones and every blooming thing.[8]

Tarry Flynn

On an apple-ripe September morning
Through the mist-chill fields I went
With a pitch-fork on my shoulder
Less for use than for devilment.

The threshing mill was set-up, I knew,
In Cassidy's haggard last night,
And we owed them a day at the threshing
Since last year. O it was delight

To be paying bills of laughter
And chaffy gossip in kind
With work thrown in to ballast
The fantasy-soaring mind.

As I crossed the wooden bridge I wondered
As I looked into the drain
If ever a summer morning should find me
Shovelling up eels again.

And I thought of the wasps' nest in the bank
And how I got chased one day
Leaving the drag and the scraw-knife behind,
How I covered my face with hay.

The wet leaves of the cocksfoot
Polished my boots as I
Went round by the glistening bog-holes
Lost in unthinking joy.

I'll be carrying bags to-day, I mused,
The best job at the mill
With plenty of time to talk of our loves
As we wait for the bags to fill.

Maybe Mary might call round . . .
And then I came to the haggard gate,
And I knew as I entered that I had come
Through fields that were part of no earthly estate.[9]

Primrose

Upon a bank I sat, a child made seer
Of one small primrose flowering in my mind.
Better than wealth it is, I said, to find
One small page of Truth's manuscript made clear.
I looked at Christ transfigured without fear—
The light was very beautiful and kind,
And where the Holy Ghost in flame had signed
I read it through the lenses of a tear.
And then my sight grew dim, I could not see
The primrose that had lighted me to Heaven,
And there was but the shadow of a tree
Ghostly among the stars. The years that pass

Like tired soldiers nevermore have given
Moments to see wonders in the grass.[10]

Wet Evening in April

The birds sang in the wet trees
And I listened to them it was a hundred years from now
And I was dead and someone else was listening to them.
But I was glad I had recorded for him
The melancholy.[11]

Louis MacNeice

Louis MacNeice (1907–1963) was a poet, a radio playwright, and a critic. In addition to his poetry and radio dramas, MacNeice also wrote the verse translation *The Agamemnon of Aeschylus* (1936), translated Goethe's *Faust* (1951), and collaborated with Auden on the travelogue *Letters from Iceland* (1937). In 1941, he joined the BBC and worked there for twenty years, creating and producing programs in the Features Department. Politically, he was a leading figure among the new generation of left-wing poets, including Stephen Spender, Cecil Day-Lewis, and W. H. Auden. MacNeice's long verse meditation *Autumn Journal*, written over the autumn and winter of 1938, chronicled his recollections on the approach of war. His war poetry continued through the 1940s, including the collections *Plant and Phantom* (1941), *Springboard* (1944), and *Holes in the Sky* (1948).[12] Despite his awareness of Irish history and politics and their influence on his poetry, MacNeice has not generally been considered an Irish poet because he lived the majority of his life in London. However, MacNeice frequently returned to the landscapes of his childhood in the west of Ireland, where his parents had their roots; and later in his life, he took great pride in his Irish heritage, and this pride of the landscapes of his youth is reflected in his nature poetry.

The Sunlight on the Garden

The sunlight on the garden
Hardens and grows cold,
We cannot cage the minute
Within its nets of gold;
When all is told
We cannot beg for pardon.

Our freedom as free lances
Advances towards its end;
The earth compels, upon it
Sonnets and birds descend;
And soon, my friend,
We shall have no time for dances.

The sky was good for flying
Defying the church bells
And every evil iron
Siren and what it tells:
The earth compels,
We are dying, Egypt, dying

And not expecting pardon,
Hardened in heart anew,
But glad to have sat under
Thunder and rain with you,
And grateful too
For sunlight on the garden.[13]

Wolves

I do not want to be reflective any more
Envying and despising unreflective things
Finding pathos in dogs and undeveloped handwriting
And young girls doing their hair and all the castles of sand
Flushed by the children's bedtime, level with the shore.

The tide comes in and goes out again, I do not want
To be always stressing either its flux or its permanence,
I do not want to be a tragic or philosophic chorus
But to keep my eye only on the nearer future
And after that let the sea flow over us.

Come then all of you, come closer, form a circle,
Join hands and make believe that joined
Hands will keep away the wolves of water
Who howl along our coast. And be it assumed
That no one hears them among the talk and laughter.[14]

Tree Party

Your health, Master Willow. Contrive me a bat
To strike a red ball; apart from that
In the last resort I must hang my harp on you.

Your health. Master Oak. You emblem of strength.
Why must your doings be done at such length?
Beware lest the ironclad ages catch up with you.

Your health, Master Blackthorn. Be live and be quick,
Provide the black priest with a big black stick
That his ignorant flock may go straight for the fear of you.

Your health, Master Palm. If you brew us some toddy
To deliver us out of by means of the body,
We will burn all our bridges and rickshaws in praise of you.

Your health, Master Pine. Though sailing be past
Let you fly your own colours upon your own mast
And rig us a crow's nest to keep a look out from you.

Your health, Master Elm. Of giants arboreal
Poets have found you the most immemorial
And yet the big winds may discover the fault in you.

Your health, Master Hazel. On Halloween
Your nuts are to gather but not to be seen
Are the twittering ghosts that perforce are alive in you.

Your health, Master Holly. Of all the trees
That decorate parlour walls you please
Yet who would have thought you had so much blood in you?

Your health, Master Apple. Your topmost bough
Entices us to come climbing now
For all that old rumour there might be a snake in you.

Your health, Master Redwood. The record is yours
For the girth that astounds, the sap that endures,
But where are the creatures that once came to nest in you?

Your health, Master Banyan, but do not get drunk
Or you may not distinguish your limbs from your trunk
And the sense of Above and Below will be lost on you.

Your health, Master Bo-Tree. If Buddha should come
Yet again, yet again make your branches keep mum
That his words yet again may drop honey by leave of you.

Your health, Master Yew. My bones are few
And I fully admit my rent is due,
But do not be vexed, I will postdate a cheque for you.[15]

Seamus Heaney

Seamus Heaney (1939–2013) was a poet, essayist, and playwright. He published his first poetry book in 1966, *Death of a Naturalist*, engaging with Ireland's natural world with powerful imagery to reflect powerful poetic representations of rural life. His later collections, including *North* (1974), *Station Island* (1984), *The Spirit Level* (1996), and *District and Circle* (2006), focused on The Troubles and their impact on Northern Ireland, leading to his winning the 1995 Nobel Prize in Literature for his poetic attention to this conflict. Heaney's legacy will ultimately reside in his poems on love, nature, and memory. Included here are some of his more popular nature poems, beginning with "Death of a Naturalist," alongside lesser-known works, including "St. Kevin and the Blackbird," with a thematic connection to Katharine Tynan's "St. Francis to the Birds" in part 3 of this anthology, and the poem "Limbo," with a connection to the cartographer Tim Robinson's exploration of the baby graveyard, "The Boneyard," from *Connemara: Listening to the Wind*, included in part 5.[16]

Death of a Naturalist

All year the flax-dam festered in the heart
Of the townland; green and heavy headed
Flax had rotted there, weighted down by huge sods.
Daily it sweltered in the punishing sun.
Bubbles gargled delicately, bluebottles
Wove a strong gauze of sound around the smell.
There were dragon-flies, spotted butterflies,
But best of all was the warm thick slobber
Of frogspawn that grew like clotted water
In the shade of the banks. Here, every spring
I would fill jampotfuls of the jellied
Specks to range on window-sills at home,
On shelves at school, and wait and watch until
The fattening dots burst into nimble-
Swimming tadpoles. Miss Walls would tell us how
The daddy frog was called a bullfrog
And how he croaked and how the mammy frog
Laid hundreds of little eggs and this was
Frogspawn. You could tell the weather by frogs too
For they were yellow in the sun and brown
In rain.

Then one hot day when fields were rank
With cowdung in the grass the angry frogs
Invaded the flax-dam; I ducked through hedges
To a coarse croaking that I had not heard
Before. The air was thick with a bass chorus.
Right down the dam gross-bellied frogs were cocked

On sods; their loose necks pulsed like sails. Some hopped:
The slap and plop were obscene threats. Some sat
Poised like mud grenades, their blunt heads farting.
I sickened, turned, and ran. The great slime kings
Were gathered there for vengeance and I knew
That if I dipped my hand the spawn would clutch it.[17]

The Salmon Fisher to the Salmon

The ridged lip set upstream, you flail
Inland again, your exile in the sea
Unconditionally cancelled by the pull
Of your home water's gravity.

And I stand in the centre, casting.
The river, cramming under me, reflects
Slung gaff and net and a white wrist flicking
Flies well-dressed with tint and fleck.

Walton thought garden worms, perfumed
By oil crushed from dark ivy berries
The lure that took you best, but here you come
To grief through hunger in your eyes.

Ripples arrowing beyond me,
The current strumming rhythms up my leg:
Involved in water's choreography
I go like you, by gleam and drag

And will strike when you strike, to kill.
We're both annihilated on the fly.
You can't resist a gullet full of steel.
I will turn home fish-smelling, scaly.[18]

Limbo

Fishermen at Ballyshannon
Netted an infant last night
Along with the salmon.
An illegitimate spawning,

A small one thrown back
To the waters. But I'm sure
As she stood in the shallows
Ducking him tenderly

Till the frozen knobs of her wrists
Were dead as the gravel,
He was a minnow with hooks
Tearing her open.

She waded in under
The sign of her cross.
He was hauled in with the fish.
Now limbo will be

A cold glitter of souls
Through some far briny zone.
Even Christ's palms, unhealed,
Smart and cannot fish there.[19]

St. Kevin and the Blackbird

And then there was St Kevin and the blackbird.
The saint is kneeling, arms stretched out, inside
His cell, but the cell is narrow, so

One turned-up palm is out the window, stiff
As a crossbeam, when a blackbird lands
And lays in it and settles down to nest.

Kevin feels the warm eggs, the small breast, the tucked
Neat head and claws and, finding himself linked
Into the network of eternal life,

Is moved to pity: now he must hold his hand
Like a branch out in the sun and rain for weeks
Until the young are hatched and fledged and flown.

•

And since the whole thing's imagined anyhow,
Imagine being Kevin. Which is he?
Self-forgetful or in agony all the time

From the neck on out down through his hurting forearms?
Are his fingers sleeping? Does he still feel his knees?
Or has the shut-eyed blank of underearth

Crept up through him? Is there distance in his head?
Alone and mirrored clear in Love's deep river,
'To labour and not to seek reward,' he prays,

A prayer his body makes entirely
For he has forgotten self, forgotten bird
And on the riverbank forgotten the river's name.[20]

Eavan Boland

Eavan Boland (1944–) was born in Dublin to the daughter of the Irish diplomat F. H. Boland, who was president of the United Nations General Assembly from 1960 until his death in 1985. Boland was educated in both London and New York and returned to Ireland to attend the Holy Child Convent in Killiney and then Trinity College. Much of her poetry and other writing has evolved from attention to the Troubles in northern Ireland and women's issues, including poems about anorexia and menstruation, motherhood, and the position of Irish women writers at the end of the twentieth century, emboldened with newfound freedoms in a changing Ireland. Boland's poetry often turns its attention to Ireland's natural world, a place often in conflict with urban development and the subsequent loss of the Irish landscape, and she writes about Ireland from a perspective outside the country. Boland and her husband, the author Kevin Casey, have two daughters, and she is currently a professor of English at Stanford University, where she directs the creative writing program.

The Lost Land

I have two daughters.

They are all I ever wanted from the earth.

Or almost all.

I also wanted one piece of ground:

One city trapped by hills. One urban river.
An island in its element.

So I could say *mine. My own.*
And mean it.

Now they are grown up and far away

and memory itself
has become an emigrant,
wandering in a place
where love dissembles itself as landscape:

Where the hills
are the colours of a child's eyes,
where my children are distances, horizons:

At night,
on the edge of sleep,

I can see the shore of Dublin Bay.
Its rocky sweep and its granite pier.

Is this, I say
how they must have seen it,
backing out on the mailboat at twilight,

shadows falling
on everything they had to leave?
And would love forever?
And then

I imagine myself
at the landward rail of that boat
searching for the last sight of a hand.

I see myself
on the underworld side of that water,
the darkness coming in fast, saying
all the names I know for a lost land:

Ireland. Absence. Daughter.[21]

The River

You brought me
    To the mouth of a river
In mid-October
    When the swamp maples
Were saw-toothed and blemished.
    I remember

how strange it felt—
    not having any
names for the red oak
    and the rail
and the slantways plunge
    of the osprey.

What we said was less
    than what we saw.
What we saw was
    a duck boat, slowly
passing us, a hunter and
    his spaniel, and

his gun poised,
    and, in the distance,
the tips of the wild
    rice drowning in
that blue which raids and
    excludes light.[22]

Mountain Time

Time is shadowless there: mornings re-occur
only as enchantments, only as time for her

to watch berries ripen by on the summer ash;
for him, at a short distance from her, to catch fish.

Afterwards, darkness will be only what is left of
a mouth after kissing or a hand laced in a hand;

a branch; a river; will be what is lost of words
as they turn to silences and then to sleep. Yet

when they leave the mountain what he will remember is
the rowan trees; that blemish, that scarlet. She will think of

the arc of salmon after sudden capture—
its glitter a larceny of daylight on slate.[23]

This Moment

A neighbourhood.
At dusk.

Things are getting ready
to happen
out of sight.

Stars and moths.
And rinds slanting around fruit.
But not yet.

One tree is black.
One window is yellow as butter.

A woman leans down to catch a child
who has run into her arms
this moment.

Stars rise.
Moths flutter.
Apples sweeten in the dark.[24]

Ode to Suburbia

Six o'clock: the kitchen bulbs which blister
Your dark, your housewives starting to nose
Out each other's day, the claustrophobia
Of your back gardens varicose
With shrubs, make an ugly sister
Of you suburbia.

How long ago did the glass in your windows subtly
Silver into mirrors which again
And again show the same woman
Shriek at a child? Which multiply
A dish, a brush, ash,
The gape of a fish.

In the kitchen, the gape of a child in the cot?
You swelled so that when you tried
The silver slipper on your foot
It pinched your instep and the common
Hurt which touched you made
You human.

No creature of the streets will feel the touch
Of a wand turning the wet sinews
Of fruit suddenly to a coach,
While this rat without leather reins
Or a whip or britches continues
Sliming your drains.

No magic here. Yet you encroach until
The shy countryside, fooled
By your plainness falls, then rises
From your bed changed, schooled
Forever by your skill,
Your compromises.

Midnight and your metamorphosis
Is now complete, although the mind
Which spinstered you might still miss
Your mystery now, might still fail
To see your power defined
By this detail:

By this creature drowsing now in every house,
The same lion who tore stripes
Once off zebras, who now sleeps
Small beside the coals and may
On a red letter day
Catch a mouse.[25]

Escape

I

It was only when a swan
made her nest
on the verge beside Leeson Street bridge,

And too near the kerb by the canal,
that I remembered
my first attempt at an Irish legend.

And stopped the car
and walked over to her.
And into my twentieth winter:

II

The window open where I left it.
The table cloth still on the table
The page at the last line I crafted.

III

I sat in the kitchen and frost
blended with kettle steam while
I crossed out and crossed out
the warm skin and huggable limbs
of Lir's children—
rhyming them into doomed swans
cursed into flight on
a coast that was only half a mile
from my flat in Morehampton Road.

IV

It was evening now. Overhead
wild stars had wheels and landing gear.

A small air of spring hung above
the verge with its bottle lids and papers,
its poplar shadows,
its opening narcissi
and passers-by hurrying home from offices,
who barely turned to see what was there:

V

A mother bird too near the road.

A middle-aged woman going
as near to her as she dared.

Neither of them willing
to stir from the actual and ordinary,
momentary danger.

One of them aware of the story.

Both of them escaped from the telling.[26]

A Sparrow Hawk in the Suburbs

At that time of year there is a turn in the road where
the hermit tones and meadow colours of
two seasons heal into
one another.

When the wild ladder of a winter scarf is stored away in
a drawer by candle-grease and lemon balm
is shaken out from
a linen press.

Those are afternoons when the Dublin hills are so close,
so mauve and blue. We can be certain dark
will bring rain and
it does to

the borrowed shears and the love-seat in the garden where
a sparrow hawk was seen through the opal
white of apple trees
after Easter. And

I want to know how it happened that those days of bloom when
rumours of wings and sightings—always seen by
someone else, somewhere else—
filled the air,

together with a citrus drizzle of petals and clematis opening,
and shadows waiting on a gradual lengthening
in the light our children
stayed up

later by, over pages of wolves and dragons and learned to
measure the sanctuary of darkness by a small
danger—how and why
they have chilled

into these April nights I lie awake listening for wings I will
never see above the cold frames and
last frosts of our
back gardens.[27]

Moya Cannon

Moya Cannon was born in County Donegal and lives in Dublin. *Keats Lives*, published by Carcanet Press, Manchester, United Kingdom, is her fifth collection of poetry. Her previous collection, *Hands*, was short-listed for the *Irish Times* Poetry Now Award. She is a winner of the Brendan Behan Award and the Laurence O'Shaughnessy Award for Poetry. She has been the editor of the *Poetry Ireland Review* and was 2011 Heimbold Professor of Irish Studies at Villanova University, Pennsylvania. As the critic Brendan Lowe notes of her collection *Keats Lives* in the *Dublin Review of Books*, for Cannon "the natural world—the inanimate included—exist in a continuum. Throughout her poems the interwoven web of life is laid out for our inspection and acknowledgement."[28] The following selections support this contention and emphasize, much like the Romantic poets and the poets of the Irish Literary Revival, a strong spiritual connection to Ireland's nature.

Bees under Snow

In a valley beside the black wood,
this year there are fifty-two beehives—
orange and blue cubes with zinc lids,
raised on long girders.

Last winter, under a foot of snow,
they were square marshmallows in a white field.
By a minuscule door lay a few dead bees
and one or two flew about distractedly
but the bees inside hovered in a great ball
shivering to keep warm, to stay alive
moving always inwards towards the globe's centre
or outward towards its surface.

As much as their hunt for sweetness
or their incidental work of fertilizing the world's
scented, myriad-coloured flowers
to bear fruit for all earthbound, airborne creatures,
this is part of their lives,
these long months of shivering, of bee-faith.[29]

Eavesdropping

Late at low tide, one June evening,
at the tip of a green promontory
which brimmed with lark song and plover cry,
I lay down on a slab of damp granite
encrusted with limpets and barnacles;
laid my head down in that rough company
and heard the whispers

of a million barnacles,
the grumbling of a hundred limpets
and behind them, the shushing
of the world's one
gold-struck, mercury sea.[30]

Two Ivory Swans

fly across a display case
as they flew across Siberian tundra
twenty thousand years ago,
heralding thaw on an inland sea—
   their wings, their necks, stretched, stretched
   vulnerable, magnificent.

Their whooping set off a harmonic
in someone who looked up,
registered the image
of the journeying birds
and, with a hunter-gatherer's hand
carved tiny white likenesses
from the tip of the tusk
of the greatest land-mammal,
wore them for a while,
traded or gifted them
before they were dropped
down time's echoing chute,
to emerge, strong-winged,
whooping,
to fly across our time.[31]

Winter View from Binn Bhriocáin

In the mountain-top stillness
the bog is heather-crusted iron.
A high, hidden mountain pond
is frozen into zinc riffles.

We have tramped across a plateau
of frost-smashed quartzite
to the summit cairn.

Far below, in February light,
lakes, bogs, sea-inlets,
the myriad lives being lived in them,
lives of humans and of trout,
of stonechats and sea-sedges,

fan out, a palette of hammered silver,
grey and silver.[32]

Primavera

A first sighting,
five low primroses,
and later, near the compost,
a sliver of white among clumped shoots—
a snowdrop splits its green sheath,
and high birdsong in the hazels—
a jolt to realise that here too,
below the snow-shawled Alps
with their tunnels and ski-stations,
this is St. Bridget's Eve.

This is the evening when my father
used to knock three times on the scullery door
and wait for an invitation to enter
with a bundle of cut rushes, saying,

Téigi ar bhur nglúine,
fosclaigí bhur súile
agus ligigí isteach Bríd.

Older, he told me his sisters used to vie
to be the one to knock three times
before entering with the first greening.
What ritual were they re-enacting?
Or we, in the warm yellow kitchen, suddenly full
of rushes and scissors and coloured wool-ends,

what ceremony were we weaving there,
folding the silky stalks into crosses
to hang above the door
of each room in the house,
or what do those little island girls celebrate
who still carry the *Brídeóg*, the spring doll,
from house to welcoming house,
if not the joyful return
of the bride of Hades after three months of deep
wintering, if not a first sighting of Persephone
among the rushes in a wet western field.

And what caution was told in the hesitation,
until that third knock granted admission,
what fear of deception, of late frosts,
of February snow and dead lambs?

Our fears are different now,
of floods and fast-calving glaciers,
of birds and beasts and fish and flowers forever lost
and the earth's old bones pressed for oil.

But our bones still bid her welcome
when she knocks three times,
when she enters, ever young,
saying
Kneel down,
open your eyes
and allow spring to come in.
   Kneel down,
   Open your eyes
   And allow Bridget to come in.[33]

The Tube-Case Makers

(LES EPHEMÈS)
This one-inch mottled twig
is built of silk and stone.
Inside it, under a larva's translucent skin,
are shadowy, almost-ready wings,
a heart which pumps and pumps.

For two or three years
it trundled about
in the shallows of a mountain river
in this stone coat, eating leaf-debris,
adding, as it grew, a little sticky silk
to one end, a few more tiny stones,
until the time came to shut itself in,
to almost seal both ends of its tube—
intent on transformation
as any medieval anchorite.

It is not true
it turns into a green soup
but how does it happen,
the breaking down of redundant muscles,
the building of flight muscles?
as a grub becomes stomachless,
rises out of the river,
for one summer's day, to mate,
alight at nightfall,
and lay the eggs
that have kept its tribe alive

since it rose in clouds
around the carbuncled feet of dinosaurs—

with each tiny,
down-drifting egg
encapsuling
a slumbered knowledge
of silk
and stone
and
flight.[34]

Crannog

Where an ash bush grows in the lake
a ring of stones has broken cover
in this summer's drought.
Not high enough to be an island,
it holds a disc of stiller water
in the riffled lake.

Trees have reclaimed the railway line behind us;
behind that, the road goes east—
as two lines parallel in space and time run away from us
this discovered circle draws us in.
In drowned towns
bells toll only for sailors and for the credulous
but this necklace of wet stones,
remnant of a wattle Atlantis,
catches us all by the throat.

We don't know what beads or blades
are held in the bog lake's wet amber
but much of us longs to live in water
and we recognise this surfacing
of old homes of love and hurt.

A troubled bit of us is kin
to people who drew a circle in water,
loaded boats with stone,
and raised a dry island and a fort
with a whole lake for a moat.[35]

Hazelnuts

I thought that I knew what they meant
when they said that wisdom is a hazelnut.
You have to search the scrub

for hazel thickets,
gather the ripened nuts,
crack the hard shells,
and only then taste the sweetness at wisdom's kernel.

But perhaps it is simpler.
Perhaps it is we who wait in thickets
for fate to find us
and break us between its teeth
before we can start to know anything.[36]

John Montague

John Montague (1929–2016) was born in Brooklyn, New York, and came to Ireland when he was four years old to live with his aunts in County Tyrone. He was educated at St. Patrick's College in Armagh and Yale University and later went on to teach at the University of California–Berkeley and at University College Cork. In the United States, Montague was influenced by American poets, especially Allen Ginsberg, Gary Snyder, and Walt Whitman, and brought these influences into his poetry, which reflected the urban life of northern Ireland and the panoramic technique used especially by Whitman in "Song of Myself." Montague's life in northern Ireland compelled him to write on the effect of the past on the present, and he became a spokesman for the Ulster Catholics, seeking to embrace both the unfolding of history and the mythic dimension in the rural life of the Irish. Much of his poetry, especially his collection *A Slow Dance* (1975), weighs in on the escape from urban life and the therapeutic power of nature as a cure for the ills of living in cities. His nature poetry carries with it the keen recognition of the interplay between life, decay, and death in the natural world.[37]

All Legendary Obstacles

All legendary obstacles lay between
Us, the long imaginary plain,
The monstrous ruck of mountains
And, swinging across the night,
Flooding the Sacramento, San Joaquin,
The hissing drift of winter rain.
All day I waited, shifting
Nervously from station to bar
As I saw another train sail
By, the San Francisco Chief or
Golden Gate, water dripping
From great flanged wheels.
At midnight you came, pale
Above the negro porter's lamp.
I was too blind with rain
And doubt to speak, but
Reached from the platform
Until our chilled hands met.
You had been travelling for days
With an old lady, who marked
A neat circle on the glass
With her glove, to watch us
Move into the wet darkness
Kissing, still unable to speak.[38]

The Wild Dog Rose

1

I go to say goodbye to the *Cailleach*
that terrible figure who haunted my childhood
but no longer harsh, a human being
merely, hurt by event.

       The cottage,
circled by trees, weathered to admonitory
shapes of desolation by the mountain winds,
straggles into view. The rank thistles
and leathery bracken of untilled fields
stretch behind with—a final outcrop—
the hooped figure by the roadside,
its retinue of dogs

         which give tongue
as I approach, with savage, whinging cries
so that she slowly turns, a moving nest
of shawls and rags, to view, to stare
the stranger down.

        And I feel again
that ancient awe, the terror of a child
before the great hooked nose, the cheeks
dewlapped with dirt, the staring blue
of the sunken eyes, the mottled claws
clutching a stick

        but now hold
and return her gaze, to greet her,
as she greets me, in friendliness.
Memories have wrought reconciliation
between us, we talk in ease at last,
like old friends, lovers almost,
sharing secrets.

        Of neighbours
she quarreled with, who now lie
in Garvaghey graveyard, beyond all hatred;
of my family and hers, how she never married,
though a man came asking in her youth.
'You would be loath to leave your own'
she signs, 'and go among strangers'—
his parish ten miles off.

        For sixty years
since she had lived alone, in one place.

Obscurely honoured by such confidences,
I idle by the summer roadside, listening,
while the monologue falters, continues,
rehearsing the small events of her life.
The only true madness is loneliness,
the monotonous voice in the skull
that never stops
                    because never heard.

2

And there
where the dog rose shines in the hedge
she tells me a story so terrible
that I try to push it away,
my bones melting.

              Late at night
a drunk came, beating at her door
to break it in, the bolt snapping
from the soft wood, the thin mongrels
rushing to cut, but yelping as
he whirls with his farm boots
to crush their skulls.

              In the darkness
they wrestle, two creatures crazed
with loneliness, the smell of the
decaying cottage in his nostrils
like a drug, his body heavy on hers,
the tasteless trunk of a seventy year
old virgin, which he rummages while
she battles for life

              bony fingers
reaching desperately to push
against his bull neck. 'I prayed
to the Blessed Virgin herself
for help and after a time
I broke his grip.'

              He rolls
to the floor, snores asleep,
while she cowers until dawn
and the dogs' whimpering starts
him awake, to lurch back across
the wet bog.

3
              And still
the dog rose shines in the hedge.
Petals beaten wide by rain, it
sways slightly, at the tip of a
slender, tangled, arching branch
which, with her stick, she gathers
into us.

              'The wild rose
is the only rose without thorns,'
she says, holding a wet blossom
for a second, in a hand knotted
as the knob of her stick.
'Whenever I see it, I remember
the Holy Mother of God and
all she suffered.'

              Briefly
the air is strong with the smell
of that weak flower, offering
its crumbling yellow cup
and pale bleeding lips
fading to white

              at the rim
of each bruised and heart-
shaped petal.[39]

The Trout

for Barrie Cooke

Flat on the bank I parted
Rushes to ease my hands
In the water without a ripple
And tilt them slowly downstream
To where he lay, tendril-light,
In his fluid sensual dream.

Bodiless lord of creation,
I hung briefly above him
Savouring my own absence,
Senses expanding in the slow
Motion, the photographic calm
That grows before action.

As the curve of my hands
Swung under his body
He surged, with visible pleasure.
I was so preternaturally close
I could count every stipple
But still cast no shadow, until

The two palms crossed in a cage
Under the lightly pulsing gills.
Then (entering my own enlarged
Shape, which rode on the water)
I gripped. To this day I can
Taste his terror on my hands.[40]

Michael Longley

Michael Longley (1939–) was born in Belfast to British parents; he attended the Royal Belfast Academical Institution, taught in Dublin, London, and Belfast, and joined the Northern Ireland Arts Council, where he was director of Combined Arts from 1970 until 1991. Much of Longley's early poetry focused on urban themes and Belfast life, particularly The Troubles and more generally the victims of all violence resulting from war. However, Longley's most profound poetry is reserved for the natural world of County Mayo; he combines keen observations of the landscape and of the flora and fauna it contains with the range of emotions—violence, decay, death, and love—that he explores in his urban poetry. In the following selection, Longley observes specific animals and landscapes of Ireland's natural world, including ospreys, badgers, hedgehogs, and kingfishers. Also included here is a conversation poem to Seamus Heaney's "St Kevin and the Blackbird," a poem Longley titles "Saint Francis to the Birds."[41]

The Osprey

To whom certain water talents—
Webbed feet, oils—do not occur,
Regulates his liquid acre
From the sky, his proper element.
There, already, his eye removes
The trout each fathom magnifies.
He lives, without compromise,
His unamphibious two lives—
An inextinguishable bird whom
No lake's waters waterlog.
He shakes his feathers like a dog.
It's all of air that ferries him.[42]

Badger

for Raymond Piper

1

Pushing the wedge of his body
Between cromlech and stone circle,
He excavates down mine shafts
And back into the depths of the hill.

His path straight and narrow
And not like the fox's zig-zags,
The arc of the hare who leaves
A silhouette on the sky line.

Night's silence around his shoulders,
His face lit by the moon, he

225

Manages the earth with his paws,
Returns underground to die.

2

An intestine taking in
Patches of dog's-mercury,
Brambles, the bluebell wood;
A heel revolving acorns;
A head with a price on it
Brushing cuckoo-spit, goose-grass;
A name that parishes borrow.

3

For the digger, the earth dog
It is a difficult delivery
Once the tongs take hold,

Vulnerable his pig's snout
That lifted cow pats for beetles,
Hedgehogs for the soft meat,

His limbs dragging after them
So many stones turned over,
The trees they tilted.[43]

Hedgehog

To begin with, the hedgehog does not
—Forgive me, John Clare—
Impale on his spines
Windfalls, rolling over

On to a bed of nails
To collect apples, soft pears
As in Pliny or
The medieval illuminations.

Pushed in his prickly cape
To the back of the mind,
He punctures with needles
Hunger and cold,

Mates with as little fuss
As he absorbs from wasp and hornet
Their poisons; the corrosives
Of the viper's mouth.

A hedgehog on the motorway
—Flattened to parchment—

Reminded me that it might be better
If these things were said.[44]

Kingfisher

A knife-thrower
Hurling himself, a rainbow
Fractured against
The plate glass of winter:

His eye a water bead,
Lens and meniscus where
The dragonfly drowns,
The water boatman crawls.[45]

Robin

Its breast a warning,
A small fire
Lit beside the snow
That does not go out—

The robin shadows
The heavy-footed, the earth—
Breakers—bull's hoof
And pheasant's too—

Is an eye that would—
If we let it in—scan
The walls for cockroaches,
For bed-bugs the beds.[46]

Out of the Sea

1. Seahorses

The eggs are incubated
By the male of the species,
Heraldic the horse's head
Though his body convulses
Pumping into the sea sons
And daughters—his stomach's
Hundred tiny versions—

Their death a dignified drift
And a slow coming to light
On the shore—an ideal gift
Or dropped off a charm bracelet.

2. Bikini Atoll

On to whose bridal sands
And out of the sea (insects'
Wings confetti on the waves)

A turtle into famine steers,
On her slow shoulders heaves
The burning hinterland,

Her ancient face hung with tears.[47]

Her Mime of the Lame Seagull

Some things come too soon for words,
Fracture syntax, from all tenses overflow,
Prove semantically impossible: and so,
Taken by surprise, your body is the bird's.

You who would sing to perfect flight again
The gull, before one syllable takes breath
Convey as part and parcel of largest death
The cut let: and with your body you explain

Its difficult lopsided freight. And since
A bird that into famine soon must steer
Is tabernacled and abiding here,
Its broken journey gathered in your silence,

I accept your body's brief vocabulary:
The gull is lame, is all you almost say,
Your little breasts, your hands like birds at play,
Rightly the last resort of such agony.[48]

Carrigskeewaun

for Penny & David Cabot

The Mountain

This is ravens' territory, skulls, bones,
The marrow of these boulders supervised
From the upper air: I stand alone here
And seem to gather children about me,
A collection of picnic things, my voice
Filling the district as I call their names.

The Path

With my first step I dislodge the mallards
Whose necks strain over the bog to where

Kittiwakes scrape the waves: then, the circle
Widening, lapwings, curlews, snipe until
I am left with only one swan to nudge
To the far side of its gradual disdain.

The Strand

I discover, remaindered from yesterday,
Cattle tracks, a sanderling's tiny trail,
The footprints of the children and my own
Linking the dunes to the water's edge,
Reducing to sand the dry shells, the toe-
And fingernail parings of the sea.

The Wall

I join all the men who have squatted here
This lichened side of the dry-stone wall
And notice how smoke from our turf fire
Recalls in the cool air above the lake
Steam from a kettle, a tablecloth and
A table she might have already set.

The Lake

Though it will duplicate at any time
The sheep and cattle that wander there,
For a few minutes every evening
Its surface seems tilted to receive
The sun perfectly, the mare and her foal,
The heron, all such special visitors.[49]

Saint Francis to the Birds

(with apologies to S. Heaney Esq.)

And, summing up, I think of when
With cloud and cloudburst you confer,
By God's sheer genius lifted there,
Lighthearted starling, nervous wren.

It is perfection you rehearse—
God placed the limpet on a rock,
He dressed the primrose in its frock upside down with its leg showing
And closed the chestnut in its purse:

Creating one more precedent,
With no less forethought, no less care
He gave you feathers and the air

To migrate to his best intent.
To useful angles well aligned,
At proper heights compelled to tilt,
Across kind landscapes yearly spilt—
Birds, you are always on his mind.

Quick emblems of his long estate,
It's good to have you overhead
Who understand when all is said,
When all is done, and it is late.

May my sermon, like your customs,
Reach suddenly beyond dispute—
Oh, birds entire and absolute,
Last birds above our broken homes.[50]

Derek Mahon

Derek Mahon (1941–) was born in Belfast and grew up in Glengormley, then attended the Royal Belfast Academical Institution and then Trinity College, Dublin, where he studied the classics. He spent time in the United States and Canada teaching before returning to Ireland to teach. He also spent time as a journalist and writer in London, where he was a reviewer, an editor, and a writer adapting novels for television. He moved to New York in the late 1980s, and without a geographic center from which to draw, Mahon's poetry reflects his own alienation from a northern Irish, Protestant, middle-class life taken from fragments of his childhood memories of Belfast and Glengormley. Mahon's most recent books of poetry include *Olympia and the Internet* (2017), *An Autumn Wind* (2010), *Life on Earth* (2008), *Somewhere the Wave* (2007), *Harbour Lights* (2005), and *Collected Poems* (1999). He also coauthored *In Their Element: A Selection of Poems with Seamus Heaney* (1977). In many of the poems throughout these collections, like many Irish urban poets of the North, Mahon finds solace in the Irish landscape, where the imagery reflects a sense of alienation. Yet in each of the poems, particularly in the selections here, the presence of the natural world offers a calming reassurance in that alienation.[51]

The Seasons

for Matthew Geden

1.

Day-stars like daisies on a field of sky.
The nuclear subs are keeping sinister watch
while sun heat focuses on the cabbage-patch.
What weird weather can we expect this July?
Tornado, hail, some sort of freak tempest?
The bonfire month, and another storm brewing:
I hear it sing I' th'wind, and among the leaves.
But out here in the hot pastures of the west,
no Google goggling at our marginal lives,
there are still corners where a lark can sing.

2.

We prospered and made hay while the sun shone.
Now autumn skies, yellow and grey, sow rain
on summer debris, Ambre Solaire, crushed bracken,
we clear the dead leaves from a blocked drain
and tap barometers since the weather's taken
a sudden turn for the worse. Contentious crows
congregate of an evening at St Multose';
the harvest hymns float out from Gothic windows
on Maersk, docked sailing-boats and guesthouses
closed for the winter now the guests have gone.

3.

The reading period, and on the writing desk
quarto and lamplight in the early dusk.
If we don't travel now we hibernate
with other locals at the Tap Tavern
beside an open hearth, our winter haven.
Glowing cinders nuzzle the warm grate
while outside, ghostly in a starlit street,
creaking signs and a novelistic breeze.
Urgent footsteps fade into the night
leaving us to our pub talk and reveries.

4.

A fly-dazzling disc in the open door,
hung on a ribbon, catches the light and blinks
as the sun spokes on gardens and seascapes,
drawing up dew, exposing hidden depths,
old shipwrecks visible from the air. A northern
draught blows flower scents to the blue horizon;
a yawl, Bermuda-rigged, shakes out its linen
watched by the yachties, blow-ins, quiet drunks
and the new girls with parasols in their drinks.
Springs gush in a shower of flowering hawthorn.[52]

Achill

*im chaonaí uaigneach nach mór go bhfeicim an lá**

I lie and imagine a first light gleam in the bay
    After one more night of erosion and nearer the grave,
Then stand and gaze from the window at break of day
    As a shearwater skims the ridge of an incoming wave;
And I think of my son a dolphin in the Aegean,
    A sprite among sails knife-bright in a seasonal wind,
And wish he were here where currachs walk on the ocean
    To ease with his talk the solitude locked in my mind.

I sit on a stone after lunch and consider the glow
    Of the sun through mist, a pearl bulb containèdly fierce;
A rain-shower darkens the schist for a minute or so
    Then it drifts away and the sloe-black patches disperse.
Croagh Patrick towers like Naxos over the water
    And I think of my daughter at work on her difficult art
And wish she were with me now between thrush and plover,
    Wild thyme and sea-thrift, to lift the weight from my heart.

---

* "a lonely chamber that must see the day"

The young sit smoking and laughing on the bridge at evening
    Like birds on a telephone pole or notes on a score.
A tin whistle squeals in the parlour, once more it is raining,
    Turf-smoke inclines and a wind whines under the door;
And I lie and imagine the lights going on in the harbor
    Of white-housed Náousa, your clear definition at night,
And wish you were here to upstage my disconsolate labour
    As I glance through a few thin pages and switch off the light.[53]

Aphrodite's Pool

I dive and rise in an explosion of spindrift
and drift to a turtle-faced inflatable raft—
evening, Cyclades, one cloud in the azure,
a brain-scan light-show swarming on blue tiles,
a flickering network of vague energies
as on dolphin murals and docked caique bows,
a murmuring hosepipe where the pool fills,
snatches of music from a quiet house,
the wash-house like a temple to the Muses;
on a marble slab flipper and apple core,
straw hat and wristwatch in a deckchair,
sandal and white sock. Nymphs have been here;
water nymphs have been here printing the blind
nap-time silence with supernatural toes
and casting magic on the ruffled water
still agitated by a dry seasonal wind.
A last plane fades beyond the glittering sound,
its wild surf-boards and somnolent fishing-boats,
as the air fills with cicadas and mosquitoes,
the sky with sunset and astronomy; goats
and donkeys nod in the god-familiar hills
among spaceship vertebrae and white asphodels.
The prone body is mine, that of a satyr,
a fat, unbronzed, incongruous visitor
under the fairy lights and paper frills
of a birthday party I was too late to attend.
Aloof from the disco ships and buzzing bikes
the pool ticks faintly among quiet rocks;
rose petals on the surface and in the air,
mimosa and jasmine fragrance everywhere,
I flirt like some corrupt, capricious emperor
with insects dithering on the rim; for this
is the mythic moment of metamorphosis
when quantitive becomes qualitative and genes
perform their atom-dance of mad mutation . . .

I climb out, shower off chlorine and sun-lotion,
and a hot turquoise underwater light
glows like Atlantis in the Aegean night;
network, stars-of-the-sea, perpetual motion,
a star-net hums in the aphrodisiac sea-lanes.[54]

The Mayo Tao

I have abandoned the dream kitchens for a low fire
and a prescriptive literature of the spirit;
a storm snores on the desolate sea.
The nearest shop is four miles away—
when I walk there through the shambles
of the morning for tea and firelighters
the mountain paces me in a snow-lit silence.
My days are spent in conversation
with deer and blackbirds;
at night fox and badger gather at my door.
I have stood for hours
watching a salmon doze in the tea-gold dark,
for months listening to the sob story
of a stone in the road, the best,
most monotonous sob story I have ever heard.

I am an expert on frost crystals
and the silence of crickets, a confidant
of the stinking shore, the stars in the mud—
there is an immanence in these things
which drives me, despite my scepticism,
almost to the point of speech,
like sunlight cleaving the lake mist at morning
or when tepid water
runs cold at last from the tap.

I have been working for years
on a four-line poem
about the life of a leaf;
I think it might come out right this winter.[55]

Penshurst Place

The bright drop quivering on a thorn
in the rich silence after rain,
lute music in the orchard aisles,
the paths ablaze with daffodils,
intrigue and venery in the air

a l'ombre des jeunes filles en fleurs,*
the iron hand and the velvet glove—
come live with me and be my love.

A pearl face, numinously bright,
shining in silence of the night,
a muffled crash of smouldering logs,
bad dreams of courtiers and of dogs,
the Spanish ships around Kinsale,
the screech-owl and the nightingale,
the falcon and the turtle-dove—
Come live with me and be my love.[56]

The Woods

Two years we spent
down there, in a quaint
outbuilding bright with recent paint.

A green retreat,
secluded and sedate,
part of a once great estate,

it watched our old
bone-shaker as it growled
with guests and groceries through heat and cold,

and heard you tocsin
meal-times with a spoon
while I sat working in the sun.

Above the yard
an old clock had expired
the night Lenin arrived in Petrograd.

Habsburgs and Romanovs
Had removed their gloves
In the drawing-rooms and alcoves

of the manor house;
but these illustrious
ghosts never imposed on us.

Enough that the pond
steamed, the apples ripened,
the chestnuts on the gravel opened.

Ragwort and hemlock
cinquefoil and ladysmock
throve in the shadows at the back;

---

* "in the shadow of blossoming girls"

beneath the trees
foxgloves and wood-anemones
looked up with tearful metamorphic eyes.

We woke the rooks
on narrow, winding walks
familiar from the story-books,

or visited
a disused garden shed
where gas-masks from the war decayed;

and we knew peace
splintering the thin ice
on the bathtub drinking-trough for cows.

But how could we
survive indefinitely
so far from the city and the sea?

Finding, at last,
too creamy for our taste
the fat profusion of that feast,

we carried on
to chaos and confusion,
our birthright and our proper portion.

Another light
than ours convenes the mute
attention of those woods tonight—

while we, released
from that pale paradise,
confront the darkness in another place.[57]

The Dream Play

What night-rule now about this haunted grove?

The spirits have dispersed, the woods
faded to grey from midnight blue
leaving a powdery residue,
night music fainter, frivolous gods
withdrawing, cries of yin and yang,
discords of the bionic young;
cobwebs and insects, hares and deer,
wild strawberries and eglantine
dawn silence of the biosphere,
among the branches a torn wing

—what is this enchanted place?
Not the strict groves of academe
but an old thicket of lost time
too cool for school, recovered space
where the brain yields to nose and ear,
folk remedy and herbal cure,
old narratives of heart and hand,
and a dazed donkey, starry-eyed,
with pearls and honeysuckle crowned,
beside her naked nibs is laid.
Wild viruses, Elysian fields—
our own planet lit by the fire
of molten substance, constant flux,
hot ice and acrobatic sex,
the electric moth-touch of desire
and a new vision, a new regime
where the white blaze of physics yields
to yellow moonlight, dance and dream
induced by what mind-altering drug
or rough-cast magic realism;
till morning bright with ant and bug
shines in a mist of glistening gism,
shifting identities, mutant forms,
angels evolved from snails and worms.[58]

Leaves

The prisoners of infinite choice
Have built their house
In a field below the wood
And are at peace.

It is autumn, and dead leaves
On their way to the river
Scratch like birds at the windows
Or tick on the road.

Somewhere there is an afterlife
Of dead leaves,
A stadium filled with an infinite
Rustling and sighing.

Somewhere in the heaven
Of lost futures
The lives we might have led
Have found their own fulfilment.[59]

Seán Lysaght

Seán Lysaght (1957–) grew up in Limerick and was educated at University College Dublin, where he received a BA and an MA in Anglo-Irish literature. He spent several years abroad, in Switzerland and Germany, before teaching at St. Patrick's College, Maynooth. He now lectures at the Galway-Mayo Institute of Technology and lives with his wife, Jessica, in Westport, County Mayo. His work on the life and writings of Robert Lloyd Praeger, *The Life of a Naturalist*, was published in 1998. In a presentation of the 2007 O'Shaughnessy Award for Poetry of the University of St. Thomas, St. Paul, Minnesota, Center for Irish Studies, Maris Kelly, dean of the College of Arts and Sciences, noted that Lysaght is an artist "whose poetry is inseparable from his engagement with Ireland's natural surroundings. Lysaght's poems abound with alert perceptions of Ireland's west, where he makes his home—its mountains, bogs, and beaches, its flora, and its birdlife. We will understand his work best (and, he reminds us, will understand our own lives best) if we remember that it rests on the bedrock of the natural world." Included in this selection is a section of "Bird Sweeney," Lysaght's modernized version of *Buile Suibhne* (*Frenzy of Sweeney*), from part 1 of the anthology; this version is realized through a more careful ornithological observation of the original poem's attention to flight.[60]

Golden Eagle

On the coast of Skye
I saw one rise,
spin and diminish,

then found preenings
at a breezy trig point
before the wind snatched them away—

sparks shot from a fire!
Watch them career
into the bygone!

The ledges are cold,
the eyries drenched
in the desert of Erris

where the last ones
flew into extinction a lifetime ago
above gillies and starvelings.[61]

The Clare Island Survey

1

I have the sketch of Clare Island,
in your hand. You drew the great brow
in silhouette from the mainland,

and scribbled gulls over a blue sound,
then etched a furze bush
with pencilled spikes in the foreground
and, in between, some trees, a slate roof
and a red gable huddling together,
No sooner had I left two years ago
than you made our trip, on your own, to Mayo.

2

It lures me back, seawards,
to a headland of thrift and stone
where July strikes cold with its bluster—
and already there's no getting away,
the native speakers are shouldering my boat
to the slipway, I float her
and fill her with my tackle (raingear,
a sooty kettle), then pay the interpreter
and row out alone into heavy waters,
where the gulls come into their own.

3

So I turn to Clare Island, and approach,
as they line up on the pier
and jostle for place, the forefathers
ready to construe my coming,
unwilling to believe that I am strange
to the old score of grant and annexation.
And I step ashore, deaf to their questions,
my pages blank for the whims of day.
Here I will inscribe readings
for the Clare Island Survey.

4

Gillie or squire in the first photographs,
going far out to give the scale
with a yardstick as a staff,
remote, unnamed, a small notch,
I would be measured against you,
and will lose face, pacing out
in the footsteps of the early workers
to where fatigue compels the heart,
and return then, my face aglow
with a booty of old words, and new echoes.[62]

Goldcrest

What's in the wood that is not ourselves?

You might well ask of our Sunday walks
through the forestry plantation,
when we defer to what is here
although so much remains unspoken.

We come together to this greying of grass
that might be a fox's path
and might be the spoor that leads
to you, after all these years;

or the scuffs in the bank, the loose tufts
that the badger must have left,
grubbing down to the root
of our silence in this quiet wood.

Show me the lichen I have bruised.
I'll show you the goldcrest,
You can't hear its high pitch anymore,
but when you were young you found its nest.[63]

From **Bird Sweeney**

Leavings

His name
a siblance of aspens,
his mark there in mud,

hoof-prints of a stag
that galloped into absence
in this wood

and left a downey plume
adrift in mid-air,
Llavings we follow

as we hunt ahead of death to hear,
beyond our bated breath.
his breath.

In the Wilderness

Sweeney whistled in the mouth of a river;
he was wigeon.

He dived in the surf of a lake;
he was smew.

His call came from the stars,
As wind reared on the guyrope of midnight;
he was redwing.

He tickled the toes of the reeds on their beds;
he was dabchick

He fenced on a catwalk of glittering water;
he was grebe.

He fell from the dome of day
To the floor of earth;
he was falcon.

Then he was phalarope, flitting in the hills of the grey sea.

Or shearwater, just clear of the waves in the wings of his life.

Eventually, he tilted homeward.

But the clerk had sported him.

All of a sudden
He roared out "Sweeney!"

And that spoiled everything.

The Flight from the Tower

Since God had cursed him with wings
Sweeney believed he owed nothing
for this artifice.

He was a collapsed brolly
around the stem of his vigil,
a body riddled with quills.

He dreamed of other extensions
as pike-loads and oars
and clattery ladders.

When the day thinned in the ivy
he reached the great span of himself
for an armful of air

and the tower delivered him.
He twisted his cockpit
as he worked the rush of his feathers.

Magpies were out in the fields
inspecting the cages of sheep
they'd picked clean.

The bodies of sea birds were tossed,
in a tangle of seaweed,
beyond the sea's fiction.

Sweeney kept going.
He stayed clear
in the metre of his flying.

A Wagtail Gloss

Sweeney danced
  on the peak of a roof,

little alpinist in his crampons
  after a fly,

so high and light!
  Then he settled again,

ahead of his own long wobbling tail—
  only to vanish in a flit,

not caring how the scribe's pen
  had to labour after him

in his economy and freedom.[64]

Desmond Egan

Desmond Egan (1936–) was born in Athlone and now lives outside Newbridge in County Kildare. Egan founded the Goldsmith Press in 1972 and edited *Era*, an occasional literary magazine, from 1974. His collections include *Midland* (1972; with drawings by Brian Bourke), *Leaves* (1974; with drawings by Charles Cullen), *Siege!* (1976); *Woodcutter* (1978), *Athlone?* (1980; with photographs by Fergus Bourke), *Seeing Double* (1983; with illustrations by Alex Sadkowsky), *Collected Poems* (1983), *Poems for Peace* (1986), *A Song for My Father* (1989), *Selected Poems* (1992), *Peninsula* (1992), *Elegies* (1996), *Famine* (1997), and *Music* (2000). He has also published a collection of essays, *The Death of Metaphor* (1990). He has been awarded the US National Poetry award for his volume *Collected Poems* and directs the Gerard Manley Hopkins Summer School. Though the struggle for freedom and a desire to maintain an Irish cultural identity are the main themes that run through his collections of poems, as is his disdain for all violence, it is his nature poetry that often does not receive the attention it deserves. The poems selected here are decidedly unique in their approach to the Irish landscape, for as one critic notes, Egan is "the first Irish poet to have broken free from the need to sound 'Irish.'"[65] His nature poetry resonates with a clear and refreshing voice yet blends elements from traditional Irish verse and Celtic themes with a veneration for the natural world.[66]

The Great Blasket

its authority
slowly drew us in

    mist islands
    a feel of the tremendous
    sea through the currach's skin

but the slipway was in moss
those proud cottages sagging
inwards like Irish and

    the imaginary crash of surf
    whitening in the distance
    cold of a summer morning

the winds of Europe
blew through blank windows

    nothing but elements
    to add to a quarter century

O Criomhthain
Peig
Muirís O Súilleabhain

I waited on a cliff-height for
for some sign from mainland Ireland

began to understand why mediocrity
never became the norm out here
where existence is an exile

past *An Tráth Bhán* icy waters
still coursed through the Sound and
over the ships of history

dear dear place
empty in the last mild collapse
Of a once great Gaelic vision
which persisted into our time[67]

Sunday Evening

hands in jeans along Dollymount I don't see
the slow line of the wave breaking far
out under Howth in mist a Tír na nÓg
I don't see the long strand quiet as another sky
nor the season the wrack dead things a saturated beam

but you who are not there
sitting any more legs crossed on a sand dune
picking at chips with musical fingers to laugh
deeper than the wine that *This is LOVEly*
while the sparse grass blows

forever as I pass.[68]

Meadowsweet

as customary on our Sunday drive we
drove in on this side of The Bay
over the tracks and went bumping
down to the edge

out across that space of water the usual car crowds
flashed and glittered under their hotel
which hovered like a church and every so often
a boat would drone past from another world

we dawdled as usual along the path
gone narrow at this stage with bushes with
that feeling of all July coming at you
in midges in weed in wild flowers

he stopped for some meadowsweet handed me a sprig

it had the last summer in it that heaviness
of milk just on the turn
by the time we got home it was already drooping
creamy white on the dashboard

but later before leaving I brought it in to him
standing waiting there at the counter
A to hell with it dump it he said
and headed for the steps to the kitchen.[69]

Snow Snow Snow Snow

like some obvious symbol snow
overnight had sifted everywhere
startling the mind's eyes into seeing again
the field forms the gentle hills of Kildare
and even a bruised sky with its line
of Russian pines the whole thing
a steppes where I began to watch
Mandelstam trudging to the death camp

having to leave a place can make it also
turn different in a day the way
hospital does to someone you knew well
and now this area that had seemed mine
has gone old is marching away on me

but landscapes of course don't matter
anything like people and is it I wonder a fact
that we the ordinary got-at allow too much
to go dulling past as if screened including
even those we love and must leave the
day after tomorrow?

is this the despairing chase of verse?
that handful of pianonotes which can
sink inwards like hot ashes or the old
desolating rush of tenderness squeezing to
tears at some subtitled film why the house of
   morning
tenses this minute like a mousetrap

so what can I do? *Nada*
about the snow dazzling into the kitchen
and round your softness where you stand
briefly dabbing at the mirror
this that eternity.[70]

unseeable lapwing
mew of distance and
   otherness

they leave you at the very
   swell
the pure winterdark

everything stripped to itself

a bark

a single light

salt down the apple tree

look for me there
generations away

A Pigeon Dead

It came as a bit of a shock to see it
Fallen on our common earth

We must have just missed
The stoop through the air the thump the
Screech
Because there was a quiet with feathers
Jiggling on the wire of the court
Opposite the familiar grey-blue body

Lacerated as if shot
Yet hardly picked-at
Just struck and let drop
You could sense the violence

Only a crow flapped past but

I caught the brown shape and pointy wings
Of a kestrel flitting across the garden banking
Upwards to alight among apple branches

Who killed it? Why? How
Could I or anyone explain to children about
All that is not allowed to realise itself
About viciousness and envy and original sin?
The death of Christ was everywhere
They studied the corpse remembered the
Badger's
Hit by a car up our road
And I lifted the pigeon by a dark underwing
It folded softly almost alive
Enough to clatter off wildly over the netting

But the eye had closed on its fate for keeps

Was there something some
Kind of imitation in the broken air?

The bird itself
Its pink exposed breast
The raw clawmarks on neck and body
The scatter of beautiful pin feathers
Were more than enough

I slung it into the field.[73]

Da ward ihr klar, wie nicht allein
Der Gottesfluch im Menschenbild
Wie er in schwerer, dumpfer Pein
Im bangen Wurm, im scheuen Wild,
Im durstgen Halme auf der Flur,
Der mit vergilbten Blattern lechzt,
In aller, aller Kreatur
Gen Himmel um Erlösung achzt.[71]
For we know that
the whole creation
groaneth and travaileth in pain
together
until now[72]

Envoi

saying goodbye for the umpteenth time the
mind like a pensioner drifts on a favourite walk
up the living road towards the bogs
that flood and colour everywhere

no doubt it could catch
this side of the tidiness of Curnabull those
obvious moments along the Shannon
but that's a bit much just now
there being so little one can cope with

so I go up and up the same way in hope
as far as the cross river
lean over the bridge and
join the weeds the ancient shadowings of water

somewhere out there
like a hint of smoke on the breeze Clonmacnois
rises in thought a graveyard wide with unheard goodbyes
the skygoats and whinnying high
high in a summer evening
cutting sad happy celtic circles over our heads

the hedges have greened I am walking very slowly
listening to my father.[74]

Mary O'Malley

Mary O'Malley was born in Connemara and educated at University College, Galway. She spent many years living in Portugal before returning to Ireland in the late 1980s and began a poetry career in 1990 with the title *A Consideration of Silk* from the Galway-based publisher Salmon Books. She has since published six other books including *The Boning Hall: New and Selected Poems* (2002). Her latest books have all been published by Carcanet Press. Her poems have been translated into several languages, and in 2016, she was awarded the Arts Council University of Limerick Writer's Fellowship. Her latest collection, *Playing the Octopus*, was published by Carcanet in July 2016. In 2009, O'Malley received the Lawrence O'Shaughnessy Award for Poetry from the University of St. Thomas Center for Irish Studies. An article published in *New Hibernia Review* notes, "Born in a western Gaeltacht in the midst of a lean decade, O'Malley often gives us poems that evoke a world in which the landscape and the domestic interior are charged with myths, both Classical and Celtic."[75]

Absent

Say mackerel shoaled through the lullabies
Wrens circled Christ's head and drank Mary's tears;
Say each love song was a festival of desire
And allow that the touch of some shapeless thing
Sickened his mind one night between bog and shore—
When he turned his back on his children
And cut their mother out of his life

He was harder than Connemara stone.
Old women pulled shawls over their faces
The silence of daughters descended
Our memories closed into a fist.[76]

The Man of Aran

But what if it were not epic.

Before the echo sounder was invented
fishermen let down weighted piano wire,
they listened for a school to hit, a note to sound.

Perhaps a scale—grace notes as single fish
hit E flat minor, say, or strange tunes
as a shoal crescendoed through the water,
minnows and sharks, sharps and flats—
heard from above at a different pitch
not perfect, but accurate, close enough for jazz;

their watery playing gave them up to slaughter
but the boatman dreamed of women singing

and the song coaxed him as he lured mackerel
with feathers that darted like blue jays
through the clear sea. He stayed out too long.

Let's leave it at that.
There would be cliffs rearing soon enough,
weather fighting,
No need for all that hauling of wrack
to the wrong side of the island,
for half drowning the locals, for shark.

We know how it works.
A pretty lure, hunger, the hook. No storm is as sweet
or deadly as the sting, the barb's sink.[77]

Porpoises

for Martin

Off Slyne Head at night
in a fifty-foot trawler
it is cold and black
even at midsummer.

The sky is close.
Out from the once manned rock
White electric light
Arcs over the water.

A mysterious life pulses
under the boat. Something
disturbs the even breathing
of the waves. A sound like wings

and a shape, indiscernible
in darkness, shaves the surface.
The fisherman hears
and leans over the bow.

The hairs on his neck rise
with the memory of old stories.
A school of invisible porpoises
is passing, 'Christ, they were lovely!'

Their perfect phosphorescent shapes
sculpted in the algae.

And there was blood on the moon.[78]

The Price of Silk Is Paid in Stone

O sweet romance in Connemara!
A soft day, a speckled hill,
a mirror bay, all certain
as the mountains swollen with heather.
All transient as thrushes' eggs,
the wild water
and a streaked chameleon sky.

O no romance in Connemara.
A speckled hen
fasting under a basket,
a whetted knife and the dance macabre,
the musk of feathers in the Sunday stew.

Yes, and when you lack the guts
to wield the knife
what use is it to the hungry child
that you dwell in gossamer and dusk?
Let them find out early
that love has a bitter edge
when life is lived among the rocks.

Yet I have seen the sedge
burn with slow fire.
I have seen the lakes rise
and make swirls of silk
in the October sky.

O the price of leaving,
the cost of coming home.[79]

The Storm

A spray of red carnations on the sill.
A fire framed in limestone waxes
in my semi-detached living room.

The habitual inventory of my men,
who is running for shore
who safe on what island, completes me.

I am waiting for the storm
and all the boats are in.
For two days I have bowstringed.

A humming deep in the ocean
vibrates me like a high tuned violin
Every muscle, drawn like wire, sizzles.

The wind rises. Locked in woodlands
I hear it turning ash and oak
as I am hauled to where the sea

is shaping new mountains. At midnight
mad airs howl like wolves
and all the trees are bending.

Swaddled in the harbour of my bed
I am rocked on seething water
absorbed in a green dance

that devours quays and laughs
at storm walls. I am a breaker
replacing beaches with boulders.

I fling wrack on a curved canvas
of ruined shore and fish drown
in my fury. The music crescendos,

ebbs, I sleep. Deep, deep, dreamless.
At evening I survey my redrawn beaches
satisfying new sand with footsteps.

The waning moon hushes me home
where I am needed and Handel
is flowing from the radio.[80]

Liadan with a Mortgage Briefly Tastes the Stars

Breasting the hill, she pauses and looks down.
In the stillness, her children sleep. She sees lights
winking in Mayo. Croagh Patrick
invisible to the right, her husband inside reading.

The house, anchored at the edge of the world
is solid, comforting. Oh, she thinks,
have we really been our own architects?

The earth gurgles as last night's rain seeps
to its subterranean level.
She would hate to live on dry land.
The house pulses like amber. It is warm
and the weather, settling at last
unsettles her. Those treacherous Septembers!

There are mounds of soft fruit ripening,
waiting to be preserved. She sees
plum and damson staining the clouds. This year
there will be no harvesting. Let those colours

ache and deepen into havoc—
she is not responsible.

A cat whispers past her feet, nightstalking.
She smiles
and sheds her garments, a light blouse and skirt
then slips into the watered sky
and holds it for a moment to her skin,
all moisture
a dress to go wandering out beyond the stars in,
stravaiging among the planets
like Zeus's daughter.
She could take in the whole universe tonight.

The house is oblivious, its roots
pierce the bedrock. Although she is glad
some god made a woman of her
she will acquiesce and go in. She dresses
and walks to her back door, quieted for now.
To the east a garnet moon rises.[81]

Rosemarie Rowley

Rosemarie Rowley (1942–), a poet, activist, and ecofeminist, has degrees in Irish and English literature and philosophy from Trinity College Dublin, an MLitt on the nature poet Patrick Kavanagh, and a diploma in psychology from National University of Ireland. Rowley is the author of the first ecofeminist poetry collection, *The Sea of Affliction* (1987). She has written extensively in form: *Flight into Reality* (1989) is the longest original work in terza rima in English. She has four times won the Epic Award in the Scottish International Open Poetry Competition and has published six books of poetry, her most recent being *Girls of the Globe* (2015). Dedicated to the preservation of Ireland's natural world, Rowley is part of the Irish green movement, and her poetry resounds with connections to nature, women, and Irish myth. *The Wooing of Etain*, based on the Old Irish myth, was published in *TRANSverse* in 2007, and she has translated the poems of the anonymous women bards of Connaught, which were published in various issues of the *Cork Literary Review* in the early 2000s. The previously unpublished selections in this anthology comprise Rowley's translations of early Irish nature poetry. As she notes about these modern translations, "Love of nature and beauty was very much entwined with Ireland's destiny and desire to be a free country."[82]

Osborn O h-Aimhirgín; A Cry from the Heart of a Poet— Morning in Beara

It is my sorrow to find that every delicate morning
That I am not in Beara standing on the strand
And the voices of birds drawing me over the ocean and hills
To the ravine of gorse where my love is to be found

It is so suddenly, sweetly, joyfully I would leap
And running free from stress, with tenderness
I would turn my back on the little clouds of this world
If I could have the full vision and apprehension of my fair darling

My losing sight of her has left me prostrate with weakness
Strictures in my heart, choked in my chest as I walk the street
As long as the realm of the rivers and the clean breeze of the sea
Are calling and shouting to this heart inside of me

It is sweet and lively to be buffeted by the winds in Beara
With the brightness of the sun generously on the grass
But alas, Queen of women endowed with abundant tresses
That we are not together, among the gorse as once we were.[83]

The Blackbird of Derry of the Cairn*

O sweet blackbird of Derry of the cairn
I never heard anywhere in the world
A music sweeter than your voice,
And you commanding your nest.

This one music the sweetest in the world
Bad cease to them that have not yet listened for tidings for it
O son of Rome of the sweet bells
You would experience again the fullness of your day.

If you, as I have myself
Had the real story of the bird
You would look diligently at it
And you wouldn't pay attention to God ever

In the Scandinavian countries of the blue streams
Fionn McCumhaill of the red horn
Found the bird you see now
Singing his song truly to you

Derry of the Cairn and the wood behind
Where still roam the Fianna
—the beauty and softness of its trees
It is where they buried the blackbird.[84]

In Praise of the Hill between of Howth

How sweet to be in Howth, the summit of Beann Eadair
Truly sweet in the clearness of the seas
This hill on a sea full with ships, abundantly
Rich with wine, melodious, valiant.

A hill where Fionn and the Fianna
Were sporting with horns and goblets
A hill which birthed bold Diarmuid O Duibhne
One day won Graine, in a wild foray

A hill where every mound vied with each other
Every green heap full of movement,
A summit leafy, sacred, rich in vegetation, antlered,
A hill pungent, full of nuts and trees

A hill as lovely as half Ireland
A radiant hill over a gull-filled sea

---

* The cairn is of an ancient burial site, at Gortcorbie, Co. Derry. The word Derry, or Doire, means an oak grove. Fionn McChumhail was the leader of the Fianna, the legendary band of warriors before the coming of Christianity to Ireland.

To abandon it is a step too cruel for me,
O beautiful hill of Howth, summit of Eadar.[85]

Blind Seamus McCourt: Welcome to the Bird

Welcome to the bird, sweetest on the bough
That speaks of the gentleness of the bush in the sunshine
How long and tiresome is this life,
As I don't see the bird when the grass sprouts.

I hear but I cannot see any aspect
Of the bird who sings, whose name is the cuckoo,
My sharp fatigue is that I cannot see it for myself—
The sight of her at the top of the branch

Every living individual who sees the form of the bird
A vision for Ireland south and north
The flowing of the outpouring on every side—
They are the ones who find it sweet to praise

My weariness that I cannot overcome my lack of sight,
So I would see in lonesome nobility the leaves growing;
Part of my sorrow is that I do not go to meet with everyone
Seeing the cuckoo on the edge of the wood—so peaceful.[86]

Kitty Dwyer*

In the early to late evening, and my flock secured from the slope,
In the bend of the leafy wood, my journey light-hearted, full of glee
The cuckoo, the blackbird and the thrush were in chorus with every true note
And at the beginning and end of each verse, the refrain that Ireland be free.

There is a little magic mound of green grass in the front of my house
And every sunny morning a fairy princess is sitting there before me
She has books of Irish, with a little bit of English through them,
And at the beginning and end of each verse the refrain that Ireland be free.

There are a thousand colours in her clothing and her shoes the colour of heather
And a dress of the new fashion on her of the kind a king's daughter would wear
And she said, "Sit down, young man, for a little while, and I will not delay,
But I tell you I'd be young again if Ireland would be free."

She sat on the little bench beside me and my limbs hanging down
I thought she was not a mortal woman, that I was in danger beside her
"Are you Pallas, or are you Helen, or the first woman who fired my heart,
Or the woman who ruined hundreds, who is related to Kitty Dwyer?"

---

* a code name for the cause of Irish freedom

"I am a woman in so much in pain since my partner went over the wave
My family are in slavery and weakened with no leap in their hearts or glee
But the clan of Ireland will rise up and every sword will be swiftly raised,
And it is the beginning and end of my story that Ireland may yet be free."[87]

NOTES TO PART IV

1. Michael Longley, "The White Butterfly," in *Collected Poems* (London: Cape Poetry, 2006), 161, lines 15–18.
2. Edward O. Wilson, *The Diversity of Life*, new ed. (New York: Norton, 1999), 206.
3. Patrick Kavanagh, "Poplars," in *The Complete Poems* (Kildare, Ireland: Goldsmith, 1972), 49.
4. Kavanagh, "Lilacs in the City," ibid., 45.
5. Kavanagh, "October," ibid., 292.
6. Kavanagh, "Canal Bank Walk," ibid., 294.
7. Kavanagh, "Having to Live in the Country," ibid., 321.
8. Kavanagh, "Inniskeen Road: July Evening," ibid., 18.
9. Kavanagh, "Tarry Flynn," ibid., 141–142.
10. Kavanagh, "Primrose," ibid., 75.
11. Kavanagh, "Wet Evening in April," ibid., 140.
12. See "Louis MacNeice," in *The Oxford Companion to Irish Literature*, ed. Robert Welch (Oxford, UK: Clarendon, 1996), 346.
13. Louis MacNeice, "The Sunlight on the Garden," in *Selected Poems* (London: Faber and Faber, 1988), 38.
14. MacNeice, "Wolves," ibid., 23.
15. MacNeice, "Tree Party," in *Collected Poems* (London: Faber and Faber, 1966), 532.
16. See "Seamus Heaney," in Welch, *Oxford Companion to Irish Literature*, 240–41. Also, see Katharine Tynan, "St. Francis to the Birds," in *Twenty One Poems by Katharine Tynan: Selected by W. B. Yeats (1861–1931)* (Dundrum, Ireland: Dun Emer, 1907), 19–22; Tim Robinson, "The Boneyard," in *Connemara: Listening to the Wind* (Dublin: Penguin Ireland, 2006), 93–116.
17. Heaney, "Death of a Naturalist," in *Poems 1965–1975* (New York: Farrar, Straus and Giroux, 1984), 5–6.
18. Heaney, "The Salmon Fisher to the Salmon," ibid., 48.
19. Heaney, "Limbo," ibid., 148.
20. Heaney, "St Kevin and the Blackbird," in *The Spirit Level: Poems* (1996; repr., Dublin: Farrar, Straus and Giroux, 2014), 24–25.
21. Eavan Boland, *The Lost Land* (New York: Norton, 1998), 260–61.
22. Boland, "The River," *New Yorker*, November 14, 1988, 120; reprinted in *New Collected Poems* (London: Carcanet, 2005), 171.
23. Boland, "Mountain Time," in *New Collected Poems*, 171–72.
24. Boland, "This Moment," ibid., 213.
25. Boland, "Ode to Suburbia," ibid., 66.
26. Boland, "Escape," ibid., 266.
27. Boland, "A Sparrow Hawk in the Suburbs," ibid., 221–22.
28. Brendan Lowe, "Earth's Old Bones," *Dublin Review of Books*, January 12, 2015, http://www.drb.ie/essays/earth-s-old-bones.
29. Moya Cannon, "Bees under Snow," in *Keats Lives* (Manchester, UK: Carcanet, 2015), 19.
30. Cannon, "Eavesdropping," ibid., 43.
31. Cannon, "Two Ivory Swans," ibid., 10.
32. Cannon, "Winter View from Binn Bhriocáin," ibid., 9.
33. Cannon, "Primavera," ibid., 21.
34. Cannon, "The Tube-Case Makers," ibid., 23.
35. Cannon, "Crannog," in *Carrying the Songs* (Dublin: Carcanet, 2007), 85.

36. Cannon, "Hazelnuts," ibid., 99.
37. See "John Montague," in Welch, *Oxford Companion to Irish Literature*, 371.
38. John Montague, "All Legendary Obstacles," in *About Love: Poems* (New York: Sheep Meadow, 1993), 109.
39. Montague, "The Wild Dog Rose," ibid., 140.
40. Montague, "The Trout," in *Selected Poems* (Winston-Salem, NC: Wake Forest University Press, 1982), 22.
41. See "Michael Longley," in Welch, *Oxford Companion to Irish Literature*, 316.
42. Longley, "The Osprey," in *Collected Poems*, 13.
43. Longley, "Badger," ibid., 48–49.
44. Longley, "Hedgehog," in "Poems by Michael Longley," Belfast Group Poetry/*Networks*, accessed March 15, 2018, https://belfastgroup.digitalscholarship.emory.edu/groupsheets/longley1 _1042/#longley1_1028.
45. Longley, "Kingfisher," ibid.
46. Longley, "Robin," in *Collected Poems*, 297.
47. Longley, "Out of the Sea," in "Poems by Michael Longley," Belfast Group Poetry/*Networks*, accessed March 15, 2018, https://belfastgroup.digitalscholarship.emory.edu/groupsheets/longley1 _10202/.
48. Longley, "Her Mime of the Lame Seagull," in "Poems by Michael Longley," Belfast Group Poetry/*Networks*, accessed March 15, 2018, https://belfastgroup.digitalscholarship.emory.edu/ groupsheets/longley1_10316/.
49. Longley, "Carrigskeewaun," in *Collected Poems*, 68–69.
50. Longley, "Saint Francis to the Birds," in *Poems by Michael Longley*, Belfast Group Poetry/*Networks*, accessed March 15, 2018, https://belfastgroup.digitalscholarship.emory.edu/groupsheets/ longley1_10282.
51. See "Derek Mahon," in Welch, *Oxford Companion to Irish Literature*, 351–52.
52. Derek Mahon, "The Seasons," in *An Autumn Wind* (Dublin: Gallery Books, 2010), 72.
53. Mahon, "Achill," in *Selected Poems* (New York: Penguin Books, 2000), 113.
54. Mahon, "Aphrodite's Pool," in *The Yellow Book* (Dublin: Gallery Books, 1997), 247–48.
55. Mahon, "The Mayo Tao," in *Selected Poems*, 37.
56. Mahon, "Penshurst Place," ibid., 47.
57. Mahon, "The Woods," ibid., 95.
58. Mahon, "The Dream Play," ibid., 208.j,,,,,,,,,,,,,,,,,,
59. Mahon, "Leaves," in *Collected Poems* (Loughcrew, Ireland: Gallery, 2000), 60.
60. See Gallery Press, "Sean Lysaght," accessed March 15, 2018, https://www.gallerypress.com/ authors/g-to-l/sean-lysaght/.
61. Seán Lysaght, "Golden Eagle," in *The Clare Island Survey* (Dublin: Gallery Books, 1991), 18.
62. Lysaght, "The Clare Island Survey," ibid., 11–12.
63. Lysaght, "Goldcrest," ibid., 36.
64. Lysaght, "Bird Sweeney," in *The Mouth of a River* (Dublin: Gallery Books, 2007), 61–79.
65. Hugh Kenner, introduction to *Selected Poems, by Desmond Egan* (Omaha, NE: Creighton University Press, 1991), 12.
66. See "Desmond Egan," in Welch, *Oxford Companion to Irish Literature*, 169.
67. Desmond Egan, "The Great Blasket," in *Elegies: Selected Poems, 1972–96* (Newbridge, Ireland: Goldsmith, 1996), 49).
68. Egan, "Sunday Evening," ibid., 74.
69. Egan, "Meadowsweet," ibid., 103.
70. Egan, "Snow Snow Snow Snow," ibid., 100.
71. "Then it became clear to her that God's curse was not laid only on humankind, but as grievous, deadening pain on the frightened worm, the timid beast, the thirsty plant in the meadow with parched yellow leaves; from the whole of creation a groan rises to heaven for deliverance": from *Die achzende Kreatur* [Groaning creation], the last poem of Annette von Droste-Hulshoff (1797–1848), trans. Ursula Prideaux (Lincoln: University of Nebraska Press, 1965), http://gutenberg.spiegel.de/ buch/gedichte-9606/34.
72. Rom. 8:22.

73. Egan, "A Pigeon Dead," in *Elegies*, 101–2.

74. Egan, "Envoi," ibid., 110.

75. "Lawrence O'Shaughnessy Award for Poetry: Mary O'Malley," *New Hibernia Review* 13, no. 4 (2009): 156–57.

76. Mary O'Malley, "Absent," in *The Knife in the Wave* (Dublin: Salmon, 1997), 41.

77. O'Malley, "The Man of Aran," in *The Boning Hall* (Dublin: Carcanet, 2002), 38.

78. O'Malley, "Porpoises," in *Where the Rocks Float* (Dublin: Salmon, 1993), 33.

79. O'Malley, "The Price of Silk Is Paid in Stone," ibid., 29.

80. O'Malley, "The Storm," ibid., 41–42.

81. O'Malley, "Liadan with a Mortgage Briefly Tastes the Stars," ibid., 50–51.

82. See Rosemarie Rowley's website, accessed March 15, 2018, http://www.rosemarierowley.ie/.

83. Rosemarie Rowley, "Osborn O h-Aimhirgín; A Cry from the Heart of a Poet—Morning in Beara," in private collection of Rosemarie Rowley. From Pádraig Ó Canainn, *Filíocht na ngael* (Dublin: An Press Náisiúnta, 1939), 242.

84. Rowley, "The Blackbird of Derry of the Cairn," in private collection of Rosemarie Rowley. From Micheal Breathnach, *Fion na Filíochta* (Dublin: Comhlucht Oideachais Na hÉireann, 1959), 203.

85. Rowley, "In Praise of the Hill between of Howth," in private collection of Rosemarie Rowley. From Breathnach, *Fion na Filíochta*, 205.

86. Rowley, "Blind Seamus McCourt: Welcome to the Bird," in private collection of Rosemarie Rowley. From Breathnach, *Fion na Filíochta*, 143.

87. Rowley, "Kitty Dwyer," in private collection of Rosemarie Rowley. From Breathnach, *Fion na Filíochta*, 31. This translation was also published by Rosemarie Rowley in *Ireland's Legendary Women* (Galway, Ireland: Arlen House, 2016), 147.

The Literature of Irish Naturalists

Introduction to Part V

"The most important function of literature today," Glen A. Love points out in his essay "Revaluing Nature," "is to redirect human consciousness to a full consideration of its place in a threatened natural world."[1] This is certainly relevant to a changing Ireland, where nature writing works to address and to preserve what remains of the natural world and to slow the rapid progress and materialism that has swept across the country. The Irish are following a new tradition in the twenty-first century by buying up land, developing it, and, as a result, paying little attention to the natural world that is being rapidly replaced by human progress. As David McWilliams observes in *The Pope's Children*, "We feel like lesser humans if we are not caught up in the great land mania that sweeps all before us [and that] has changed the psychology of the nation and the way we see ourselves and others."[2] Because of progress, the Irish no longer see themselves, like Patrick Kavanagh's Patrick McGuire of *The Great Hunger*,[3] tied to the land. The Irish are finally free from their land, living the dream of wealth and opportunity, of money and material things that make life more bearable. There is no wish to return to that necessary marriage to the land, so nature no longer holds power.

"Where are the environmentalists?" David McWilliams asks in *The Pope's Children*, "where is the sense of the common good? Where is the sacrifice for the 'good of the country?'"[4] Despite all of the abrupt changes to the Irish landscape and the modern antiseptic culture that McWilliams outlines in his book, and despite the twenty-first-century mind-set of the consumerism that seems all but unstoppable, there *is* an undercurrent of concern for the environment, an ecological undercurrent that has been more or less running through Irish culture since the early part of the twentieth century. These concerns for the change in Irish landscape, in fact, are evinced as early as 1937 in Æ's *The Living Torch*, and it has been the writing of Irish environmental writers who have kept this current flowing.[5]

The goal of both nature writing and nature literature should be a balanced intimacy with the landscape that does not interfere with or distort an objective attention to that landscape; instead, the artistic representation of writing from a scientific perspective adds a literary approach that in fact deepens that attention on both a realistic and a spiritual plane. Scott Slovic, who emphasizes that the role of "necessary watchfulness" is enhanced by the writing process, notes, "Contemporary nature writers tend to resist openly espousing one particular attitude toward nature, their goal being instead the empirical study of their own psychological responses to the world—or, in other words, objective scrutiny of subjective experience"—and he adds that most nature writers who predominate any country or geography "walk a fine line . . . between rhapsody and detachment, between aesthetic celebration and scientific explanation."[6]

The writers in this final part of the anthology represent that balance between Slovic's "rhapsody and detachment" in their observations of Ireland's natural world.

The first writer and scientist represented in part 5 is John Tyndall, a prominent nineteenth-century physicist. His initial scientific fame arose in the 1850s from his study of diamagnetism. Later he made discoveries in the realms of infrared radiation and the physical properties of air. Tyndall also published more than a dozen science books that brought state-of-the-art nineteenth-century experimental physics to a wide audience. Tyndall played his part in communicating to the educated public what he thought were the virtues of having a clear separation between a rational, knowledge-based view of the world (science) and one based on emotion and spirituality (faith). After he was elected president of the British Association for the Advancement of Science in 1874, he gave a long keynote speech at the association's annual meeting, held that year in Belfast, which included the scientific process in observing the natural world, leading to the important evolutionary theory proposed by Darwin, a name he repeated in the speech more than twenty times; Tyndall concluded his address by asserting that religious sentiment should not be permitted to "intrude on the region of knowledge, over which it holds no command."[7] Because he was the first prominent scientist to back Darwin and to promote his scientific explanation for humanity's relationship to the natural world, newspapers carried the report of the address and his comments on their front pages—in the British Isles, North America, even the European Continent—and many critiques of it appeared soon after, which led to an explosion of nature writing that made more objective and rational observations of the various components that make up the parts of the whole of the natural world.

Though Tyndall's address seemingly endorses an objective view of the natural world, Ruth Barton has noted that Tyndall does not entirely discount a view of nature based on emotion, religion, and God; she cites the critic Anna Therese Cosslett, who argued that "science and humanistic values are reconciled in Tyndall's account of scientific thought and his awareness that scientific explanations do not remove mystery from the universe, his perception of the universe as living, and the integration of his scientific knowledge and moral experience."[8] Tyndall, in other words, blends an objective and subjective view of the natural world through the lens of his experience—first as a scientist, then as a humanist.

This view can be said of the rest of the *scientific* or *objective* nature writing in this section. As Slovic notes of this scientific process, "the very mysteriousness of nature contributes to the independence and, presumably, the self-awareness of the observer."[9]

This awareness is readily apparent in the travelogue *The Way That I Went* by the Irish naturalist and writer Robert Lloyd Praeger. For modern environmentalists and nature poets, Praeger's *The Way That I Went*, published in the same year as Æ's *The Living Torch*, became an important resource for other environmental writers and for poets to understand and value the natural world around them. "To my mind," the poet Seán Lysaght (whose poetry is included in part 4) noted in a personal interview, "the greatest omission from the *Field Day* are the writings of Robert Lloyd Praeger," who "was very much on the map by the 1930's as the elder statesman of Irish environmental science, Irish landscape, and even Irish heritage."[10]

Praeger's seminal work is essentially a narrative of five years of his life traversing the Irish landscape, and as he notes at the beginning of the volume, "The way that I went was an Irish way, with extraorbital aberrations" comprising "a thousand or fifteen hundred miles" that became "a way of flowers and stones and beasts."[11] During the course of his journey, Praeger explores the natural world of Ireland, from its western islands to the tops of mountains, deep into bogs and caves, around and across the lakes and rivers. The narrative, as a whole, is an ecological treatise on Ireland, at once an environmental and literary perspective of places and species. As he notes, *The Way That I Went* is for "the Ireland of the man who goes with reverent feet through the hills and valleys, accompanied by neither noise nor dust to scare away wild creatures; stopping often, watching closely, listening carefully. Only thus can he, if he is fortunate, make friends by degrees with the birds and flowers and rocks, learn all the signs and sounds of the country-side, and feel at one with . . . his natural environment."[12]

The Way That I Went is a polemic on the importance of Ireland's natural history through close observation of the natural world, an aspect of Ireland that Praeger contends is often overlooked in favor of political matters. "If St. Patrick had banished from Ireland politics instead of snakes," Praeger writes, "he would have conferred a far greater boon, and this lovely land would have had peace and charity as well as faith and hope."[13] Praeger's observation and the way that he goes is the same journey that Ireland's nature poets and fiction writers have taken before and after him: he is leaving the stage of history and politics and observing a natural world freed from human constraint.

Praeger's observations on the "peace and charity" implicit in Ireland's nature at times border on the sublime, as he discovers, through the course of his observations, entirely new phenomena, evident in this entry on the Irish boglands: "It was on a barren storm-swept, half-sandy, half-peaty flat intersected with shallow pools, on the edge of the Atlantic in a place that shall be nameless, . . . that we found ourselves suddenly among fairy-like little birds, quite unknown to us, but evidently belonging to the Plover family. The most extraordinary thing about them was that they displayed absolutely no fear of us."[14] The discovery becomes at once objective and poetic, as Praeger cites the otherworldly, fairy-like quality of his experience in a place, from his immediate observations, where man has never ventured.

The Way That I Went is a departure from the traditional academic narratives of naturalists observing species in the field. Instead, Praeger infuses vivid descriptions of Ireland's unique landscape with the poetic mannerisms indicative of Æ. In his description of the Connemara boglands, for example, Praeger writes, "On a day of bright sky, when the hills are of that intoxicating misty blue that belongs especially to the west, the bogland is a lovely, far-reaching expanse of purple and rich brown; and the lakelets take on the quite indescribable colour that comes from clear sky reflected in bog-water, while the sea-inlets slow with an intense but rather greener blue. On such a day the wanderer will thank his lucky star that it has brought him to Connemara."[15] The journey itself, through Ireland's richly diverse topography, is all worth the feeling it evokes to the author, who is fully immersed in nature and is bound by an innate appreciation for all that it offers: "There is something infinitely satisfying about these wide, treeless, houseless undulations, clothed with heather and Purple moor-grass, so filled with lakes and so intersected by arms of the Atlantic that water entangled in a network of land becomes almost imperceptibly land entangled in a network of water."[16] The author's observation of the Connemara wilderness is witness to a mirage of entangled land and waters, but it is also a tribute to its mysterious beauty and to the spell it weaves into his consciousness, where a merging of conscious and unconscious are woven like land and water.

Praeger's successors likewise embrace this merging, including the observations of the naturalist Michael Viney, whose musings on the natural world stem from his residence in the wilds of County Mayo and who contributes a weekly column to the *Irish Times*, "Another Life." Viney lives in a small self-sustaining home along the coast in County Mayo with his wife, Ethna, with whom he most recently collaborated on the important book *Ireland's Ocean*, which explores the marine ecosystem that inhabits "the pump" of the Gulf Stream that flows through the Atlantic around Ireland.[17] Included in this anthology are sections from Viney's book *A Year's Turning*, which chronicles a year living in this house and his observations and interactions with the natural world of Ireland's rugged west coast.

Tim Robinson, another prominent Irish writer who blends both objective and subjective approaches to Ireland's natural world, is also a cartographer. He began a detailed study of the landscape of the West of Ireland, producing maps of the Aran Islands, Connemara, and the Burren; these are published by Folding Landscapes, the imprint that he and his wife, Máiréad, run from their Roundstone base.[18] Robinson's most important contribution to a study of Ireland's natural world, however, is his nature writing, which forms a true literary connection to his detailed and scientific observations with its blend of poetic ruminations of the beautiful and unique Irish landscape. Robinson's two-volume study of the Aran Islands, *Stones of Aran*, is a poetic blend of topographical and culture lore. *Stones of Aran: Pilgrimage* (1984) follows, in the spirit of Robert Lloyd Praeger, a coastal exploration, while *Stones of Aran: Labyrinth* (1986) explores the interior. His most recent work has been the publication of a three-volume study of Connemara: *Listening to the Wind* (2006), *The Last Pool of Darkness* (2008), and *A Little Gaelic Kingdom* (2011). The sections included in this anthology are from the introduction to *Connemara: Listening to the Wind* and also include "The Boneyard," which draws a parallel to Heaney's poem "Limbo" (included in part 4) in its description of the graveyards of unbaptized infants and its haunting interaction with the rugged Connemara landscape.

Slovic notes of the importance of nature literature, "Nature writing is a 'literature of hope' in its assumption that the elevation of consciousness may lead to wholesome political change, but this literature is also concerned, and perhaps primarily so, with interior landscapes, with the mind itself."[19] It is on this notion that the anthology concludes with a selection from *Invoking Ireland*, by the late Irish philosopher John Moriarty, in which he urges, much like the writers of the Irish Literary Revival, a return to a glorious Celtic past that embraces the natural world and all of the beauty and immortality it offers—by paying attention not only to nature but also to the ancient Irish myths derived from that nature. Moriarty emphasizes throughout the work a central message: humanity has taken a wrong turn somewhere along the way and is not paying attention to what the myths from every continent and the characters who inhabit them are telling us about ourselves and our vital connection to nature. In *Invoking Ireland*, he focuses almost entirely on Irish myths to illustrate his belief that there has been a schism between what we as humans instinctively are and what we have become and how we choose to live. In the book, he becomes a character living in a parallel Ireland called Fódhla, lamenting the wrong turn that his fellow countrymen and the rest of the Western world has taken. The way to correct course, finally, for Moriarty, for Ireland, for the world, is to pay more attention not only to the myths of the past but also to the natural world of the present that is rapidly retreating.

John Tyndall

John Tyndall (1820–1893) was an Irish naturalist and experimentalist whose most notable accomplishment was the discovery that carbon dioxide is a greenhouse gas—meaning
that it traps heat and keeps it from escaping the Earth's atmosphere into outer space. This
scientific observation, which evolved into climatology and the concern over global climate
change, was made as the Industrial Revolution was rapidly changing the relationship between
humanity and its environment and at a time when the dangers of man-made climate change
were largely unknown. Later in the early twentieth century, the Swedish geochemist Svante
Arrhenius developed Tyndall's observations and theorized that carbon dioxide released into
Earth's atmosphere through the burning of fossil fuels could alter the atmosphere and warm
the planet. In 1874, Tyndall gave his famous Belfast Address before the annual meeting of the
British Association for the Advancement of Science.[20] It was one of the most prestigious places
from which to speak on the importance of scientific advancement, and he emphasized in this
address the need for scientific impulse. Tyndall famously used his address to argue for the
superior authority of science over religious or nonrationalist explanations. The address was
popularly believed to advocate materialism as the true philosophy of science. It remains a
powerful call for rationalism, consistency, and skepticism.

Belfast Address

An impulse inherent in primeval man turned his thoughts and questionings be-
times towards the sources of natural phenomena. The same impulse, inherited and
intensified, is the spur of scientific action to-day. Determined by it, by a process of
abstraction from experience we form physical theories which lie beyond the pale of
experience, but which satisfy the desire of the mind to see every natural occurrence
resting upon a cause. In forming their notions of the origin of things, our earliest
historic (and doubtless, we might add, our prehistoric) ancestors pursued, as far as
their intelligence permitted, the same course. They also fell back upon experience,
but with this difference—that the particular experiences which furnished the weft
and woof of their theories were drawn, not from the study of nature, but from what
lay much closer to them, the observation of men. Their theories accordingly took an
anthropomorphic form. To supersensual beings, which, "however potent and invisible, were nothing but a species of human creatures, perhaps raised from among
mankind, and retaining all human passions and appetites,"* were handed over the
rule and governance of natural phenomena. Tested by observation and reflection,
these early notions failed in the long run to satisfy the more penetrating intellects
of our race. Far in the depths of history we find men of exceptional power differen-
tiating themselves from the crowd, rejecting these anthropomorphic notions, and
seeking to connect natural phenomena with their physical principles. But long prior
to these purer efforts of the understanding the merchant had been abroad, and rendered the philosopher possible; commerce had been developed, wealth amassed,
leisure for travel and speculation secured, while races educated under different

---

* Hume, *Natural History of Religion.*

conditions, and therefore differently informed and endowed, had been stimulated and sharpened by mutual contact. In those regions where the commercial aristocracy of ancient Greece mingled with its eastern neighbours the sciences were born, being nurtured and developed by free-thinking and courageous men. The state of things to be displaced may be gathered from a passage of Euripides quoted by Hume. "There is nothing in the world; no glory, no prosperity. The gods toss all into confusion; mix everything with its reverse, that all of us, from our ignorance and uncertainty may pay them the more worship and reverence." Now, as science demands the radical extirpation of caprice and the absolute reliance upon law in nature, there grew with the growth of scientific notions a desire and determination to sweep from the field of theory this mob of gods and demons, and to place natural phenomena on a basis more congruent with themselves.

The problem which had been previously approached from above was now attacked from below; theoretic effort passed from the super- to the sub-sensible. It was felt that to construct the universe in idea it was necessary to have some notion of its constituent parts—of what Lucretius subsequently called the "First Beginnings." Abstracting again from experience, the leaders of scientific speculation reached at length the pregnant doctrine of atoms and molecules, the latest developments of which were set forth with such power and clearness at the last meeting of the British Association. Thought, no doubt, had long hovered about this doctrine before it attained the precision and completeness which it assumed in the mind of Democritus,* a philosopher who may well for a moment arrest our attention. "Few great men," says Lange, a non-materialist, in his excellent "History of Materialism," to the spirit and to the letter of which I am equally indebted, "have been so despitefully used by history as Democritus. In the distorted images sent down to us through unscientific traditions there remains of him almost nothing but the name of 'the laughing philosopher,' while figures of immeasurably smaller significance spread themselves out at full length before us." Lange speaks of Bacon's high appreciation of Democritus—for ample illustrations of which I am indebted to my excellent friend Mr. Spedding, the learned editor and biographer of Bacon. It is evident, indeed, that Bacon considered Democritus to be a man of weightier metal than either Plato or Aristotle, though their philosophy "was noised and celebrated in the schools, amid the din and pomp of professors." It was not they, but Genseric and Attila and the barbarians, who destroyed the atomic philosophy. "For at a time when all human learning had suffered shipwreck these planks of Aristotelian and Platonic philosophy, as being of a lighter and more inflated substance, were preserved and came down to us, while things more solid sank and almost passed into oblivion."

The son of a wealthy farmer, Democritus devoted the whole of his inherited fortune to the culture of his mind. He travelled everywhere; visited Athens when Socrates and Plato were there, but quitted the city without making himself known. Indeed, the dialectic strife in which Socrates so much delighted had no charms for Democritus, who held that "the man who readily contradicts and uses many words is unfit to learn anything truly right." He is said to have discovered and educated Protagoras the sophist, being struck as much by the manner in which he, being

---

* Born 460 B.C.

a hewer of wood, tied up his faggots as by the sagacity of his conversation. Democritus returned poor from his travels, was supported by his brother, and at length wrote his great work entitled "Diakosmos," which he read publicly before the people of his native town. He was honoured by his countrymen in various ways, and died serenely at a great age.

The principles enunciated by Democritus reveal his uncompromising antagonism to those who deduced the phenomena of nature from the caprices of the gods. They are briefly these—1. From nothing comes nothing. Nothing that exists can be destroyed. All changes are due to the combination and separation of molecules. 2. Nothing happens by chance. Every occurrence has its cause from which it follows by necessity. 3. The only existing things are the atoms and empty space; all else is mere opinion. 4. The atoms are infinite in number and infinitely various in form; they strike together, and the lateral motions and whirlings which thus arise are the beginnings of worlds. 5. The varieties of all things depend upon the varieties of their atoms, in number, size, and aggregation. 6. The soul consists of fine, smooth, round atoms, like those of fire. These are the most mobile of all. They interpenetrate the whole body, and in their motions the phenomena of life arise. The first five propositions are a fair general statement of the atomic philosophy, as now held. As regards the sixth, Democritus made his fine smooth atoms do duty for the nervous system, whose functions were then unknown. The atoms of Democritus are individually without sensation; they combine in obedience to mechanical laws; and not only organic forms, but the phenomena of sensation and thought are the result of their combination.

That great enigma, "the exquisite adaptation of one part of an organism to another part, and to the conditions of life," more especially the construction of the human body, Democritus made no attempt to solve. Empedocles, a man of more fiery and poetic nature, introduced the notion of love and hate among the atoms to account for their combination and separation. Noticing this gap in the doctrine of Democritus, he struck in with the penetrating thought, linked, however, with some wild speculation, that it lay in the very nature of those combinations which were suited to their ends (in other words, in harmony with their environment) to maintain themselves, while unfit combinations, having no proper habitat, must rapidly disappear. Thus more than 2,000 years ago the doctrine of the "survival of the fittest," which in our day, not on the basis of vague conjecture, but of positive knowledge, has been raised to such extraordinary significance, had received at all events partial enunciation.*

Epicurus,† said to be the son of a poor schoolmaster at Samos, is the next dominant figure in the history of the atomic philosophy. He mastered the writings of Democritus, heard lectures in Athens, went back to Samos, and subsequently wandered through various countries. He finally returned to Athens, where he bought a garden, and surrounded himself by pupils, in the midst of whom he lived a pure and serene life, and died a peaceful death. Democritus looked to the soul as the ennobling part of man; even beauty without understanding partook of animalism. Epicurus also rated the spirit above the body; the pleasure of the body was that of

---

* Lange, 2nd edit., p. 23.
† Born 342 B.C.

the moment, while the spirit could draw upon the future and the past. His philosophy was almost identical with that of Democritus; be he never quoted either friend or foe. One main object of Epicurus was to free the world from superstition and the fear of death. Death he treated with indifference. It merely robs us of sensation. As long as we are, death is not; and when death is, we are not. Life has no more evil for him who has made up his mind that it is no evil not to live. He adored the gods, but not in the ordinary fashion. The idea of divine power, properly purified, he thought an elevating one. Still he taught, "Not he is godless who rejects the gods of the crowd, but rather he who accepts them." The gods were to him eternal and immortal beings, whose blessedness excluded every thought of care or occupation of any kind. Nature pursues her course in accordance with everlasting laws, the gods never interfering. They haunt

"The lucid interspace of world and world
Where never creeps a cloud or moves a wind,
Nor ever falls the least white star of snow,
Nor ever lowest roll of thunder moans,
Nor sound of human sorrow mounts to mar
Their sacred everlasting calm."*

Lange considers the relation of Epicurus to the gods subjective; the indication probably of an ethical requirement of his own nature. We cannot read history with open eyes, or study human nature to its depths, and fail to discern such a requirement. Man never has been, and he never will be, satisfied with the operations and products of the Understanding alone; hence physical science cannot cover all the demands of his nature. But the history of the efforts made to satisfy these demands might be broadly described as a history of errors—the error, in great part, consisting in ascribing fixity to that which is fluent, which varies as we vary, being gross when we are gross, and becoming, as our capacities widen, more abstract and sublime. On one great point the mind of Epicurus was at peace. He neither sought nor expected, here or hereafter, any personal profit from his relation to the gods. And it is assuredly a fact that loftiness and serenity of thought may be promoted by conceptions which involve no idea of profit of this kind. "Did I not believe," said a great man to me once, "that an Intelligence is at the heart of things, my life on earth would be intolerable." The utterer of these words is not, in my opinion, rendered less noble but more noble by the fact that it was the need of ethical harmony here, and not the thought of personal profit hereafter, that prompted his observation.

There are persons, not belonging to the highest intellectual zone, nor yet to the lowest, to whom perfect clearness of exposition suggests want of depth. They find comfort and edification in an abstract and learned phraseology. To some such people Epicurus, who spared no pains to rid his style of every trace of haze and turbidity, appeared, on this very account, superficial. He had, however, a disciple who thought it no unworthy occupation to spend his days and nights in the effort to reach the clearness of his master, and to whom the Greek philosopher is mainly indebted for the extension and perpetuation of his fame. A century and a half after

---

* Tennyson's *Lucretius*.

the death of Epicurus, Lucretius* wrote his great poem "On the Nature of Things," in which he, a Roman, developed with extraordinary ardour the philosophy of his Greek predecessor. He wishes to win over his friend Memnius to the school of Epicurus; and although he has no rewards in a future life to offer, although his object appears to be a purely negative one, he addresses his friend with the heat of an apostle. His object, like that of his great forerunner, is the destruction of superstition; and considering that men trembled before every natural event as a direct monition from the gods, and that everlasting torture was also in prospect, the freedom aimed at by Lucretius might perhaps be deemed a positive good. "This terror," he says, "and darkness of mind must be dispelled, not by the rays of the sun and glittering shafts of day, but by the aspect and the law of nature." He refutes the notion that anything can come out of nothing, or that that which is once begotten can be recalled to nothing. The first beginnings, the atoms, are indestructible, and into them all things can be resolved at last. Bodies are partly atoms, and partly combinations of atoms; but the atoms nothing can quench. They are strong in solid singleness, and by their denser combination all things can be closely packed and exhibit enduring strength. He denies that matter is infinitely divisible. We come at length to the atoms, without which, as an imperishable substratum, all order in the generation and development of things would be destroyed.

The mechanical shock of the atoms being in his view the all-sufficient cause of things, he combats the notion that the constitution of nature has been in any way determined by intelligent design. The inter-action of the atoms throughout infinite time rendered all manner of combinations possible. Of these the fit ones persisted, while the unfit ones disappeared. Not after sage deliberation did the atoms station themselves in their right places, nor did they bargain what motions they should assume. From all eternity they have been driven together, and after trying motions and unions of every kind, they fell at length into the arrangements out of which this system of things has been formed. "If you will apprehend and keep in mind these things, nature, free at once, and rid of her haughty lords, is seen to do all things spontaneously of herself, without the meddling of the gods."†

To meet the objection that his atoms cannot be seen, Lucretius describes a violent storm, and shows that the invisible particles of air act in the same way as the visible particles of water. We perceive, moreover, the different smells of things, yet never see them coming to our nostrils. Again, clothes hung up on a shore which waves break upon become moist, and then get dry if spread out in the sun, though no eye can see either the approach or the escape of the water particles. A ring, worn long on the finger, becomes thinner; a water-drop hollows out a stone; the ploughshare is rubbed away in the field; the street pavement is worn by the feet; but the particles that disappear at any moment we cannot see. Nature acts through invisible particles. That Lucretius had a strong scientific imagination the foregoing references prove. A fine illustration of his power in this respect is his explanation of the apparent rest of bodies whose atoms are in motion. He employs the image of a flock of sheep with

---

* Born 99 B.C.

† Monro's translation. In his criticism of this work, *Contemporary Review*, 1867, Dr. Hayman does not appear to be aware of the really sound and subtle observations on which the reasoning of Lucretius, though erroneous, sometimes rests.

skipping lambs, which, seen from a distance, presents simply a white patch upon the green hill, the jumping of the individual lambs being quite invisible.

His vaguely-grand conception of the atoms falling eternally through space suggested the nebular hypothesis to Kant, its first propounder. Far beyond the limits of our visible world are to be found atoms innumerable, which have never been united to form bodies, or which, if once united, have been again dispersed, falling silently through immeasurable intervals of time and space. As everywhere throughout the All the same conditions are repeated, so must the phenomena be repeated also. Above us, below us, beside us, therefore, are worlds without end; and this, when considered, must dissipate every thought of a deflection of the universe by the gods. The worlds come and go, attracting new atoms out of limitless space, or dispersing their own particles. The reputed death of Lucretius, which forms the basis of Mr. Tennyson's noble poem, is in strict accordance with his philosophy, which was severe and pure.

During the centuries lying between the first of these three philosophers and the last, the human intellect was active in other fields than theirs. The sophists had run through their career. At Athens had appeared Socrates, Plato, and Aristotle, who ruined the sophists, and whose yoke remains to some extent unbroken to the present hour. Within this period also the School of Alexandria was founded, Euclid wrote his "Elements," and made some advance in optics. Archimedes had propounded the theory of the lever and the principles of hydrostatics. Pythagoras had made his experiments on the harmonic intervals, while astronomy was immensely enriched by the discoveries of Hipparchus, who was followed by the historically more celebrated Ptolemy. Anatomy had been made the basis of Scientific medicine; and it is said by Draper* that vivisection then began. In fact, the science of ancient Greece had already cleared the world of the fantastic images of divinities operating capriciously through natural phenomena. It had shaken itself free from that fruitless scrutiny "by the internal light of the mind alone," which had vainly sought to transcend experience and reach a knowledge of ultimate causes. Instead of accidental observation, it had introduced observation with a purpose; instruments were employed to aid the senses; and scientific method was rendered in a great measure complete by the union of Induction and Experiment.

What, then, stopped its victorious advance? Why was the scientific intellect compelled, like an exhausted soil, to lie fallow for nearly two millenniums before it could regather the elements necessary to its fertility and strength? Bacon has already let us know one cause; Whewell ascribes this stationary period to four causes—obscurity of thought, servility, intolerance of disposition, enthusiasm of temper—and he gives striking examples of each.† But these characteristics must have had their antecedents in the circumstances of the time. Rome and the other cities of the Empire had fallen into moral putrefaction. Christianity had appeared, offering the gospel to the poor, and, by moderation if not asceticism of life, practically protesting against the profligacy of the age. The sufferings of the early Christians, and the extraordinary exaltation of mind which enabled them to triumph over the diabolical tortures to which

---

* *History of the Intellectual Development of Europe*, p. 295.
† *History of the Inductive Sciences*, vol. i.

they were subjected,* must have left traces not easily effaced. They scorned the earth, in view of that "building of God, that house not made with hands, eternal in the heavens." The Scriptures which ministered to their spiritual needs were also the measure of their Science. When, for example, the celebrated question of antipodes came to be discussed, the Bible was with many the ultimate court of appeal. Augustine, who flourished A.D. 400, would not deny the rotundity of the earth; but he would deny the possible existence of inhabitants at the other side, "because no such race is recorded in Scripture among the descendants of Adam." Archbishop Boniface was shocked at the assumption of a "world of human beings out of the reach of the means of salvation." Thus reined in, Science was not likely to make much progress. Later on the political and theological strife between the Church and civil governments, so powerfully depicted by Draper, must have done much to stifle investigation.

Whewell makes many wise and brave remarks regarding the spirit of the Middle Ages. It was a menial spirit. The seekers after natural knowledge had forsaken that fountain of living waters, the direct appeal to nature by observation and experiment, and had given themselves up to the remanipulation of the notions of their predecessors. It was a time when thought had become abject, and when the acceptance of mere authority led, as it always does in science, to intellectual death. Natural events, instead of being traced to physical, were referred to moral causes; while an exercise of the phantasy, almost as degrading as the spiritualism of the present day, took the place of scientific speculation. Then came the mysticism of the Middle Ages, Magic, Alchemy, the Neo-platonic philosophy, with its visionary though sublime abstractions, which caused men to look with shame upon their own bodies as hindrances to the absorption of the creature in the blessedness of the Creator. Finally came the Scholastic philosophy, a fusion, according to Lange, of the least-mature notions of Aristotle with the Christianity of the West. Intellectual immobility was the result. As a traveller without a compass in a fog may wander long, imagining he is making way, and find himself after hours of toil at his starting point, so the schoolmen, having "tied and untied the same knots and formed and dissipated the same clouds," found themselves at the end of centuries in their old position. With regard to the influence wielded by Aristotle in the Middle Ages, and which, though to a less extent, he still wields, I would ask permission to make one remark. When the human mind has achieved greatness and given evidence of extraordinary power in any domain, there is a tendency to credit it with similar power in all other domains. Thus theologians have found comfort and assurance in the thought that Newton dealt with the question of revelation, forgetful of the fact that the very devotion of his powers, through all the best years of his life, to a totally different class of ideas, not to speak of any natural disqualification, tended to render him less instead of more competent to deal with theological and historic questions. Goethe, starting from his established greatness as a poet, and indeed from his positive discoveries in Natural History, produced a profound impression among the painters of Germany when he published his "Farbenlehre" in which he endeavoured to overthrow Newton's theory of colours. This theory seemed so obviously absurd that he considered the author a charlatan, and attacked him with a corresponding vehemence of language. In the

---

* Depicted with terrible vividness in Renan's *Antichrist*.

domain of Natural History Goethe had made fully considerable discoveries; and we have high authority for assuming that, had he devoted himself wholly to that side of science, he might have reached in it an eminence comparable with that which he attained as a poet. In sharpness of observation, in the detection of analogies, however apparently remote, in the classification and organization of facts according to the analogies discerned, Goethe possessed extraordinary powers. These elements of scientific inquiry fall in with the discipline of the poet. But, on the other hand, a mind thus richly endowed in the direction of natural history may be almost shorn of endowment as regards the more strictly called physical and mechanical sciences. Goethe was in this condition. He could not formulate distinct mechanical conceptions; he could not see the force of mechanical reasoning; and in regions where such reasoning reigns supreme he became a mere *ignis fatuus* to those who followed him.

I have sometimes permitted myself to compare Aristotle with Goethe, to credit the Stagirite with an almost superhuman power of amassing and systematizing facts, but to consider him fatally defective on that side of the mind in respect to which incompleteness has been just ascribed to Goethe. Whewell refers the errors of Aristotle, not to a neglect of facts, but to "a neglect of the idea appropriate to the facts; the idea of Mechanical cause, which is Force, and the substitution of vague or inapplicable notions, involving only relations of space or emotions of wonder." This is doubtless true; but the word "neglect" implies mere intellectual misdirection, whereas in Aristotle, as in Goethe, it was not, I believe, misdirection, but sheer natural incapacity which lay at the root of his mistakes. As a physicist, Aristotle displayed what we should consider some of the worst attributes of a modern physical investigator—indistinctness of ideas, confusion of mind, and a confident use of language, which led to the delusive notion that he had really mastered his subject, while he had as yet failed to grasp even the elements of it. He put words in the place of things, subject in the place of object. He preached Induction without practising it, inverting the true order of inquiry by passing from the general to the particular, instead of from the particular to the general. He made of the universe a closed sphere, in the centre of which he fixed the earth, proving from general principles, to his own satisfaction and to that of the world for near 2,000 years, that no other universe was possible. His notions of motion were entirely unphysical. It was natural or unnatural, better or worse, calm or violent—no real mechanical conception regarding it lying at the bottom of his mind. He affirmed that a vacuum could not exist, and proved that if it did exist motion in it would be impossible. He determined *à priori* how many species of animals must exist, and shows on general principles why animals must have such and such parts. When an eminent contemporary philosopher, who is far removed from errors of this kind, remembers these abuses of the *à priori* method, he will be able to make allowance for the jealousy of physicists as to the acceptance of so-called *à priori* truths. Aristotle's errors of detail, as shown by Eucken and Lange, were grave and numerous. He affirmed that only in man we had the beating of the heart, that the left side of the body was colder than the right, that men have more teeth than women, and that there is an empty space at the back of every man's head.

There is one essential quality in physical conceptions which was entirely wanting in those of Aristotle and his followers. I wish it could be expressed by a word untainted by its associations; it signifies a capability of being placed as a coherent picture before the mind. The Germans express the act of picturing by the word *vorstellen*, and the picture they call a *Vorstellung*. We have no word in English which comes nearer to our requirements than *Imagination*, and, taken with its proper limitations, the word answers very well; but, as just intimated, it is tainted by its associations, and therefore objectionable to some minds. Compare, with reference to this capacity of mental presentation, the case of the Aristotelian who refers the ascent of water in a pump to Nature's abhorrence of a vacuum, with that of Pascal when he proposed to solve the question of atmospheric pressure by the ascent of the Puy de Dome. In the one case the terms of the explanation refuse to fall into place as a physical image; in the other the image is distinct, the fall and rise of the barometer being clearly figured as the balancing of two varying and opposing pressures.

During the drought of the Middle Ages in Christendom, the Arabian intellect, as forcibly shown by Draper, was active. With the intrusion of the Moors into Spain, he says, order, learning, and refinement took the place of their opposites. When smitten with disease, the Christian peasant resorted to a shrine, the Moorish one to an instructed physician. The Arabs encouraged translations from the Greek philosophers, but not from the Greek poets. They turned in disgust "from the lewdness of our classical mythology, and denounced as an unpardonable blasphemy all connexion between the impure Olympian Jove and the Most High God." Draper traces still further than Whewell the Arab elements in our scientific terms, and points out that the under garment of ladies retains to this hour its Arab name. He gives examples of what Arabian men of science accomplished, dwelling particularly on Alhazen, who was the first to correct the Platonic notion that rays of light are emitted by the eye. He discovered atmospheric refraction, and points out that we see the sun and the moon after they have set. He explains the enlargement of the sun and moon, and the shortening of the vertical diameters of both these bodies, when near the horizon. He is aware that the atmosphere decreases in density with increase of elevation, and actually fixes its height at 58½ miles. In the Book of the Balance of Wisdom, he sets forth the connexion between the weight of the atmosphere and its increasing density. He shows that a body will weigh differently in a rare and dense atmosphere: he considers the force with which plunged bodies rise through heavier media. He understands the doctrine of the centre of gravity, and applies it to the investigation of balances and steelyards. He recognises gravity as a force, though he falls into the error of making it diminish simply as the distance increased, and of making it purely terrestrial. He knows the relation between the velocities, spaces, and times of falling bodies, and has distinct ideas of capillary attraction. He improved the hydrometer. The determination of the densities of bodies as given by Alhazen approach very closely to our own. "I join," says Draper, in the pious prayer of Alhazen, "that in the day of judgment the All-Merciful will take pity on the soul of Abur-Raihân, because he was the first of the race of men to construct a table of specific gravities." If all this be historic truth (and I have entire confidence in Dr. Draper), well may he "deplore the systematic manner in which the literature of Europe has contrived to put out of sight our scientific obligations to the Mahommedans."*

---

* *Intellectual Development of Europe*, p. 359.

The strain upon the mind during the stationary period towards ultra-terrestrial things, to the neglect of problems close at hand, was sure to provoke reaction. But the reaction was gradual; for the ground was dangerous, a power being at hand competent to crush the critic who went too far. To elude this power and still allow opportunity for the expression of opinion, the doctrine of "two-fold truth" was invented, according to which an opinion might be held "theologically" and the opposite opinion "philosophically."* Thus in the thirteenth century the creation of the world in six days, and the unchangeableness of the individual soul which had been so distinctly affirmed by St. Thomas Aquinas, were both denied philosophically, but admitted to be true as articles of the Catholic faith. When Protagoras uttered the maxim which brought upon him so much vituperation, that "opposite assertions are equally true," he simply meant that human beings differed so much from each other that what was subjectively true to the one might be subjectively untrue to the other. The great Sophist never meant to play fast and loose with the truth by saying that one of two opposite assertions made by the same individual could possibly escape being a lie. It was not "sophistry," but the dread of theologic vengeance that generated this double dealing with conviction; and it is astonishing to notice what lengths were possible to men who were adroit in the use of artifices of this kind.

Towards the close of the stationary period a word-weariness, if I may so express it, took more and more possession of men's minds. Christendom had become sick of the School philosophy and its verbal wastes, which led to no issue, but left the intellect in everlasting haze. Here and there was heard the voice of one impatiently crying in the wilderness, "Not unto Aristotle, not unto subtle hypothesis, not unto church, Bible, or blind tradition, must we turn for a knowledge of the universe, but to the direct investigation of Nature by observation and experiment." In 1543 the epoch-making work of Copernicus on the paths of the heavenly bodies appeared. The total crash of Aristotle's closed universe with the earth at its centre followed as a consequence, and "the earth moves!" became a kind of watchword among intellectual freemen. Copernicus was Canon of the Church of Frauenburg, in the diocese of Ermeland. For three-and-thirty years he had withdrawn himself from the world and devoted himself to the consolidation of his great scheme of the solar system. He made its blocks eternal; and even to those who feared it and desired its overthrow it was so obviously strong that they refrained for a time from meddling with it. In the last year of the life of Copernicus his book appeared: it is said that the old man received a copy of it a few days before his death, and then departed in peace.

The Italian philosopher Giordano Bruno was one of the earliest converts to the new astronomy. Taking Lucretius as his exemplar, he revived the notion of the infinity of worlds; and, combining with it the doctrine of Copernicus, reached the sublime generalization that the fixed stars are suns, scattered numberless through space and accompanied by satellites, which bear the same relation to them that our earth does to our sun, or our moon to our earth. This was an expansion of transcendent import; but Bruno came closer than this to our present line of thought. Struck with the problem of the generation and maintenance of organisms, and duly pondering it, he came to the conclusion that Nature in her productions does not imitate the

---

* Lange, 2nd edit. pp. 181, 182.

technic of man. Her process is one of unravelling and unfolding. The infinity of forms under which matter appears were not imposed upon it by an external artificer; by its own intrinsic force and virtue it brings these forms forth. Matter is not the mere naked, empty *capacity* which philosophers have pictured her to be, but the universal mother who brings forth all things as the fruit of her own womb.

This outspoken man was originally a Dominican monk. He was accused of heresy and had to fly, seeking refuge in Geneva, Paris, England, and Germany. In 1592 he fell into the hands of the Inquisition at Venice. He was imprisoned for many years, tried, degraded, excommunicated, and handed over to the civil power, with the request that he should be treated gently and "without the shedding of blood." This meant that he was to be burnt; and burnt accordingly he was, on the 16th of February, 1600. To escape a similar fate Galileo, thirty-three years afterwards, abjured, upon his knees, and with his hand upon the holy gospels, the heliocentric doctrine which he knew to be true. After Galileo came Kepler, who from his German home defied the power beyond the Alps. He traced out from pre-existing observations the laws of planetary motion. Materials were thus prepared for Newton, who bound those empirical laws together by the principle of gravitation.

In the seventeenth century Bacon and Descartes, the restorers of philosophy, appeared in succession. Differently educated and endowed, their philosophic tendencies were different. Bacon held fast to Induction, believing firmly in the existence of an external world, and making collected experiences the basis of all knowledge. The mathematical studies of Descartes gave him a bias towards Deduction; and his fundamental principle was much the same as that of Protagoras, who made the individual man the measure of all things. "I think, therefore I am," said Descartes. Only his own identity was sure to him; and the development of this system would have led to an idealism in which the outer world would be resolved into a mere phenomenon of consciousness. Gassendi, one of Descartes's contemporaries, of whom we shall hear more presently, quickly pointed out that the fact of personal existence would be proved as well by reference to any other act as to the act of thinking. I eat, therefore I am; or I love, therefore I am, would be quite as conclusive: Lichtenberg showed that the very thing to be proved was inevitably postulated in the first two words, "I think;" and that no inference from the postulate could by any possibility be stronger than the postulate itself.

But Descartes deviated strangely from the idealism implied in his fundamental principle. He was the first to reduce, in a manner eminently capable of bearing the test of mental presentation, vital phenomena to purely mechanical principles. Through fear or love, Descartes was a good churchman; he accordingly rejects the notion of an atom, because it was absurd to suppose that God, if he so pleased, could not divide an atom; he puts in the place of the atoms small round particles and light splinters, out of which he builds the organism. He sketches with marvellous physical insight a machine, with water for its motive power, which shall illustrate vital actions. He has made clear to his mind that such a machine would be competent to carry on the processes of digestion, nutrition, growth, respiration, and the beating of the heart. It would be competent to accept impressions from the external sense, to store them up in imagination and memory, to go through the internal movements of the appetites and passions, the external movement of limbs. He deduces these functions of his machine from the mere arrangement of its organs, as the movement of a clock or other automaton is deduced from its weights and wheels. "As far as these functions are concerned," he says, "it is not necessary to conceive any other vegetative or sensitive soul, nor any other principle of motion or of life, than the blood and the spirits agitated by the fire which burns continually in the heart, and which is in no wise different from the fires which exist in inanimate bodies." Had Descartes been acquainted with the steam-engine, he would have taken it, instead of a fall of water, as his motive power, and shown the perfect analogy which exists between the oxidation of the food in the body and that of the coal in the furnace. He would assuredly have anticipated Mayer in calling the blood which the heart diffuses "the oil of the lamp of life;" deducing all animal motions from the combustion of this oil, as the motions of a steam-engine are deduced from the combustion of its coal. As the matter stands, however, and considering the circumstances of the time, the boldness, clearness, and precision with which he grasped the problem of vital dynamics constitute a marvellous illustration of intellectual power.*

During the Middle Ages the doctrine of atoms had to all appearance vanished from discussion. In all probability it held its ground among sober-minded and thoughtful men, though neither the church nor the world was prepared to hear of it with tolerance. Once, in the year 1348, it received distinct expression. But retraction by compulsion immediately followed, and, thus discouraged, it slumbered till the seventeenth century, when it was revived by a contemporary and friend of Hobbes and Malmesbury, the orthodox Catholic provost of Digne, Gassendi. But before stating his relation to the Epicurean doctrine, it will be well to say a few words on the effect, as regards science, of the general introduction of monotheism among European nations.

"Were men," says Hume, "led into the apprehension of invisible intelligent power by contemplation of the works of Nature, they could never possibly entertain any conception but of one single being, who bestowed existence and order on this vast machine, and adjusted all its parts to one regular system." Referring to the condition of the heathen, who sees a god behind every natural event, thus peopling the world with thousands of beings whose caprices are incalculable, Lange shows the impossibility of any compromise between such notions and those of science, which proceeds on the assumption of never-changing law and causality. "But," he continues, with characteristic penetration, "when the great thought of one God, acting as a unit upon the universe, has been seized, the connexion of things in accordance with the law of cause and effect is not only thinkable, but it is a necessary consequence of the assumption. For when I see ten thousand wheels in motion, and know, or believe, that they are all driven by one, then I know that I have before me a mechanism the action of every part of which is determined by the plan of the whole. So much being assumed, it follows that I may investigate the structure of that machine, and the various motions of its parts. For the time being, therefore, this conception renders scientific action free." In other words, were a capricious God at the circumference of every wheel and at the end of every lever, the action of the machine would be incalculable by the methods of science. But the action of all its parts being rigidly

---

* See Huxley's admirable Essay on Descartes. *Lay Sermons*, pp. 364, 365.

determined by their connexions and relations, and these being brought into play by a single self-acting driving wheel, then, though this last prime mover may elude me, I am still able to comprehend the machinery which it sets in motion. We have here a conception of the relation of Nature to its Author which seems perfectly acceptable to some minds, but perfectly intolerable to others. Newton and Boyle lived and worked happily under the influence of this conception; Goethe rejected it with vehemence, and the same repugnance to accepting it is manifest in Carlyle.*

The analytic and synthetic tendencies of the human mind exhibit themselves throughout history, great writers ranging themselves sometimes on the one side, sometimes on the other. Men of warm feelings and minds open to the elevating impressions produced by Nature as a whole, whose satisfaction, therefore, is rather ethical than logical, lean to the synthetic side, while the analytic harmonizes best with the more precise and more mechanical bias which seeks the satisfaction of the understanding. Some form of pantheism was usually adopted by the one, while a detached Creator, working more or less after the manner of men, was often assumed by the other. Gassendi is hardly to be ranked with either. Having formally acknowledged God as the great first cause, he immediately dropped the idea, applied the known laws of mechanics to the atoms, deducing thence all vital phenomena. He defended Epicurus, and dwelt upon his purity, both of doctrine and of life. True he was a heathen, but so was Aristotle. He assailed superstition and religion, and rightly, because he did not know the true religion. He thought that the gods neither rewarded nor punished, and adored them purely in consequence of their completeness; here we see, says Gassendi, the reverence of the child instead of the fear of the slave. The errors of Epicurus shall be corrected, the body of his truth retained; and then Gassendi proceeds, as any heathen might do, to build up the world, and all that therein is, of atoms and molecules. God, who created earth and water, plants and animals, produced in the first place a definite number of atoms, which constituted the seed of all things. Then began that series of combinations and decompositions which goes on at present, and which will continue in future. The principle of every change resides in matter. In artificial productions the moving principle is different from the material worked upon; but in Nature the agent works within, being the most active and mobile part of the material itself. Thus, this bold ecclesiastic, without incurring the censure of the church or the world, contrives to outstrip Mr. Darwin. The same cast of mind which caused him to detach the Creator from his universe led him also to detach the soul from the body, though to the body he ascribes an influence so large as to render the soul almost unnecessary. The aberrations of reason were in his view an affair of the material brain. Mental disease is brain disease; but then the immortal reason sits apart, and cannot be touched by the disease. The errors of madness are errors of the instrument, not of the performer.

It may be more than a mere result of education, connecting itself probably with the deeper mental structure of the two men, that the idea of Gassendi above enunciated

---

* Boyle's model of the universe was the Strasburg clock with an outside Artificer. Goethe, on the other hand, sang

"Ihm ziemt's die Welt im Innern zu bewegen,
Natur in sich, sich in Natur zu hegen."

See also Carlyle, *Past and Present*, Chap. V.

is substantially the same as that expressed by Professor Clerk Maxwell at the close of the very able lecture delivered by him at Bradford last year. According to both philosophers, the atoms, if I might understand aright, are the *prepared materials* which, formed by the skill of the highest, produce by their subsequent inter-action all the phenomena of the material world. There seems to be this difference, however, between Gassendi and Maxwell. The one *postulates*, the other *infers* his first cause. In his "manufactured articles," as he calls the atoms, Professor Maxwell finds the basis of an induction which enables him to scale philosophic heights considered inaccessible by Kant, and to take the logical step from the atoms to their Maker.

Accepting here the leadership of Kant, I doubt the legitimacy of Maxwell's logic; but it is impossible not to feel the ethic glow with which his lecture concludes. There is, moreover, a very noble strain of eloquence in his description of the steadfastness of the atoms:—"Natural causes, as we know, are at work, which tend to modify, if they do not at length destroy, all the arrangements and dimensions of the earth and the whole solar system. But though in the course of ages catastrophes have occurred and may yet occur in the heavens, though ancient systems may be dissolved and new systems evolved out of their ruins, the molecules out of which these systems are built— the foundation stones of the material universe—remain unbroken and unworn."

The atomic doctrine, in whole or in part, was entertained by Bacon, Descartes, Hobbes, Locke, Newton, Boyle, and their successors, until the chemical law of multiple proportions enabled Dalton to confer upon it an entirely new significance. In our day there are secessions from the theory, but it still stands firm. Loschmidt, Stoney, and Sir William Thomson sought to determine the sizes of the atoms, or rather to fix the limits between which their sizes lie; while only last year the discourses of Williamson and Maxwell illustrate the present hold of the doctrine upon the foremost scientific minds. In fact, it may be doubted whether, wanting this fundamental conception, a theory of the material universe is capable of scientific statement.

Ninety years subsequent to Gassendi the doctrine of bodily instruments, as it may be called, assumed immense importance in the hands of Bishop Butler, who, in his famous "Analogy of Religion," developed, from his own point of view, and with consummate sagacity, a similar idea. The Bishop still influences superior minds; and it will repay us to dwell for a moment on his views. He draws the sharpest distinction between our real selves and our bodily instruments. He does not, as far as I remember, use the word soul, possibly because the term was so hackneyed in his day as it had been for many generations previously. But he speaks of "living powers," "perceiving" or "percipient powers," "moving agents," "ourselves," in the same sense as we should employ the term soul. He dwells upon the fact that limbs may be removed, and mortal diseases assail the body, the mind, almost up to the moment of death, remaining clear. He refers to sleep and to swoon, where the "living powers" are suspended but not destroyed. He considers it quite as easy to conceive of existence out of our bodies as in them: that we may animate a succession of bodies, the dissolution of all of them having no more tendency to dissolve our real selves, or "deprive us of living faculties—the faculties of perception and action—than the dissolution of any foreign matter which we are capable of receiving impressions from, or making use of for the common occasions of life." This is the key of the Bishop's position; "our organized bodies are no more a part of ourselves than any other matter around us." In proof of this he calls attention to the use of glasses, which "prepare objects" for the "percipient power" exactly as the eye does. The eye itself is no more percipient than the glass; is quite as much the instrument of the true self, and also as foreign to the true self, as the glass is. "And if we see with our eyes only in the same manner as we do with glasses, the like may justly be concluded from analogy of all our senses."

Lucretius, as you are aware, reached a precisely opposite conclusion; and it certainly would be interesting, if not profitable, to us all, to hear what he would or could urge in opposition to the reasoning of the Bishop. As a brief discussion of the point will enable us to see the bearings of an important question, I will here permit a disciple of Lucretius to try the strength of the Bishop's position, and then allow the Bishop to retaliate, with the view of rolling back, if he can, the difficulty upon Lucretius.

The argument might proceed in this fashion:—

"Subjected to the test of mental presentation (*Vorstellung*), your views, most honoured prelate, would present to many minds a great, if not an insuperable difficulty. You speak of 'living powers,' 'percipient or perceiving powers,' and 'ourselves;' but can you form a mental picture of any one of these apart from the organism through which it is supposed to act? Test yourself honestly, and see whether you possess any faculty that would enable you to form such a conception. The true self has a local habitation in each of us; thus localized, must it not possess a form? If so, what form? Have you ever for a moment realized it? When a leg is amputated the body is divided into two parts; is the true self in both of them or in one? Thomas Aquinas might say in both; but not you, for you appeal to the consciousness associated with one of the two parts to prove that the other is foreign matter. Is consciousness, then, a necessary element of the true self? If so, what do you say to the case of the whole body being deprived of consciousness? If not, then on what grounds do you deny any portion of the true self to the severed limb? It seems very singular that, from the beginning to the end of your admirable book (and no one admires its sober strength more than I do), you never once mention the brain or nervous system. You begin at one end of the body and show that its parts may be removed without prejudice to the perceiving power. What if you begin at the other end, and remove, instead of the leg, the brain? The body, as before, is divided into two parts; but both are now in the same predicament, and neither can be appealed to to prove that the other is foreign matter. Or, instead of going so far as to remove the brain itself, let a certain portion of its bony covering be removed, and let a rhythmic series of pressures and relaxations of pressure be applied to the soft substance. At every pressure, 'the faculties of perception and of action' vanish; at every relaxation of pressure they are restored. Where, during the intervals of pressure, is the perceiving power? I once had the discharge of a large Leyden battery passed unexpectedly through me: I felt nothing, but was simply blotted out of conscious existence for a sensible interval. Where was my true self during that interval? Men who have recovered from lightning-stroke have been much longer in the same state; and indeed in cases of ordinary concussion of the brain, days may elapse during which no experience is registered in consciousness. Where is the man himself during the period of insensibility? You may say that I beg the question when I assume the man to have been unconscious, that he was really conscious all the time, and has simply forgotten what had occurred to him.

In reply to this, I can only say that no one need shrink from the worst tortures that superstition ever invented if only so felt and so remembered. I do not think your theory of instruments goes at all to the bottom of the matter. A telegraph-operator has his instruments, by means of which he converses with the world; our bodies possess a nervous system, which plays a similar part between the perceiving power and external things. Cut the wires of the operator, break his battery, demagnetize his needle: by this means you certainly sever his connexion with the world; but inasmuch as these are real instruments, their destruction does not touch the man who uses them. The operator survives, *and he knows that he survives*. What is it, I would ask, in the human system that answers to this conscious survival of the operator when the battery of the brain is so disturbed as to produce insensibility, or when it is destroyed altogether?

"Another consideration, which you may consider slight, presses upon me with some force. The brain may change from health to disease, and through such a change the most exemplary man may be converted into a debauchee or a murderer. My very noble and approved good master had, as you know, threatenings of lewdness introduced into his brain by his jealous wife's philter; and sooner than permit himself to run even the risk of yielding to these base promptings he slew himself. How could the hand of Lucretius have been thus turned against himself if the real Lucretius remained as before? Can the brain or can it not act in this distempered way without the intervention of the immortal reason? If it can, then it is a prime mover which requires only healthy regulation to render it reasonably self-acting, and there is no apparent need of your immortal reason at all. If it cannot, then the immortal reason, by its mischievous activity in operating upon a broken instrument, must have the credit of committing every imaginable extravagance and crime. I think, if you will allow me to say so, that the gravest consequences are likely to flow from your estimate of the body. To regard the brain as you would a staff or an eyeglass—to shut your eyes to all its mystery, to the perfect correlation of its condition and our consciousness, to the fact that a slight excess or defect of blood in it produces the very swoon to which you refer, and that in relation to it our meat and drink and air and exercise have a perfectly transcendental value and significance—to forget all this does, I think, open a way to innumerable errors in our habits of life, and may possibly in some cases initiate and foster that very disease, and consequent mental ruin, which a wiser appreciation of this mysterious organ would have avoided."

I can imagine the Bishop thoughtful after hearing this argument. He was not the man to allow anger to mingle with the consideration of a point of this kind. After due reflection, and having strengthened himself by that honest contemplation of the facts which was habitual with him, and which includes the desire to give even adverse facts their due weight, I can suppose the Bishop to proceed thus:—"You will remember that in the 'Analogy of Religion,' of which you have so kindly spoken, I did not profess to prove anything absolutely, and that I over and over again acknowledged and insisted on the smallness of our knowledge, or rather the depth of our ignorance, as regards the whole system of the universe. My object was to show my deistical friends, who set forth so eloquently the beauty and beneficence of Nature and the Ruler thereof, while they had nothing but scorn for the so-called absurdities of the Christian scheme, that they were in no better condition than we were, and that, for every difficulty found upon our side, quite as great a difficulty was to be found upon theirs. I will now, with your permission, adopt a similar line of argument. You are a Lucretian, and from the combination and separation of insensate atoms deduce all terrestrial things, including organic forms and their phenomena. Let me tell you, in the first instance, how far I am prepared to go with you. I admit that you can build crystalline forms out of this play of molecular force; that the diamond, amethyst, and snow-star are truly wonderful structures which are thus produced. I will go further and acknowledge that even a tree or flower might in this way be organized. Nay, if you can show me an animal without sensation, I will concede to you that it also might be put together by the suitable play of molecular force.

"Thus far our way is clear; but now comes my difficulty. Your atoms are individually without sensation, much more are they without intelligence. May I ask you, then, to try your hand upon this problem? Take your dead hydrogen atoms, your dead oxygen atoms, your dead carbon atoms, your dead nitrogen atoms, your dead phosphorus atoms, and all the other atoms, dead as grains of shot, of which the brain is formed. Imagine them separate and sensationless, observe them running together and forming all imaginable combinations. This, as a purely mechanical process, is *seeable* by the mind. But can you see, or dream, or in any way imagine, how out of that mechanical act, and from those individually dead atoms, sensation, thought, and emotion are to arise? Are you likely to extract Homer out of the rattling of dice, or the Differential Calculus out of the clash of billiard-balls? I am not all bereft of this *Vorstellungs-Kraft* of which you speak, nor am I, like so many of my brethren, a mere vacuum as regards scientific knowledge. I can follow a particle of musk until it reaches the olfactory nerve; I can follow the waves of sound until their tremors reach the water of the labyrinth and set the otoliths and Corti's fibres in motion; I can also visualize the waves of ether as they cross the eye and hit the retina. Nay more, I am able to pursue to the central organ the motion thus imparted at the periphery, and to see in idea the very molecules of the brain thrown into tremors. My insight is not baffled by these physical processes. What baffles and bewilders me, is the notion that from those physical tremors things so utterly incongruous with them as sensation, thought, and emotion can be derived. You may say, or think, that this issue of consciousness from the clash of atoms is not more incongruous than the flash of light from the union of oxygen and hydrogen. But I beg to say that it is. For such incongruity as the flash possesses is that which I now force upon your attention. The flash is an affair of consciousness, the objective counterpart of which is a vibration. It is a flash only by your interpretation. *You* are the cause of the apparent incongruity and *you* are the thing that puzzles me. I need not remind you that the great Leibnitz felt the difficulty which I feel, and that to get rid of this monstrous deduction of life from death he displaced your atoms by his monads, which were more or less perfect mirrors of the universe, and out of the summation and integration of which he supposed all the phenomena of life—sentient, intellectual, and emotional—to arise.

"Your difficulty, then, as I see you are ready to admit, is quite as great as mine. You cannot satisfy the human understanding in its demand for logical continuity between molecular processes and the phenomena of consciousness. This is a rock on which materialism must inevitably split whenever it pretends to be a complete philosophy of life. What is the moral, my Lucretian? You and I are not likely to indulge in ill-temper in the discussion of these great topics, where we see so much room for honest differences of opinion. But there are people of less wit or more bigotry (I say it with humility) on both sides, who are ever ready to mingle anger and vituperation with such discussions. There are, for example, writers of note and influence at the present day who are not ashamed to assume the 'deep personal sin' of a great logician to be the cause of his unbelief in a theologic dogma. And there are others who hold that we, who cherish our noble Bible, wrought as it has been into the constitution of our forefathers, and by inheritance into us, must necessarily be hypocritical and insincere. Let us disavow and discountenance such people, cherishing the unswerving faith that what is good and true in both our arguments will be preserved for the benefit of humanity, while all that is bad or false will disappear."

I hold the Bishop's reasoning to be unanswerable, and his liberality to be worthy of imitation.

It is worth remarking that in one respect the Bishop was a product of his age. Long previous to his day the nature of the soul had been so favourite and general a topic of discussion, that, when the students of the University of Paris wished to know the leanings of a new Professor, they at once requested him to lecture upon the soul. About the time of Bishop Butler the question was not only agitated but extended. It was seen by the clear-witted men who entered this arena that many of their best arguments applied equally to brutes and men. The Bishop's arguments were of this character. He saw it, admitted it, accepted the consequences, and boldly embraced the whole animal world in his scheme of immortality.

Bishop Butler accepted with unwavering trust the chronology of the Old Testament, describing it as "confirmed by the natural and civil history of the world, collected from common historians, from the state of the earth, and from the late inventions of arts and sciences." These words mark progress; and they must seem somewhat hoary to the Bishop's successors of to-day.* It is hardly necessary to inform you that since his time the domain of the naturalist has been immensely extended—the whole science of geology, with its astounding revelations regarding the life of the ancient earth, having been created. The rigidity of old conceptions has been relaxed, the public mind being rendered gradually tolerant of the idea that not for six thousand, nor for sixty thousand, nor for six thousand thousand thousand, but for aeons embracing untold millions of years, this earth has been the theatre of life and death. The riddle of the rocks has been read by the geologist and palaeontologist, from subcambrian depths to the deposits thickening over the sea-bottoms of to-day. And upon the leaves of that stone book are, as you know, stamped the characters, plainer and surer than those formed by the ink of history, which carry the mind back into abysses of past time compared with which the periods which satisfied Bishop Butler cease to have a visual angle.

The lode of discovery once struck, those petrified forms in which life was at one time active increased to multitudes and demanded classification. They were grouped in genera, species, and varieties, according to the degree of similarity subsisting

---

* Only to some; for there are dignitaries who even now speak of the earth's rocky crust as so much building material prepared for man at the Creation. Surely it is time that this loos language should cease.

between them. Thus confusion was avoided, each object being found in the pigeon-hole appropriated to it and to its fellows of similar morphological or physiological character. The general fact soon became evident that none but the simplest forms of life lie lowest down, that as we climb higher among the super-imposed strata more perfect forms appear. The change, however, from form to form was not continuous, but by steps—some small, some great. "A section," says Mr. Huxley, "a hundred feet thick will exhibit at different heights a dozen species of Ammonite, none of which passes beyond its particular zone of limestone, or clay, into the zone below it, or into that above it." In the presence of such facts it was not possible to avoid the question:—Have these forms, showing, though in broken stages and with many irregularities, this unmistakable general advance, been subjected to no continuous law of growth or variation? Had our education been purely scientific, or had it been sufficiently detached from influences which, however ennobling in another domain, have always proved hindrances and delusions when introduced as factors into the domain of physics, the scientific mind never could have swerved from the search for a law of growth, or allowed itself to accept the anthropomorphism which regarded each successive stratum as a kind of mechanic's bench for the manufacture of new species out of all relation to the old.

Biassed, however, by their previous education, the great majority of naturalists invoked a special creative act to account for the appearance of each new group of organisms. Doubtless there were numbers who were clear-headed enough to see that this was no explanation at all, that in point of fact it was an attempt, by the introduction of a greater difficulty, to account for a less. But having nothing to offer in the way of explanation, they for the most part held their peace. Still the thoughts of reflecting men naturally and necessarily simmered round the question. De Maillet, a contemporary of Newton, has been brought into notice by Professor Huxley as one who "had a notion of the modifiability of living forms." In my frequent conversations with him, the late Sir Benjamin Brodie, a man of highly philosophic mind, often drew my attention to the fact that, as early as 1794, Charles Darwin's grandfather was the pioneer of Charles Darwin.* In 1801, and in subsequent years, the celebrated Lamarck, who produced so profound an impression on the public mind through the vigorous exposition of his views by the author of "Vestiges of Creation" endeavoured to show the development of species out of changes of habit and external condition. In 1813 Dr. Wells, the founder of our present theory of Dew, read before the Royal Society a paper in which, to use the words of Mr. Darwin, "he distinctly recognises the principle of natural selection; and this is the first recognition that has been indicated." The thoroughness and skill with which Wells pursued his work, and the obvious independence of his character, rendered him long ago a favourite with me; and it gave me the liveliest pleasure to alight upon this additional testimony to his penetration. Professor Grant, Mr. Patrick Matthew, Von Buch, the author of the "Vestiges," D'Halloy, and others,† by the enunciation of opinions more or less clear and correct, showed that the question had been fermenting long prior to the year

---

* *Zoonomia*, vol. i. pp. 500–510.

† In 1855 Mr. Herbert Spencer (*Principles of Psychology*, 2nd edit., vol. i. p. 465) expressed "the belief that life under all its forms has arisen by an unbroken evolution, and through the instrumentality of what are called natural causes."

1858, when Mr. Darwin and Mr. Wallace simultaneously but independently placed their closely concurrent views upon the subject before the Linnean Society.

These papers were followed in 1859 by the publication of the first edition of "The Origin of Species." All great things come slowly to the birth. Copernicus, as I informed you, pondered his great work for thirty-three years. Newton for nearly twenty years kept the idea of Gravitation before his mind; for twenty years also he dwelt upon his discovery of Fluxions, and doubtless would have continued to make it the object of his private thought had he not found that Leibnitz was upon his track. Darwin for two and twenty years pondered the problem of the origin of species, and doubtless he would have continued to do so had he not found Wallace upon his track.* A concentrated but full and powerful epitome of his labours was the consequence. The book was by no means an easy one; and probably not one in every score of those who then attacked it had read its pages through, or were competent to grasp their significance if they had. I do not say this merely to discredit them; for there were in those days some really eminent scientific men, entirely raised above the heat of popular prejudice, willing to accept any conclusion that science had to offer, provided it was duly backed by fact and argument, and who entirely mistook Mr. Darwin's views. In fact, the work needed an expounder; and it found one in Mr. Huxley. I know nothing more admirable in the way of scientific exposition than those early articles of his on the origin of species. He swept the curve of discussion through the really significant points of the subject, enriched his exposition with profound original remarks and reflections, often summing up in a single pithy sentence an argument which a less compact mind would have spread over pages. But there is one impression made by the book itself which no exposition of it, however luminous, can convey; and that is the impression of the vast amount of labour, both of observation and of thought, implied in its production. Let us glance at its principles.

It is conceded on all hands that what are called varieties are continually produced. The rule is probably without exception. No chick and no child is in all respects and particulars the counterpart of its brother and sister; and in such differences we have "variety" incipient. No naturalist could tell how far this variation could be carried; but the great mass of them held that never by any amount of internal or external change, nor by the mixture of both, could the offspring of the same progenitor so far deviate from each other as to constitute different species. The function of the experimental philosopher is to combine the conditions of nature and to produce her results; and this was the method of Darwin.† He made himself acquainted with what could, without any manner of doubt, be done in the way of producing variation. He associated himself with pigeon-fanciers—bought, begged, kept, and observed every breed that he could obtain. Though derived from a common stock, the diversities of these pigeons were such that "a score of them might be chosen which, if shown to an ornithologist, and he were told that they were wild birds, would certainly be ranked by him as well-defined species." The simple principle which guides the

---

* The behaviour of Mr Wallace in relation to this subject has been dignified in the highest degree.
† The first step only towards experimental demonstration has been taken. Experiments now begun might, a couple of centuries hence, furnish data of incalculable value, which ought to be supplied to the science of the future.

pigeon-fancier, as it does the cattle-breeder, is the selection of some variety that strikes his fancy, and the propagation of this variety by inheritance. With his eye still directed to the particular appearance which he wishes to exaggerate, he selects it as it reappears in successive broods, and thus adds increment to increment until an astonishing amount of divergence from the parent type is effected. The breeder in this case does not produce the *elements* of the variation. He simply observes them, and by selection adds them together until the required result has been obtained. "No man," says Mr. Darwin, "would ever try to make a fantail till he saw a pigeon with a tail developed in some slight degree in an unusual manner, or a pouter until he saw a pigeon with a crop of unusual size." Thus nature gives the hint, man acts upon it, and by the law of inheritance exaggerates the deviation.

Having thus satisfied himself by indubitable facts that the organization of an animal or of a plant (for precisely the same treatment applies to plants) is to some extent plastic, he passes from variation under domestication to variation under nature. Hitherto we have dealt with the adding together of small changes by the conscious selection of man. Can Nature thus select? Mr. Darwin's answer is, "Assuredly she can." The number of living things produced is far in excess of the number that can be supported; hence at some period or other of their lives there must be a struggle for existence; and what is the infallible result? If one organism were a perfect copy of the other in regard to strength, skill, and agility, external conditions would decide. But this is not the case. Here we have the fact of variety offering itself to nature, as in the former instance it offered itself to man; and those varieties which are least competent to cope with surrounding conditions will infallibly give way to those that are most competent. To use a familiar proverb, the weakest comes to the wall. But the triumphant fraction again breeds to overproduction, transmitting the qualities which secured its maintenance, but transmitting them in different degrees. The struggle for food again supervenes, and those to whom the favourable quality has been transmitted in excess will assuredly triumph. It is easy to see that we have here the addition of increments favourable to the individual still more rigorously carried out than in the case of domestication; for not only are unfavourable specimens not selected by nature, but they are destroyed. This is what Mr. Darwin calls "Natural Selection," which "acts by the preservation and accumulation of small inherited modifications, each profitable to the preserved being." With this idea he interpenetrates and leavens the vast store of facts that he and others have collected. We cannot, without shutting our eyes through fear or prejudice, fail to see that Darwin is here dealing, not with imaginary, but with true causes; nor can we fail to discern what vast modifications may be produced by natural selection in periods sufficiently long. Each individual increment may resemble what mathematicians call a "differential" (a quantity indefinitely small); but definite and great changes may obviously be produced by the integration of these infinitesimal quantities through practically infinite time.

If Darwin, like Bruno, rejects the notion of creative power acting after human fashion, it certainly is not because he is unacquainted with the numberless exquisite adaptations on which this notion of a supernatural artificer has been founded. His book is a repository of the most startling facts of this description. Take the marvellous observation which he cites from Dr. Crüger, where a bucket with an aperture, serving as a spout, is formed in an orchid. Bees visit the flower: in eager search of material for their combs they push each other into the bucket, the drenched ones escaping from their involuntary bath by the spout. Here they rub their backs against the viscid stigma of the flower and obtain glue; then against the pollen-masses, which are thus stuck to the back of the bee and carried away. "When the bee, so provided, flies to another flower, or to the same flower a second time, and is pushed by its comrades into the bucket, and then crawls out by the passage, the pollen-mass upon its back necessarily comes first into contact with the viscid stigma," which takes up the pollen; and this is how that orchid is fertilized. Or take this other case of the *Catasetum*. "Bees visit these flowers in order to gnaw the labellum; in doing this they inevitably touch a long, tapering, sensitive projection. This, when touched, transmits a sensation or vibration to a certain membrane, which is instantly ruptured, setting free a spring, by which the pollen-mass is shot forth like an arrow in the right direction, and adheres by its viscid extremity to the back of the bee." In this way the fertilising pollen is spread abroad.

It is the mind thus stored with the choicest materials of the teleologist that rejects teleology, seeking to refer these wonders to natural cases. They illustrate, according to him, the method of nature, not the "technic" of a man-like Artificer. The beauty of flowers is due to natural selection. Those that distinguish themselves by vividly contrasting colours from the surrounding green leaves are most readily seen, most frequently visited by insects, most often fertilized, and hence most favoured by natural selection. Coloured berries also readily attract the attention of birds and beasts, which feed upon them, spread their manured seeds abroad, thus giving trees and shrubs possessing such berries a greater chance in the struggle for existence.

With profound analytic and synthetic skill, Mr. Darwin investigates the cell-making instinct of the hive-bee. His method of dealing with it is representative. He falls back from the more perfectly to the less perfectly developed instinct—from the hive-bee to the humble bee, which uses its own cocoon as a comb, and to classes of bees of intermediate skill, endeavouring to show how the passage might be gradually made from the lowest to the highest. The saving of wax is the most important point in the economy of bees. Twelve to fifteen pounds of dry sugar are said to be needed for the secretion of a single pound of wax. The quantities of nectar necessary for the wax must therefore be vast, and every improvement of constructive instinct which results in the saving of wax is a direct profit to the insect's life. The time that would otherwise be devoted to the making of wax is now devoted to the gathering and storing of honey for winter food. He passes from the humble bee with its rude cells, through the Melipona with its more artistic cells, to the hive-bee with its astonishing architecture. The bees place themselves at equal distances apart upon the wax, sweep and excavate equal spheres round the selected points. The spheres intersect, and the planes of intersection are built up with thin laminae. Hexagonal cells are thus formed. This mode of treating such questions is, as I have said, representative. He habitually retires from the more perfect and complex to the less perfect and simple, and carries you with him through stages of *perfecting*, adds increment to increment of infinitesimal change, and in this way gradually breaks down your reluctance to admit that the exquisite climax of the whole could be a result of natural selection.

Mr. Darwin shirks no difficulty; and, saturated as the subject was with his own thought, he must have known better than his critics the weakness as well as the strength of his theory. This of course would be of little avail were his object a temporary dialectic victory instead of the establishment of a truth which he means to be everlasting. But he takes no pains to disguise the weakness he has discerned; nay, he takes every pains to bring it into the strongest light. His vast resources enable him to cope with objections started by himself and others, so as to leave the final impression upon the reader's mind that, if they be not completely answered, they certainly are not fatal. Their negative force being thus destroyed, you are free to be influenced by the vast positive mass of evidence he is able to bring before you. This largeness of knowledge and readiness of resource render Mr. Darwin the most terrible of antagonists. Accomplished naturalists have levelled heavy and sustained criticisms against him—not always with the view of fairly weighing his theory, but with the express intention of exposing its weak points only. This does not irritate him. He treats every objection with a soberness and thoroughness which even Bishop Butler might be proud to imitate, surrounding each fact with its appropriate detail, placing it in its proper relations, and usually giving it a significance which, as long as it was kept isolated, failed to appear. This is done without a trace of ill-temper. He moves over the subject with the passionless strength of a glacier; and the grinding of the rocks is not always without a counterpart in the logical pulverization of the objector.

But though in handling this mighty theme all passion has been stilled, there is an emotion of the intellect incident to the discernment of new truth which often colours and warms the pages of Mr. Darwin. His success has been great; and this implies not only the solidity of his work, but the preparedness of the public mind for such a revelation. On this head a remark of Agassiz impressed me more than anything else. Sprung from a race of theologians, this celebrated man combated to the last the theory of natural selection. One of the many times I had the pleasure of meeting him in the United States was at Mr. Winthrop's beautiful residence at Brookline, near Boston. Rising from luncheon, we all halted as if by a common impulse in front of a window, and continued there a discussion which had been started at table. The maple was in its autumn glory; and the exquisite beauty of the scene outside seemed, in my case, to interpenetrate without disturbance the intellectual action. Earnestly, almost sadly, Agassiz turned, and said to the gentleman standing round, "I confess that I was not prepared to see this theory received as it has been by the best intellects of our time. Its success is greater than I could have thought possible."

In our day grand generalizations have been reached. The theory of the origin of species is but one of them. Another, of still wider grasp and more radical significance, is the doctrine of the Conservation of Energy, the ultimate philosophical issues of which are as yet but dimly seen— that doctrine which "binds nature fast in fate" to an extent not hitherto recognized, exacting from every antecedent its equivalent consequent, from every consequent its equivalent antecedent, and bringing vital as well as physical phenomena under the dominion of that law of causal connexion which, so far as the human understanding has yet pierced, asserts itself everywhere in nature. Long in advance of all definite experiment upon the subject, the constancy and indestructibility of matter had been affirmed; and all subsequent experience justified the affirmation. Later researches extended the attribute of indestructibility to force. This idea, applied in the first instance to inorganic, rapidly embraced organic nature. The vegetable world, though drawing almost all its nutriment from invisible sources, was proved incompetent to generate anew either matter or force. Its matter is for the most part transmuted gas; its force transformed solar force. The animal world was proved to be equally uncreative, all its motive energies being referred to the combustion of its food. The activity of each animal as a whole was proved to be the transferred activity of its molecules. The muscles were shown to be stores of mechanical force, potential until unlocked by the nerves, and then resulting in muscular contractions. The speed at which messages fly to and fro along the nerves was determined, and found to be, not as had been previously supposed, equal to that of light or electricity, but less than the speed of a flying eagle.

This was the work of the physicist: then came the conquests of the comparative anatomist and physiologist, revealing the structure of every animal, and the function of every organ in the whole biological series, from the lowest zoophyte up to man. The nervous system had been made the object of profound and continued study, the wonderful and, at bottom, entirely mysterious, controlling power which it exercises over the whole organism, physical and mental, being recognized more and more. Thought could not be kept back from a subject so profoundly suggestive. Besides the physical life dealt with by Mr. Darwin, there is a psychical life presenting similar gradations, and asking equally for a solution. How are the different grades and order of Mind to be accounted for? What is the principle of growth of that mysterious power which on our planet culminates in Reason? These are questions which, though not thrusting themselves so forcibly upon the attention of the general public, had not only occupied many reflecting minds, but had been formally broached by one of them before the "Origin of Species" appeared. With the mass of materials furnished by the physicist and physiologist in his hands, Mr. Herbert Spencer, twenty years ago, sought to graft upon this basis a system of psychology; and two years ago a second and greatly amplified edition of his work appeared. Those who have occupied themselves with the beautiful experiments of Plateau will remember that when two spherules of olive-oil, suspended in a mixture of alcohol and water of the same density as the oil, are brought together, they do not immediately unite. Something like a pellicle appears to be formed around the drops, the rupture of which is immediately followed by the coalescence of the globules into one. There are organisms whose vital actions are almost as purely physical as that of these drops of oil. They come into contact and fuse themselves thus together. From such organisms to others a shade higher, and from these to others a shade higher still, and on through an ever-ascending series, Mr. Spencer conducts his argument. There are two obvious factors to be here taken into account—the creature and the medium in which it lives, or, as it is often expressed, the organism and its environment. Mr. Spencer's fundamental principle is that between these two factors there is incessant interaction. The organism is played upon by the environment, and is modified to meet the requirements of the environment. Life he defines to be "a continuous adjustment of internal relations to external relations."

In the lowest organisms we have a kind of tactual sense diffused over the entire body; then, through impressions from without and their corresponding adjustments, special portions of the surface become more responsive to stimuli than others. The senses are nascent, the basis of all of them being that simple tactual sense which the sage Democritus recognised 2,300 year ago as their common progenitor. The action of light, in the first instance, appears to be a mere disturbance of the chemical processes in the animal organism, similar to that which occurs in the leaves of plants. By degrees the action becomes localized in a few pigment-cells, more sensitive to light than the surrounding tissue. The eye is here incipient. At first it is merely capable of revealing differences of light and shade produced by bodies close at hand. Followed as the interception of the light is in almost all cases by the contact of the closely adjacent opaque body, sight in this condition becomes a kind of "anticipatory touch." The adjustment continues; a slight bulging out of the epidermis over the pigment-granules supervenes. A lens is incipient, and, through the operation of infinite adjustments, at length reaches the perfection that it displays in the hawk and eagle. So of the other senses; they are special differentiations of a tissue which was originally vaguely sensitive all over.

With the development of the senses the adjustments between the organism and its environment gradually extend in *space*, a multiplication of experiences and a corresponding modification of conduct being the result. The adjustments also extend in *time*, covering continually greater intervals. Along with this extension in space and time the adjustments also increase in specialty and complexity, passing through the various grades of brute life, and prolonging themselves into the domain of reason. Very striking are Mr. Spencer's remarks regarding the influence of the sense of touch upon the development of intelligence. This is, so to say, the mother-tongue of all the senses, into which they must be translated to be of service to the organism. Hence its importance. The parrot is the most intelligent of birds, and its tactual power is also greatest. From this sense it gets knowledge unattainable by birds which cannot employ their feet as hands. The elephant is the most sagacious of quadrupeds—its tactual range and skill, and the consequent multiplication of experiences, which it owes to its wonderfully adaptable trunk, being the basis of its sagacity. Feline animals, for a similar cause, are more sagacious than hoofed animals—atonement being to some extent made, in the case of the horse, by the possession of sensitive prehensile lips. In the *Primates* the evolution of intellect and the evolution of tactual appendages go hand in hand. In the most intelligent anthropoid apes we find the tactual range and delicacy greatly augmented, new avenues of knowledge being thus open to the animal. Man crowns the edifice here, not only in virtue of his own manipulatory power, but through the enormous extension of his range of experience, by the invention of instruments of precision, which serve as supplemental senses and supplemental limbs. The reciprocal action of these is finely described and illustrated. That chastened intellectual emotion to which I have referred in connexion with Mr. Darwin is not absent in Mr. Spencer. His illustrations possess at times exceeding vividness and force; and from his style on such occasions it is to be inferred that the ganglia of this Apostle of the Understanding are sometimes the seat of a nascent poetic thrill.

It is a fact of supreme importance that actions the performance of which at first requires even painful effort and deliberation may by habit be rendered automatic. Witness the slow learning of its letters by a child, and the subsequent facility of reading in a man, when each group of letters which forms a word is instantly, and without effort, fused to a single perception. Instance the billiard-player, whose muscles of hand and eye, when he reaches the perfection of his art, are unconsciously coordinated. Instance the musician, who, by practice, is enabled to fuse a multitude of arrangements, auditory, tactual, and muscular, into a process of automatic manipulation. Combining such facts with the doctrine of hereditary transmission, we reach a theory of Instinct. A chick, after coming out of the egg, balances itself correctly, runs about, picks up food, thus showing that it possesses a power of directing its movements to definite ends. How did the chick learn this very complex coordination of eye, muscles, and beak? It has not been individually taught; its personal experience is *nil*; but it has the benefit of ancestral experience. In its inherited organization are registered all the powers which it displays at birth. So also as regards the instinct of the hive-bee, already referred to. The distance at which the insects stand apart when they sweep their hemispheres and build their cells is "organically remembered."

Man also carries with him the physical texture of his ancestry, as well as the inherited intellect bound up with it. The defects of intelligence during infancy and youth are probably less due to a lack of individual experience than to the fact that in early life the cerebral organization is still incomplete. The period necessary for completion varies with the race and with the individual. As a round shot outstrips a rifled one on quitting the muzzle of the gun, so the lower race in childhood may outstrip the higher. But the higher eventually overtakes the lower, and surpasses it in range. As regards individuals, we do not always find the precocity of youth prolonged to mental power in maturity; while the dullness of boyhood is sometimes strikingly contrasted with the intellectual energy of after years. Newton, when a boy, was weakly, and he showed no particular aptitude at school; but in his eighteenth year he went to Cambridge, and soon afterwards astonished his teachers by his power of dealing with geometrical problems. During his quiet youth his brain was slowly preparing itself to be the organ of those energies which he subsequently displayed.

By myriad blows (to use a Lucretian phrase) the image and superscription of the external world are stamped as states of consciousness upon the organism, the depth of the impression depending upon the number of the blows. When two or more phenomena occur in the environment invariably together, they are stamped to the same depth or to the same relief, and indissolubly connected. And here we come to the threshold of a great question. Seeing that he could in no way rid himself of the consciousness of Space and Time, Kant assumed them to be necessary "forms of intuition," the moulds and shapes into which our intuitions are thrown, belonging to ourselves solely and without objective existence. With unexpected power and success Mr. Spencer brings the hereditary experience theory, as he holds it, to bear upon this question. "If there exist certain external relations which are experienced by all organisms at all instants of their waking lives—relations which are absolutely constant and universal—there will be established answering internal relations that are absolutely constant and universal. Such relations we have in those of Space and Time. As the substratum of all other relations of the Non-Ego, they must be responded to by conceptions that are the substrata of all other relations in the Ego. Being the constant and infinitely repeated elements of thought, they must become the automatic elements of thought—the elements of thought which it is impossible to get rid of—the 'forms of intuition.'"

Throughout this application and extension of the "Law of Inseparable Association," Mr. Spencer stands upon his own ground, invoking, instead of the experiences of the individual, the registered experiences of the race. His overthrow of the restriction of experience to the individual is, I think, complete. That restriction ignores the power of organizing experience furnished at the outset to each individual; it ignores the different degrees of this power possessed by different races and by different individuals of the same race. Were there not in the human brain a potency antecedent to all experience, a dog or cat ought to be as capable of education as a man. These predetermined internal relations are independent of the experiences of the individual. The human brain is the "organised register of infinitely numerous experiences received during the evolution of life, or rather during the evolution of that series of organisms through which the human organism has been reached. The effects of the most uniform and frequent of these experiences have been successively bequeathed, principal and interest, and have slowly mounted to that high intelligence which lies latent in the brain of the infant. Thus it happens that the European inherits from twenty to thirty cubic inches more of brain than the Papuan. Thus it happens that faculties, as of music, which scarcely exist in some inferior races, become congenital in superior ones. Thus it happens that out of savages unable to count up to the number of their fingers, and speaking a language containing only nouns and verbs, arise at length our Newtons and Shakespeares."

At the outset of this Address it was stated that physical theories which lie beyond experience are derived by a process of abstraction from experience. It is instructive to note from this point of view the successive introduction of new conceptions. The idea of the attraction of gravitation was preceded by the observation of the attraction of iron by a magnet, and of light bodies by rubbed amber. The polarity of magnetism and electricity appealed to the senses; and thus became the sub-stratum of the conception that atoms and molecules are endowed with definite, attractive, and repellent poles, by the play of which definite forms of crystalline architecture are produced. Thus molecular force becomes *structural*. It required no great boldness of thought to extend its play into organic nature, and to recognize in molecular force the agency by which both plants and animals are built up. In this way out of experience arise conceptions which are wholly ultra-experiential. None of the atomists of antiquity had any notion of this play of molecular polar force, but they had experience of gravity as manifested by falling bodies. Abstracting from this, they permitted their atoms to fall eternally through empty space. Democritus assumed that the larger atoms moved more rapidly than the smaller ones, which they therefore could overtake, and with which they could combine. Epicurus, holding that empty space could offer no resistance to motion, ascribed to all the atoms the same velocity; but he seems to have overlooked the consequence that under such circumstances the atoms could never combine. Lucretius cut the knot by quitting the domain of physics altogether, and causing the atoms to move together by a kind of volition.

Was the instinct utterly at fault which caused Lucretius thus to swerve from his own principles? Diminishing gradually the number of progenitors, Mr. Darwin comes at length to one "primordial form;" but he does not say, as far as I remember, how he supposes this form to have been introduced. He quotes with satisfaction the words of a celebrated and divine who had "gradually learnt to see that it is just as noble a conception of the Deity to believe He created a few original forms, capable of self-development into other and needful forms, as to believe that He required a fresh act of creation to supply the voids caused by the action of His laws." What Mr. Darwin thinks of this view of the introduction of life I do not know. But the anthropomorphism, which it seemed his object to set aside, is as firmly associated with the creation of a few forms as with the creation of a multitude. We need clearness and thoroughness here. Two courses and two only, are possible. Either let us open our doors freely to the conception of creative acts, or, abandoning them, let us radically change our notions of Matter. If we look at matter as pictured by Democritus, and as defined for generations in our scientific text-books, the notion of any form of life whatever coming out of it is utterly unimaginable. The argument placed in the mouth of Bishop Butler suffices, in my opinion, to crush all such materialism as this. But those who framed these definitions of matter were not biologists, but mathematicians, whose labours referred only to such accidents and properties of matter as could be expressed in their formulae. The very intentness with which they pursued mechanical science turned their thoughts aside from the science of life. May not their imperfect definitions be the real cause of our present dread? Let us reverently, but honestly, look the question in the face. Divorced from matter, where is life to be found? Whatever our *faith* may say, our *knowledge* shows them to be indissolubly joined. Every meal we eat, and every cup we drink, illustrates the mysterious control of Mind by Matter.

Trace the line of life backwards, and see it approaching more and more to what we call the purely physical condition. We come at length to those organisms which I have compared to drops of oil suspended in a mixture of alcohol and water. We reach the *protogenes* of Haeckel, in which we have "a type distinguishable from a fragment of albumen only by its finely granular character." Can we pause here? We break a magnet and find two poles in each of its fragments. We continue the process of breaking, but, however small the parts, each carries with it, though enfeebled, the polarity of the whole. And when we can break no longer, we prolong the intellectual vision to the polar molecules. Are we not urged to do *something* similar in the case of life? Is there not a temptation to close to some extent with Lucretius, when he affirms that "nature is seen to do all things spontaneously of herself without the meddling of the gods?" or with Bruno, when he declares that Matter is not "that mere empty capacity which philosophers have pictured her to be, but the universal mother who wrings forth all things as the fruit of her own womb?" Believing as I do in the continuity of Nature, I cannot stop abruptly where our microscopes cease to be of use. Here the vision of the mind authoritatively supplements the vision of the eye. By an intellectual necessity I cross the boundary of the experimental evidence, and discern in that Matter which we, in our ignorance of its latent powers, and notwithstanding our professed reverence for its Creator, have hitherto covered with opprobrium, the promise and potency of all terrestrial Life.

If you ask me whether there exists the least evidence to prove that any form of life can be developed out of matter, without demonstrable antecedent life, my reply is that evidence considered perfectly conclusive by many has been adduced; and that were some of us who have pondered this question to follow a very common example, and accept testimony because it falls in with our belief, we also should eagerly close with the evidence referred to. But there is in the true man of science a wish stronger than the wish to have his beliefs upheld; namely, the wish to have them true. And this stronger wish causes him to reject the most plausible support if he has reason to suspect that it is vitiated by error. Those to whom I refer as having studied this question, believing the evidence offered in favour of "spontaneous generation" to be thus vitiated, cannot accept it. They know full well that the chemist now prepares from inorganic matter a vast array of substances which were some time ago regarded as the sole products of vitality. They are intimately acquainted with the structural power of matter as evidenced in the phenomena of crystallization. They can justify scientifically their *belief* in its potency, under the proper conditions, to produce organisms. But in reply to your question they will frankly admit their inability to point to any satisfactory experimental proof that life can be developed save from demonstrable antecedent life. As already indicated, they draw the line from the highest organisms through lower ones down to the lowest, and it is the prolongation of this line by the intellect beyond the range of the senses that leads them to the conclusion which Bruno so boldly enunciated.*

The "materialism" here professed may be vastly different from what you suppose, and I therefore crave your gracious patience to the end. "The question of an external world," says Mr. J. S. Mill, "is the great battleground of metaphysics."† Mr. Mill himself reduces external phenomena to "possibilities of sensation." Kant, as we have seen, made time and space "forms" of our own intuitions. Fichte, having first by the inexorable logic of his understanding proved himself to be a mere link in that chain of eternal causation which holds so rigidly in Nature, violently broke the chain by making Nature, and all that it inherits, an apparition of his own mind.‡ And it is by no means easy to combat such notions. For when I say I see you, and that I have not the least doubt about it, the reply is, that what I am really conscious of is an affection of my own retina. And if I urge that I can check my sight of you by touching you, the retort would be that I am equally transgressing the limits of fact; for what I am really conscious of is, not that you are there, but that the nerves of my hand have undergone a change. All we hear, and see, and touch, and taste, and smell, are, it would be urged, mere variations of our own condition, beyond which, even to the extent of a hair's breadth, we cannot go. That anything answering to our impressions exists outside of ourselves is not a *fact*, but an *inference*, to which all validity would be denied by an idealist like Berkeley, or by a sceptic like Hume. Mr. Spencer takes another line. With him, as with the uneducated man, there is no doubt or question as to the existence of an external world. But he differs from the uneducated, who think that the world really is what consciousness represents it to be. Our states of consciousness are mere symbols of an outside entity which produces them and determines the order of their succession, but the real nature of which we can never

---

* Bruno was a "Pantheist," not an "Atheist" or a "Materialist."
† *Examination of Hamilton*, p. 154.
‡ *Bestimmung des Menschen*.

know.* In fact, the whole process of evolution is the manifestation of a Power absolutely inscrutable to the intellect of man. As little in our day as in the days of Job can man by searching find this Power out. Considered fundamentally, then, it is by the operation of an insoluble mystery that life on earth is evolved, species differentiated, and mind unfolded from their prepotent elements in the immeasurable past. There is, you will observe, no very rank materialism here.

The strength of the doctrine of evolution consists, not in an experimental demonstration (for the subject is hardly accessible to this mode of proof), but in its general harmony with scientific thought. From contrast, moreover, it derives enormous relative strength. On the one side we have a theory (if it could with any propriety be so called) derived, as were the theories referred to at the beginning of this Address, not from the study of Nature, but from the observation of men—a theory which converts the Power whose garment is seen in the visible universe into an Artificer, fashioned after the human model, and acting by broken efforts, as man is seen to act. On the other side, we have the conception that all we see around us, and all we feel within us—the phenomena of physical nature as well as those of the human mind—have their unsearchable roots in a cosmical life, if I dare apply the term, an infinitesimal span of which is offered to the investigation of man. And even this span is only knowable in part. We can trace the development of a nervous system, and correlate with it the parallel phenomena of sensation and thought. We see with undoubting certainty that they go hand in hand. But we try to soar in a vacuum the moment we seek to comprehend the connexion between them. An Archimedean fulcrum is here required which the human mind cannot command; and the effort to solve the problem, to borrow a comparison from an illustrious friend of mine, is like the effort of a man trying to lift himself by his own waistband. All that has been here said is to be taken in connexion with this fundamental truth. When "nascent senses are spoken of, when "the differentiation of a tissue at first vaguely sensitive all over" is spoken of, and when these processes are associated with "the modification of an organism by its environment," the same parallelism, without contact, or even approach to contact, is implied. Man the *object* is separated by an impassable gulf from man the *subject*. There is no motor energy in intellect to carry it without logical rupture from the one to the other.

Further, the doctrine of evolution derives man in his totality from the inter-action of organism and environment through countless ages past. The Human Understanding, for example—that faculty which Mr. Spencer has turned so skillfully round upon its own antecedents—is itself a result of the play between organism and

---

* In a paper, at once popular and profound, entitled *Recent Progress in the Theory of Vision*, contained in the volume of Lectures by Helmholtz, published by Longmans, this symbolism of our states of consciousness is also dwelt upon. The impressions of sense are the mere *signs* of external things. In this paper Helmholtz contends strongly against the view that the consciousness of space is inborn; and he evidently doubts the power of the chick to pick up grains of corn without preliminary lessons. On this point, he says, further experiments are needed. Such experiments have been since made by Mr. Spalding, aided, I believe, in some of his observations by the accomplished and deeply lamented Lady Amberly; and they seem to prove conclusively that the chick does not need a single moment's tuition to enable it to stand, run, govern the muscles of its eyes, and to peck. Helmholtz, however, is contending against the notion of pre-established harmony; and I am not aware of his views as to the organisation of experiences of race or breed.

environment through cosmic ranges of time. Never surely did prescription plead so irresistible a claim. But then it comes to pass that, over and above his understanding, there are many other things appertaining to man whose perspective rights are quite as strong as those of the understanding itself. It is a result, for example, of the play of organism and environment that sugar is sweet and that aloes are bitter, that the smell of henbane differs from the perfume of a rose. Such facts of consciousness (for which, by the way, no adequate reason has yet been rendered) are quite as old as the understanding; and many other things can boast an equally ancient origin. Mr. Spencer at one place refers to that most powerful of passions—the amatory passion—as one which, when it first occurs, is antecedent to all relative experience whatever; and we may pass its claim as being at least as ancient and valid as that of the understanding. Then there are such things woven into the texture of man as the feeling of Awe, Reverence, Wonder—and not alone the sexual love just referred to, but the love of the beautiful, physical, and moral, in Nature, Poetry, and Art. There is also that deep-set feeling which, since the earliest dawn of history, and probably for ages prior to all history, incorporated itself in the Religions of the world. You who have escaped from these religions into the high-and-dry light of the intellect may deride them; but in so doing you deride accidents of form merely, and fail to touch the immovable basis of the religious sentiment in the nature of man. To yield this sentiment reasonable satisfaction is the problem of problems at the present hour. And grotesque in relation to scientific culture as many of the religions of the world have been and are— dangerous, nay destructive, to the dearest privileges of freemen as some of them undoubtedly have been, and would, if they could, be again—it will be wise to recognize them as the forms of a force, mischievous, if permitted to intrude on the region of *knowledge*, over which it holds no command, but capable of being guided to noble issues in the region of *emotion*, which is its proper and elevated sphere.

All religious theories, schemes and systems, which embrace notions of cosmogony, or which otherwise reach into the domain of science, must, *in so far as they do this*, submit to the control of science, and relinquish all thought of controlling it. Acting otherwise proved disastrous in the past, and it is simply fatuous to-day. Every system which would escape the fate of an organism too rigid to adjust itself to its environment must be plastic to the extent that the growth of knowledge demands. When this truth has been thoroughly taken in, rigidity will be relaxed, exclusiveness diminished, things now deemed essential will be dropped, and elements now rejected will be assimilated. The lifting of the life is the essential point; and as long as dogmatism, fanaticism, and intolerance are kept out, various modes of leverage may be employed to raise life to a higher level. Science itself not unfrequently derives motive power from an ultra-scientific source. Whewell speaks of enthusiasm of temper as a hindrance to science; but he means the enthusiasm of weak heads. There is a strong and resolute enthusiasm in which science finds an ally; and it is to the lowering of this fire, rather than to the diminution of intellectual insight, that the lessening productiveness of men of science in their mature years is to be ascribed. Mr. Buckle sought to detach intellectual achievement from moral force. He gravely erred; for without moral force to whip it into action, the achievements of the intellect would be poor indeed.

It has been said that science divorces itself from literature; but the statement, like so many others, arises from lack of knowledge. A glance at the less technical writings of its leaders—of its Helmholtz, its Huxley, and its Du Bois-Reymond—would show what breadth of literary culture they command. Where among modern writers can you find their superiors in clearness and vigour of literary style? Science desires not isolation, but freely combines with every effort towards the bettering of man's estate. Single-handed, and supported not by outward sympathy, but by inward force, it has built at least one great wing of the many-mansioned home which man in his totality demands. And if rough walls and protruding rafter-ends indicate that on one side the edifice is still incomplete, it is only by wise combination of the parts required with those already irrevocably built that we can hope for completeness. There is no necessary incongruity between what has been accomplished and what remains to be done. The moral glow of Socrates, which we all feel by ignition, has in it nothing incompatible with the physics of Anaxagoras which he so much scorned, but which he would hardly scorn today.

And here I am reminded of one amongst us, hoary, but still strong, whose prophet-voice some thirty years ago, far more than any other of this age, unlocked whatever of life and nobleness lay latent in its most gifted minds—one fit to stand beside Socrates or the Maccabean Eleazar, and to dare and suffer all that they suffered and dared—fit, as he once said of Fichte, "to have been the teacher of the Stoa, and to have discoursed of Beauty and Virtue in the groves of Academe." With a capacity to grasp physical principles which his friend Goethe did not possess, and which even total lack of exercise has not been able to reduce to atrophy, it is the world's loss that he, in the vigour of his years, did not open his mind and sympathies to science, and make its conclusions a portion of his message to mankind. Marvellously endowed as he was—equally equipped on the side of the Heart and of the Understanding—he might have done much towards teaching us how to reconcile the claims of both, and to enable them in coming times to dwell together in unity of spirit and in the bond of peace.

And now the end is come. With more time, or greater strength and knowledge, what has been here said might have been better said, while worthy matters here omitted might have received fit expression. But there would have been no material deviation from the views set forth. As regards myself, they are not the growth of a day; and as regards you, I thought you ought to know the environment which, with or without your consent, is rapidly surrounding you, and in relation to which some adjustment on your part may be necessary. A hint of Hamlet's, however, teaches us all how the troubles of common life may be ended; and it is perfectly possible for you and me to purchase intellectual peace at the price of intellectual death. The world is not without refuges of this description; nor is it wanting in persons who seek their shelter and try to persuade others to do the same. The unstable and the weak will yield to this persuasion, and they to whom repose is sweeter than the truth. But I would exhort you to refuse the offered shelter and to scorn the base repose—to accept, if the choice be forced upon you, commotion before stagnation, the leap of the torrent before the stillness of the swamp.

In the course of this Address I have touched on debatable questions and led you over what will be deemed dangerous ground—and this partly with the view of telling you that as regards these questions science claims unrestricted right of search. It is not to the point to say that the views of Lucretius and Bruno, of Darwin and Spencer, may be wrong. Here I should agree with you, deeming it indeed certain that these views will undergo modification. But the point is, that, whether right or wrong, we ask the freedom to discuss them. For science, however, no exclusive claim is here made; you are not urged to erect it into an idol. The inexorable advance of man's understanding in the path of knowledge, and those unquenchable claims of his moral and emotional nature which the understanding can never satisfy, are here equally set forth. The world embraces not only a Newton, but a Shakespeare—not only a Boyle, but a Raphael—not only a Kant, but a Beethoven—not only a Darwin, but a Carlyle. Not in each of these, but in all, is human nature whole. They are not opposed, but supplementary—not mutually exclusive, but reconcilable. And if, unsatisfied with them all, the human mind, with the yearning of a pilgrim for his distant home, will turn to the Mystery from which it has emerged, seeking so to fashion it as to give unity to thought and faith; so long as this is done, not only without intolerance or bigotry of any kind, but with the enlightened recognition that ultimate fixity of conception is here unattainable, and that each succeeding age must be held free to fashion the Mystery in accordance with its own needs—then, casting aside all the restrictions of Materialism, I would affirm this to be a field for the noblest exercise of what, in contrast with the *knowing* faculties, may be called the *creative* faculties of man.

"Fill thy heart with it," said Goethe, "and then name it as thou wilt." Goethe himself did this in untranslateable language.* Wordsworth did it in words known to all Englishmen, and which may be regarded as a forecast and religious vitalization of the latest and deepest scientific truth,—

> "For I have learned
> To look on nature; not as in the hour
> Of thoughtless youth; but hearing oftentimes
> The still, sad music of humanity,
> Nor harsh nor grating, though of ample power
> To chasten and subdue. *And I have felt*
> *A presence that disturbs me with the joy*
> *Of elevated thoughts; a sense sublime*
> *Of something far more deeply interfused,*
> *Whose dwelling is the light of setting suns,*
> *And the round ocean, and the living air,*
> *And the blue sky, and in the mind of man:*
> *A motion and a spirit, that impels*
> *All thinking things, all objects of all thought,*
> *And rolls through all things."*†[21]

---

* Procœmium to "Gott und Welt."
† Tintern Abbey.

Robert Lloyd Praeger

Robert Lloyd Praeger (1865–1953) was one of the first prominent naturalists to explore Ireland's natural world. Born in Hollywood, County Down, he was the son of a Dutch linen merchant and the grandson of the Belfast naturalist Robert Patterson. He graduated from Queen's University Belfast and began a career as a civil engineer; later, he joined the National Library of Ireland, where he retired as its chief librarian. Over his lifetime, Praeger had a keen interest in nature, joining the Dublin Field Club, the Horticultural Society of Ireland, and the Geographical Society of Ireland. His endeavors in these organizations earned him honors from the Association of Linnaeans and the Botanical Society of the British Isles for his study of plant forms. He was also president of the Royal Irish Academy from 1931 to 1934. Praeger's works include *The Botanist in Ireland* (1934), *Some Irish Naturalists* (1949), *Natural History of Ireland* (1950), and *Irish Landscape* (1953). However, he is best known for *The Way That I Went* (1947), a classic example of Irish nature literature that works as a travel journal and a topographical analysis of the Irish landscape, written with insight and humor that culminates in a philosophical rumination of the decay of modern twentieth-century life in Ireland. The following selections are taken from chapters 1 and 8 of *The Way That I Went*, a title Praeger took from a poem by Robert Bridges.[22]

From **The Way That I Went**

FROM CHAPTER 1: IRELAND

> He made you all fair,
>   You in purple and gold,
> You in silver and green,
> Till no eye that has seen
>   Without love can behold.
> —Dora Sigerson Shorter[23]

The way that I went was an Irish way, with extraorbital aberrations, especially in later years, to the extent of a thousand or fifteen hundred miles. It was from the beginning a way of flowers and stones and beasts. When I was old enough to toddle, my father had to put a fence around a garden patch in front of the house, because I picked all the blossoms; and I knew belemnites and harebells and flint-flakes before I was five. That obsession has remained with me throughout life, and I make no apology for the predominant place which it will occupy in what I am about to write. For we are ourselves creations of nature, and spend our lives amid natural objects. Who does not wish on a fine day to escape from the town into the country? And when you get there, it adds enormously to your interest and enjoyment if you understand something about the architecture of the hills and plains, and about their teeming population of birds and butterflies and trees. So I launch my paper ships boldly, in the desire to stimulate an interest in natural things. I venture to hope that—

> Away down the river,
> A hundred miles or more,

Other little children
Shall bring my boats ashore.

I have traversed Ireland to and fro from end to end, and from sea to sea. Mostly on foot, for that is the only way to see and get to know intimately any country; sometimes by cycle; seldom by car, because the motor travels much too fast for the serious observer. Used as one uses the train, for rapid transit to some desired spot, it is often a boon beyond price: it can take the town-dweller rapidly beyond the zone of bungalows, and the less sturdy far afield. But for the nature-lover, and for the mind jaded with the meaningless noise and hurry of modern life, with "the rush and glare of the interminable hours," quiet wandering on foot along brown streams and among the windy hills can bring a solace and a joy that is akin only to the peace of God that passed understanding.

But, finite and worldly creatures that we are, we cannot exist long on that high plane. Hunger and a westering sun soon drive us back towards the abodes of men, and in the evening the bus or clattering tram is often a godsend as great as was the welcome freedom of the heather in the forenoon. And so the following chapters, built up chiefly of impressions gained in many years' wayfaring in Ireland, must recognize the interest of the populous places as well as those of the country-side. But this is not a guide-book—heaven forfend! Rather have I, in memory, wandered over the country, picking out places and things that have interested me, and which I have hoped may interest others. Nor is the Ireland I describe, like that of many recent writings, the Ireland the motorist, who, like the "wind-borne mirroring soul" of Matthew Arnold's *Ernpedocles*,

A thousand glances wins,
And never sees a whole;
Looks once, and drives elsewhere, and leaves its last employ.

There are plenty of books for him. It is rather the Ireland of man who goes with reverent feet through the hills and accompanied by neither noise nor dust to scare away wild creatures; stopping often, watching closely, listening carefully. Only thus can he, if he is fortunate, make friends by degrees with the birds and flowers and rocks, learn all the signs and sounds of the country-side, and at length feel at one with what is, after all, his natural environment. I hold that in this mood he will also be better fitted for appraisement of the many monuments of man's industry and faith that he will meet in this Ireland of ours, be, it a cairn of the Bronze Age, a medieval church, or some marvel of modern science.

There is no need to begin with any general description of Ireland; that has been done over and over again, and by hands more skilled than mine. But it may be desirable to recall a few topographical features which have affected and still affect much that is within the country. There is, first of all, its unique position—an island out in the North Atlantic, doubly cut off from direct continental influences by intervening seas. At the same time, it lies, along with the adjoining and larger island of Great Britain, on a shallow shelf, projecting into the ocean between Spain and Norway, so that a slightly higher level of the land, by spilling the water off this shelf, would allow, and has allowed at certain periods in the past, free immigration from the

Continent. These times were too long ago to have affected human affairs as we know them, but they had a considerable influence as regards the peopling of the land with the animals and plants which still occupy it, and possibly as regards movements of the earlier races of man.

Next, there is the unusual nature of the surface. Ancient crumplings of the Earth's crust have resulted in the formation of mountain ranges in the coastal regions, leaving a broad low plain in the centre. Easy access to the interior has consequently been limited to gaps in the high rim, thus fixing trade routes and the position of coastal towns; but free dispersal over the central parts has been possible once the coastal barrier was passed or evaded. This has profoundly influenced the effect of the various human invasions which Ireland has endured, tending to push pre-existing cultures not into an inaccessible centre, as in most islands, but into the mountain-fringe: witness the present and recent distribution of the native Irish tongue. Again, geological vicissitudes have produced an astonishing variety of rocks, as compared with most areas of similar size: this has given us delightfully varied scenery, and also different kinds of soils, with obvious repercussions on human life. The wholesale mixing-up of superficial deposits caused by the moving ice of the Glacial Period has tended to more uniform and also better soil conditions than would otherwise have been the case. Climate also intrudes itself strikingly in Ireland. The position of the island relative to the warm Atlantic results in high rainfall, cool summers, mild winters, and much wind; these factors influence all life within the island, from man down to mosses. This peculiar position is also at the root of that most delightful of Irish climatic phenomena, its ever-changing cloud-effects, so different from the monotonous and more settled skies—whether cloudy or cloudless—that characterize continental areas. The western hills and the clouds which are their legitimate accompaniment are inseparable; the eye is carried upward from the hill-tops for thousands of feet into the infinite blue. The cloudland is indeed so wonderful a creation that Ireland would be a dull place without it: here it is almost always with us, as vital to our enjoyment as the landscape itself. And if frequent condensation and consequent precipitation is the necessary corollary to the frequent temperature changes which give us our snowy cumulus and colourful cloud curtains, we can afford to take with grateful hearts whatever comes. As J. W. Riley sings:

> It ain't no use to grumble and complain;
>   It's jest as cheap and easy to rejoice;
> When God sorts out the weather and sends rain,
>   W'y, rain's my choice.

Perhaps the most marked effect of the wet climate is the vast development of peat-bog on the plains, which has rendered one-seventeenth of the lowlands of Ireland useless for purposes of agriculture, but has provided the people with a widespread and almost inexhaustible supply of fuel. It is curious to speculate what would have been the history of the treeless, coal-less rainy western areas had peat not been present almost everywhere.

A marked result of the marginal distribution of high ground is seen if the river-courses are studied. The streams which rise on the seaward slope of the mountains are short and rapid, while those whose sources lie on the inland side have mostly long and devious courses, and their mouths often lie many times further away from their springs than does the nearest sea. The Shannon, whose "basin" occupies over one-seventh of the whole of Ireland, is a case in point. Its source is distant 24 miles from Donegal Bay; the river is 214 miles long, and its mouth is on the confines of Kerry. The Bann, whose length is 97 miles, rises within 7 miles of Dundrum Bay in Down.

Ireland does not extend through a sufficient range of latitude to show a marked difference between north and south, and there is actually a greater amount of divergence between east and west. The combination of maximum rainfall, maximum exposure and minimum range of temperature which one encounters along the Atlantic seaboard produces effects, especially as regards vegetation, which are very noticeable, and of much importance to agriculturists, horticulturists, botanists and zoologists.

If we imagine Ireland as it was until some couple of thousand years ago, before drainage and peat-cutting had affected the surface, we get a striking picture. The central area in particular was little more than an archipelago—ridges and knolls of firm ground set in a sea of shallow lakes, deep swamps, and wide peat-bogs. Traffic within this region must have been much constricted, and no doubt the frequent coincidence of esker-ridges with present-day roads gives a hint of past conditions.

The former prevalence of lake, marsh and bog has a bearing on the question of past forests. We know that within the period of deposition of our peat-bogs drier spells permitted of the growth over immense areas of the Scotch Fir, and that the slightly warmer climate that prevailed during Neolithic times allowed such forests to spread even to the exposed islands of the west coast. By the way, Caleb Threlkeld in his *Synopsis Stirpium Hibernicarum* puts forward an explanation of the presence of these now buried pine-forests which has at least the charm of novelty: "But whether the Firr-wood taken out of Mosses or Bogges, which being split into small Sticks do burn like a Torch, or Link, be of this Tree [Scotch Fir] or the *Abies mas* in Irish *Crann Giumnais*, planted by the Danes and after their expulsion cut down, and left to be burryed in the Earth by the Natives to extinguish the Badges of their Servitude, is not to be determined by me."

When Oak began to replace Pine, the forests tended to become increasingly restricted to the better drained and more sheltered ground. At present the extensive woods of Oak in the Wicklow and Kerry valleys, and of Oak mixed with Birch, Holly, Arbutus, etc., about Killarney, are the best representatives of the ancient woodlands. Wherever the ground was fit for pasture or tillage, the forests have been destroyed long since. Our existing native woods, whether of Oak or of mixed species, are delightful, for they are not so dense as to exclude a rich ground-vegetation of flowers and ferns.

The recent complete disappearance of the Pine as a native is the most notable event in the history of Irish trees. In comparatively recent times there were several species of tall Conifers in Ireland: now the only representatives of that great and ancient family are the Yew and the Juniper. We have none of the grand forests of Central Europe, where the Pine stems rise like gigantic columns into a canopy which the sun cannot penetrate, where the silence is complete,

And the gloom divine is all around,
And underneath is the mossy ground.

But I do not think, having traversed them in Switzerland and Germany and Bulgaria and Scandinavia, that I mourn the absence from Ireland of the dense dark gnome-haunted forests of the Continent. You soon get too much of them, and long for open glades and tree-free hill-sides where you can have sun and wind and a wide prospect. When you are in Switzerland or Tyrol, the reason for your steady thumbing through the two or three thousand feet of forest zone is, after all, your desire to get out of it! The mind does not work at its best there; and the shadow and restriction of the imprisoning trees produce at length a feeling of depression and in some minds even of fear. So you hurry upward towards the crags, and there anywhere, with the round earth below you and the sky above, you may achieve freedom of spirit.

I can claim a fairly extensive knowledge of every county in Ireland—particularly as regards its topography and botany—otherwise this book would not be written; and in order that the reader may understand the kind of information which I mean (which is a very small portion of what might be acquired) and which it shall be my endeavour in some measure to transmit to him, it will simplify matters if I indicate briefly the sources of both my knowledge and my ignorance: to do this I am compelled to be briefly autobiographical. . . .

FROM CHAPTER 8: THE LAND OF NAKED LIMESTONE (CLARE, EAST GALWAY, EAST MAYO)

It is not altogether easy to explain why, while along the eastern side of the great Central Plain the passing away of the ice of the Glacial Period has left the limestone thickly covered with detritus, generally in the form of Boulder-clay, these deposits become thinner as one goes westward, till along the western edge of the plain, from Lough in Mayo down to the Fergus estuary in Clare, a length of miles, the limestone lies in many places quite devoid of covering. Its beds still rest almost everywhere horizontally, just as they were deposited as limy mud on the bottom of the Carboniferous sea millions of years ago. Long-continued aerial denudation has worn away almost everywhere in the plain the newer beds which may at one time or another have been deposited upon them, and the ice completed the process, if there was anything left to complete. If the limestone is now exposed by the removal of over-Glacial clay, it is seen to be smooth and polished by the passage of the ice. But where this protection is not afforded, it has been re-carved by the weather in the most interesting way. Percolating water has enlarged the parallel vertical joints which, mostly in two series more or less at right angles, everywhere traverse the horizontal beds, forming little canons about a foot wide and often six or ten feet deep; and the flat face of the rock has suffered also, and is full of shallow solution-pans and channels and little rounded ridges. Whole solid beds of limestone have often been dissolved away, leaving only wreckage behind in the form of loose blocks. Over considerable areas even west of the Shannon and Suck a stony clay still protects the limestone, and is sometimes heavily covered with peat; but the characteristic feature of this western region is the wide expanse of bare grey rock, which attains its maximum in northern Clare, in the famous district of Burren; there the limestone, unlike its extensions in Galway and Mayo, rises into terraced hills of over 1000 feet. In the northern part of the area, where the low plain abuts on the ancient meta-morphic rocks of Connemara and west Mayo, the surface of the limestone sinks gently below drainage level, resulting in the large lakes of Corrib, Mask, Carra and Conn. Possibly the more acidic waters descending from the western highlands have helped to produce these lakes, by accelerating the rate of solution. But why does the Boulder-clay diminish in thickness and extent all the way from Dublin to Galway? No doubt it is connected with the fact that the main centres of dispersal of the ice-sheet layout near the western coast. The new ice formed there would be clean and more or less free of debris, which would become more abundant in and under the ice as it slowly ground its way across the country. And out in the east, especially if the ice were melting, the mud and stones contained in it would be thrown down in increasing quantity.

The Mayo-Galway part of the area—that is, Mayo and Galway east of the line of large lakes—is a wide flat region, which has but little attraction for the visitor save for the interest that attaches to the lakes—their geology, fauna and flora. Lough Conn, on the edge of the limestone, is a jewel in a dull setting, so far as everything east of it is concerned, and the same may be said of Lough Carra. The larger lakes, Lough Mask and Lough Corrib, have like Conn been mentioned already. When we get to Cong (Cunga, a narrow river-strait), we come into a region that offers a good deal to the archaeologist. At the village itself, underground drainage between Mask and Corrib comes to producing some curious effects. Standing on the narrow which separates the two lakes, Cong commands an important way between east and west. Beside the stream, on a little oasis among the limestone rocks, St. Fechin of Fore is stated to have founded a church in 624. Later, in the twelfth century, arose an abbey tenanted by Canons Regular of the Order of St. Augustine. To judge by what is left of it, this must have been a very beautiful building, and it is unfortunate that so little remains. Much of the land around Cong, richly wooded, is enclosed in the demesne of Ashford, and strictly preserved on account of its famous woodcock shooting. Undoubtedly the most curious feature of the neighbourhood is the canal, built to provide for traffic between the two lakes. The channel was cut through solid limestone, but the fickle rock proved to be a mere sieve, and the expensive exca-vation, waterless, four miles in length, still remains, a monument of engineering futility. Out in the great flat east of Lough Corrib stand the ruins of two monasteries, unusually complete and undefaced, giving an interest to an otherwise dull region. The monastery of Ross, on the banks of the Black River a mile north-west of Head-ford, needs only a roof to make it again habitable. It presents an extensive range of buildings, with many beautiful architectural features, though, like of the Irish ecclesiastical settlements, it shows little of the richness of contemporary buildings in England. The abbey was erected for the Franciscans in 1351, and owes its present excellent state of preservation to the fact that after the suppression of the monaster-ies the monks returned to it again and again, and it was not finally abandoned until 1765. Not only are the ecclesiastical buildings intact, but you may study the arrange-ment of the kitchens and other domestic annexes. The whole presents a more com-plete picture of Irish monastic life than may be obtained at any other site in Ireland.

Claregalway monastery stands by the Clare River twelve miles from Ross, and eight miles north-east of Galway. It is half a century later in date than the former, having been built by John de Cogan for the Franciscans in 1290. It had a somewhat similar history, since suppression did not mean its entire abandonment, and a small chapel still kept in repair probably points to continuous or almost continuous limited occupation during the whole of the intervening period. The buildings are more ruined than those of Ross, but much that is beautiful and interesting remains. The solid castle ruin which adjoins is one of the De Burgo strongholds, and witnessed in its day a good deal of fighting.

Far and wide over this flat region are dotted small castles which were the fortified residences of the holders of the land for several centuries, and there are also the ruins of smaller ecclesiastical establishments well worth a visit by the antiquary. This is a wide lonely country of great distances and broad skies, with few houses or trees, and endless walls of grey stone. If you want to see how lonely it can be take the new road from Galway towards Headford. After a couple of miles of hummocky limestone ground (into which the mysterious Terryland River disappears) you drop past the old castle and little lake at Ballindooly (Baile an dubhlaoigh, the town of the dark-visaged chief) and enter a stretch of six miles of road, dead level, dead straight, with neither hedges nor houses—just flat wet meadow or bog on either side, stretching away to Lough Corrib on the west, and to slightly rising ground on the east. The first time I traversed that heart-breaking thoroughfare the land was wrapped in a wet mist driving before a wind that moaned: and so, like the visitor to Castle Carabas in the *Book of Snobs* "for a mile and a half I walked—alone, and thinking of death"[24]—save that the mile and a half was six! But on a sparkling western day all is different. One notices with delight the white and yellow Water-lilies in black wayside pools, the masses of Bog-bean and Marsh St. John's wort and Orchids in the wet ground, the lovely colours over bog and meadow, and, ever beckoning, the hills of Connemara out beyond the silver gleams that betray Lough Corrib.[25]

Michael Viney

Michael Viney (1933–) has been writing for the *Irish Times* for fifty years, with a parallel career in broadcasting, in filmmaking, and as a natural history author. His Saturday column "Another Life" began in 1977, when he moved with his family from Dublin to settle on the Mayo coast. "Another Life" has developed from experiments in self-reliance to a deep concern with nature and ecology and is illustrated with Viney's drawings and paintings through his observations of Ireland's rugged west coast. His more recent works about the natural world include the books *Ireland: A Smithsonian Natural History* (2003)and *Ireland's Ocean* (written with his wife, Ethna Viney; 2008). In addition to selections from "Another Life," the following excerpts are from *A Year's Turning*, Viney's Thoreau-like observations of seasonal changes to the natural world of County Mayo and his own interaction with these changes in his quest for self-reliance.[26]

From A Year's Turning

JANUARY

The sky in the west was darkening on cue, the waves already panicky and jostling where the channel meets the sea. There was a gleam of borrowed light on the far swells, but beyond them the horizon had vanished in a smoky pall. It seemed time to batten down the hatches. The hens complained at being ushered to bed so early but better that, I thought, than try to round them up as errant shuttlecocks in the violent gusts promised by dusk. I cut enough logs with the bush-saw for two days and then took the hammer and a tin of four-inch nails and went around the windbreak fences, making firm. They were creaking and shifting in the wind like the timbers of an old boat.

In the event, we'd known worse, as winter storms go, and we didn't lose the electricity until dawn. Then, venturing out between the hedges to visit the nest-boxes (three eggs, and they can't have slept very much), I had the illusion of moving in a personal capsule of calm while the whine and rush of wind continued all around. But within the house, the great press of air on the walls and windows webbed the rooms with unfamiliar drafts. On the second night I stuffed my ears with cotton wool, so that the squalls rumbled and shook in the depths of my pillow. Ethna slept on imperturbably.

What made the storm memorable was the way it piled up the breakers at the mouth of the channel and then drove the sea ahead, drowning the *duach* in a silvery green flood, subsuming both lakes and swirling on through the reeds to mingle with the streams from the hill. The ebbing tide left the fences strung blackly with seaweed, and here and there the drag of water toppled a whole line of stakes. We needed waders to cross the ford on the boreen. A coppery flood from the mountain tugged at our knees and rolled the rocks from under our feet; the rush of water was giddying, so that we felt for our footholds without looking down.

The whole landscape, for that matter, was still shuddering and excited after the gale. The fences and briars were flying white pennants of wool, and sinister flags of black plastic torn from silage covers. At the channel from the lake there were waves around the stepping stones—waves from the wrong direction, from the land—and out on the beach the sand seethed in long, wintry skeins, like the snow in films about Antarctic explorers. Grains rattled on my boots and hissed through the banners of wrack. We had to lean to walk, as if hauling an invisible sledge.

Trudging there, monitoring a tideline monotonously innocent of whatever it is I hope to find on these occasions, my mind skipped back forty years to winter days on Brighton beach, to the town's fisherman strung out in silhouette against the surf beside the pier. They walked the wet shingle at this same angle, heads lowered, bellies bulging their jerseys, hands clasped behind their buttocks. They paced back and forth in a slow trance, ignoring each other, as if summoned there to consider some enormous problem on humanity's behalf. But they were watching for money: for half-crowns, florins, shillings, sixpences. The coins, fumbled and rolling irrecoverably, sifted through the planks of the pier all summer, glinting briefly like fish in the waves. The sea rolled them landwards, burying them deep in the beach, and the winter gales, hammering at a shuttered promenade, dragged back the shingle to expose them. The fisherman descried them as of right, stalking, intent as herons, in the salt-mist beyond the hauled-up boats. No one else went near.

Half a lifetime has passed since my youth in that town. I have fetched up at a farther shore, a deeper ocean, with no one to covet whatever it is that I watch for.

The strand, this particular arena, has played an odd part in our lives. It has obsessed us separately and together, like some echoing ampitheatre waiting for a pair of actors (for what use is one?).

In my first winter in Ireland, more than thirty years ago, I used to look across the bay from Connemara to this long, pale gleam of dunes below the mountain, so apparently remote and wild. I focused upon it all the yearning for what was unspoiled, all the young outsider's fantasy of life in a simple, secret place. I did not need to go there with any urgency, simply to have it there in the distance, to store it up in the mind.

JUNE

The house breathes gently, all doors and windows open to whatever breeze there is. Raised up on the hillside, we seem besieged by light. It burnishes the ocean, bleaches the islands to a distant slatey blue. Temperate people, at home with the cool, moist and luminous, we step out reluctantly, and stoop among the crops in wide-brimmed Italian straw hats.

Just for once, just for now, there is a glossy perfection to everything that grows: to the crisp whorls of sweet corn, to the grape-sheen on red cabbage, to the polished green spikes of onions and shallots. You could put them in a gallery, each on its plinth: plants posing as themselves. But also, just for once, there is point and satisfaction in the hiss of the hoe, stroking away grass and groundsel. Some weeds I leave, to shade the soil and save its moisture: cool fleeces of dead-nettle and jostling chickweed. Others I spare because they are beautiful. Fumaria, the wispy "smoke of the earth," wreathes the Welsh onions in lacy stems, waxy bells. Pink stars of cranesbill and herb Robert infiltrate the cauliflowers. ("You remember all these names," Ethna says, "but you won't remember people or who's married to whom." She is right: the parish goes on without me.)

Even the grasses have names: old names we are forgetting because "grass" is what farmers grow, and of one sort only meant to be mowed for silage before it flowers. We are missing nothing—the flower of perennial rye-grass is a ratty little pigtail. But in June, in any sheltered spot away from grazing animals, the true grasses of Ireland find their own stature and magnificence, across the stream in The Hollow, where I have not yet penetrated with the scythe, cocksfoot, red fescue and Yorkshire fog join with flowering sorrel in a rampant, rosy meadow.

Cocksfoot is an easy one to know. Its flower-heads are spread in fat, spiky lobes, smothered now in anthers of pale purple. This is the grass for the human nibbler. Pulled at the right time, the stalk comes away with a squeak to offer a white base full of sugar; later, as the seed-head develops, it uses up the sugar and leaves only a crunchy stem to chew on. Yorkshire fog is also worth a bite, and the velvety, purplish fox-tail of its flowers worth brushing on one's cheek, for softness.

Looming presences beyond the ditch, heavy breathing through the hedge: the closest I get to cattle is when we can't see each other. On my side, grunts and mutterings as I lever up the weeds; on their side, coughs and tummy-rumbles and that disconcerting, calico-ripping sound which is a cow wrapping its tongue around a tuft of grass and pulling. Eamon Grennan, who spends weeks in a cottage across the bay when he is not teaching English at Vassar, has written the most evocative poem about cows that I know (the only poem about cows, if I am honest). A sample:

I love the way a torn tuft
of grassblades, stringy buttercup and succulent clover
sway-dangles towards a cow's mouth, the mild teeth
taking it in—purple flowers, green stems and yellow petals
lingering on those hinged lips fringed with spittle . . .

I do stand and watch cattle sometimes, struck by the sculpture they make lying down, or the bits of paintings they compose, clustered at the lake or strung out, backlit, in procession across the strand. I call them all cows, even though I know better: they are usually bullocks or heifers. I know an "elder" is really an udder, I know—now—that a cow isn't bellowing because she's hungry.

There are cattle right up on the ridge today, a jotting of little black marks along the skyline. Only a very dry spell would let them up that high; only a very fine day would keep them there so long, glad of the breeze on their rocky prominence. Left to themselves, cattle seek out variety; they like landscape with hollows and hillocks and out-of-the-way places. On this side of the hill, their groups are small: cows and their followers, and calves bought in for stores. They are the sort to be herded slowly, by one boy with a stick, or a tractor creeping in bottom gear.

A young friend over at Drummin, a blue-cheese-maker of some accomplishment, used to take his flock of dairy goats for walks on a little-used road through the mountains. More accurately, they took him, since goats have a dominant nanny to make decisions about stopping for a browse, or moving on. As honorary billy, his role was that of consort or guardian, and the leisurely meander from whin to bramble, bells tinkling, suited his meditative nature, or so he claimed.

Our own goats, while we had them, were not a flock, but a succession of mothers and daughters, shrewd, self-willed and teasing. Even two goats are too many on an acre given over, at the same time, to gardening, ducks, hens, bees, sometimes a pony. The shifting and untangling of tethers two or three times a day did not suit either of our natures.

Milking, however, had its moments. I find my fingers curling at the thought—that special, two-part squeeze that traps the milk and squirts it in the pail. I felt sure I would never learn to use both hands at once. But, "Barby stands still only while she's eating" was the message that came with our prize Saanen, so milking became a race against time. As she chased the last nut around the bottom of her bucket, her rear leg began to twitch, and a few seconds later, if the milk pail had not been snatched up, one dainty but shitty hoof was plunged into it. But there were times when knack and rhythm coincided. A great calm would descend in the shed as two jets of milk converged and foamed in the beam of the flashlamp. This is remembered from dusk in winter. Outside, a smoky blue afterglow above the islands: in the cave of the shed, goats and milker rapt on a mattress of rushes; in the shadows, black and white ducks. Sounds: hiss of milk, munching goat, muttering ducks, whispers of stream and wind.

June was when our second goat, Sally, gave birth to twins, ejecting them in pink balloons in a moment when my back was turned. They were silky and winsome, and within a week were butting at my wellingtons and leaping up and down from the boulder in the hen run, a most engaging display. Part of the charm in a kid's appearance are the two tight curls of hair on top of its head. Within a few days of birth, two bumps can be felt at the centre of the curls. Left alone, these erupt in sharp little horns like those on the classical Pan. We forget, in a countryside of hornless cattle, that calves which are not of a naturally polled breed are routinely disbudded at a couple of weeks old. Dairy goats, too, must conform, for the sake of human comfort in small spaces.

The disbudding of kids at a few days old is not yet within the casual competence of the average Irish vet. Our goat-keepers' manual seemed to anticipate this, since it described the technique of using a red-hot disbudding iron, to be applied "briefly" (six seconds) but firmly to the horn buds, searing down to the skull. Even with the kid properly anaesthetised, the book confessed, "the human operator is often in agony."

We did not own a disbudding iron, but an expert consulted by telephone was happy to describe an alternative contrived from copper tubing. "You stick it in the fire, and while it's heating." He went on to detail the anaesthetising of a kid with chloroform, sprinkled on cotton wool inside a cocoa tin. "You can't really go wrong," he reassured me. "You're an intelligent chap, good with your hands and all that. You won't burn through the skull."

In thanking him, my gratitude already fought with dread. The more I rehearsed the scene in my mind, the more unthinkable it became. Ethna, on the other hand, while every bit as humane, has a dogged, stoical streak which she attributes to a Catholic childhood. Confronted with an unpleasant solution to a problem, she will put her head down and go through with it while I am still procrastinating. Fortunately, in our marriage, we each do what we can. Ethna cannot go very far up ladders and I cannot cauterise a kid with a red-hot iron. Thus, as we knelt together on the kitchen floor, giving the first kid whiffs of chloroform, it was Ethna who was bracing herself for an ultimate ordeal. I would merely be holding the little animal "firmly between the knees."

In the event, her nerve was not to be tested. It took much longer than expected for the chloroform to take effect. Each time we decided the kid was asleep, and withdrew its little muzzle from the cocoa tin, it would raise its head and bleat for its mother. By the time Ethna reached for the home-made disbudding iron, left to heat between the bars of the range, the copper tube had gone soft and collapsed. I could, perhaps, have made another, but the excuse was too providential. We abandoned the surgery (later completed, not very well, by a vet with a red-hot screwdriver) and got tipsy together, rather quickly, on home-made parsley wine.

A friend lives among trees beyond the village. We were standing at his door at dusk, making farewells after a convivial evening, when a cuckoo called from somewhere close at hand. My friend wet his palms with spit, then cupped them together and blew between his thumbs to mimic the fluting call to perfection. At once, the cuckoo's hawk-like silhouette arrived above us, full of territorial angst. Finding no intruder, it vanished again—then returned to a second summons. I was most impressed.

On our side of the hill, I more often see than hear the cuckoo, my eye drawn by the procession of meadow pipits the big bird trails behind it, like a sky-sign towed by an aeroplane. The little birds mob and harass the cuckoo whenever it rests, teetering, on a wall or wire. Yet, when the damage has long been done, and the baby cuckoo is out of the pipit's nest, the same birds will follow and fawn upon it, feeding it titbits like a fat young prince. Across in stony Connemara, where such scandals are even more in the open, an ornithologist watched eleven pipits and one skylark feeding a young cuckoo as it rested on a fencepost. The birds took turns to perch on its shoulder, and it accepted their insect offerings with a languid turn of the head. Such triumphant perversion of parental altruism deserves a special footnote in the record of the selfish gene.

Europe's cuckoos are divided into races, according to the species they habitually choose as foster parents to their young. Thus, most of Connacht's birds are pipit-cuckoos, while those in other regions and habitats might be dunnock-cuckoos or reed-warbler-cuckoos. In each race, the cuckoo is faithful, if that is the word, to the species that reared it, but we do not know if this happens through genetic inheritance or by imprinting when the cuckoo is a chick. In any event, the female flies in from Africa already programmed with its host's identity, ready to mimic the size and mottling of its eggs. How this pattern is maintained between generations of cuckoo, when male cuckoos mate across the races, is still a mystery.

The whole story of the cuckoo's parasitic lifestyle greatly troubled my early, plain man's grapplings with evolutionary biology. How many million chances did it take, after all, how many solitary and random repetitions, to build this bizarre contrivance and deceit into normal behaviour for one species? But of course it is not just one species, merely the one we are used to, and we are always more ready to accept the bizarre if examples can be multiplied. Across the world, brood parasitism is practised by some eighty kinds of birds, fifty of them various sorts of cuckoo. In Africa, rather than heaving fellow nestlings over the edge, the baby honey guide hacks them to death with an especially sharp, hooked beak. In India, the male koel approaches a crow's nest with loud cries and lets itself be driven off; the female koel, meanwhile, nips in to lay her egg. Thus I can go on believing in the neo-Darwinian ordering of chance. But I have yet to see how life is made much easier for the female cuckoo, which has to hang about for hours, watching for the critical moment to swoop in and lay—this, at anything up to twenty-five different nests over a period of seven or eight weeks. Nor can it make much odds to the eventual survival of her chick, since the world is scarcely overrun by cuckoos. But nature abounds in different ways of doing everything, not all of them efficient or economical.

Our fuchsia windbreaks, barbered every month or two to keep them thick and vigorous, carve out quadrangles of calm from the hillside breezes. Flying insects congregate in these restful spaces, sampling unexpected flowers (chives, chicory, strawberries) or hovering, bright as beads, like fixed points in a quantum diagram.

Midges, unfortunately, like to dawdle here too: clouds of them dance perpetually above the water tap. Midges can drive strong men from the bog and scatter haymakers homewards. The sweet little trout of the mountain lake are safe enough from me, for any day dark enough to fish them is a day when the midges are biting, too. They make the cottongrass bogs especially their own because their larvae can live in peaty mud, low in oxygen, but there are midges for every niche and contour. Some sorts are for heathery slopes, others for mossy flushes and the high springheads among the rocks. "Fistigruffs" is one name for them in Connemara, as in "them bloody fistigruffs have the cow's elder ate—it's all swelled."

Does it help to know that the intensity of biting is governed precisely by the level of the light? As radiation from the sun declines below a critical level of 260 watts per square yard, clouds of midges take wing. Hence the special torment at dusk and on dark days.

Three or four crossroads towards Louisburgh, at Carrowniskey, hidden among bushes, a thatched cabin with tiny windows and green-stained walls is waiting to fall down. The bushes are elders, rampant. In June their flowers reflect the sunshine, like mirrors, into the sooty interior of the house, and the scent of them, on a dry day, is medievally sensual. It has to be a dry day, the flowers fluffed up like lace, if the blossom is to carry its fragrance into the wine: an hour on tiptoe, with scissors and buckets, stretching up through the creamy light.

Elder needs phosphate and feeds greedily on bones and ashes, which is why, like nettles, it thrives outside back doors. Once this side of Louisburgh, however, human habitation and the elder both begin to peter out. The Carrowniskey bushes are a lonely grove on moorland and there is one more thicket, in a ditch, at a crossroads near the sea. But for the last five miles towards the mountain, *Sambucus nigra* (*Sambucus* for a Greek penny whistle, *nigra* for the ebony berries) has no roothold. In our vestigial spinneys, its absence among oak and hazel is proof of their wild antiquity.

Wine-making explains this intimate knowledge of the elder's biogeography. For years it was the queen of the flower wines we mashed in the big red dustbin, five or ten gallons at a time. Gorse was, if anything, mellower, and could be started in spring, but the prickles made the harvesting a diffident investment: half a gallon of golden petals for a mere half-dozen bottles. Honeysuckle seemed a good idea, but yielded wine with a cloying bouquet, like cachous or old dressing tables. Meadowsweet, frothing into bloom on the damp bank beside the stream, carried aspirin-like principles into the wine along with the fragrance of almonds: we sipped and—later—sweated.

Flower wines are a pleasant illusion; they hurry a summer bouquet to Christmas alcohol conjured chiefly from the added sugar, raisins and oranges. Almost any sugary vegetable, too, can be persuaded to ferment. Once, harvesting peas for the freezer and finding ourselves with basins of pristine pods, we were happy to discover pea-pod wine in the manual we keep on the dresser. "Like a light Sauternes" was the promise, so we made five gallons of it. Every six months we sampled a bottle and the flavour was of pea-pods. The wine became increasingly smooth and clear, and found great favour with a cousin home from the Gulf. But the hoped-for miracle never occurred: it remained pea-pod wine, even if you weren't told. After three years, we smuggled it in cupfuls into the gooseberry wine, to which it brought a subdued (and anonymous) gravitas.

Of all our vintages, the best have been the berry wines, fermenting their own sugars along with pagan flavours. Blackberry is probably the finest, the wine sneaked by druids in the vestry. Rowan and rosehip, mashed together, make a bitter, addictive elixir in small glasses. Blackcurrant, from bushes we share with the birds, has been the *vin ordinaire* for parties and the droppers-in of summer. "You're really very comfortable" they beam after the second glass. The labour has been Ethna's: hours no, days—on her knees in the perfumed blackcurrant thickets, juice dripping down her wrists; hours of boiling kettles for the mash; days more of squeezing, straining, bottling, heaving in and out. Thirty gallons in some years, and she doesn't even drink it.

"A June Day" was my *Irish Times* column for 14 June 1986—one of the difficult summers. It belongs here, warts and all:

"You write about the odd things," a reader says, "but try giving us an average, boring old day—then I might know if I'd like it." Yesterday will do.

4.45 A.M.

We beat the alarm—must be in training. Ethna sits up in bed to write, lost at once in her story. I pad out to the studio, to catch up on letters. A still, pretty morning, islands stretched out in a haze, the surf silent. I write to Norway, to a hut above a fjord, where a young German is translating "Another Life" for a book the Greens might like. What, he needs to know, is a JCB? What are sea rods? Some of the headings come out well in German: for "Wimp of the West," read "Softe Des Westens."

7.15 A.M.

Short jog before breakfast—just as far as Paddy's silage pit. Jeered by grey crow on an ESB pole. Try the new batch of rye bread at breakfast. Well-risen but still a bit soggy; Ethna quite put out. Radio tells about a plan to put mailboxes at the ends of bore ends, to save the postman time. Michael Fergus, just retired, used to wade the channel to the last house.

8.15 A.M.

Feed hens, collect two eggs; feed ducks, steal one egg. "Steal" because it feels like that: the duck has a drake, covers her egg, has obvious hopes. I sidle by as they shovel up their mash, the egg palmed. Measure the rain in the gauge on the lawn: 0.5 mm. Better than May: 167 mm, over twice normal.

8.30 A.M.

We are a two-wheelbarrow family. Ethna takes the small one to Báinín's field, to shake nitrogen on the bare bits. What isn't bare he has dunged on, and thus won't eat. We tether him at the gable to eat the lawn until the rain has melted the nitrogen: he'll have to spend his nights in the hen run.

With the big barrow, I start shifting the last ton of cowmuck we tipped outside Michele's window. She is in Paris, au-pairing to improve her French. How're we going to keep her down on the farm, after she's seen Paree? We're not, if she can help it.

Meg runs at my heels as I trundle down and up the path (thank goodness for the slope: the heavy, wet manure almost runs away with the barrow). The cats laze among the strawberry flowers, watching. Bimbo and her kitten got into the cold frame last night and slept on the sweet corn seedlings. They see all the plastic cloches as summer pavilions put up specially for them. Cinnamon gives me less trouble, but he does piss on the turf.

Take off my anorak—about time! It's June, but where are the flies? Three bumble-bees burrow into the catmint, grateful for a decent drop of nectar.

10.30 A.M.

The postman's van at the gate. Among the mail, a Dublin housewife wants to say how much she enjoys WWOOFing—"Working Weekends On Organic Farms." WWOOFers would shift this muck for me, but we're not the hospitable, outgoing kind. I should have a beard and play the tin whistle until two o'clock in the morning.

11.00 A.M.

A young neighbour arrives with an American cousin: could they take Báinín to ride? Keep him for a week, we say (but no one has that much spare grass).

NOON

A farmer and his collie gather sheep in the rocky field across the road. I lean on my fork to watch, taking pleasure in the work of an intelligent dog. But the sheep are uncooperative and keep breaking ranks as they near the gate. Another neighbour, passing in his car, pulls up and gets out to help in the last push. I feel mortified, as usual—I was just standing there. Nine years alongside farmers and I still never know when to offer a hand.

1.00 P.M.

Egg salad for lunch. I could eat fresh-laid eggs at every meal. Before cholesterol, did people worry? The hens have another two when I take them their feed. Rooks and jackdaws perch on the fence, waiting their turn at the bowl.

3.00 P.M.

Finish the muck at last and turn to planting out winter cabbage. On my knees, scooping holes, when a strange sound rasps out from the field-bank beside me. Not quite a belch, not quite a growl, but a beastly, mammalian sort of a sound. I creep close and peer into the dark behind the nettles. It comes again at intervals, but its source eludes me. Settle for a hedgehog—perhaps a family. Creep away again, delighted.

3.30 P.M.

Ethna has been trying to mow the steep bank of The Hollow, across the stream where the pony won't go. She is using our new Italian machine, but the growth in this sheltery place keeps choking it into silence. I am appealed to: "I've been waiting for years to mow that grass!" I take down the scythe and open up an arc into the soft, green stuff. Finding my rhythm, I begin to enjoy it . . . swish . . . swish, The sun comes out and sweat begins to drip from my eyebrows—which is, I suppose, what they're for.

4.30 P.M.

Fish swam at the gate: spotless, well-iced, worth a medal. Our own ray in the freezer is almost gone and we can't start fishing with the spillet until I'm on top of the planting. We buy plaice and cod and fresh mackerel. Do we eat the mackerel or freeze them for bait? Prudence wins.

5.00 P.M.

Too sunny now for planting (the seedlings wilt). Start hoeing weeds off a bed to plant out French beans under plastic, but decide the hedge needs cutting back first. Get out the electric hedge-cutter—not the luxury it seems when you have sixfoot hedges within hedges, like Hampton Court maze. Plug in two hundred feet of cable, bring end over right shoulder where it won't get cut, and prepare to concentrate. Goes through fuchsia like butter—"Magic!" as Selwyn Froggitt would say. Get carried away and do the next hedge as well.

6.00 P.M.

Dinner. "How is it," asks Ethna, "that however many potatoes I do there are never enough left over for potato salad?"

7.00 P.M.

Night chores. Bring in sack of turf to fill the box, and bucket of clods to bank down range. Take Báinín down to the hen run, close in hens. Lure ducks into shed with bowl of mash. Passing belt of infant spruces (for more shelter), start pulling grass from around them. Stop me, somebody.

8.00 P.M.

Nothing on RTE—is there ever, in Summer? Take Meg for walk round the boreen. Thorn hedges still withered by the Big Wind, willows barely in leaf, ferns just uncoiled above the primroses. The fields are green, but cattle come running to me, mistaking my figure. The hay lorry swoops down the hill, blowing its home like a French *camion*. "I don't see any dead beasts," I said to a neighbour a week or two back. He looked at me quizzically. " 'Not a drum was heard, not a funeral note'—do you know that one? 'We buried him darkly at dead of night, the sods with our bayonets turning.'"

9.00 P.M.

To bed, with the *London Review of Books*.

The first big sailboat of summer clears Renvyle Point and glides northwards, so slowly that its white triangle is a presence like the shadow of a sundial, tipping the islands one by one through the long afternoon. Working at weeds, I keep straightening up to see where the yacht is now. I'm reminded how, alone on an island, one comes to sense if the sea is empty. There was an old stone sundial on Inishvickillane, one of the Blaskets off Kerry: an island that helped, you could say, to set my own course, all the way here to Thallabawn. I camped on the island alone for most of June, thirty years ago. It was an exercise in solitude, a small adventure all my own. I weathered a train of summer gales, shot rabbits and cooked them over sheep's dung; swam naked and uneasy in the grey seals' cove; braved the midnight petrels that crashed into my tent; kept a diary. Day Fourteen takes a typical tone for posterity:

> This evening I climbed the sea-crag to watch the sun go down: for once there was no low, leaden bank of cloud to snare it prematurely. A theatrical clarity of light lent the islands new perspectives: deep avenues of cliffs like vistas in a Piranesi, gleaming and gold-enameled (slow bursts of spun-glass spray). I stayed on the crag until the gulls flew black against the afterglow and the wind grew unfriendly. Walking back along the fringe of the southern cliffs, I found a colony of puffballs shining white in the dusk, and picked the youngest of them to slice and fry for breakfast . . .

The gales had a few people worried: among them Ethna, then beginning to have "notions" of me, as her mother might have said. She drove to Dingle, and organised a trawler on the first good day to sail the twenty miles to Inishvickillane. In a cove wheeling with excited puffins, she was left to hold the throttle while the skipper rowed in to get me.

Islands, thereafter, seemed to celebrate so much of what we had in common. Our mutual immersion in the West's more rugged effects seemed to speak for some sort of choice between the natural and the sophisticated, the real and the ritual; there was a general lack of interest in the details of living it up. We honeymooned (in a hotel) on Clare Island, just round the corner from us now, and spent our next holiday marooned on Caher, an empty island on the way from Clare to Inishturk.

Camped on Caher among the seals and peewits and early Christian crosses, we drew the curiosity of the lobstermen of Inishturk. They circled us in currachs and landed at last to brew tea and talk. It puzzled them that we should have cast ourselves away on this bare wedge of rock and grass, when a couple of sea miles further would have brought us to their own, more hospitable, isle. "There are days," said one enticingly, "when the smell of the flowers comes out to meet you. It would do your heart good."

Inishturk now reclines in our kitchen window, all hips and hollows like a Henry Moore sculpture. Close up, the obdurate toughness of the rock, the way the island twists along its Ordovician grain, is a matter for some awe. The people could be dour, but are not. They do know their own minds. When the gold in our ridge was tracked down to the sea and out under the waves, surfacing again in Inishturk's switchback strata, the islanders thought about it and talked together, and then they asked the mining company not to call again. The island has no signposts, nor a single public notice: it seems to know all it needs to know. Once, following a track from the northern cliffs, we came unexpectedly into the heart of a farmstead. Cocks of hay were being hauled bodily to the rick with a rope looped behind a pony. Father was up the ladder, children led the pony, a heroic line of washing flapped brightly in the breeze; Dev's Ireland, smiling and waving in a clean check shirt. More than once after settling here, we thought of taking that last step westwards, out into the ocean. But we shrank from drawing such a tight and final knot around our lives, and from the fretful improvisations of island living. Now I wish we had been braver and less practical.

Our daughter, if not quite conceived on an island, chose one on which to make her presence known. To the south of Inishbofin, at the left of our horizon, is Ardoilean, High Island. In winter it is hunched amid huge gouts of foam, but in summer it calms down for the nesting of sea birds, which wheel in and out the black shadows and cave-echoes of the cliffs. Ethna and I were delivered by trawler from Cleggan and set up camp high among the sea pinks, where the old monks built their hermitage. We caught a lobster in a pot we had brought with us, a huge creature studded with white barnacles. We ate all of him at one sitting (the weather was hot). When Ethna was struck with nausea that refused to go away, we grew anxious and hailed a passing half-decker. It used its new radio in a garbled and overexcited fashion. Our return to Cleggan drew black-shawled women to the skyline, like figures from Synge, and Ethna, who was feeling much better, had to lie down and look sick all over again. Later, there were bills from boat-owners who had put to sea to rescue us, or so they said.

Michele, reared on this and other stories about islands, had her turn at the Crusoe caper when she was twelve years old. The island was Inishdegil, straight below Mweelrea and just far enough out from the mouth of Killary to be foam-girt and mysterious. It is no bigger than St Stephen's Green in Dublin, but fits into its few acres a hill with lazy-beds, a rushy valley, a web of grassy roads. On the lee side the harbour is just big enough to swing a currach, and right beside it are the ruins of two tiny cabins, home of the O'Tooles until they were coaxed ashore in the 1920s. They had lived with a currach at the door, like a gondola in Venice, and when a stormy spring tide swirled into the house, the fire was scooped into a cooking pot and hoisted up the chimney.

We camped at the harbour, a creek between rocks embroidered brilliantly with lichen, a tarpaulin lashed over driftwood spars made a kitchen in a corner of a ruin. We gathered more driftwood for a fire and cooked periwinkles picked from the harbour bottom, where they grazed among shards of stoneware, glazed crocks, and fragments of sepia willow-pattern plates.

There were hundreds and thousands of periwinkles. Michele would clear a square yard of them for our supper and find it carpeted again at the next low tide. I have this image of her, kneeling, the shadowed water glowing where the sun shone through her hair. She was never more of a red-head than among the island's greens and blues, a maverick gene that last cropped up in a Cavàn great-great-grandfather, Ned Mhice Rua. It was one more mystery for the questions that suggest themselves on islands: who is she? who am I? how did it come to this?

Michele, watching the winkles' slow perambulations underwater, took her cue: "What are they for?" Stuck in the rucksack was a book still in its wrappings from the post, one that seemed to have sought out its perfect occasion: *Life on Earth*, by

David Attenborough. What winkles are for, and why the question is improper to evolutionary theory, took us beautifully into Chapter One, "The Infinite Variety," and on into the magic shapes of trilobites and feather stars. The island seemed made for the performance of my life as father, guide and reader-aloud. We hung over rock pools, watching scenes from primitive life among the prawns and sea urchins. We set a lobster pot in the sound, where the big compass jellyfish drifted like art nouveau lamp shades. We discussed the crabs before we cooked them.

All this really had less to do with explaining life on earth than with explaining me to my daughter. When I took up a curlew's skull, with the long, curved tweezers of a bill, and used it as a prop for a sermon on adaptation, she had other things to read in my face and voice: why any of it mattered to me, why I cared if she were interested. At twelve and a half, the reason for our change of lifestyle must still have seemed deeply mysterious, a thing of constantly shifting focus and enthusiasm, of unassuagable curiosity and finding-out. This was, if I could communicate it, the state of grace I wanted her to share.

Expecting that solitude meant silence, she was a little appalled by the clamour of the island, disconcerted by the manic alarm of the gulls that nagged at us night and morning from their colony across the sound and by the unrelenting boom and boil of surf. Even the engines of the fishing boats, echoing among the reefs, were noisier than the few cars and tractors she was used to.

There is a special sound we both remember, a tremulous hooting that seemed to fill the air above our tent in the half-light just before dawn. It was the sound a child makes with a sheet over its head, playing ghosts, but had a tense vibrato that spoke of something not human. For a second, dragging awake, I shared Michele's clutch of alarm; then recognised the drumming of a snipe, the "heatherbleat," the "goat of the air." I explained to her how the bird rises up in towering circles, then shoots steeply down, spreading its tail-feathers stiffly against the rush of air. She was interested, but less so than in the novelty of being frightened, in a tent on an island, with her father's arm around her.

The snipe of Inishdegil now has an almost heraldic presence in our family album. For Inishbofin, too, there are bird-sounds of a summer's night to be cut out and pasted in, these all the more poignant because, just like a photograph, their moment is utterly lost. There were nights not long ago on Gustin's island when, walking home late from Dea's Hotel through that magical, rocky defile between the two harbours, you could hear two, three, even four corncrakes calling in the little flaggy fields at either side. Listening to their ratchety mantras floating out of the dark, I had just one face to go with the voice: a corncrake glimpsed beyond the hedge of our home at the edge of Dublin (we bordered on a wheat field, rich farmland now concreted over for a suburban shopping centre).

Nothing has changed in the damp little meadows on Irlishbofin; they still wait for the scythe in July. Yet the corncrakes have deserted the island, crashing from eleven pairs in 1991 to two to none at all—part, it seems, of the wider crisis in the species.

Why go on chiselling mottoes for a tomb,
Counting on a scythe to spare
Your small defenceless home?

Quicken your tune, improvise before
The combine and the digger come
Little bridegroom.

Richard Murphy, whose life as a poet has been so much bound up with these islands,
wrote his "Song for a Corncrake" almost twenty years ago. But the story of decline
goes back long before the words "combine" and "digger" took on their mechanical meanings. For a century in Ireland, longer still in Britain and France, almost
everything that changed in grassland farming had some baneful significance for
the corncrake: "reclamation" of moist meadows, the switch from haymaking to
silage-mowing, the coming of bigger and faster machines. Now, in a flurry of concern, a few scores of farmers are being paid to delay their mowing for a month, then
to start in the middle and mow outwards, to give the mother and her chicks a chance
to run. It is as if we are trying to unwind the past.

But there was always something about the corncrake that suggested a species
pressing to its limits. Take the mere fact of its migration from East Africa: how
absurdly taxing a venture on those stubby, rounded wings! The corncrake is not
one of nature's flyers: on its breeding grounds, at least, it hides and skulks, that
rasping *crex-crex* its only sense of community. When Irish lighthouses had keep-
ers, they would sometimes find dozens of corncrakes on a spring morning, newly
arrived in the night and lying exhausted under rocks: was there, on passage, some
transient togetherness?

Once, in our early days here, days when I was full of my own manly pioneering,
a neighbour's children arrived at the gate with a shoe box. Pressed together in one
corner were half a dozen balls of trembling, ashy black fluff. I could see the forage
harvester still at work in a meadow at the edge of the strand, its red neck spewing
minced-up grass. The children wanted advice on how to rear the chicks. I was not
encouraging. "Are you really going to be able to feed them on squashed insects,
every fifteen minutes from dawn to dusk, for weeks?" This was only approximately,
hastily, true, but as much as I knew at the time. The children turned from the gate,
their faces dosed. Thus the corncrake was lost to Thallabawn, probably forever.

SEPTEMBER

September finds the acre under siege: from parachuting thistle-down, from heli-
copter squads of cabbage whites, from grapnel-lines of bramble shoots tossed over
the boundary hedge as if by some invisible army. Invasion is clearly on the cards.
For each slender green briar, dropping to earth, takes root at its tip to seize a new
bridgehead for its parent plant. Next summer it will arch on again—and again. In
fact, said Pliny the Elder (thinking, perhaps, of the country estate he was neglecting
for his scholarship in Nero's Rome), blackberry briars "would fill up the whole place
if resistance were not offered by cultivation, so that it would be positively possible to
imagine that mankind is created for this service of the earth."

Some of the briars I do, indeed, chop back, and tug from the soil if they have
rooted. But others, springing out from plants with the biggest, juiciest berries, are
carefully woven back into the hedge, for next year's crop. *Rubus fruticosus*, the
blackberry, achieves its many forms through variations in its seeds. Each successful

variation, spread in the droppings of starlings or foxes, is potentially a microspecies, adapted to particular conditions of temperature or soil chemistry and cloning itself repeatedly by the arching of its shoots. There are at least seventy sorts of blackberry along the hedges of Ireland now, some hauling themselves about with briars the thickness of my thumb and armed with hooked prickles of a medieval ferocity. The rooted arches of briars figure in rural "cures" (like a hole in a rock or a split in a tree, it was one more natural loop or orifice through which to crawl from one state of grace to another) and some microspecies of *R. fruticosus*, threatened as a remedy for boils or hernia, must have added elements of genuine ordeal.

Pauses to straighten one's back and sample the blackberries are the prerogative of the potato-digger. The job takes a good many days (a few together now and then) and can't be hurried. Nothing suits the new silence of the acre better than the hiss of spade in earth, the small whispery sounds as I search out the tubers and lob them gently together, the whir of a robin darting to snatch a worm from my shadow; above all, the measured buzz of working bumblebees. They fumble the last few hollyhock blossoms, stuck to the tops of their stems like stubborn pink butterflies, and the purple sheafs of Michaelmas daisies sprawled beside the pond. Sometimes, the very pointlessness of their industry overwhelms me: they will all die. Only the queens will live past winter and there will be no more queen bumblebees in Connacht next year than there were this: perhaps even fewer, as more field-banks are bulldozed away. I go back to the potatoes, digging blackberry pips out with my tongue, even less ready to die than I was before.[27]

From **Another Life**

FROM SWERVE OF SHORE TO BEND OF BAY:
THE WARMING GLOBE IS ERODING IRELAND'S COAST

At the bend in the road at the top of the hill the summer tourists tread hard on the brakes, not so much for caution as in sudden awe of the view. It is partly the grand spread of it all—so much landscape at once—but partly its near-primitive disposition.

There's the size of the strand, for a start, sprawling back around the dunes to a big lawn of level, grassy machair; then the channel of the mountain river, winding through the sand. This curls back to a couple of lakes or lagoons, one glittering under a low, wooded cliff with a plateau of bog beyond. All this is virtually roadless and couched below the mountains as if for revelation: Mweelrea on this side, lofty Benwhatsit across in Connemara. The mouth of the fjord, Killary Harbour, opens darkly in between.

The soft bits of Thallabawn are distinctly dynamic, their sculpting and shifting over the centuries ruled by wind and wave. A map from 1838 shows dunes at either end of the strand but great tongues of bare sand licking far back into the shore. By 1919 the dunes had grown across from the south, and the machair and lakes were forming behind them. But the little graveyard perched on the northern dunes was now an isolated pyramid in the sand.

This "burial mound," as everyone knew it, has since been melted by storms into a flat mandala of stone slabs. The dunes have been trimmed back and cliffed on the seaward side. A new rampart of rocks has been built to resist the flood when spring tide and swollen river combine to attack the lowest, sandy pastures. A farmer tried to persuade the channel to take a more direct course to the sea—he took his digger to the strand and carved a new course for it, straight out. The tides erased it, and the channel resumed its leisurely loop of an estuary: it is where it wants to go.

So, even without global warming, this soft stretch of the west has known enormous change, as storms, tides and currents have played with available sediments— offshore sand and gravel swept out in the melt of the glaciers or carried down in the river from the mountain. A summer as calm as the last one let the waves build up the strand—a new soft and fluffy selvedge at the edge. The autumn gales have been clawing the sand back again, the breakers spinning like wheels.

Looking out from my desk I wonder, of course, how far fiercer and steeper storm-piled waves will bring a rising sea. Round and over the dunes, I suppose, into the lakes, and as far as the reedy marsh where the hillside rock begins to rise. I shan't see it, but somebody will.

With Ireland taking much of the brunt of Europe's future Atlantic storms, our coastline has been under close study since the late 1970s. Ireland's leading authority on likely sea-level impact is Dr Robert Devoy, professor of geography at University College Cork's Coastal and Marine Research Centre. For the immediate future, his work is relatively reassuring. Much of our coast, as he describes, already has high resilience, conditioned to environmental extremes of big tides, frequent storms and heavy rainfall. Our western continental shelf, the inshore shallows that run into rocky platforms, and our wide and often island-studded bays all help to blunt and dissipate the power of hurricane-heaped Atlantic swells and slow initial erosion from a rising sea level. Even so, about a third of coastal wetlands like the one below me seem doomed to disappear.

Erosion already bites hardest at the soft cliffs of glacial till at the southeast corner of the island, averaging as much as a metre a year. But the south and east coasts at least have an abundant supply of sediment for the beaches, lying in banks offshore. Elsewhere, the supply from these old glacial deposits has almost ceased. Instead, sand and gravel in beach barriers is being swept along the shore and dissipated, and tractorloads scooped up for construction have robbed the budget further.

How fast will the sea level rise? A survey of 90 sea-level experts in 18 countries, just published (go to realclimate.org) offers a consensus of 40–60 cm in this century if the human world takes determined action to limit carbon dioxide and 70–120 cm if it does not. Devoy, like all his colleagues, wrestles with the uncertainties of modelling, melting ice, and political commitment. The latest conference fiasco in Poland will not have encouraged him.

He does, however, think it's time—long, long past time—we prepared for it. Integrated coastal zone management, well discussed through the 1990s and strongly urged by Europe, would bang heads together in the several Government departments concerned, and involve coastal communities as stakeholders. UCC's website on the subject, however, has found nothing new to say since 2004.

I think, while there's time, I must walk to the far lake and listen to the whooper swans gossiping under the cliff.[28]

Tim Robinson

Tim Robinson was born in England in 1935, studied mathematics at the University of Cambridge, and taught the subject in Turkey. He then worked as a visual artist under the name of Timothy Drever, first in Vienna and later in London, where there were several exhibitions of his abstract paintings and environmental installations in the 1960s. In 1972, he went to live in the Aran Islands and began writing and making maps. He now lives in Roundstone, Connemara. His detailed study of the Aran Islands, *Stones of Aran: Pilgrimage*, was published in 1986 to critical acclaim. Known for his excellent cartography, Robinson has produced maps of the Aran Islands, Connemara, and the Burren in County Clare; these are published by Folding Landscapes, the imprint he and his wife, Máiréad, run from their Roundstone base, a specialist publishing house and information resource center for Galway Bay, including the Aran Islands, the Burren, and Connemara. Robinson's maps, renowned for scholarly exactitude and artistry, are widely used in university departments and schools. They inform the discriminating visitor about the region's culture and landscapes and nourish community spirit by identifying the irreplaceable uniqueness of local environment and history. Robinson's most recent work has been the publication of a three-volume study of Connemara: *Listening to the Wind*, *A Little Gaelic Kingdom*, and *The Last Pool of Darkness*. The following excerpt is the preface from *Connemara: Listening to the Wind*, followed by the section "The Boneyard," which describes both the natural world of Ireland's west coast and the tragedies of Ireland's discarded infants, which were also the subject of Heaney's poem "Limbo."

From Connemara: Listening to the Wind

PREFACE: THE SOUND OF THE PAST AND THE MOMENT OF WRITING

A small concrete cross stands by the road that follows the river from Ballynahinch to the sea. The proprietor of the Angler's Return, two bends of the road and the river further on, told me it marks the place where one of the gillies was found dead of a heart attack. "Wasn't it good that he died looking out at the river he'd worked on all his life?" she added. But from the time of the tyrannical Tadhg O'Flaherty, who forbade fishing in the lake by his castle, to the fish-ins of the Gaelic Civil Rights Movement in the sixties, the fisheries of Connemara have been occasions of resentment. Perhaps the man died cursing the river that had brought him a lifetime of midge bites and the condescension of the rich.

Whatever the burden of the gillie's last breath, it was dispersed into the air to be degraded by the hiss of rain or eroded molecule by molecule in the Brownian fidget of drifting pollen grains, and captured, a little of it, by the tilting, spilling cups and saucers of the water surface, dissolved, hurried under the old bridge at Tuaim Beola and added to the sea. So one can imagine it infinitesimally present in, and persuasively interpreting, the sough (which we should not delude ourselves is a sighing) of the Ballynahinch woods, the clatter (not a chattering) of the mountain streamlets, the roar (not a raging) of the waves against the shore.

These indefinite but enormous noises are part of Connemara. Sometimes from my doorstep on a still night I become aware that the silence is set in a velvet background like a jewel in a display case, a hushing that, when attended to, becomes ineluctable. It is compounded of the crash of breakers along distant strands, variously delayed, attenuated, echoed and re-echoed. A frequently falsified but never quite discredited forewarning of gales, it is an effect that, from our perspective here, precedes its cause: a depression moving across the Atlantic and advancing its concentric rollers towards our coast. By the morning, perhaps, a tumult of air will be battering the windows, all its wavelengths, from the vast heft of gusts over the hill that half shelters us, to the spasms of the garden shrubs and the fluting of a dry leaf caught between two stones, merging into one toneless bulk noise. Going here and there in thought through the pandemonium, only the most analytic listening can disengage its elements: shriek of sedge bent double out on the heath, grinding of shingle sucked back by the reflux, slow chamfering of a stone's edge by blown sand grains.

Such vast, complex sounds are produced by fluid generalities impacting on intricate concrete particulars. As the wave or wind breaks around a headland, a wood, a boulder, a tree trunk, a pebble, a twig, a wisp of seaweed or a microscopic hair on a leaf, the streamlines are split apart, flung against each other, compressed in narrows, knotted in vortices. The ear constructs another wholeness out of the reiterated fragmentation of pitches, and it can be terrible, this wide range of frequencies coalescing into something approaching the auditory chaos and incoherence that sound engineers call white noise: zero of information-content, random interference obliterating all messages, utterly dire, a metaphysical horror made audible, sometimes dinned into prisoners' heads to drive them mad in the cells of their brains.

Similar too is the sound of the past, the wreck of time's grand flow in tortuous passages. It includes and sometimes drowns the sound of history. History has rhythms, tunes and even harmonies; but the sound of the past is an agonistic multiplicity. Sometimes, rarely, a scrap of a voice can be caught from the universal damage, but it may only be an artefact of the imagination, a confection of rumours. Chance decides what is obliterated and what survives if only to be distorted and misheard. Of the gillie who died by the river, I know nothing more, but may yet find out something. But who, for one of the crowding shades besieging my book, was Cuach na Coille, the "cuckoo of the wood"? I hear of her from a single source only, and only this: that she was a beautiful horsewoman who lived in Derryclare Wood. I fear that nobody living can tell me more. Even in the ancient forest itself, where slender shafts of sunlight look almost material enough to cast a greenish shadow and sometimes in the restless canopy a cuckoo claims to be "here/there," the mysterious horsewoman does not appear, tantalizing with her untold tale. Hers, with his, may stand for all Connemara's abolished voices.

A preface represents the moment of writing, a fictive moment in which the book is declared complete, or abandoned as incompletable within the limits of time and talent available, and is delivered to that longed-for response, the moment of reading, which stands in the same labyrinthine relation to hearing as writing does to speech. The moment of writing, outcome of the potentially endless reshapings of sense and intricate adjustments of word to context that true writing allows and indeed consists in, is a fractal construction out of all the subsidiary moments in which words, phrases, paragraphs, chapters, have been completed.

Whatever curse or blessing the gillie may have uttered, on someone or on everyone who was not there to receive it, it would have been true speech, spontaneous, out of the unfathomable depth of personhood. As such it would have been the very opposite of true writing. (The material differences between speech and writing are immaterial to this opposition; rehearsed speech is writing, and a dashed-off love-note can be true speech.) How can writing, writing about a place, hope to recuperate its centuries of lost speech? A writing may aspire to be rich enough in reverberatory internal connections to house the sound of the past as well as echoes of immediate experience, but it is also intensely interested in its own structure, which it must preserve from the overwhelming multiplicity of reality. I am aware of the selectivity of my written response to living in Connemara. I concentrate on just three factors whose influences permeate the structures of everyday life here: the sound of the past, the language we breathe, and our frontage onto the natural world. I don't propose these as philosophical categories, merely use them as organizing principles, interplaying with the general topographical drive of the work. And if, as seems possible, this book becomes three books, each might privilege one of these factors while remaining open to all of them. The fact of language (not "the language question," which scarcely interests) might predominate in writing about the conflictually bilingual southern region of Connemara. The ocean, inescapable symbol of the ever-changing, almost-eternal, other-than-human setting of human affairs, would especially direct me when I come to the cliffs and isles and promontories of the Atlantic seaboard. The present book concerns a huge tract of south-west and central Connemara; after wandering in Roundstone Bog for a while it works its way from the beaches west of Roundstone, where I live, by Ballynahinch, for centuries the heart of Connemara and the seat of its various masters, to the eastern extremity of Roundstone Parish, the legendary mountain pass of Mam Ean; the sound of the past is particularly insistent throughout this territory.

That is the schema emerging under my hands, at the moment of writing. I may have to abandon it if subsequent volumes lead me another way. And as to this volume, I am aware that, even leaving out of account the writer's ignorance and misapprehensions, the truest of writing about the past can hardly offer more than an appalled recognition of the injustice of time, its brutally hasty recourse to mass graves for irreplaceable individualities and to landfill for delicate discriminations.

—Tim Robinson
Roundstone, 2006

THE BONEYARD

There should always be flowing water between consecrated ground and a plot set aside for the burial of unbaptized infants. That was the belief in the old times, according to an elderly man of the locality with whom I was discussing the children's burial ground at Goirtín, two miles west of Roundstone village. Indeed there is a little stream between the hillock topped by a stone bearing the words "In memory of the deceased infants" and the wall of the official cemetery just west of it. This memorial is a recent mark of reconciliation with the past; it was erected by the

Roundstone Development Committee as a Millennium Year project, and the spot was consecrated by the parish priest, Fr McCarthy, on 2 January 2000.

When I was exploring Connemara for my map in the 1980s I was shown about forty children's burial grounds, only a very small number of them marked on official maps or recorded in any way other than in folk memory, and most of them known only to people of the immediate vicinity. A few of them are noticeable scatterings of small set stones, uninscribed but obviously not a random assemblage; others I would discover only because some oddity of the terrain would attract my attention: why does the little road down to Lettermore, near Renvyle, have a kink in it? Why are there so many small boulders under the thorn-bushes on a tiny peninsula of the shoreline of Camas Íochtair? Why does the boundary wall between the townlands of Canower and Rosroe, near Cashel, bisect a small hummock a few yards from the highwater level? Many of these burial places are totally obscured by bracken and brambles; an old man pointing out one such meagre memorial in the corner of a field behind his cottage added, "Some of my own are buried there." Often a stillborn child would be buried by night in some ancient earthwork whose origins as a stock-yard around a dwelling had been forgotten for centuries and which bore an anom-alous otherworldly repute as a fairy fort, or under a fence between two properties, as if neither side would accept responsibility for it, or on the no man's land of the seashore. Although disused for some decades now, children's burial grounds are still tender spots of the rural landscape and have to be approached with tact.

In their obscurity and ambiguity these sites match the Catholic doctrine of limbo, that shadowy province of the afterworld reserved for those who, through no fault of their own, have not been saved by the word of Christ. As the *Catholic Encyclopaedia* of 1912 explains in its article on baptism:

The Catholic teaching is uncompromising on this point, that all who depart this life without baptism are perpetually excluded from the vision of God . . . Many Catho-lic theologians have declared that infants dying without baptism are excluded from the beatific vision; but as to the exact state of these souls in the next world they are not agreed. In speaking of souls who have failed to attain salvation, these theolo-gians distinguish the pain of loss (*paena damni*), or privation of the beatific vision, and the pain of sense (*paena sensus*). Though these theologians have thought it certain that unbaptized infants must endure the pain of loss, they have not been similarly certain that they are subject to the pain of sense. St. Augustine held that they would not be exempt from the pain of sense, but at the same time he thought it would be of the mildest form . . . Since the twelfth century, the opinion of the majority of theologians has been that unbaptized infants are immune from all pain of sense. This was taught by St. Thomas Aquinas, Scotus, St. Bonaventure, Peter Lombard, and others, and is now the common teaching in the schools . . . As to the question, whether in addition to freedom from the pain of sense, unbaptized infants enjoy any positive happiness in the next world, theologians are not agreed, nor is there any pronouncement of the Church on the subject. Many, following St. Thomas, declare that these infants are not saddened by the loss of the beatific vision, either because they have no knowledge of it, and hence are not sensible of their privation; or because, knowing it, their will is entirely conformed to God's will and they are conscious that they have missed an undue privilege through no fault of their own. In addition to this freedom from regret at the loss of heaven, these infants may also enjoy some positive happiness.

While the opinion, then, that unbaptized infants may enjoy a natural knowledge and love of God and rejoice in it, is perfectly tenable, it has not the certainty that would arise from a unanimous consent of the Fathers of the Church, or some a favourable pronouncement of ecclesiastical authority.

Nevertheless, in its article on limbo the *Catholic Encyclopaedia* is confident in asserting that "as a result of centuries of speculation on the subject, we ought to believe that these souls enjoy and will eternally enjoy a state of perfect natural happiness." And the 1992 *Catechism of the Catholic Church* takes an optimistic, if rather vague, view:

> As regards children who have died without Baptism, the Church can only entrust them to the mercy of God, as she does in her funeral rites for them. Indeed, the great mercy of God who desires that all men should be saved, and Jesus' tenderness toward children which caused him to say: "Let the children come to me, do not hinder them," allows us to hope that there is a way of salvation for children who have died without Baptism.

That was the mellow mood of Vatican II, and in its aftermath some retrospective measures are being taken for the sake of the poor souls whose mortal remains went into the children's burial grounds before these mild modern understandings. Fortunately (and after a mere 1,500 years of reflection) theologians have found ingenious ways out of their own trap; for instance, Christ's general will to save all may be deemed equivalent to a baptism by desire. Thus those formerly regarded as the unbaptized can be disinterred and reburied in a proper cemetery, or a proxy baptismal service may be conducted on their behalf. In 1994 a children's burial ground in Raheenduff Renvyle, was consecrated, as a result of a campaign led by Mary Salmon, whose two stillborn children lay there, having been denied Christian burial some sixty years previously. By courageously exposing the depth of her anguish and resentment she made herself the spokesperson for the generations of women who had been so cruelly misled by their spiritual fathers:

> I felt very let down by the Catholic Church . . . I remember one priest saying to me "surely you did not cry for that baby," to which I replied "I did cry for that baby and I think there's no God in heaven to take him away from me." I told him my baby was not in purgatory or limbo and that I did not believe in such places. I also told him that I would see my baby very soon. I had taken the baby's death so hard that I felt like dying. In those days it was customary for the local priest to bless a pregnant woman before giving birth and to consecrate her with oil two or three weeks after the birth. After I had the dead babies the priests never came near me and because of this I stopped going to the church to be consecrated after giving birth of my other children. I was very bitter towards the clergy, because I believed at the time that they wanted almost to pretend that nothing had ever happened. I stopped attending Mass and it was only after Fr. Keane visited me and pleaded with me to return to Mass that I eventually agreed to go again. In recent years I have had many visits

from priests in America who knew my sons over there. These priests have all talked to me about my loss and these conversations have brought me some consolation but they will never fully make up for the clergy's uncaring attitude back then.

Since then children's burial grounds have been blessed by the local priest in a few other places in Connemara, but these gestures of atonement and reclamation have been prompted by the parishioners; the Hierarchy remains silent on them and offers no guidance. As one priest said to me, "The cardinals do their own thing. They work out the logic of the doctrine, and it's the logic of the head, not of the heart. They despise emotions. So we do this discreetly. Say too much about it and you'd get a rap from Rome. It comforts people today, but it's too late for all those in the past. The Church will never admit that it was wrong. It fears that if it did so the whole structure would crumble—which might be no great harm." So priests and the leaders of congregations improvise the inauguration of a more humane regime, and not always without discomfiting those they would comfort. Some elderly parishioners may not want anything to do with such matters even today, their feelings being understandably confused and embittered. Very few people turned out for the ceremony at Goirtín in the year 2000.

It would not be right to blame solely the Church for the stream of tears that flows between the children's burial ground and the cemetery. Death is mysterious, and so is birth; doubly so is death-in-birth. Suspicion lurked around it, of abortion, infanticide, witchcraft. Up to a few generations ago, a question would have shadowed the mind of the sorrowful parents: did the envious fairies steal away our lovely vigorous baby and leave this wretched limp thing in its place? The decline of such superstitions, the medicalization of childbirth, the pressures of secularism and feminism, have all contributed to the abandonment of the old ways and the evolution of a charitable assumption that all infants are baptized, by the very fact of their parents' having desired them to be so. Nevertheless, I cannot pass by the burial place of these failed attempts at life without registering my amazement and distress over the persistence of the gargoyle-logic of limbo into such recent times. Stony throats continued for centuries to roar forth the consequences of their false premises high above the heads of suffering humanity, oblivious to the fact that what matters once an infant is dead is not the welfare of a non-existent entity in a fictional hereafter, but the feelings of the parents, and perhaps particularly of the mother, who brought this scrap of humanity so briefly, or so nearly, into the world. A funeral, with the words set down to be spoken over each of us in our turns, and burial in the ground set aside for all our corpses, would have been a continual recognition of the little body's attempt at personhood, and would have helped the bereaved to begin to let their loss fall into the past. When at a child's funeral I hear our kind-hearted parish priest say, "God must have loved little Jane so much that He called her to Him so soon," and the parents repeat the formula to themselves and even to me, I recognize once again that what to me is a sentimental inanity is a source of strength to others and is not to be despised. So, the centuries-long Catholic ban on burying the unbaptized in consecrated ground, necessitating the furtive, unceremonious spading-in of the dead baby or foetus under a boundary wall, in the haunted rath or along the stones of the seashore, was a bitter wrong.

The stream, this little Jordan of such millennial consequence, a mere trickle in dry weather but quite busy after a downpour, carves a miniature valley around the western side of the knoll on which the memorial now stands, then spills through a culvert under the path leading to the cemetery gate and makes its way down to meet the tide through improvised canyons a few inches deep in the sand of the beach. A few yards to the west of it, the consecrated ground within the walls of salvation is hummocky, sandy and grassy. The graves are in irregular close proximity, almost as neighbourly or as mutually intrusive as those of *Cré na Cille*, Máirtín Ó Cadhain's famous novel that imagines an eternity of gossip, flirting and backbiting between the corpses in a south Connemara graveyard. But in compensation Goirtín cemetery is awash with spacious colours: often, the blue-grey of the Atlantic blowing over it from the south; sometimes, the severe enamel blue of Mary's mantle; occasionally, that Mediterranean quintessence of blue, the *azure* of Valéry's *Cimetière Marin*. In winter the mourners cower under blasts of slanting rain; in summer the graves are self-strewn with the low nodding blossoms of sand-dune flora.

I like fossicking and yoricking about in graveyards, scanning the headstones, stopping for a closer look at one or another, as one takes down a book from a bookshop shelf to see if its opening words live up to its title. One of my desiderata for a well-run world would be that every tombstone carry a brief biography (and, at the foot, "For notes and sources, see over"). But how reductively uninformative are the inscriptions here! John Barlow, fondly remembered; Margaret Dundass, sadly missed. Mr Barlow I knew as the deaf, mannerly old gentleman who sold me my newspaper every day, and who once told me that he had not expected to spend his life behind the counter of a shop. He exercised great caution in stocking the shop; a phrase I several times heard from him, for instance when I suggested he might get in a few guidebooks, or even some of my own maps, was "You could have a lot of money tied up in those things!" This most peaceable of men often held me there for half an hour reminiscing about his glory days as a member of the Local Defence Force; he would explain to me that in manning a machine gun "you need to be able to work all around you," and his whole frame would shudder with the imagined recoil as he directed a withering spray of bullets into every corner of the shop. Miss Dundass, a schoolteacher retired for many a year, was in her nineties when I used to call in on her with queries about village history; I remember her sitting crouched like a cricket by a smoky fire in her rather derelict little house on Marine Terrace, which she would allow no one to repair or tidy up because she was losing her sight and could only manage in unchanging circumstances. The last time I saw her she was mooching about outside the house on a sunny afternoon; "I'm mooching about," she said, as if she were taking the opportunity of teaching me the word, the reflexes of her calling as prompt as ever.

The cemetery also houses the bones of some notable personalities that figure in history books: Bulmer Hobson, the gentle Quaker revolutionary who retired to the house at the bottom of the road down to Goirtín after the debacle of the Easter Rising, and wrote his book *Ireland Today and Tomorrow* there; Maurice McGonigal, President of the Royal Hibernian Academy and painter of many Roundstone landscapes; the Duchess de Stacpoole, local patron of the Lady Dudley Nursing Scheme and chatelaine of Errisbeg House. All three died before I came to live in Roundstone, but local people remember them and have given me the odd non-historical particular about them. Hobson had a bicycle fitted with a little petrol motor, and Joe Rafferty, who kept a shop on the coast road not far away, placed a stone by its door to help him mount and dismount. When Hobson's sight was failing he studied the mechanism of the eye and devised a reading aid, a sheet of glass of some kind suspended from his forehead so that it would swing out of the way if he nodded off. McGonigal, I am told, was buried with his palette, which had been given to him by Paul Henry, who had it from Sir William Orpen—a nice emblem of the continuity of Roundstone's artistic tradition. The Duchess, I hear, was a ruthless and erratic motorist; when a local lad was buying his first car, his father warned him of the three terrors of driving in Connemara: "the ditches, the donkeys and the Duchess."

One of the deepest difficulties of disbelief in a hereafter is the implication that so much suffering remains forever unrevenged and uncompensated; but such is the case, or so it appears to me. I think here of Fidelma, a kindly, obsequious, shapeless old lady who did some cleaning jobs, and was married to a sly, malicious and probably marginally deranged joker from Mayo, who it is said sometimes beat her and threw her out of her house at night, and for some years before her death dragged her off to live here and there far away from her familiar neighbours. When the hearse bringing her remains from that distant town was approaching the village and her husband heard that people were waiting in the street there to follow it to the cemetery in the customary procession, he persuaded the driver to detour around by Ballyconneely, avoiding Roundstone, and so cheated her of respect to the last and beyond. But all graves are memorials to time's disrespect; the knowledge even of who lies in the older ones is mouldering in the newer, just as library shelves are filling with books on other books, which will never be opened and must eventually be pulped to give room for more. Cemeteries themselves get buried in cemeteries; the Ordnance Survey map of 1839 shows a burial ground at Goirtín as a roughly oval unenclosed patch about thirty yards by fifteen; on the 1899 map it is seventy yards long by thirty across; today's cemetery is a walled rectangle about two hundred yards by a hundred, and is fully occupied, while a new tract to the west, recently taken in, is sparsely tenanted as yet, a green forethought.

The terrain out of which the cemetery is taking successive bites is a stretch of *muirbheach* or machair, a smooth sward kept trimmed by exposure and grazing, based on long-consolidated sand. It spans the base of a peninsula, the *iorras beag* or little headland, from which the townlands of Errisbeg East and Errisbeg West, extending inland from it, derive their names. The peninsula consists of a narrow sandbar, with a beach on either side of it, linking the mainland to what would otherwise be an island about a mile offshore. The whole area is loosely called Goirtín, anglicized as Gorteen and meaning "small field," a name that perhaps primarily applied to the head of the peninsula, on which there used to be potato fields. Seen from the slopes of Errisbeg Hill rising just inland of it, the whole landform looks like a long arm bone and a knobbly fist thrust out into the sea. The beaches rimming the bays on either side of the sandbar—Dog's Bay to the west, and Port na Feadóige (bay of the plovers), also known as Gorteen Bay, to the east—are themselves bone-white and consist of minute shards of mollusc shells and the exoskeletons of the single-celled sea-creatures called foraminifera. The whole formation is a place of bones. Buried in it or exhumed by scouring winds are the remains of humans and their kitchen refuse. George Petrie, in the early 1830s, was the first to take note of the abundant traces of early settlement here:

> A few years since on the shore of Roundstone Bay, a bank of sand 300 feet high, being removed by a storm, discovered on the strand beneath a cluster of nine oval houses of stone in perfect condition including their roofs; they have since been reburied by a new accumulation of sand.

Although not exactly part of the shoreline of Roundstone Bay, Goirtín is the only nearby location where great movements of sand occur, and Petrie must be referring to the duneland west of the graveyard or the sandbar south of it (although his "300 feet" is surely a mistake, perhaps for "30 feet"). In 1895 F. J. Bigger discovered hut sites on the mainland close to the neck of the peninsula, presumably the remains of Petrie's "stone houses," and investigated them in the following year in the company of Robert Lloyd Praeger and others:

> A hasty survey of the place would show here and there small clumps of stones which indicated the positions of hearths that were probably the centres of hut sites . . . Where we found a good site from which the covering had not long been removed and from which the remains had not been collected, it was a most instructive sight, as we could see the hammer-stones just as they had been last used by their pre-historic owners, the flakes lying probably on the spots where they had fallen on being struck off, or where they had been laid down after being used; and amongst these objects broken and split bones and small heaps of shell fish, the remains of their meals, were also visible.

The description of Bigger's finds suggests the Neolithic period, and it is clear that humans have occupied the Goirtín peninsula at least intermittently since then. Until recently two or three blackish layers could be seen in the faces of the dunes where westerly storms had carved them into low cliffs all around Dog's Bay. These soot-blackened "soil horizons" with their spills of seashells showed very graphically that at various periods in the distant past people had foregathered here, perhaps seasonally, to live off the harvest of the sea, and that after a time each of these habitation surfaces had been buried by a further building-up of the dune system. They have largely been obscured by loose sand again, as a result of coastal protection work. In one area, near the south end of the bay, an archaeological dig was carried out in advance of this work, in 1991, by a team led by Erin Gibbons. The oldest ruins were found at the level of the beach and represent human activity here in the Neolithic, before the dunes began to form. They included a small scraper and some worked flint, and two stretches of drystone wall. In a soil horizon about half a yard above the beach there were plentiful signs of occupation: animal and fish bones, burnt stone and charcoal, pits containing shells, and holes left by wooden posts. On an exposed shelf of sand about three yards above the beach, among severely eroded dunes, more considerable structures were found. A well-constructed drystone wall could be traced for some fifty yards southwards, with an intact kiln on the seaward side of it. The kiln seemed to have been used for drying corn, as carbonized oats were found in it and elsewhere nearby. It was built into the sandy soil and consisted of a bowl lined with cut granite stone and a flue. It had been abandoned when the stones began to flake from repeated firings, and had been backfilled with soil and stones including a large fragment of a saddle quern. Finally, the place had been reused as a children's burial ground; three little burials were excavated, one of them in the flue of the kiln itself.

A puzzling feature of the shell middens seen by Bigger and his colleagues is that some of the shells had been gathered into separate heaps according to their species, which included limpets, oysters, flat periwinkles, mussels and common whelks. Similarly, separate deposits of limpet, periwinkle and whelk shells were found here in 1944 when F. J. O'Rourke opened a trial trench near the north end of the dunes. It is difficult to imagine why these common food-species should have been segregated; perhaps they were gathered at different times of the year. Even more interesting is Bigger's find of a deposit, fifty-five yards long and up to fifteen yards broad, of dogwhelk shells, in which all the shells were broken, the topmost whorls having been smashed, leaving the lower whorls and the mouth intact. The dogwhelk (*Nucella lapillus*, until recently known as *Purpura lapillus*), like the closely related *Murex* that was the source of the famous Tyrian purple of classical times, has, just under the point of the shell, a gland that secretes a whitish slimy substance rich in potent chemicals including a nerve poison and an antibiotic; the substance may play a role in carrying extraneous particles out of the shell, in rendering the animal or its eggs unpalatable, or in protecting the eggs against disease. From the human point of view its important constituent is a pigment chemically similar to indigo, which turns a rich purple colour on exposure to light and air. This substance was the foundation of the prosperity of the Phoenician city of Tyre (now known as Sur, to the south of Beirut); according to the Greek geographer Strabo, writing some two thousand years ago, "Although the great number of dye works makes the city unpleasant to live in, yet it makes the city rich through the superior skills of its inhabitants." The original discovery of shellfish purple is of course lost in prehistory, but it was important enough to have its representation in Greek myth. One day Hercules was walking on the beach with a Tyrian nymph whose favours he hoped to win. His dog came across a *Murex* and devoured it, and the nymph, seeing the stains on the dog's mouth, bargained with Hercules for a robe of that same glorious colour. So Hercules took the shellfish, extracted the dyestuff and made her the first robe of Tyrian purple. Since it took about 25,000 shellfish to provide a tenth of an ounce of dyestuff, Tyrian purple was literally worth its weight in gold and was used only for the most prestigious and luxurious garments. In Rome only the Emperor, the highest officials and priests were allowed to wear purple. At the Battle of Actium, it is said, Mark Antony's ship flaunted purple-bordered sails. In the great days of Byzantium, emperors used to sign their names in shellfish purple. The dyers' skills were closely guarded trade secrets, not written down, and it seems that knowledge of them died with the Byzantine Empire after the capture of Constantinople by the Ottomans in 1453.

Was there some reflection of all this oriental splendour in the lives of the un-recorded folk of Dog's Bay? Emily Murray of Queen's University, Belfast, has collected the evidence for a dogwhelk-dye industry in the west of Ireland. Middens of broken dogwhelk shells have been found at Ballyconneely and in various dune systems around the south-western peninsula of Connemara, at Omey Island and at a few places in Mayo, Sligo and Donegal. Recent radiocarbon dating of the surviving sites places them all within a period roughly from AD 360 to 800, that is, in early Christian times. However, there are no known references to the use of shellfish purple in writings of the period. The Venerable Bede in his *Ecclesiastical History of the English People*, written in about 731, states that in "Albion" there is "a great abundance of whelks, from which a scarlet-coloured dye is made, a most beautiful red which neither fades through the heat of the sun nor exposure to the rain; indeed the older it is the more beautiful it becomes"—but this passage occurs in a eulogy of "Albion" that lends it all the charms of ancient days, and is perhaps not to be taken literally. All other medieval references to the use of shellfish purple in Britain or Ireland seem to derive from Bede. Despite many speculations and assertions in twentieth-century sources on the topic, scientific analysis, with one possible very recent exception, has failed to confirm that shellfish purple was used in illuminated manuscripts from Ireland or Britain. In the many accounts of ancient Irish dress, from Giraldus Cambrensis down to contemporary scholars, if purple is mentioned its source is given as a lichen, and technical analysis of old textiles tends to confirm this. But there is substantial written evidence for the use of shellfish purple from the seventeenth and eighteenth centuries. A William Cole offered his "observations on the Purple Fish" to the Royal Society in 1685:

> For in October 1684, there were two ladies of Myne head [Somerset] who told me, there was a certain person living by the seaside in some port or Creek in Ireland, who made considerable gain, by marking with a delicate durable crimson colour, fine linen of ladies, gent. etc. sent from many parts of that island, with their names or otherwise as they please; which they told me was made by some liquid substance taken out of a shellfish . . . these shells, being harder than most of other kinds are to be broken with a smart stroke of a hammer on a plate of iron, or firm piece of Timber (with their mouths downwards) so as not to crush the body of the Fish within: the broken pieces being picked off there will appear a white vein, lying transversely in a little furrow or cleft, next to the head of the fish, which must be digg'd out with the stiff point of the Horse hair pencil.

J. C. Walker, in an essay of 1788 on Irish dress, states that dyeing with shellfish purple "is still practised in the counties of Wicklow, Wexford and other counties on the east coast of Ireland," while an anonymous writer in the *Annual Register* of 1760 gives us this charming scene from the west:

> I happened some years ago, to be at a gentleman's house upon the western coast of Ireland, where I took particular notice of a gown which the lady of the house wore one day. It was a muslin flowered with the most beautiful violet colour I had ever seen. Upon my expressing my admiration of it, the lady told me, with a smile, it was her own work and seeing me wonder at her saying so took me down to the seaside, among the rocks, when the tide was out, where she gathered some little shellfishes . . . and to convince me brought a handful of the fishes home with her, and breaking

them open, and extracting the liquor with the point of a clean pen, marked some spots directly before me . . . Though the fishes were sufficiently plenty, the drop that was extracted from each was so little that I suppose the contents of a hundred would make a drop so large as a small pea.

Finally, there is some evidence from placenames of the existence of a dye industry only a few miles from Dog's Bay: a townland near Slyne Head is called Creggoduff, which represents the Irish Creig an Duibh, "the rocky place of the black stuff," and in a seventeenth-century source the place is named as Creagacorcron, which would mean "the rocky place of the purple stuff." The "black stuff" is probably the intensely black, iron-rich sediment collected from the bottom of bog-holes, widely used for dyeing wool until a couple of generations back and referred to in numerous Connemara placenames; it gives a dull black colour, or, with the addition of oak chips, a glossy jet black. The "purple stuff" could be from a lichen; but Creggoduff lies close to all the dogwhelk sites of south-western Connemara listed above, and it might be that it was once a centre for producing seashell purple, and that when this luxury item was no longer in demand the dye trade lingered on, dealing in humbler materials. Since a single dogwhelk yields only ten or twenty milligrams of dye, which is much less than the product of the Mediterranean *Murex* species, the Irish shellfish-purple business must always have been on a small scale. Emily Murray suggests that it involved the dyeing of skeins of wool by direct application from the live shellfish, the wool being used in the fringes of mantles and similar sparing applications, rather than the wholesale production of dyed fleeces and robes. Goirtín, then, was never the Tyre of the West, and traces of whatever eminence it once enjoyed in the trade are hard to find nowadays. Bigger's fifty-yard-long deposit of shells seems to have vanished, lost no doubt to the fierce erosion of the dunes rimming Dog's Bay. I have never even come across a scattering of broken dogwhelk shells here, but a Roundstone lady tells me that in her childhood she and her playmates used to collect them, and string them into necklaces. Nothing goes to waste; the nymph of Tyre needs the juice of the creature, and the girls of Roundstone its bones; both are moments in the Earth's ruthless self-adornment.

Because the wind perpetually dusts the sward of Goirtín with lime-rich seashell stuff off the beaches, and because it is underlain by more or less consolidated sand, the pasturage here is nutritious and dry underfoot, and therefore is a valuable resource in this region of wet, peaty soils; it "puts bone" on the cattle, as they say. The whole peninsula is commonage, in the limited sense that each landholder of the townland in which it lies, Errisbeg West, has the right to a share of its grazing. The regulations governing these rights are complicated, and evidently ancient. Each holding is called a "band." The holder of a band may put fifteen sheep and one ram onto Goirtín, from the first of November to the first of December; nowadays the agreed total of sheep is 345. Cattle may be grazed here from 15 May to the last Sunday in July and from 15 August to 1 November, the allowance per band being three cows with their calves, or nine yearlings, or a half-collop plus one yearling. (A half-collop is a cow "with two teeth up," i.e. a one-year-old, I am informed. The Anglo-Irish word "collop" is from the Irish *colpa*, meaning a fullgrown cow or horse, or its equivalent as a unit of grazing, six sheep.) The beasts are counted on to and counted off from the commonage on the assigned days, their owners meeting for the purpose at 3 p.m. by the gate of Thomas Griffin, a farmer of Errisbeg West. The best of the grazing is on the level land just west of the cemetery and among the granite knolls of the head of the peninsula; the sandbar joining these two areas has a spine of rough grassland, now largely planted with marram grass and fenced to keep cattle and tourists off it.

A sandbar of this sort, connecting an island to the shore, is called a "tombolo" by the physical geographers, who have borrowed the term from the Italian for a sand dune. The dune systems of Ireland are evidently the result of waves and wind bringing sand ashore from the ocean bed, and they are thought to have begun to form after a fall in relative sea level six thousand years ago. A quirk of geography has led to the construction of the tombolo here. The one-time island that now forms the head of the peninsula is about a mile long, and lies almost parallel to the shore and a half mile off it. The dominant wind direction here is southwest, so the island absorbs most of the shock of incoming waves and the channel inshore of it is sheltered. Waves refracted around the two ends of the island meet head to head in its lee and cancel each other's impetus, so that their cargos of sand are deposited in relatively still water. As the zone between island and coast becomes shallower and shallower it becomes more and more effective in robbing the waves of their energy, and deposition accelerates. Once the growing sandbar reaches sea level the wind takes over, scouring sand from the beaches and heaping it above high-water mark, where vegetation soon begins to bind it into dry land.

But this cumulatively constructive process can be reversed, and an equally cumulative destruction ensue. Since the lower deposits of organic material in the dunes have been dated to some two thousand years ago, the sandbar is at least that old, while the alternation of blackish strata representing habitation levels with bright layers representing the burial of those habitation levels under further depths of sand shows that building of the tombolo has continued ever since then: so it might appear to be a fixed and stable item of local geography. However, the huge increase in human traffic, especially in summer, now amounts to a force that threatens to undo nature's millennial work. At present the sandbar is well vegetated, but only through a continuous effort of conservation. In recent decades it seems to have been denuded by erosion at times, perhaps in a natural and cyclical alternation. Old photographs show that it was virtually all bare sand in the 1950s but had begun to recover in the 1960s; by 1976 there was a good coverage of vegetation all along the core of the spit. Some of this variation may have been due to early attempts to stabilize the spit by planting it with marram grass; this species has the ability to grow upwards through many feet of sand, and if it can be established its stalks and leaves filter the flying sand grains out of the wind blowing through it so that they fall, accumulate and are eventually bound together by the grass's root systems. The Land Commission had certain areas fenced off to keep the cattle out of the marram grass, but the fences were neglected, and spring tides undermined them and dragged them down the beaches. Eventually the Land Commission handed the problem over to the County Council, which had the fences removed. In the 1980s the east side lost most of its plant cover. By 1990 the beaches were encroaching on the vegetated sand from either side, and the grassland was further reduced by blowouts, sandy pits where the cover had been totally worn away and the wind was excavating the underlying dunes. During the January storms of 1991 it looked as if the sea might break through the spit, leading to the wreckage of the famous beaches and the loss of grazing on the headland. The landholders of the townland, advised by Teagasc, the Agriculture and Food Development Authority, formulated the Roundstone Beaches Project and won the support of the County. During spring of that year a lot of reclamation work was done under a community employment scheme. A gang of men went off with lorries to Belmullet to dig up clumps of marram grass, planted the shifting sands with it, fenced off the planted areas, fortified the exposed faces of the dunes by setting rows of pine branches along the tops of the beaches to trap the flying sand, and, later on, armoured the most vulnerable stretch, at the south end of the Dog's Bay beach, with gabions, big boxes of thick wire mesh filled with boulders. All this interference with nature was unsightly for a time, and I was tempted to think that it would have been better to let wind and tide have their way, that perhaps the bar has come and gone many times; but then Erin Gibbons' excavations showed quite uncontrovertibly that it has been in continuous formation for at least two thousand years, and if it is breaking up now it is because of cumulative human interference, from the introduction of rabbits by the Normans down to the pleasure-seeking invaders of our own days. We can no longer delude ourselves that there is a Nature whose wild destructive and constructive forces derive a certain validation in our minds from their impartiality, their independence of our hopes and desires; rather, we are part of the problem and so must be part of the solution, if such there be. In the meantime, piled sand and a healthy coverage of plant life are burying the tattered fences of Goirtín in their depths and restoring a simulacrum of untouched naturalness.

A curious episode in May 1991 underlined for the Roundstone community what an unusual and vulnerable feature of their environment the tombolo is. Word suddenly spread that two large container lorries had arrived at six o'clock in the morning and were parked on the main road above Dog's Bay, that one of the fences protecting the newly planted marram grass had been cut, and that two tractors were driving up and down a gully in the eroding dune face, bringing loads of sand up to a smaller lorry which was transporting it up the side road to the container lorries. The tenants of Errisbeg West immediately blocked the side road with their own tractors and compelled the intruders to replace the sand. It turned out that a contractor from Carna had been employed to collect this material, under a licence issued by the Department of the Marine. The licence limited them to thirty tons, to be gathered from below high-water mark, but they assured the tenants they had been given the nod for the removal of fifty tons. It was also clear that they were saving themselves some effort by taking the loose sand above high-water mark at the foot of the eroding dune. Their employers, we learned to our amazement, included Italian university institutions that needed samples of the sand because, as mentioned, it is largely composed of the shells of foraminifera. Since foraminifera (or forams as scientists call them for short) are single-celled creatures, one might have thought that a sample would be something of the order of a teaspoonful, but it transpired that the Italians—the Technical University of Turin, the Institute for Research on Models and Structures, in Bergamo, and the Italian National Electricity Board—were not studying the beautiful structure of foram shells but the crushability of calcareous sands, as part of a research programme ultimately relating to marine engineering projects, and that the type of sand found in Dog's Bay was unobtainable in bulk onshore anywhere else in the northern hemisphere.

I was called upon by the Roundstone Community Council to draft a letter to the Minister for the Marine, in my grandest manner, demanding that the licence be immediately rescinded since its provisions had been breached, and pointing out that the area had recently been designated as one of Scientific Importance and that its Neolithic-to-medieval archaeology was currently being investigated. Scientists from the Italian institutions hurried to Roundstone to try to placate us; their offers of funding for social development projects and scientific research into the precious terrain were rejected loftily. They even promised to bring the sand back once they had finished with it. We became absurdly obdurate and told them that return of the sand would only be acceptable if we could count the forams off the beach and count them back on again, and that we would not tolerate any breakages. A newspaper report of all this even has me saying grimly, "A line has been drawn in the sand!", and perhaps I did indeed get carried away to that extent. Eventually the scientists went away and we heard no more of the matter; I don't know how they solved their problem. There may have been more to this affair than met our eyes at the time, for on rereading a document that "came into my hands" during the controversy I find this annotation: "The research reported in this document is being sponsored by the U.S. Government through the European research office of the U.S. Army. The document is only intended for distribution within the U.S. Government and the above named contractor."

So the forani is a consequential creature, by reason of its numbers. Single-celled organisms more complex than bacteria, in that their DNA is contained in a nucleus, they are classed as Protozoa and represent a halfway stage of evolution between bacteria and the animal kingdom. The earliest ones in the fossil record are over 550 million years old; nevertheless they share half the genes that define us as human beings. There are about sixty thousand species worldwide, including those known only as fossils; over two hundred species have been recorded from Dog's Bay. Some might be a millimetre across, others a tenth of that. Each species builds shells of a characteristic form, most of them being divided by partitions into several chambers connected by small openings called "foramina" (from which the creatures get their name). Under the microscope foram shells are of extraordinary variety. Many look like triumphs of the baker's art: plaited bread rolls, fancy cupcakes, tarts with elaborate spiral trelliswork of piped icing. The organism builds the chambers of its shell one by one and occupies all except one or two of the outermost and most recently constructed. It trawls for its food—bacteria, single-celled algae and other tiny floaters—with a network of hair-like extensions of its substance that radiates from the aperture of its outer chamber. Most forams have shells of calcite and extract the material for them from seawater, and therefore are an important part of the "carbon cycle" that stabilizes the amount of carbon dioxide in the atmosphere and so keeps the Earth habitable. It has been estimated that 1.23 billion tons of foram shells are deposited on the sea floor each year, representing the death of 226 billion billion individuals—each one of which had its own life-history, proposed by its sac of DNA, and disposed by the chaos of the sea, some of them, into such prodigies of order as the tombolo of Goirtín.

Having walked the length of the vast necropolis of forams, along either of the beaches, one can scramble up a little slope onto the broad head of the peninsula. The ground is the smooth swellings of consolidated dunes, covered with a sward that feels elastic underfoot, nibbled as neat as a lawn by rabbits and rich with lime-loving herbs. Outcrops of granite interrupt it here and there, together with big round boulders of granite dropped at random by the retreating glaciers ten thousand years ago, sometimes in piles that make visitors think they have discovered prehistoric dolmens and stone circles. Patches of this fertile terrain were cultivated in harder times; here and there the traces of old potato ridges show in the green turf like ribs in a famished beast. But the field walls have long been reduced to gapped rows of stones, and cattle wander unconstrained by them. The land's edge is low, rocky and intricate. On the south-facing shore of the peninsula is a small sandy bay called An Trá Gharbh, the rough strand, backed by broken dunes that spill prehistoric shell middens. Near the western point of the headland an alert eye might spot some hundreds of beach pebbles a few inches long laid out in a regular pattern on a flat marshy area of the shore; the stones have almost sunk into the soft ground, but the pattern is still just legible, and walkable, as a maze of the classical Greek form known as the Walls of Troy. A well-informed Englishwoman of the locality told me that it was made by the British land-artist Richard Long, but I doubted this, since it was rather untypical of his work, until I found a photograph of it in his book *Walking in Circles*, published in connection with his 1991 exhibition in London. In an interview reported in that book Long said:

> In *Connemara Sculpture*, which is that maze, I'd gone to the museum in Dublin and had seen that particular image on an early rock carving, a sacred stone. I drew it in my notebook. Then, a week later, when I was in the west of Ireland and wanted to make a sculpture out of beach pebbles, I had the image in my notebook.

I have enquired of the National Museum and am informed that the carving in question can only be the so-called Hollywood Stone, which is now off display in the Reserve Collections. It is a labyrinth stone of the Christian era originally located by St. Kevin's Road, the ancient pilgrims' way to Glendalough in County Wicklow. The connection with pilgrimage is apposite, for Richard Long's life has been largely devoted to a divinatory worldwide journeying through wildernesses, and his own road has been marked by his sculptural works; I say "divinatory" because what he divines is the match between site and construct, the latter usually being a rearrangement of whatever the terrain provides, such as sticks or stones, seaweed or mud, in an elemental configuration, frequently a circle, straight lines or a cross. The *Connemara Sculpture* is uncharacteristically complex; it is an early work, dating from 1971. Having intervened in nature thus, he photographs the result in its setting, and passes onwards, leaving its future in the hands of nature. For his audience, the real artwork is a photograph, and perhaps a short text, exhibited in an art gallery, and the persistence or otherwise of what he leaves behind him is apparently irrelevant; but it is not so to me. I have had a brief exchange of letters with Richard

Long on the afterlife of the traces of his passage. I had marked the sites of two of his circles on my map of the Aran Islands, and in 1997 his wife, Denny, telephoned my partner, M, looking for a copy of the map to give him for his birthday, which we happily provided. However, the birthday gift was apparently not well received, for soon afterwards we heard from him as follows:

> Dear M, As a matter of fact, the edition of the map you kindly sent Denny didn't have my sculpture on it—which is fine by me, as it was never my intention for my sculptures to be marked "sites." I was originally very surprised and aghast when someone told me years ago that my work was marked on a map. (It was without my knowledge or intention.) Anyway, it's good it has been deleted. Also the way my 2 works are mentioned in the book [*Stones of Aran: Pilgrimage*] is appropriate & fitting to the spirit in which they were made.

Naturally I sprang to the defence of my cartography:

> Actually your circle of upright stones *is* marked on the Aran map M sent Denny (the little figure at the east end of the island, south of Túr Mártin); but in this new edition the note on it is in the companion book rather than on the map itself as in the previous edition.
>
> I'm sorry to learn that you were aghast when someone told you it had been marked on a map. If I had been reproducing one of your photos of it I would have looked for permission, naturally; but marking its position on a map is a different matter. I would never treat one of your works with anything less than great respect, but the primary loyalty of maps is to what is there. Think of it this way: once an artist has made a visible intervention in the landscape and left it there, it contributes to other people's experience of the place, which may well be expressed in someone else's work of art. Placelore will start to accumulate around it—and my subject matter is the web of placelore. Just as a text is relinquished to other people's interpretations once it has left the writer's hands, so your marks on the landscape will have a career of their own; they are no longer defined by their origin in your creativity. If they are of a persistent substance like stone they may play roles other than that of a work of art (fox's den, pilot's landmark), or revert to being mere stones. Your other Aran circle on the coast a mile or so further west actually functioned as a fairy circle once, I see from my diary . . .

. . . and I finished with a reminiscence of taking two children to visit the circle, and jumping into it hand-in-hand with them. Richard Long was clearly mollified by this, and his next letter was purely friendly, which is why I have not hesitated to pinpoint his *Connemara Sculpture* and raise the question of the role of his artefacts in their natural setting. The essence of his works is, according to his intentions, what he brings home to the art world: a photographic image in many cases, not primarily of value for its merits as landscape photography or as a record of a site-specific sculpture, but as the entry-point to a concept, the idea of a journey, the passage of a particular human being through certain places. But if the spirit of the work has flown off into the realms of thought, its bones, remaining in actuality for at least a time, have equally complex destinies. If identified, as I have identified a few of them in Aran, the Burren and Connemara, they may even be preserved as memorabilia, objects imbued by touch with the charisma of the artist, contemplation of which might reveal the stages of his or her self-creation as a creator. One might take them as markers of exemplary terrains in which the formative processes of Nature are particularly clearly displayed at work. Unidentified, their origins unknown to the passer-by, they are minor enigmas of the landscape. As they slowly founder in the interplay of the elements, their status as the product of an intention becomes as hard to be sure of as those of the nearly effaced potato ridges or the random clutches of glacial erratics. Eventually they will be anonymous contributions to the compilation of the Earth, like the soft bones of stillborn babies rotted into that knoll by the seashore, or the husks of uncountable forams heaped onto the tombolo. We find ourselves in a world compacted out of our forebears. In art we take responsibility for this fact, or at least recognize our ineluctable complicity in its processes. It is as if we choose that our parents have to die; it is our fault. In growing out of childhood we drive them on before us into middle age; in adding a birthday to our lives we burden them with another year; finally, one more day packed with hours and minutes for us is enough to push them over the edge. This is how we make room, make time, make the world, for ourselves. This is the gargoyle-logic of creation.[29]

John Moriarty

John Moriarty (1938–2007) grew up in Kerry and later attended University College Dublin, where he gained a double degree, in philosophy and English literature. Later, he taught literature at the University of Manitoba, Canada. As noted in his obituary in the *Guardian*, "he was uncomfortable as an academic and decided to return to his beloved Ireland and search for his biological, cultural and spiritual roots, seeking to develop a relationship with the earth and his fellow creatures."[30] Moriarty turned to gardening to mesh his philosophy with a love of the natural world, working with landscapes in both England and Ireland, in Connemara and County Galway. Moriarty also hosted the radio discussion program *The Blackbird and the Bell* for Raidió Teilifís Éireann (RTÉ) and lectured widely, using his extensive knowledge of mythology and religion to enliven his talks with entrancing storytelling. In 2002, he began to explore his vision of a Christian monastic "hedge school," Slí na Firinne, and bought land near Kilgarvan for the purpose of fostering the same union with nature as did the early Irish monks. His writing blends mythology, philosophy, and a love for the natural world, and he saw in the Irish landscape the same spiritual energy that inhabited the Irish Revivalists Yeats and Æ. He lived down from the Horse's Glen at the foot of Mangerton Mountain in north Kerry and died there in 2007. His publications include *Dreamtime* (1994, rev. 1999), *Turtle Was Gone a Long Time: Crossing the Kedron* (1996), *Horsehead Nebula Neighing* (1997), *Anaconda Canoe* (1999), *Nostos* (autobiography; 2001), *Invoking Ireland, Slí na Fírinne* (2006), *Night Journey to Buddh Gaia* (2006), and *One Evening in Eden* (2007)—a CD box set containing a collection of stories narrated by Moriarty. The following selection is from *Invoking Ireland*, in which the author invokes an Irish past, with its mythologies and rituals, and weaves it through philosophy into a modern twenty-first-century Ireland in need of a mirror to its past.

From Invoking Ireland

GENERAL INTRODUCTION

Q. Limiting yourself to a sentence or two, would you say what it is you are up to here?

A. The endeavour, such as it is, has its source in a question: how, working from within our tradition, might we reconstitute ourselves as a people?

Q. It hadn't occurred to me that we need to do any such thing.

A. The first story enacts a struggle between two peoples who have chosen two different ways of being in the world. The Fomorians have chosen to shape nature to suit them. Surrendering to it, the Tuatha De Danann have chosen to let nature shape them to suit it. Our way now is wholly Fomorian. It isn't working, or, rather, it has proved to be utterly disastrous; so it is that we go back out over nine waves and, wiser now we hope, we come back into an alternative experience of ourselves in a world alternatively experienced. It will make little sense to you until you have read their stories but I will say it anyway. In Fintan mac Bochra we experience ourselves alternatively in a world alternatively experienced. In Ollamh Fódhla we experience ourselves alternatively in a world alternatively experienced. And then, in one hand a beheading block and in the other an axe, a god called Cu Roi mac Daire erupts among us and all too soon we have learned that being a self of no matter what kind in a world of no matter what kind isn't the whole story. Life at the level of the subjective-objective divide, even when it is as blessed as it is in Magh Meall, isn't the final destination. All this, and more, we mean when we sing

Ailiu lath n-hErend.

In invoking Ireland we are seeking to evoke it. In invoking it we are seeking to call it into being. And how better to call it into being than to call it into an image or archetype of itself. That image or archetype I seek neither to name nor to define, but I do seek to suggest it in a safari of stories. In our journey inland we do have to reckon with cormorant and boar and bear and badger and wolf and fox and carrion crow and hawk and stag and goat and, out of our underworld, with spectral terrors catlike in form and ferocity, all of them instinctively in ourselves as well as actually in the land. Here, in this safari into the centre, we seek to deal with them not murderously but Orphically, living with them in a great Ecumene, in Irish called In Enflaith, in English called the Birdreign.

Q. So it isn't by accident that this adventure inland begins where and when it does, in lath nAnann at a time when two peoples are fighting for the soul of the country, one people seeking to turn it into a human convenience, the other finding fulfilment in being of one mind with the wind and the rain?

A. In the course of this battle, preoccupied as they were with it, the Tuatha De Danann took their eye off what is essential, and so it was that the Fomorians were able to steal their music, their very soul that is, that soul being the Orphic note that harmonized them to all things.

Q. So, in your sense of it, soul isn't a substance?

A. As I understand it here, no. Here, I think of it as a constituting disposition or attitude. Here, I think of it as a way of being oneself in a world.

Q. In that sense of soul, who or what are we now in Ireland?

A. We are Fomorians. Predominantly our collective eye is a Balar's eye, poisoned and poisoning, reducing everything in sight to commodity. And as is the collective eye so is the collective soul.

In an old account of the battle in one of Ireland's oldest books, *Cath Maige Tuiread*, is the following simple yet, in its meaning, immense sentence:

Tocauher a malae dia deirc Baloir.

Its lid was lifted off Balar's eye.

We are talking here not about its natural lid but about a multilayered, manufactured lid set in place to make sure that it didn't look at anything because anything it looked at it would destroy.

Sadly, histories of Ireland are silent about the event that has mostly driven all subsequent Irish history, the opening of what in old Irish is called the

Suil Mildagach.

Concentrated though it is in one bad eye, in Balar's bad eye, it is nonetheless the collective bad eye. It is also the bad tongue, the Nemtenga, imagined here in its likeness to a cormorant's tongue and, later, in its likeness to the muscle that opens and closes a crab's claw.

So there you have it,

The Suil Midagach

The Nemtenga

distinguishing us as Fomorians. It is what we have become.

Q. So, where Blake sees Urizen you see Balar?

A. Thinking of him as a collective condition, Balar is what the tradition sees.

Q. Is Balar as we find him in the Irish tradition in a way comparable to Medousa as we find her in the Greek tradition?

A. On initial inspection, there is one very obvious difference between them: whereas it is deadly to look at Medousa it is deadly to be looked at by Balar.

However, taking her myth where Greeks didn't take it, we can think of Medousa as the perra-flying principle in perception. Whatever she looks at she turns to stone, and in this she is not unlike Balar. In that we have reduced our originally stupendous planet to economic size, we are their all too successful offspring, inheriting their ecological deadliness in instinct, eye and mind.

Q. And the remedy, if there is one?

A. Silver-branch perception, the Orphic note and the path that Jesus pioneered.

Q. What of that path?

A. Well, the thought of Jesus crossing the Torrent has left the Upanishads gasping for breath. It has left all Buddhist Sutras gasping for breath. It has left the Tao Te Ching gasping for breath. It has left the Bible speechless.

Q. Silence therefore?

A. Our tradition doesn't only know of the Suil Mildagach and the Nemtenga. Sponsored by Manannan mac Lir at sea as well as by Christ on land, it knows of In Tenga Bithnua, the ever-new tongue:

As is the case with all other rivers, our river has its source in Connla's Well. And that is why we learn to speak. For us, to learn to speak is to learn to say:

Our river has its source in the Otherworld Well.

And anything we say about the hills and anything we say about the stars is a way of saying:

A hazel grows over the Otherworld Well our river has its source in.

Our time being so other than Otherworld time, it isn't often, in our time, that a hazelnut falls into Connla's Well, but when it does it is carried downstream and if, passing from current to current, it is brought to your feet and you eat it, then though in no way altered, sight in you will be pure wonder. Then, seeing ordinary things in the ordinary way you had always seen them, sight in you will be more visionary than vision . . .

Q. Are you implying that such sight isn't native to us?

A. No, I am not. As Bran mac Feabhail who set out in quest of it discovered, the Otherworld is a way of perceiving this world. Quite simply, the Otherworld is silver-branch perception, and this fits in with the persistent claim that ours is a land of three immaculate dimensions, Banbha, Fodhla and Eire. And be sure of this: however ravaged and spoiled and polluted it might be by our Fomorian abuse of it, Eire in itself is still immaculate. And this isn't only true of Ireland. It is true of no matter what country. It is true of the world at large. The Bhagavad Gita, the Song of God that Manannan, god of the sea, sang to us at sea—that he could as easily sing to us in New York or in Tokyo, because reality there is as immaculate as it is here this morning in the mountains of Kerry. Banbha, Fodhla and Eire are immaculate dimensions of New York as much as they are immaculate dimensions of the furze-yellow world between me and Torc Mountain, silver-branch perception is as possible in the Ruhr Valley as it is here. There too, the corn is orient and immortal wheat.

Time, meeting Banbha on Slieve Mish, to shake their apprehensive hawk talons out of our hands.

Time, meeting Fodhla on Cnoc Grene, to shake their apprehensive hawk talons out of our eyes.

Time, meeting Eire on Uisnech, to shake their apprehensive hawk talons out of our minds.

Q. No small matter in that case to come ashore into Ireland, no small matter to settle in Ireland?

A. We have come ashore into Ireland and we have settled here when we know that any well we dip our buckets into is Connla's Well.

Q. But who is Connla?

A. If you do not know him from within yourself as yourself, then you will never know him at all.

Q. And Ireland? Again I ask, what of Ireland?

A. My hope is that it is still a dangerous place.

Q. Meaning what?

A. My hope is that the Owenmore River, and rivers like it, and that Torc Mountain, and mountains like it, can still subvert us back into sanity.

Q. And the stories you tell?

A. Better imagined and better told than they are here, they could be forms of our sensibility and categories of our understanding.

Better imagined and better told than they are here, they could be an alternative to Balar's evil eye, to the national nemtenga.

Better imagined and better told than they are here, they could be In Tenga Bithnua.

Better imagined and better told than they are here, they could be a way of saying

Ailiu lath n-hErend.

Q. But if to reach and settle in Ireland we have to come in not over but through nine waves, each wave a yet deeper initiation into yet deeper wonder. And if, having come through all that, we must continue into and through a swordless safari of stories, each story a challenge to further integration not just of instinct but of insight, if we must be thrown on the bonefire of all our incarnations past and to come, and if, not there yet, we must now respond to the invitations extended to us by Danu, Manannan, Cu Roi and Christ, then who will make it?

A. We are talking about realizing our highest human possibilities, and what is wrong with that? What is wrong about emerging into a sense of wonder? What is wrong about the integration of deepest instinct and highest insight? What is wrong about silver-branch perception? What is wrong about the road of ashes? What is wrong about metanoesis? What is wrong about a graduation from anthropus to deinan-thropus? What is wrong about a mystical ascent between the Paps of Danu? What is wrong about the gap between those divine breasts being the ultimate gap into Ultimate Ireland? If the alternative is a republic such as we have now, what is so wrong about an Enflaith? What is so wrong about the democracy of royalty in Tara? What is so wrong about the royalty of everyone? Not institutional royalty or royalty by coronation, but royalty that Conaire and Cormac emerged into, royalty of nature.

Oldest democracy, newest democracy, truest democracy, surest democracy, is the democracy of the Road of Initiations. From the moment the Paschal Candle is set up by my cradle to the moment it is set up by my coffin, the Christian road is a road of initiations. In the sense that everyone is welcome onto it, it is the most democratic of roads, but how vastly foolish we would be were we to set out upon it if waving a bill of human rights. Seek to inscribe no such bill on the Paschal Candle. Seek to hang no such bill from the solstice sunspear.

FROM TAILTIU REVISITED

I have discovered for myself that the old human and animal life, indeed the entire prehistory and past of all sentient being, works on, loves on, hates on, thinks on, in me.

When it comes down to it, Amhairghin Glungheal, the poet who was prow to the Celtic invasion of Ireland, is claiming nothing particularly more than our common phylogenetic inheritance. The difference between him and Nietzsche is that while he parades it Nietzsche is perturbed by it. Given what it is we are talking about, surely the perturbation is safer than the parade.

We are after all talking about something as serious as our emergence into Ireland. So the question is: with what vision of ourselves and our world do we sail up Kenmare Bay? With what vision of ourselves and our world do we set foot on that single shore?

What is clear is this: now in our day we need someone who has the gifts and the ability and the willingness to be Amhairghin Glungheal to a new emergence, to a new anodos, into Ireland; we need someone who, having gone back out over nine waves, re-emerges singing the new song among us.

The truth is this: those nine waves that surround Ireland and its islands are nine initiations into nine wholly unexpected dimensions of reality. To properly come ashore into Ireland therefore we need to sail, not over them, but into them and through them. Taking them at face value, the Celts sailed in over them. Hence the sadness of their subsequent history here.

True of Celts, true of Christians, true of Vikings, true of Anglo-Normans.

True of the English who came.

In over the waves they all came.

Also, who now walks out of the common dimension of Ireland called Eire and sets up house by a river in Fodhla, its more mystical dimension? Since when has a great teacher and legislator come back among us out of Fodhla? Since when, passing him on the road, have we said, that is him, among us in our day he is

Ollamh Fodhla

Ireland without an Amghairghin, a poet who with his song opens a way into Ireland for us.

Ireland without an Ollamh Fodhla, a sage who comes back speaking Upanishads among us.

Having failed to come poetically ashore into Ireland the Celt has failed in Ireland.

Biodh bron ort a Roisin

And yet, a doubt remains. And so, having recourse to a possibly creative misreading, can we not think that, in singing his Song of Himself, Amhairgin is as it were carving a totem pole of who we elementally and phylogenetically are, indeed of who we microcosmically are, right there before our eyes?

Singing it with him we are carving it with him:

Am gaeth i mmuir
Am tond trethan
Am fuaim mara
Am dam secht ndrenn . . .

Ireland's first totem pole set up where it was first sung, and where it has now been carved, at the head of Kenmare Bay.

Catching sight of it as we come in from the sea, it puts it to us that to come ashore into Ireland is to come ashore into ourselves.

Reaching Uisnech, what better can we do than to give the benefit of the doubt, if not yet to the singer, then to the song, and this we can do by proclaiming a constitution that acknowledges the One in the Many, that the philosophical justification for enfranchising all things, equally, a bush having equal rights with a bear, a calf or a dropped fawn having equal rights with a child.

Soon in Ireland

The Birdreign

Ailiu lath n-hErend.

OLLAMH FODHLA

As is the case with all other rivers, our river has its source in Connla's Well. And that is why we learn to speak. For us, to learn to speak is to learn to say:

Our river has its source in the Otherworld Well.

And anything we say about the hills and anything we say about the stars is a way of saying:

A hazel grows over the Otherworld Well our river has its source in.

Our time being so other than Otherworld time, it isn't often, in our time, that a hazelnut falls into Connla's Well, but when it does it is carried downstream and if, passing from current to current, it is brought to your feet and you eat it, then though in no way altered, sight in you will be pure wonder. Then, seeing ordinary things in the ordinary way you had always seen them, sight in you will be more visionary than vision.

To know, and to continue to know, that any well we dip our buckets into is Connla's Well is why we are a people.

We are a river people.
Exile for us is to live in a house that isn't river-mirrored.
Our river isn't only a river. It is also the moon-white cow who will sometimes walk
    towards us, but not all the way towards us, on one or another of its banks.
The river and the cow we call by the same name. We call them Boann.

Boann, the moon-white cow.
Boann, the gleaming river.
In dreams I know it as cow.
Awake I know it as river.

And my house isn't only river-mirrored. It is mirrored in Linn Feic, its most sacred pool. And this is so because, by difficult and resisted destiny, I am ollamh to my people. They call me Ollamh Fodhla. In their view of me, Boann, the gleaming river, has carried a hazelnut to my feet.

As these things often do, it began in sleep, in dreams in the night: standing in my door I'd be tempted to think he was only a short morning's walk away, and yet it would often be nightfall before I'd at last turn back, not having made it. A sense I had is that the man I was seeking to reach was myself as I one day would be. In the most frightening of all the dreams I dreamed at that time a man who had no face came towards me and said, "You are worlds away from him." When he next came towards me he had a face and he said, "You are as far away from him as waking is from dreaming." In the end it was my own voice, more anguished than angry, that I heard: it isn't distance, measurable in hours or days of walking, that separates you from what you would be. It is states of mind, yours more than his.

Defeated, I settled back into my old ways. At this time of year that meant that one morning I'd pull my door shut behind me and drive my cattle to the high grazing ground between the Paps of Morrigu.

My father who quoted his father had always assured me that there was no sacrilege in this. According to the oldest ancestor we had hearsay of, it was in no sense a right that we claimed. Fearfully, it was a seasonal rite we were called upon to undergo. This I took on trust, allowing that there was something more than good husbandry at stake.

Up here, summer after summer since I was a boy, we shook off the vexations and
    the weariness of winter enclosure.
Up here the gods were not fenced in.
Up here, when we heard him neighing, we knew that the horse god couldn't be cut
    down to cult size, couldn't be made to serve religious need.

Up here there is a rock. It so challenges our sane sense of things that I long ago
capitulated to the embarrassment of crediting what my father and his father
before him used to say about it, that every seven years, at Samhain, it turns into
an old woman driving a cow.

Sensing my difficulties, my father was blunt: if in the eyes of the world you
aren't embarrassed by your beliefs about the world then you may conclude that the
wonder-eye that is in all of us hasn't yet opened in you.

That's how it was with me in those days. No sooner had I learned the world and
learned my way in it than, standing in front of a rock or a tree, I'd have to unlearn it.
I'd hear a story and think that's it, that's how the world is, that story will house me,
but then there she'd be, the old woman driving her cow in through my front door
and out through my back door, leaving me homeless yet again.

And it wasn't just anywhere I was homeless. I was homeless on the high grazing
ground between the Paps of Morrigu, and it wasn't by hearsay that, however red-
mouthed she was, Morrigu vas divine, all the more divine in my eyes because, like
the horse god who neighed only at night, she would never submit to religious servility. Though a people prayed to her she wouldn't send rain in a time of drought or
stand in battle with them against an invader.

Worship of Morrigu, of red-mouthed Morrigu, had to be pure.

And that's what I did up here.

Up here every summer I lived between the breasts of a goddess who, in her form
as skald crow, called above me every day, circled and called, searching for after-
births, searching for corpses, searching for carrion.

The contradiction ploughed me. It ploughed me and harrowed me. 'Twas as if the
breasts of the Mother Goddess had become the Paps of the Battle Goddess. And to
live between the Paps was to live in trepidation of the divine embrace.

Sometimes bearing her call as a skald crow calls I would hear a demand: you must
be religious but in being religious you must have no recourse to religion. So that is
it, I thought. That is the seasonal rite. To be religious here is to fast from religion.

These were heights I wasn't continuously able for. Always by summer's end
I'd have lost my nerve, and now again I would pull a door shut behind me and I
would go down, me and my cattle, my cattle going down to the shelter of the woods
and swards along the river, and I going down to the shelter of traditional religion
and story.

Here, as well as being a moon-white cow, the goddess is Boann, the gleaming
river.

Down here, we are river-mirrored. And since it is the same sacred river that mirrors us, we are a people.

My house is mirrored in Linn Feic.

In a sense therefore I sleep in Linn Feic, I dream in Linn Feic.

At a sleeping depth of me that I'm not aware of, maybe I am a salmon in Linn
Feic, and maybe I swim upstream every night, all the way up into the Otherworld,
all the way up into Connla's Well. At that depth of myself, maybe the shadows of the
Otherworld hazel are always upon me. Are always upon all of us, letting wisdom
and wonder drop down into us.

Could it be that we are safer in our depths than we are in our heights? Or could it be that we will only be safe in our heights when we already know that we are safe in our depths?

This time the old woman didn't drive her cow through the conclusion I came to. This time, bringing a six years' solitude in the Loughcrew Hills to a sudden end, it was like a stroke, it was like waking up from waking. During an endless instant, all heights and depths had disappeared, leaving only a void, or what seemed like a void.

Twenty-six years later, sitting in my house by Linn Feic, I was able to say, it is in Divine Ground behind all depths and heights that we are safe.

That summer, sitting in my reconstructed hut between the Paps, I was able to say, it is from Divine Ground behind and within them that we become able for our depths and heights.

Coming down, at a turn on the path where I was only a short morning's walk away from them, I felt I was able for the sense that people had of me. I felt I was able to be their ollamh. Opening my door, knowing that I was mirrored by the sacred river, I felt that in that depth of me that is overarched by the Otherworld hazel I had consented to be Ollamh Fodhla.

FINTAN MAC BOCHRA

The geography of my mind is the geography of the world I walk in. In the geography of my mind and, therefore, also in the geography of the world I walk in, are Sidh ar Feimhin, Linn Feic, Da Chich na Morrigna and Connla's Well. And if you ask me about life, about what we haven't eyes for in this life, I will talk to you about Da Chich na Morrigna and the paths to Sidh ar Feimbin. And the stars, if you ask me about the stars I will tell you that only they who have seen them mirrored in that divine deep within themselves can call themselves astronomers. And Connla's Well, at Connla's Otherworld Well it was I first realized that being human is a habit. It can be broken. Like the habit of going down to the river by this path rather than that, I broke it. And so it is that, although I always know who I am, I can never be sure that what I am going to sleep at night is what I will be when I wake in the morning. In me the shape-shifts of sleep survive into waking. What I'm saying is, my shape depends on my mood. In one mood, as you can see, I'm an old man, old in the way weather-lore is old, old in the way old stories are old. In another mood I'm a salmon in Lough Derg. In a mood that lasted from the coming of Partholon to the coming of the Milesians I was a hawk in Achill.

Yes, that's how it is. You only need to break the habit once, the habit of being human I mean, and then you will be as you were between death and rebirth. Between death and rebirth our bodies are mind-bodies, and that means they are alterable. Alterable at will. We only have to will it and it happens, we flow from being a swan in Lough Owel into being a hind on Slieve Bloom into being a hare on Beara.

If for some reason he crosses into our world, the hare will have one red ear.

That's how it is.

What's possible for all of us there is possible for some of us here.

Mostly, though, we've forgotten all this, but folktales remember. Folktales aren't afraid. On its way to the well at the world's end, a folktale will stop by a rock and tell you that every seventh year, at Samhain, it turns into an old woman driving a cow.

On its way to Linn Feic, a folktale will sit with you under a bush and, where a bard might tell you the history of your people awake, that bush will tell you the much more serious history of your people asleep.

And the folktale knows what so many people no longer know. It knows how to walk the path to Connla's Well. On the way to Connla's Well we come to see that the world's habit of being more worldly is not in the world, it is in our eyes.

As the folktale sees I see.
As the folktale lives I live.
And the path to my door, that too is folktale.

Coming here, you either undergo what people undergo in a folktale or you'll never lift my latch.

Little wonder I so rarely hear my latch being lifted.
Little wonder I so rarely hear my latch being lifted.
Little wonder I so rarely hear my latch being lifted.[31]

NOTES TO PART V

1. Glen A. Love, "Revaluing Nature: Toward an Ecological Criticism," in *The Ecocriticism Reader: Landmarks in Literary Ecology*, ed. Cheryll Glotfelty and Harold Fromm (Athens: University of Georgia Press, 1996), 236.
2. David McWilliams, *The Pope's Children: Ireland's New Elite* (Dublin: Gill and Macmillan, 2005), 71.
3. Patrick Kavanagh, *The Great Hunger*, in *The Complete Poems* (Kildare, Ireland: Goldsmith, 1972), 79–104.
4. McWilliams, *Pope's Children*, 212.
5. Æ, *The Living Torch*, ed. Monk Gibbon (London: Macmillan, 1937).
6. Scott Slovic, "Nature Writing and Environmental Psychology: The Interiority of Outdoor Experiences," in Glotfelty and Fromm, *Ecocriticism Reader*, 367, 353.
7. John Tyndall, *Address Delivered before the British Association Assembled at Belfast, with Additions* (London: Longmans, Green, 1874), 61, http://www.victorianweb.org/science/science_texts/belfast.html.
8. Ruth Barton, "John Tyndall, Pantheist: A Rereading of the Belfast Address," *Osiris*, 2nd ser., 3 (1987): 112, citing Anna Therese Cosslett, "Science and Value: The Writings of John Tyndall," in *John Tyndall, Essays on a Natural Philosopher*, ed. W. H. Brock, N. D. McMillan, and R. C. Mollan (Dublin: Royal Dublin Society, 1981), 184.
9. Slovic, "Nature Writing," 353.
10. Seán Lysaght, interview by the author, Castlebar, Ireland, January 9, 2008.
11. Robert Lloyd Praeger, *The Way That I Went: An Irishman in Ireland* (Dublin: A. Figgus, 1980), 1.
12. Ibid., 2.
13. Ibid., 385.
14. Ibid., 199.
15. Ibid., 161.
16. Ibid., 160.
17. Michael Viney and Ethna Viney, *Ireland's Ocean: A Natural History* (Cork, Ireland: Cork Collins, 2008).
18. Folding Landscapes, home page, accessed March 15, 2018, http://www.foldinglandscapes.com.
19. Slovic, "Nature Writing," 368.
20. See "John Tyndall," in *Britannica Academic*, accessed March 15, 2018, https://academic-eb-com.proxy.library.vcu.edu/levels/collegiate/article/John-Tyndall/73992.

21. Tyndall, *Address Delivered before the British Association*, 1–64.

22. See "Robert Lloyd Praeger," in *The Oxford Companion to Irish Literature*, ed. Robert Welch (Oxford, UK: Clarendon, 1996), 481.

23. Dora Sigerson Shorter, "Ireland," in *The Collected Poems of Dora Sigerson Shorter* (London: Hodder Stoughton, 1907), 130.

24. William Makepeace Thackeray, *The Book of Snobs*, in *The Works of William Makepeace Thackeray* (Boston: James R. Osgood, 1872), 7.

25. Praeger, *Way That I Went*, 1–7, 211–18.

26. See "Michael Viney's Ireland: 50 Years a Blow-In," *Irish Times*, March 19, 2016, https://www.irishtimes.com/life-and-style/people/michael-viney-s-ireland-50-years-a-blow-in-1.2578762.

27. Michael Viney, *A Year's Turning* (Belfast: Blackstaff, 1996), 1–3, 99–117, 166–67.

28. Michael Viney, "From Swerve of Shore to Bend of Bay: The Warming Globe Is Eroding Ireland's Coast," Another Life, *Irish Times*, November 30, 2013, https://www.irishtimes.com/news/environment/another-life-from-swerve-of-shore-to-bend-of-bay-1.1612113.

29. Tim Robinson, *Connemara: Listening to the Wind* (Dublin: Penguin Ireland, 2006), 1–4, 93–116.

30. Peter Clare, obituary of John Moriarty, *Guardian*, 30 August 2007, https://www.theguardian.com/news/2007/aug/30/guardianobituaries.booksobituaries1.

31. John Moriarty, *Invoking Ireland: Ailiu Iath n-hErend* (Dublin: Lilliput Press, 2007), 7–13, 37–45.

Appendix

Environmental Organizations in Ireland

Appropriate Roads Group, http://www.theapplefarm.com/n24.htm. This group is dedicated to the overturning of a decision to build a dual carriageway between Cahir and Clonmel.

Crann, http://www.mde.ie/crann. Crann is an organization that works with trees, including the afforestation of Ireland with broadleaf trees. The website describes basics of the organization and work, including a tree-sponsorship scheme and how to join.

ECO-UNESCO's Young Environmentalist Awards (YEA). This program is an all-Ireland environmental awards program for young people. The awards honor the work of young people between the ages of twelve and eighteen who protect, conserve, and enhance the Irish environment through local environmental projects.

Environment and Heritage Service. This service is a Northern Ireland Executive conservation agency within the Department of the Environment that aims to promote and conserve both the natural environment and the built environment and to promote their appreciation by present and future generations.

Environmental Protection Agency, http://www.epa.ie/. The EPA is Ireland's statutory body for the balanced and sustainable protection and management of the environment. The website includes organization history, educational and technical material, notes on licensing, and interactive water-quality maps.

Friends of the Earth Northern Ireland. This organization campaigns for environmental justice and inspires people to take action to improve their lives.

Friends of the Irish Environment, http://www.friendsoftheirishenvironment.net/. This is a network of environmentally concerned groups and individuals that offers detailed news, campaign information, and archives on its work in Ireland.

GRIAN, Greenhouse Ireland Action Network, http://homepage.eircom.net/~grian/. This climate-change-awareness and solutions-promoting network offers news, details of its work, suggestions on how to help, press releases, and a newsletter.

Irish Cooperative Society Organisation, http://www.icos.ie/home/index.asp. This organization seeks, according to its mission statement, "to provide leadership for the co-operative movement and to promote, develop, co-ordinate, and represent agri-business and rural related co-operatives in the interests of their user members."

Irish Environmental Forum. This forum includes more than twenty different groups from around the country.

Irish Peatland Conservation Council, http://www.ipcc.ie/. This is one of Ireland's leading environmental campaigning groups, offering information on bogs, press releases, fund-raising, education, and contacts.

Irish Seedsavers Association, http://www.irishseedsavers.ie/. This conservation organization is dedicated to the preservation of Ireland's special and disappearing
varieties of fruit, grains, and vegetable. The website provides background information, details of projects, membership and sponsorship notes, events, and contact information.

Just Forests, http://www.iol.ie/~woodlife. This volunteer group, concerned with sustainable development and global deforestation, is involved with the Forest Stew-
ardship Council and fosters campaigns and exhibitions and provides listings of
timber suppliers and links.

Native Woodland Trust, http://www.nativewoodtrust.ie/. This group, which aims to
protect remaining native woodlands, provides details about itself and its various
campaigns, news, and articles on its website.

Tree Council of Ireland, http://www.treecouncil.ie/. This group works with organizations concerned with trees in Ireland, providing details of its work, members
and publications, and contact information.

Wildwatch (The Irish Wildlife Trust), http://www.iwt.ie. Formerly the Irish Wildlife
Federation, this is a leading nongovernmental conservation and environmental
education and campaigning group. The website offers information on its structure, positions, joining up, and affiliated bodies.

Zero Waste Alliance Ireland, http://www.zerowastealliance.ie/. The website includes
an outline of the alliance's purpose, activity summaries, press releases, and news
on current environmental issues.

Acknowledgments

A special thank-you to Maureen O'Connor, University College Cork, for her advice and work with permissions.

Also a thank-you to Adam Zimmerle, the librarian at Virginia Union University, for his help converting hard copies of books to Word files.

⚘

Eavan Boland, "The Lost Land" and "Escape," from *The Lost Land* (1998); "Mountain Time" and "The River" from *Outside History* (1990); "This Moment" and "A Sparrow Hawk in the Suburbs" from *In a Time of Violence* (1994); and "Ode to Suburbia" in *An Origin like Water* (1996), reprinted with permission from Carcanet Press Limited.

Moya Cannon, "Bees under Snow," "Eavesdropping," "Two Ivory Swans," "Winter View from Binn Bhriocáin," "Primavera," "The Tube-Case Makers," "Crannog," and "Hazelnuts," reprinted by kind permission of the author.

Desmond Egan, "The Great Blasket," "Sunday Evening," "Meadowsweet," "Snow Snow Snow Snow," "A Pigeon Dead," and "Envoi," from *Elegies* (1996), reprinted by kind permission of the author and The Goldsmith Press Ltd. Dublin, Ireland.

Seamus Heaney, "Death of a Naturalist" from *Death of a Naturalist* (2006); "The Salmon Fisher to the Salmon" from *Door into the Dark* (1969); "Limbo" from *Wintering Out* (2002); "St Kevin and the Blackbird" from *The Spirit Level* (2014), reprinted by permission of Faber & Faber Ltd., London, and Farrar, Straus and Giroux for U.S. rights.

Michael Longley, "The Osprey," "Badger," "Robin," "Out of the Sea," and "Carrigskeewaun," reprinted from *Collected Poems* (2006) with permission from Jonathan Cape Poetry.

Louis MacNeice, "The Sunlight in the Garden" and "Wolves" from *Selected Poems* (1988); and "Tree Party" from *The Burning Perch* (1963), reprinted with permission from Faber & Faber Ltd., London.

Derek Mahon, "The Seasons," "Achill," "Aphrodite's Pool," "The Mayo Tao," "Penshurst Place," "The Woods," "The Dream Play," and "Leaves," reprinted from *New Collected Poems* (2011) by kind permission of the author and the Gallery Press.

John Montague, "All Legendary Obstacles," "The Wild Dog Rose," and "The Trout," reprinted from *Collected Poems* (1995) with permission from Wake Forest University Press.

John Moriarty, from *Invoking Ireland* (2007), reprinted with permission from The Lilliput Press, Dublin.

Robert Lloyd Praeger, from *The Way That I Went* (1937), reprinted with permission from Collins Press.

Tim Robinson, preface and "The Boneyard" from *Connemara: Listening to the Wind* (2008), reprinted with permission from Penguin Random House UK.

Bibliography

Æ (George William Russell). *The Candle of Vision*. London: Macmillan, 1918. http://www.archive.org/stream/candleofvisionooae18/candleofvisionooae18_djvu.txt.

——. *Collected Poems by A.E.* London: Macmillan, 1913. http://www.bartleby.com/br/253.html.

——. "Connla's Well." In *Irish Literature*, vol. 8, edited by Justin McCarthy, 3001. Philadelphia: J. D. Morris, 1904.

——. *The Living Torch*. Edited by Monk Gibbon. [London]: Macmillan, 1937.

Allen, Paula Gunn. "The Sacred Hoop: A Contemporary Perspective." In *The Ecocriticism Reader: Landmarks in Literary Ecology*, edited by Cheryll Glotfelty and Harold Fromm, 241–63. Athens: University of Georgia Press, 1996.

Allingham, William. *The Music Master: A Love Story and Two Series of Day and Night Songs*. With contributions by Arthur Hughes, D. G. Rossetti, and John E. Millais. London: Routledge, 1855.

——. *Rhymes for Young Folk*. London: Cassell, 1887. Project Gutenberg, 2017. http://www.gutenberg.org/files/46702/46702-h/46702-h.htm.

——. *Selected Poems from the Works of William Allingham*. Edited by Helen Paterson Allingham. London: Macmillan, 1912. https://babel.hathitrust.org/cgi/pt?id=njp.32101067627305.

——. *Sixteen Poems by William Allingham: Selected by William Butler Yeats*. Dundrum, Ireland: Dun Emer, 1905. Project Gutenberg, 2005. http://www.gutenberg.org/files/16839/16839.txt.

——. *William Allingham: A Diary*. Edited by Helen Paterson Allingham and Dollie Radford. London: Macmillan, 1907.

Amergin. *The Mystery*. Translated by Douglas Hyde. In *Voices and Poetry of Ireland*, 3. London: HarperCollins, 2003.

Barton, Ruth. "John Tyndall, Pantheist: A Rereading of the Belfast Address." *Osiris*, 2nd ser., 3 (1987): 111–34.

Boland, Eavan. *The Lost Land*. New York: Norton, 1998.

——. *New Collected Poems*. London: Carcanet, 2005.

——. "The River." *New Yorker*, November 14, 1988, 120. Reprinted in *New Collected Poems*. London: Carcanet, 2005.

Boland, Eavan, Paula Meehan, and Mary O'Malley. *Three Irish Poets: An Anthology*. Dublin: Carcanet, 2003.

Brearton, Fran, and Alan Gillis, eds. *The Oxford Handbook of Modern Irish Poetry*. Oxford: Oxford University Press, 2012.

Buile Suibhne. ca. 1100. Edited by J. G. O'Keeffe. Dublin: Dublin Institute for Advanced Studies, 1931. Compiled by Beatrix Färber, proof corrections by Vibeke Dijkman and Maxim Fomin. CELT: Corpus of Electronic Texts. Cork: University College Cork, 2001, 2008, 2013. http://www.ucc.ie/celt/published/G302018/index.html.

Campbell, Sueellen. "The Land and Language of Desire: Where Deep Ecology and Post-Structuralism Meet." In *The Ecocriticism Reader: Landmarks in Literary Ecology*, edited by Cheryll Glotfelty and Harold Fromm, 124–36. Athens: University of Georgia Press, 1996.

Cannon, Moya. *Hands*. Manchester, UK: Carcanet, 2011.

——. *Keats Lives*. Manchester, UK: Carcanet, 2015.

——. *The Parchment Boat*. Dublin: Gallery Books, 1998.

Carleton, William. *The Black Prophet: A Tale of Irish Famine*. In *Traits and Stories of the Irish Peasantry*, vol. 3 of *The Works of William Carleton*. New York: P. F. Collier, 1881. Project Gutenberg. 2004. http://www.gutenberg.org/files/16018/16018-h/16018-h.htm.

Colum, Padraic. "The Crane." In *The Collected Poems of Padraic Colum*, 166. New York: Devin-Adair, 1916.

——. "Dublin Roads." In *The Collected Poems of Padraic Colum*, 50. New York: Devin-Adair, 1916.

——. *Wild Earth and Other Poems*. New York: Henry Holt, 1916. https://archive.org/details/wildearthandothoicolugoog.

Connolly, S. J., ed. *The Oxford Companion to Irish History*, 2nd ed. Oxford: Oxford University Press, 2002.

Cromwell, Oliver. *Oliver Cromwell's Letters and Speeches: Including Supplements to the First Edition*. Contributions by Thomas Carlyle. 2 vols. New York: Harper and Brothers, 1860.

Davies, John. *A Discovery of the True Causes Why Ireland Was Never Entirely Subdued and Brought under Obedience of the Crown of England until the Beginning of His Majesty's Happy Reign* (1612). Edited by James P. Myers Jr. Washington, DC: Catholic University of America Press, 1989.

Deane, Seamus, ed. *The Field Day Anthology of Irish Writing*. 3 vols. Cork: Cork University, 2002.

"Deer's Cry or St. Patrick's Breastplate." In *A Taste of Ireland's Poets*, Servants of the Word, accessed October 8, 2017, http://dailyscripture.servantsoftheword.org/ireland/early7.htm.

Droste-Hulshoff, Annette von. *Die achzende Kreatur*. Translated by Ursula Prideaux. Lincoln: University of Nebraska Press, 1965.

Drummond, William Hamilton. *The Giants' Causeway: A Poem*. Belfast: Joseph Smyth for Longman et al., 1811. http://babel.hathitrust.org/cgi/pt?id=loc.ark:/13960/t6ww8rk3p;view=1up;seq=11.

Eagleton, Terry. *Heathcliff and the Great Hunger: Studies in Irish Culture*. London: Verso, 1995.

Egan, Desmond. *Elegies: Selected Poems, 1972–96*. Newbridge, Ireland: Goldsmith, 1996.

Encyclopaedia of Ireland. Dublin: Allen Figgis, 1968.

Feehan, John. "The Heritage of the Rocks." In *Nature in Ireland: A Scientific and Cultural History*, edited by John Wilson Foster and Helena C. G. Cheney, 3–22. Dublin: Lilliput, 1997.

———. "Threat and Conservation: Attitudes to Nature in Ireland." In *Nature in Ireland: A Scientific and Cultural History*, edited by John Wilson Foster and Helena C. G. Cheney, 573–96. Dublin: Lilliput, 1997.

Flower, Robin, trans. *Poems and Translations*. London: Constable, 1931. Reprint, Dublin: Lilliput, 1994.

Foster, John Wilson, and Helena C. G. Cheney, eds. *Nature in Ireland: A Scientific and Cultural History*. Dublin: Lilliput, 1997.

Frawley, Oona. *Irish Pastoral: Nostalgia in Twentieth-Century Irish Literature*. Dublin: Irish Academic Press, 2005.

Frazer, James G. *The Golden Bough: The Roots of Religion and Folklore*. New York: Gramercy Books, 1993.

Gainsford, Thomas. *A Description of Ireland: A.D. 1618*. *The Other Clare* 36 (2012): 33–37. Modernized by Luke McInerney. CELT: Corpus of Electronic Texts. Cork: University College Cork, 2013. http://www.ucc.ie/celt/published/E610006.html.

Glotfelty, Cheryll. "Introduction: Literary Studies in an Age of Environmental Crisis." In *The Ecocriticism Reader: Landmarks in Literary Ecology*, edited by Cheryll Glotfelty and Harold Fromm, xv–xxxvii. Athens: University of Georgia Press, 1996.

Gore-Booth, Eva. *Poems of Eva Gore-Booth*. London: Longmans, Green, 1929.

———. *The Poetry Foundation, 1870–1926*. Chicago: Poetry Foundation, 2017. http://www.poetryfoundation.org/bio/eva-gore-booth.

Green, Miranda J. *The World of the Druids*. London: Thames and Hudson, 1997.

Haggerty, Bridget. "St. Columcille of Iona." Irish Culture and Customs. Accessed February 3, 2019. http://www.irishcultureandcustoms.com/ASaints/Columcille.html.

Harrison, Robert Pogue. *Forests: The Shadow of Civilization*. Chicago: University of Chicago Press, 1992.

Heaney, Seamus. *Death of a Naturalist*. London: Faber and Faber, 1966.

———. *Selected Poems 1966–1987*. New York: Noonday, 1990.

———. *The Spirit Level: Poems*. Dublin: Farrar, Straus and Giroux, 1996. Reprint, 2014.

———. *Station Island*. Dublin: Farrar, Straus and Giroux, 2014.

———, trans. *Sweeney Astray*. London: Faber and Faber, 1983.

Howarth, William. "Some Principles of Ecocriticism." In *The Ecocriticism Reader: Landmarks in Literary Ecology*, edited by Cheryll Glotfelty and Harold Fromm, 69–91. Athens: University of Georgia Press, 1996.

"Ireland's Lost Glory." *Birds and All Nature* 7, no. 4 (April 1900). Reprint, edited by C. C. Marble, 188. Chicago: A. W. Mumford, 1900. https://books.google.com/books?id=PpYhHI3CTicC&pg=PA188.

"James Clarence Mangan." In *The Oxford Companion to Irish Literature*, edited by Robert Welch, 355. Oxford, UK: Clarendon, 1996.

Kavanagh, Patrick. *Collected Poems*. New York: Devin-Adair, 1964.

———. *Patrick Kavanagh: The Complete Poems*. Kildare, Ireland: Goldsmith, 1972.

Lawless, Emily. *Hurrish: A Study*. Edinburgh and London: William Blackwood and Sons, 1886. https://archive.org/details/hurrishastudyo1lawlgoog.

Longley, Michael. *Collected Poems*. London: Cape Poetry, 2006.

———. *Poems by Michael Longley*. Belfast Group Poetry/Networks. Accessed March 16, 2018, https://belfastgroup.digitalscholarship.emory.edu/groupsheets/longley1_10282/.

———. *Snow Water*. Winston-Salem, NC: Wake Forest University Press, 2004.

Love, Glen A. "Revaluing Nature: Toward an Ecological Criticism." In *The Ecocriticism Reader: Landmarks in Literary Ecology*, edited by Cheryll Glotfelty and Harold Fromm, 225–40. Athens: University of Georgia Press, 1996.

Lowe, Brendan. Review of *Keats Lives*, by Moya Cannon. *Dublin Review of Books*, 2015. http://poems.com/special_features/prose/essay_lowe_cannon.php.

Lynas, Mark, with Iva Pocock. "The Concrete Isle." *Guardian* (London), Guardian Weekend, final ed., December 4, 2004, 16.

Lysaght, Seán. *The Clare Island Survey*. Dublin: Gallery Books, 1991.

———. *The Mouth of a River*. Dublin: Gallery Books, 2007.

———. Personal interview with author, Castlebar, Ireland, January 9, 2008.

———. *Robert Lloyd Praeger: The Life of a Naturalist*. Dublin: Four Courts, 1998.

MacNeice, Louis. *Selected Poems*. Edited by Michael Longley. Dublin: Faber and Faber, 2015.

Mahon, Derek. *Collected Poems*. Loughcrew, Ireland: Gallery, 2000.

Maignant, Catherine. "Rural Ireland in the Nineteenth Century and the Advent of the Modern World." In *Rural Ireland, Real Ireland?*, edited by Jacqueline Genet, 21–30. Gerrards Cross, UK: Smythe, 1996.

Mangan, James Clarence. *James Clarence Mangan: His Selected Poems*. Boston: Lamson, Wolffe, 1897. https://archive.org/stream/jamesclarenceman1897mang/jamesclarenceman1897mang_djvu.txt.

McWilliams, David. *The Pope's Children: Ireland's New Elite*. Dublin: Gill and Macmillan, 2005.

Meyer, Kuno. Introduction to *Selections from Ancient Irish Poetry*, translated by Kuno Meyer, vii–xiv. London: Constable, 1911. Project Gutenberg, 2010. http://www.gutenberg.org/files/32030/32030-h/32030-h.htm.

———, trans. *Selections from Ancient Irish Poetry*. London: Constable, 1911. Project Gutenberg, 2010. http://www.gutenberg.org/files/32030/32030-h/32030-h.htm.

Montague, John. *Collected Poems*. Winston-Salem, NC: Wake Forest University Press, 1995.

———. *A Slow Dance*. Dublin: Dolmen; Winston-Salem, NC: Wake Forest University Press, 1975.

Moore, George Augustus. *The Lake*. London: William Heinemann, 1921. Project Gutenberg, 2004. http://www.gutenberg.org/ebooks/11304.

Moriarty, John. *Invoking Ireland: Ailiu Iath n-hErend*. Dublin: Lilliput, 2007.

Murphy, Neil. "Political Fantasies: Irish Writing and the Problems of Reading Strategies." In *The Current Debate about the Irish Literary Canon: Essays Reassessing "The Field Day Anthology of Irish Writing,"* edited by Helen Thompson, 59–83. Lewiston, NY: Edwin Mellen, 2006.

Neeson, Eoin. "Woodland in History and Culture." In *Nature in Ireland: A Scientific and Cultural History*, edited by John Wilson Foster and Helena C. G. Cheney, 133–56. Dublin: Lilliput, 1997.

O'Malley, Mary. *The Boning Hall: New and Selected Poems*. Manchester, UK: Carcanet, 2006.

———. *A Consideration of Silk*. Galway, Ireland: Salmon Books, 1990.

———. *The Knife in the Wave*. Dublin: Salmon, 1997.

———. *Playing the Octopus*. Manchester, UK: Carcanet, 2016.

———. *Where the Rocks Float*. Dublin: Salmon, 1993.

Praeger, Robert Lloyd. *The Way That I Went: An Irishman in Ireland*. Dublin: A. Figgus, 1980.

Robinson, Tim. *Connemara: Listening to the Wind*. Dublin: Penguin Ireland, 2006.

———. *Stones of Aran: Pilgrimage*. New York: New York Review Books, 1986.

Rowley, Rosemarie. *Flight into Reality*. Chicago: Rowan Tree, 1989.

———. *Girls of the Globe*. Galway, Ireland: Arlen House, 2015.

———. *The Sea of Affliction*. Dublin: Rowan Tree, 1987. 2nd ed., 2010.

Schama, Simon. *Landscape and Memory*. New York: Vintage Books, 1995.

Sedulius, Caelius. "Invocation." In *Carmen Paschale [Easter Song]*. Inspirational Stories. Accessed October 8, 2017, http://www.inspirationalstories.com/poems/invocation-caelius-sedulius-poems/.

Shorter, Dora Sigerson. *The Collected Poems of Dora Sigerson Shorter*. London: Hodder Stoughton, 1907.

Slovic, Scott. "Nature Writing and Environmental Psychology: The Interiority of Outdoor Experiences." In *The Ecocriticism Reader: Landmarks in Literary Ecology*, edited by Cheryll Glotfelty and Harold Fromm, 351–70. Athens: University of Georgia Press, 1996.

St. Columcille of Iona. "Columcille Fecit." In *The Oxford Companion to Irish Literature*, edited by Robert Welch, 108–9. Oxford, UK: Clarendon, 1996.

Synge, John Millington (J. M.). "The Aran Islands." In *The Complete Works of John M. Synge*, 313–475. New York: Random House, 1904.

——. *Poems and Translations*. Dublin: Maunsel, 1911. https://archive.org/stream/translationoopoems syngrich/translationoopoemssyngrich_djvu.txt.

——. *Riders to the Sea: A Play in One Act*. In *The Complete Works of John M. Synge*, 81–97. New York: Random House, 1904.

Tacitus. *The Sacred Grove*. In *Tacitus*, translated by M. Hutton, revised by E. H. Warmington. Cambridge, MA: Harvard University Press, 1980. http://www.sacred-texts.com/cla/tac/.

Thackeray, William Makepeace. *Irish Sketchbook*. Edited by Walter Jerrold. London: J. M. Dent, 1903. https://books.google.com/books/about/The_Irish_sketch_book.html?id=5ecMAAAAYAAJ.

Thompson, Helen. "Introduction: Field Day, Politics and Irish Writing." In *The Current Debate about the Irish Literary Canon: Essays Reassessing "The Field Day Anthology of Irish Writing,"* edited by Helen Thompson, 1–37. Lewiston, NY: Edwin Mellen, 2006.

Trevor, William. *A Writer's Ireland: Landscape in Literature*. New York: Viking, 1984.

Tynan, Katharine. *Flower of Youth: Poems in War Time*. London: Sidgwick and Jackson, 1915. https://en.wikisource.org/wiki/Flower_of_youth,_poems_in_war_time.

——. *Herb o' Grace: Poems of War-Time*. London: Sidgwick and Jackson, 1918. https://babel.hathitrust.org/cgi/pt?id=njp.32101067645703.

——. "High Summer." In *A Treasury of War Poetry: British and American Poems of the World War, 1914–1919*, edited by George Herbert Clarke, 166. Boston: Houghton Mifflin, 1919.

——. *Twenty One Poems by Katharine Tynan: Selected by W. B. Yeats*. Dundrum, Ireland: Dun Emer, 1907. http://www.digital.library.upenn.edu/women/tynan/poems/poems.html.

——. *The Wind in the Trees: A Book of Country Verse*. London: Grant Richards, 1898. https://archive.org/details/windintreesbookoootynarich.

Tyndall, John. *Address Delivered before the British Association Assembled at Belfast, with Additions*. London: Longmans, Green, 1874. http://www.victorianweb.org/science/science_texts/belfast.html.

Viney, Michael. "Another Life: From Swerve of Shore to Bend of Bay, the Warming Globe Is Eroding Ireland's Coast." *Irish Times*, November 30, 2013. https://www.irishtimes.com/news/environment/another-life-from-swerve-of-shore-to-bend-of-bay-1.1612113.

——. *Ireland: A Smithsonian Natural History*. Belfast: Blackstaff, 2003.

——. *A Year's Turning*. Belfast: Blackstaff, 1996.

Viney, Michael, and Ethna Viney. *Ireland's Ocean: A Natural History*. Cork, Ireland: Cork Collins, 2008.

Whitman, Walt. "Song of Myself." In *Leaves of Grass*, 13–56. Brooklyn, NY: Rome Brothers, 1855.

Wilson, Edward O. *The Diversity of Life*. New ed. New York: Norton, 1999.

Wordsworth, William. "I Wander'd Lonely as a Cloud." In *The Collected Poems of William Wordsworth*, 219. London: Wordsworth Editions, 1998.

Yeats, W. B. *Autobiography: Consisting of Reveries over Childhood and Youth, The Trembling of the Veil, and Dramatis Personae*. New York, Macmillan, 1953.

——. *The Collected Poems of W. B. Yeats*. London: Wordsworth Editions, 1994.

——. *The Collected Works of W. B. Yeats*. Vol. 1, *The Poems*, 2nd ed. Edited by Richard J. Finneran. New York: Simon and Schuster, 1997.

——. *The Collected Works of W. B. Yeats*. Vol. 4, *Early Essays*. Edited by Richard J. Finneran and George Bornstein. New York: Scribner, 2007.

——. *The Wanderings of Oisin, and Other Poems*. London: Kegan Paul, Trench, 1889.

——. *The Wild Swans at Coole*. New York: Macmillan, 1919. http://www.bartleby.com/148/.

——. *The Wind among the Reeds*. New York: J. Lane, Bodley Head, 1899. http://www.bartleby.com/146/.

Index

About the Editor

Tim Wenzell is an associate professor of English in the Department of Languages and Literature at Virginia Union University in Richmond, Virginia. He has published widely, including a novel, *Absent Children*, many short stories and poems in literary magazines, articles on Irish ecocriticism, and *Emerald Green: An Ecocritical Study of Irish Literature* (2009). Wenzell is now working on a collection of ecocritical essays on Arthurian legend.